COMPREHENSIVE CHORD THEORY FOR GUITAR

MW00450803

BY DOUGLAS BALDWIN

To access audio visit:
www.halleonard.com/mylibrary

"Enter Code"
6375-3075-6013-5612

ISBN 978-1-4234-9614-4

7777 W. BLUEMOUND RD. P.O. BOX 13819 MILWAUKEE, WI 53213

Visit Hal Leonard Online at
www.halleonard.com

All audio tracks were perfomed, recorded, and produced by
Douglas Baldwin at Coyote Music, 1 Flowerfield, St. James, NY.

Douglas Baldwin would like to give special thanks to Doug West at
Mesa/Boogie Amplifiers and Brian Vance at D'Addario Strings for their support.

Most importantly, the author is forever indebted to
Debbie and Taylor for their love and support.

Douglas Baldwin can be contacted through his website at www.TheCoyote.org

Table of Contents

Introduction

Chords are the foundation of almost all of Western music, and the most common function of the guitar is as an accompaniment instrument—i.e., one that plays chords while someone sings or plays another instrument. Most people, whether they are listeners or musical companions, don't care how blazingly fast you can play the guitar if you don't have much of a grasp of chords.

In my experience with students and many professional musicians, chords are used far more often than they're understood. Initially, this is perfectly normal; we all want to play songs as we hear them played by others around us, and that usually means playing lots of chords on the guitar. But sooner or later, curiosity or necessity leads us to try to understand chords a little better. How are chords put together? How did they get these weird names? How do I figure out what notes are in a B♭13♯11 chord? Where's a C♯ minor chord? Why do some chords sound "good" and some sound "bad?" We also discover in this process that sometimes our hands simply can't play the chords we ask them to.

Because of this, I've felt that a practical book of chord theory for the guitar has been long overdue. Many approaches to chord construction rely on the terminology, rules, and examples developed during the "common practice" period of classical music[1]; often they're nothing more than a collection of "dos and don'ts" that evolved from keyboard music. Others devolve into mere lists and charts of "all the major chords, all the minor chords, chords in the Dorian mode," etc. Both of these approaches have their place in the organization of information, and I will certainly use them in this book when they're appropriate. However, I will focus on a more practical use and understanding of chords.

Specifically, I expect a practical study will address two major issues. First, the information here can be put to use in a practical way. It relates to the music of this time and culture and, if I do my work well, it may function as a guide to what may come next. Second, a practical guide will require practice. You will often want to use a pencil and paper to work out musical problems. It is assumed that you will study, absorb, and retain information as you work through this book and audio. Most importantly, I assume throughout the text that you will pick up your guitar and practice the examples and etudes in this guide. I certainly hope the audio tracks will whet your appetite for the sounds I discuss, but creating those sounds with your own hands and experiencing your own sound with your own ears is essential.

It is impossible to discuss traditional chord construction without using the nomenclature of traditional music theory. I have made a great effort throughout this book to introduce technical terms slowly and carefully, to define these terms immediately, and to give several practical examples along with definitions. When a new term appears, I will indicate it in ***italicized, boldface text***, which I hope will help the reader to quickly find the term, should he or she travel to some distant and exotic chapter before learning the language of the locals.

I will employ circle diagrams (Schillinger circles for voice-leading and diatonic and chromatic circles for musical pattern recognition) for much of the information. Chromatic circles are becoming more common in advanced discussions of twelve-tone serial composition, but I have found them (along with diatonic circles and the more obscure Schillinger circles) extremely useful for conveying many basic musical concepts such as voice-leading, all possible progressions in a given key, identifying symmetric chords, and identifying intervals in a chord.

---

[1]   The common practice period of classical music refers to the rules and styles used by male European composers that were supported by the ruling classes between 1600 and 1900.

I will address problems of technique wherever appropriate. I've developed numerous exercises and tips for barre-chord playing, finger dexterity, etc. You will find these as **sidebars** or **special sections** labeled **Technique Tips** throughout the book.

I've recorded numerous examples of the chords, progressions, and etudes in this book so you can actually hear what I'm writing about. Numerous short etudes will be used to demonstrate the concepts as they are presented and will be played with a wide range of instruments and tones appropriate to the common styles in which the music might be heard.

My hope is that this text and audio package will prove useful to a wide range of musicians. I'll refer to three levels of musicianship throughout this text:

- **The Beginner** is actually an advanced beginner who has already begun to understand some basic musical ideas, tools, and skills on the guitar. These ideas, tools, and skills are defined in the next section of the text: A Prelude in Musicspeak and the Rosetta Stone for Chord Diagrams.

- **The Intermediate musician** has established a reliable practice with her or his instrument. An intermediate musician has enough experience to know what skills they lack and can work towards attaining those skills in a self-directed way.

- **The Advanced musician** may be approaching music as a profession or as a lifelong study. More than just knowing what they know, advanced musicians use and feel what they know and are often eager to embrace what they don't know. Advanced musicians also look for ways to transmit musical information to others as a way of better understanding themselves and their own relationship to music.

There's another level of musicianship that should be acknowledged—that of the **Master**, or perhaps even the **Genius**. Acknowledging (and hopefully transcending) the gender-identified origin of "master," we recognize a master of music as one who has the ability to call upon music and allow it to work its magic through them, without attachment. The master speaks so freely in the musical language that it appears effortless. Once in a very rare while, the genius appears—someone who realigns the world we know and opens us up to new worlds. Mastery is something to which we can all aspire. Genius is angelic.

I won't presume to address either mastery or genius in this text, but I will often address how Beginner, Intermediate, and Advanced musicians might work to master the material presented.

A Prelude in Musicspeak and the Rosetta Stone for Guitar Diagrams

One of the biggest hurdles that aspiring musicians face when attempting to learn about music is the confusing terminology of music theory. I call this kind of terminology "musicspeak" and prefer to avoid it whenever possible. When it must be used, I will introduce it in a boldfaced, italicized font with a definition soon to follow.

Basic Ideas, Tools, and Skills You Should Know

I am going to make brief mention of the following musical ideas, tools, and skills, and then I'm going to assume that you know and understand them from here on in:

- You know the names of the strings in standard tuning: (low to high) E–A–D–G–B–E. You also have at least a basic understanding of where notes are on all six strings of the guitar.

- You can experience, understand, and identify a sense of pitch. ***Pitch*** is the relative "highness" or "lowness" of a sound. When a sound has a relatively clear fundamental pitch, we can work with it as a traditional musical pitch. Think of changes on the strings of a guitar as changes in the direction of pitch— not as physical directions in space. For example, when you remain on a single string and move from the first fret to the 13th fret, you are moving *up the neck*, even though the physical direction is probably slightly *downward* in space. When you begin a pattern on the low E string and then move to the A string, the D string, and the G string, you are also moving *up* the neck, even though (again) the physical direction is *downward* in space.

- You understand the music staff. A ***staff*** is a graphic image of five parallel lines that, along with the spaces between them, is used to represent musical pitch. ***Ledger lines*** temporarily extend the range of a staff.

- You understand the treble and bass clefs. The treble and bass clefs show a specific range of pitches. Guitar music is commonly written using the treble clef.

- I expect that you can read music on a staff. When I say that you can read music, I mean that as you look at notes on a staff with a clef at the beginning of it, you can do the following:

  → Name these notes by their proper letter names: A, B, C, D, E, F, and G, plus "sharp" and/or "flat" where appropriate.

  → You are familiar with the symbols for **sharp** (♯), **flat** (♭), and **natural** (♮), and you know that a sharp raises a note by one **half step** or **minor 2nd**, a flat lowers a note by one half step or minor 2nd, and a natural cancels a sharp or flat that has been used previously. (A half step or minor 2nd is an **interval**. We'll define intervals a little further on.) The most common practical application of sharps and flats is in **key signatures**—groups of one or more sharps or flats at the beginning of a piece of music. A key signature indicates which notes will remain sharped or flatted throughout a piece or section of music, but they can be temporarily cancelled (for the duration of a measure) by a natural symbol ♮.

  → You understand the concept of **enharmonic equivalence**. This is a fancy term for a pitch that can have two names, such as C♯ and D♭.

  → You won't be thrown off by the bass clef. Most of the music reading in this book will be in the treble clef, but when we venture into the bass clef, you should be able to take your time to puzzle out the notes by name.

- As much as I would hope otherwise, I understand that you may not yet have all of your key signatures memorized. Keep working with them; you'll get to know them better as you progress through this book and through your study of music. Here's a useful guide to key signatures, shown in a circle of 5ths.

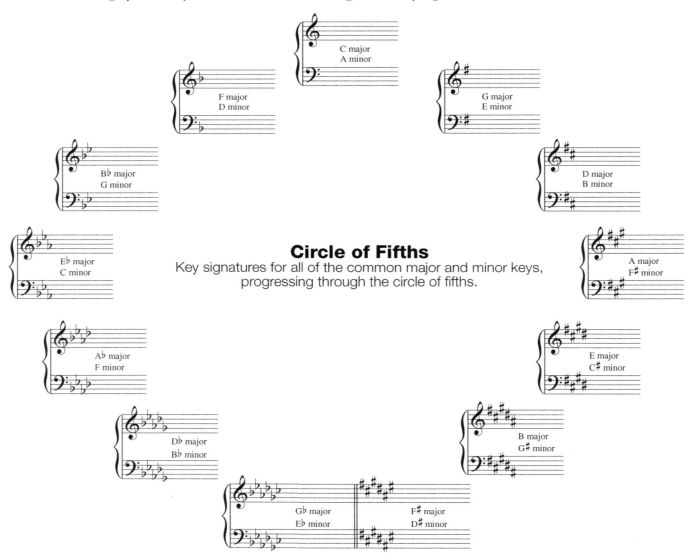

Circle of Fifths
Key signatures for all of the common major and minor keys, progressing through the circle of fifths.

- You understand the basics of **time signatures** and are familiar with the most common ones in use at the beginning of the 21st century; 4/4, 3/4, 2/4, and 6/8 are good ones with which to start.

- You can count the basic rhythmic values of notes and rests.

- You have basic music-writing skills. You can use a pencil on music staff paper and notate the previously mentioned symbols clearly, so that another musician can read them.

- You understand basic scale construction. A **scale** is a group of **notes** derived from a portion of music (usually a melody or a melody and its accompaniment), which is then arranged in a stepwise ascending or descending order. Hopefully, you aldready have a couple of scale-fingerings under your fingertips.

- You can apply all of these skills to the guitar in the standard tuning of the early 21st century.[1] You don't have to be a great **sight-reader**—someone who can play written music really quickly and accurately— but you should be able to puzzle through standard music notation and translate it onto the guitar.

If you don't have these skills available to some small degree, acquire them, and this book/audio package will be much easier to use.

Now hang on, because here's one of the trickiest bits of musicspeak we should clarify: What is a **note**?

Some musicians use the terms **note** and **tone** interchangeably. I try not to. When I refer to a note in the general sense, I will call it a **note**. But when I refer to a specific note, I will refer to it as being higher or lower in pitch than another note. And since this is a book primarily for guitarists, I will also identify notes in their specific locations on the guitar. Sometimes I will specify a note by its frequency, which defines its pitch very specifically. For example, there's a note we call C that's found on the A string at the third fret. The ideal fundamental frequency of this note is 130.813 cycles per second, or 130.813 Hz (hertz). The same note C also resides on the low E string at the eighth fret.

Then there's a note called C that's higher in pitch than these. You'll find it on the D string at the tenth fret, and it will, if prodded, vibrate at 261.626 Hz. This same C is also found on the G string at the fifth fret, on the B string at the first fret, on the A string at the fifteenth fret, and—if your guitar has it—the low E string at the twentieth fret.

Another C, still higher in pitch, can be found on the high E string at the eighth fret. Pluck it, and it vibrates primarily at 523.251 Hz. The very same C can be coaxed from the B string at the thirteenth fret, the G string at the seventeenth fret and—again, if your guitar has it—the D string at the twenty-second fret.

Finally, there's a teensy tiny squeaky C found on the high E string at the twentieth fret, which has an ideal fundamental frequency of 1046.504 Hz.

It's very important to recognize that I just identified three different kinds of notes, all called C: First, there's the general C note that can be any C at all. This generalized C can be referred to simply with the letter "C." Second, there's a C of a specific pitch, or frequency, which will be shown in standard music notation. Third, there are several different notes called C, many of them with identical pitch, with specific locations on the guitar fretboard. These will be shown using tablature and/or chord block diagrams. All of these ways of identifying notes will be used throughout this book. And I assume you found and played each of these notes that I just described.

Intervals

An interval is the musical or pitch-related distance between two notes. Intervals can be **melodic** (when two notes are sounded one at a time in sequence) or **harmonic** (when two notes are sounded more or less at the same time so that they sound together for a recognizable period of time). Usually, harmonic intervals are played simultaneously as two notes at the same time, but sometimes one note can sound and continue to ring while a second note is sounded. I will always refer to intervals as follows:

- Two notes that are the same pitch will be called a **unison**, abbreviated as "U."

- The smallest distance between two notes in standard, tempered tuning will be a **minor 2nd**, abbreviated as "m2." Guitarists will recognize a minor second as the distance of one fret on the same string. Notice that the distance of a minor 2nd can be one fret *above* or one fret *below* the starting note.

---

1   The current standard tuning for guitar is low E (82.4 Hz), A (110 Hz), D (146.8 Hz), G (196.0 Hz), B (246.9 Hz), and high E (329.6 Hz). If you don't understand Hz, don't worry. Make a note of it and do a little studying on the physics of sound.

- The next smallest distance will be a **major 2nd**, abbreviated as "M2." Guitarists will recognize a major second as the distance of two frets on the same string.

- I won't use the terms **half step**, **half tone**, **semitone**, **whole step**, **tone**, or **whole tone** unless I'm referring to some kind of musical construction that's been historically identified with these terms, such as a whole tone scale or a whole-half diminished scale.

- Continuing through larger intervals, I will use the names **minor 3rd** (the distance of three frets on the same string, abbreviated m3), **major 3rd** (the distance of four frets on the same string, abbreviated M3), and **perfect 4th** (the distance of five frets on the same string, abbreviated P4).

- To name the tricky interval of six minor seconds (or six frets) above or below a given note, I will use any of the following terms: **augmented 4th** (aug4), **tritone** (TT), and **diminished 5th** (dim5).

- The distance of seven frets on a single string is a perfect 5th (P5), eight frets on a single string is a **minor 6th** (m6), nine frets on a single string is a **major 6th** (M6), ten frets on a single string is a **minor 7th** (m7), eleven frets on a single string is a **major 7th** (M7), and twelve frets on a single string is an **octave** (8ve). We'll discuss intervals greater than an octave when we reach them.

Circle Diagrams

Music can be put on the page in many ways. The European music tradition has had a pretty good run with standard music notation, and we guitarists use **tablature** and **chord diagrams**[2] because of their practical, mechanical, and geometric clarity. There's another way of visualizing music that has been curiously ignored in the Western tradition. This is the **circle diagram**. A circle diagram places the twelve notes of our musical system in a circle without regard for what octave the note might be in. Enharmonic notes are shown as one point on the diagram.

If you are used to thinking of notes as a continuously rising or falling pattern, as in standard music notation, the abstraction of a circle diagram might be difficult to understand. Here's a physical model of how a circle diagram is constructed: Imagine we isolated a B string on a guitar and made a mark at each fret—from the first fret for where the note C sounds, up to the thirteenth fret, where C sounds an octave higher. If we took the string off the guitar, snipped it from the first fret mark to the thirteenth fret mark, and labeled each mark with its corresponding note name, we'd have something like this.

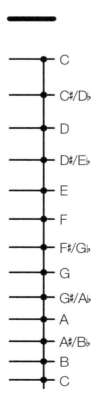

---

2   See p. 9 for a discussion of tablature and chord diagrams.

Now imagine stretching the string so that the distance between each note was equal.

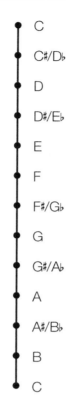

Finally let's form it into a circle, aligning the low C with the high C. Now we have a circle of 12 different notes.

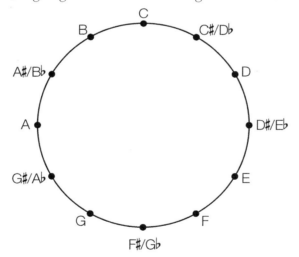

This particular circle diagram is a **chromatic circle**. (Notice, by the way, that the circle of key signatures on page 2 was a circle of fifths.) If we wanted to add some esoteric musicspeak, we could call these circles **dodeca-hedral diagrams**, or diagrams showing the **dodecaphonic symmetry** of our system of music.

A circle diagram is somewhat abstract, and it's good to recognize how it differs from concrete reality. First, notice that in the steps we just took, when we stretched the imaginary string to equalize the fret distance, we eliminated the diminishing size of the notes as they get higher in pitch. (In a way, this is much like standard music notation, where notes remain the same size on the page, even though the vibrating string must get smaller and smaller as notes go up in pitch.) Then, when we formed our snipped-off string into a circle, we eliminated any physical relationship between the notes as they occur on a guitar and the notes of the circle diagram. Once we envision notes in this way, there's no longer any "higher" or "lower" note. Since we overlapped the note C onto itself, that C can represent any C. By extension, the B can represent any B, the B♭/A♯ can represent any B♭/A♯, etc.

So what good is a circle diagram? Let us count the ways...

- **A circle diagram clearly shows the smallest intervallic distance between two notes without regard for note names.** Our traditional system of note naming and notation is built around the seven-note, seven-letter approach, which makes some musical patterns difficult to grasp. For example, many beginning musicians have a hard time with the concept of the six-note whole tone scale as a symmetric scale made up of major seconds (or whole steps) because neither standard notation nor the letter-naming of notes reveals this pattern. But when you connect every other note in a circle diagram, not only does the symmetric structure become clear, but the more advanced concept that there are only two different whole tone scales in our system of music becomes quite clear as well.

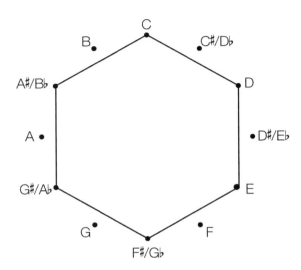

A circle diagram of a whole-tone scale.

- **A circle diagram can be easily rotated.** Below we see a C major chord next to an E major chord using circle diagrams. Most people have little trouble seeing that the distance from C to G is the same as the distance from E to B, and that by mentally rotating the image, the two triangles are congruent (showing that the two chords have the same structure). Even if a person is spatially challenged, the two shapes can be physically rotated to align.

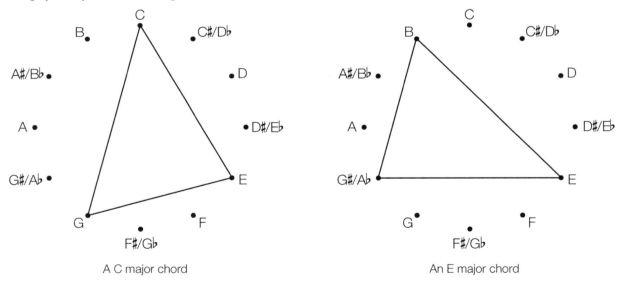

A C major chord   An E major chord

- **Circle diagrams reveal patterns in how we perceive music.** Referring back to the previous figures, it's easy to see that the whole tone scale is a symmetric hexagon, while the major chords are asymmetric triangles. The whole tone scale sounds a little weird and ethereal to most people, while major chords sound pleasant and stable. A little experience with circle diagrams shows that visual symmetry on a chord diagram usually translates to a sensation of musical unrest.

- **Circle diagrams are fun to play with.** Grab a pencil and paper and draw a few scales or chords using circle diagrams. I'm sure you'll find yourself rapidly filling pages with them.

So why aren't circle diagrams used more often in music? My own observations are as follows:

- We are a linear culture and a left-brained culture. We like things that line up in a cause-and-effect way. We like our musical symbols to mimic our written language and our mathematical symbols (left-to-right, top-to-bottom). The possibility that information can be shown in a non-linear form like a circle is so anti-thetical to our usual ways of conveying information that we tend to ignore it or minimize it.

- A circle diagram requires just a bit of right-brained drawing skill. If you wish to make a circle diagram with, say, twelve equal points around the circle, you must first be able to draw a fair circle on paper, then subdivide that circle into twelve equal sections. We don't place much value to that skill in our society. (The next page gives instructions on how to draw a 12-point circle diagram.)

- In a circle diagram, the information is being conveyed in a shape—not an abstract set of symbols or names. Our culture has minimized the value of shapes and instead favors deeply symbolic and verbal communication.

- The circular form of the diagram conveys a centered, motionless, meditative quality that, again, has been minimized in our culture.

How to Draw a Freehand Circle Diagram

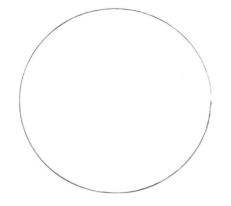

Use a pencil.
Lightly draw a circle about 2 inches in diameter.
Leave plenty of room around it.

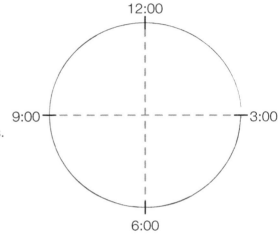

Imagine a clock face.
Mark points at 12:00, 6:00, 3:00 and 9:00.
Notice that you've divided the circle into quarters.

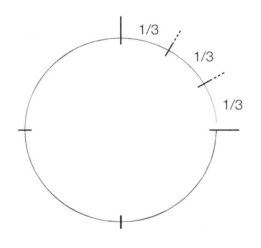

Subdivide each quarter into thirds.

You can visually cross-check your 12-pointed circle
by visualizing lines connecting opposite points. These
lines should pass through the center of the circle.

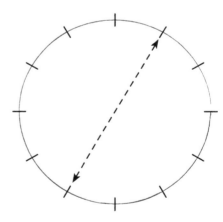

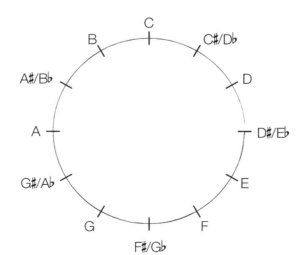

Add note names to the circle. Put the most important
note (the first note of a scale, the root of a chord, etc.)
at the 12:00 point.

Tablature and Chord Diagrams

There are several ways to show the notes of a chord as they are played on the guitar. Most guitarists are familiar with tablature, or tab. Briefly, the six horizontal lines of tab represent the six strings of the guitar. The lowest line represents the lowest pitched string, the low E string, with the other strings following logically, low to high. A chord in tab will appear as a vertical stack of numbers, where each number represents a fret being pressed down. Notation of note lengths and rhythm can become clumsy in tab, so it's usually paired with standard music notation. Below is an example of tablature paired with standard music notation.

The best all-purpose chord diagram is the graphic "block diagram" or "chord frame" shown below.

How a drawing of the guitar neck becomes a block diagram

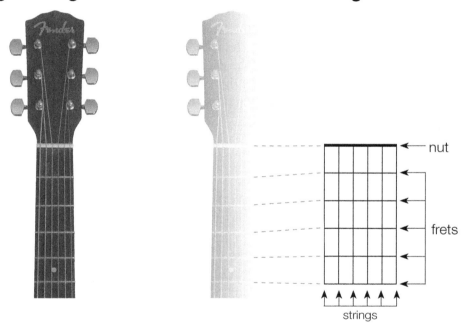

A block diagram is like the drawing of the neck of the guitar showing only the frets (horizontal lines) and strings (vertical lines), as shown here. (Note that the top horizontal line is made thicker than the others, indicating the nut of the guitar.

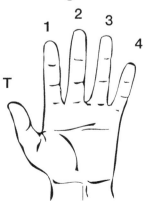

By indicating the fingers of the fretting hand (the hand that presses down the strings) with the numbers 1, 2, 3, and 4 and the letter "T" for the thumb, we can see which fingers are pressing down which strings.

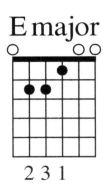

We indicate where the fingers press the strings down with dots on the lines representing the strings. The specific fingers used are shown below each string. It should be clear in the diagram and the drawing above that the first finger is pressing down the G (or third) string at the first fret, the second finger is pressing down the A (or fifth) string at the second fret, and the third finger is pressing down the D (or fourth) string at the second fret. Strings that are not fretted but which ring open are shown with circles above them. It should be clear that the high E, B, and low E strings should be played in the chord. Notice that the chord gets a name: E major.

Here we see a more advanced chord diagram. The location on the neck is defined by the location of the first finger and is shown to the right of the first fret of the diagram (in this case, the first finger is in the sixth fret). An alternate fingering is shown in parentheses below the primary fingering. A ***functional analysis*** is shown in a smaller font below the fingerings. We'll discuss functional analysis in the next chapter.

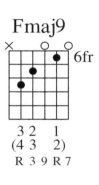

Are you familiar with the Rosetta Stone? It's a block of granite that was engraved in 196 BC with a proclamation in Egyptian hieroglyphics, Egyptian Demotic script, and Greek. When it was discovered by a French expedition to Egypt in 1799, Greek was commonly understood, Demotic script was somewhat understood, and hieroglyphics seemed like just a bunch of wacky cartoon drawings of bird-headed people walking sideways. With the Rosetta Stone, linguists were able to correlate the three languages to "break the codes" of hieroglyphics and Demotic script. On the next page is your Rosetta Stone for guitar chords.

The Rosetta Stone for Guitar Chords

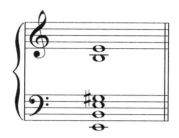

The chord as it is written for piano

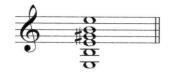

The chord as it is written for guitar in standard music notation. Note that music for the guitar is written an octave higher than it sounds on piano.

The chord as it is notated in tablature

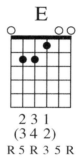

2 3 1
(3 4 2)
R 5 R 3 5 R

The chord as it is shown in a block diagram with fingering, alternate fingering, and functional analysis.

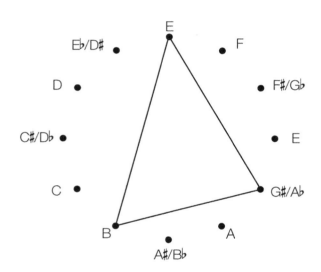

The chord as it is shown in a circle diagram.

Another useful system for indicating chords is to show the frets and strings played numerically. The E chord as shown above can be numerically abbreviated as 022100, representing the strings left to right, low to high: open, second fret, second fret, first fret, open, open. I "invented" this system when I first started playing guitar and used it for any chord I couldn't easily name. Then I found out that other people "invented" it as well. Necessity is the true mother.

Finally, string pitches can be written in "Helmholtz notation." Developed by the German scientist Hermann von Helmholtz, it uses a combination of upper and lower case letters (A to G) and the sub- and super-prime symbols (, and ') to describe each individual note. The Helmholtz scale always starts on the note C and ends at B (C–D–E–F–G–A–B). The note C is shown in different octaves by using upper-case letters for low notes, lower-case letters for high notes, and adding sub-primes and primes in the following sequence: $C_{\prime\prime}$, $C_{\prime}$, C, c, c', c'', c'''. The E chord as shown above can be written in Helmholtz notation as E, B, e, g#, b, e'. You may find this notation useful when you want to write down a pitch-based idea and no staff paper is handy. I often use this notation myself, but I won't in this text.

The Naming of Chords

A huge number of strange chord names will be given throughout this book, and sometimes I'll even present them outside of any logical order of presentation. For instance, the next section (A Beginners Collection of Chords in Open Position) will include some rather exotic-looking names. You don't need to understand chord names to use the chords, but some understanding of these names will help you to organize your own use of these chords as well as communicate with other musicians.

To begin to understand chord names, let's jump back in time to the beginning of the twentieth century. The European era of cultural dominance is coming to an end, and the guitar is ascending in popularity. It's portable, inexpensive, adaptable to different styles of music and different tunings (including microtonal bent notes), and you can play all kinds of melodies on it as well as those juicy old European chords. Recorded music and electronically broadcast music has arrived, along with a desire to recreate the resulting rapidly changing stream of popular songs. A system of naming those juicy European chords developed—a system that could be interpreted faster than reading standard music notation.

Somewhere around 1910 to 1920, on the sheet music for popular songs, there began to appear chord names above the melody. Names evolved according to the common usage of a chord type. Major chords were so common that they were simply named by their root note. A C major triad would be named "C," an F♯ major triad would be named "F♯," a B♭ major triad would be named "B♭," etc. Minor chords, almost nearly as common, would have a lowercase "m" or "mi" suffixed to their root note name. A C minor triad would be named "Cm" or "Cmi," an F♯ minor triad would be named "F♯m" or "F♯mi," etc. The single most common four-note chord of this time was the so-called "dominant seventh" chord, which would be shown by adding the number 7 after the chord, such as C7, F♯7, or B♭7. With these three chord types—major, minor, and dominant 7—you could play an accompaniment to most of the popular songs of the first thirty years of the twentieth century. As different chords came into common use, these basic names were (and still are) continually modified. The following chart is a guide to understanding chord names. We'll recall it and refer to it throughout this book.

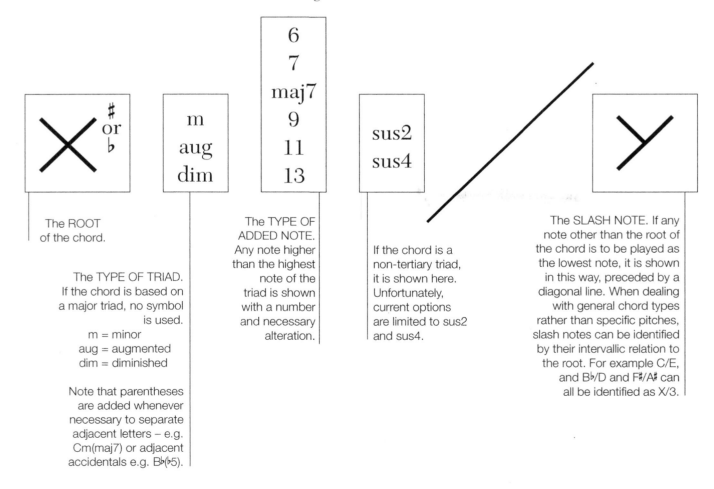

A Beginner's Collection of Chords in Open Position

The following collection of chord block diagrams are what we call **_open position_** chords. Chords in open position are played within the first five frets of the guitar neck and include one or more open strings as part of the chord. It's not necessary to understand the theory and naming of chords before using them, and this collection should prove particularly useful for guitarists who need a quick guide to a wide range of open position chords, perhaps before fully understanding how they got those funny names and what notes are included in them. This kind of collection is also useful in lighting a fire under guitarists who want to grow their skills as musicians, as a search for certain chords will reveal that no open position fingerings exist for that particular chord. This will hopefully lead to a questioning of why that chord doesn't have an open position, how that chord can be played in a closed or movable fingering, and what mental and physical skills are required to use that fingering.

MAJOR

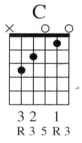

C

3 2   1
R 3 5 R 3

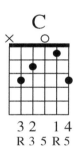

C

3 2   1 4
R 3 5 R 5

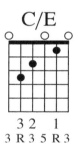

C/E

3 2   1
3 R 3 5 R 3

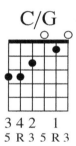

C/G

3 4 2   1
5 R 3 5 R 3

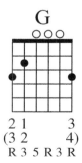

G

2 1   3
(3 2   4)
R 3 5 R 3 R

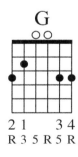

G

2 1   3 4
R 3 5 R 5 R

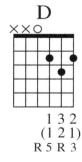

D

1 3 2
(1 2 1)
R 5 R 3

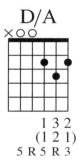

D/A

1 3 2
(1 2 1)
5 R 5 R 3

D/F♯

T   1 3 2
(1   2 4 3)
3 5 R 5 R 3

A

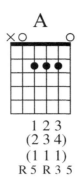

1 2 3
(2 3 4)
(1 1 1)
R 5 R 3 5

A/E

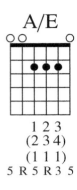

1 2 3
(2 3 4)
(1 1 1)
5 R 5 R 3 5

E

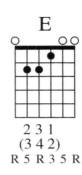

2 3 1
(3 4 2)
R 5 R 3 5 R

E/G♯

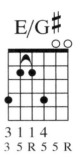

3 1 1 4
3 5 R 5 5 R

F

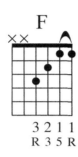

3 2 1 1
R 3 5 R

Note: this is not an open chord, as there are no open strings. However, it leads to several useful open fingerings.

F/A

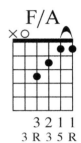

3 2 1 1
3 R 3 5 R

MINOR

Dm

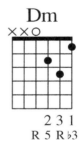

2 3 1
R 5 R ♭3

Dm/A

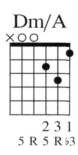

2 3 1
5 R 5 R ♭3

Am

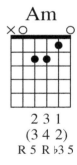

2 3 1
(3 4 2)
R 5 R ♭3 5

Am/E

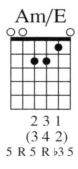

2 3 1
(3 4 2)
5 R 5 R ♭3 5

Em

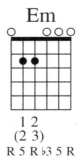

1 2
(2 3)
R 5 R ♭3 5 R

Gm/D

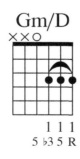

1 1 1
5 ♭3 5 R

Gm/B♭

1   3 4
♭3 5 R 5 R

SEVENTH

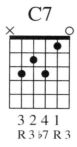

C7

3 2 4 1
R 3 ♭7 R 3

C7/E

3 2 4 1
3 R 3 ♭7 R 3

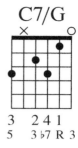

C7/G

3　2 4 1
5　3 ♭7 R 3

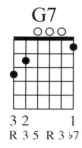

G7

3 2　　1
R 3 5　R 3 ♭7

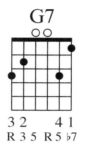

G7

3 2　4 1
R 3 5　R 5 ♭7

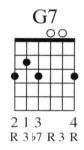

G7

2 1 3　4
R 3 ♭7 R 3 R

D7

2 1 3
R 5 ♭7 3

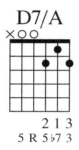

D7/A

2 1 3
5 R 5 ♭7 3

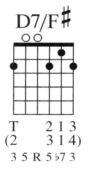

D7/F♯

T　2 1 3
(2　3 1 4)
3 5 R 5 ♭7 3

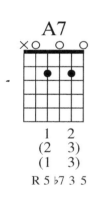

A7

1　2
(2　3)
(1　3)
R 5 ♭7 3 5

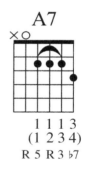

A7

1 1 1 3
(1 2 3 4)
R 5 R 3 ♭7

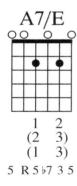

A7/E

1　2
(2　3)
(1　3)
5 R 5 ♭7 3 5

Look at the root!

SEVENTH (Cont.)

A7/E

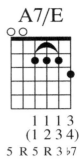

1 1 1 3
(1 2 3 4)
5 R 5 R 3 ♭7

E7

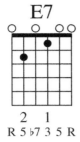

2   1
R 5 ♭7 3 5 R

E7

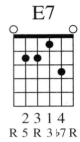

2 3 1 4
R 5 R 3 ♭7 R

E7

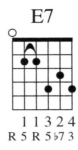

1 1 3 2 4
R 5 R 5 ♭7 3

B7

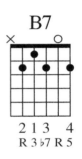

2 1 3   4
R 3 ♭7 R 5

B7/F♯

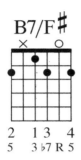

2   1 3   4
5   3 ♭7 R 5

F♯7

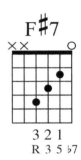

3 2 1
R 3 5 ♭7

F♯7

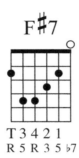

T 3 4 2 1
R 5 R 3 5 ♭7

F♯7/C♯

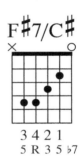

3 4 2 1
5 R 3 5 ♭7

MINOR SEVENTH

Dm7

2 1 1
R 5 ♭7 ♭3

Dm7/A

2 1 1
5 R 5 ♭7 ♭3

Am7

2 1
R 5 ♭7 ♭3 5

Am7

2 3 1 4
R 5 R ♭3 ♭7

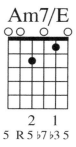

Am7/E

2 1
5 R 5 ♭7 ♭3 5

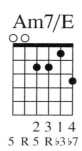

Am7/E

2 3 1 4
5 R 5 R ♭3 ♭7

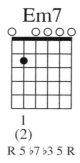

Em7

1
(2)
R 5 ♭7 ♭3 5 R

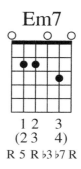

Em7

1 2   3
(23 4)
R 5 R ♭3 ♭7 R

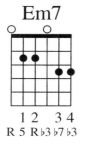

Em7

1 2   3 4
R 5 R ♭3 ♭7 ♭3

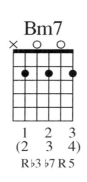

Bm7

1   2   3
(2   3   4)
R ♭3 ♭7 R 5

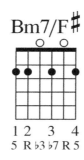

Bm7/F♯

1 2   3   4
5 R ♭3 ♭7 R 5

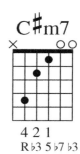

C♯m7

4 2 1
R ♭3 5 ♭7 ♭3

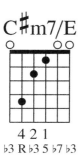

C♯m7/E

4 2 1
♭3 R ♭3 5 ♭7 ♭3

MAJOR SEVENTH

Fmaj7

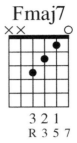

3 2 1
R 3 5 7

Fmaj7

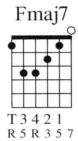

T 3 4 2 1
R 5 R 3 5 7

Fmaj7/A

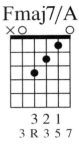

3 2 1
3 R 3 5 7

Fmaj7/C

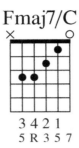

3 4 2 1
5 R 3 5 7

Cmaj7

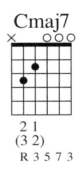

2 1
(3 2)
R 3 5 7 3

Cmaj7/E

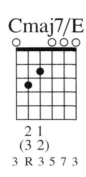

2 1
(3 2)
3 R 3 5 7 3

Cmaj7/G

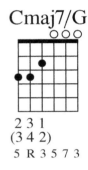

2 3 1
(3 4 2)
5 R 3 5 7 3

Gmaj7

3 2   1
R 3 5 R 3 7

Gmaj7

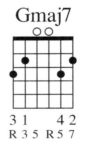

3 1   4 2
R 3 5 R 5 7

Dmaj7

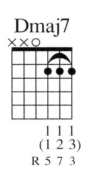

1 1 1
(1 2 3)
R 5 7 3

Dmaj7/A

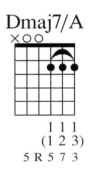

1 1 1
(1 2 3)
5 R 5 7 3

Dmaj7/F#

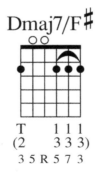

T   1 1 1
(2   3 3 3)
3 5 R 5 7 3

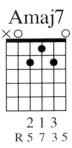

Amaj7

2 1 3
R 5 7 3 5

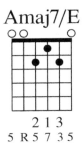

Amaj7/E

2 1 3
5 R 5 7 3 5

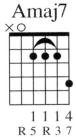

Amaj7

1 1 1 4
R 5 R 3 7

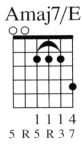

Amaj7/E

1 1 1 4
5 R 5 R 3 7

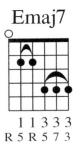

Emaj7

1 1 3 3 3
R 5 R 5 7 3

MINOR SEVEN FLAT FIVE

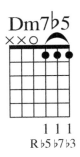

Dm7b5

1 1 1
R b5 b7 b3

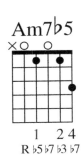

Am7b5

1 2 4
R b5 b7 b3 b7

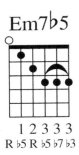

Em7b5

1 2 3 3 3
R b5 R b5 b7 b3

Bm7b5

2 3 1
R b3 b7 R b5

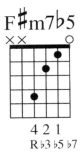

F#m7b5

4 2 1
R b3 b5 b7

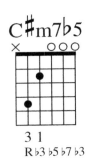

C#m7b5

3 1
R b3 b5 b7 b3

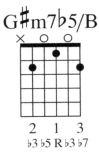

G#m7b5/B

2 1 3
b3 b5 R b3 b7

DIMINISHED SEVENTH

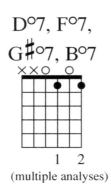

$D^{\circ}7, F^{\circ}7,$
$G^{\#\circ}7, B^{\circ}7$

1 2
(multiple analyses)

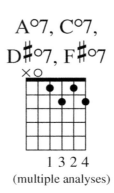

$A^{\#\circ}7, C^{\#\circ}7,$
$E^{\circ}7, G^{\circ}7$

1 2 3
(multiple analyses)

$A^{\circ}7, C^{\circ}7,$
$D^{\#\circ}7, F^{\#\circ}7$

1 3 2 4
(multiple analyses)

SUSPENDED SECOND (sus2)

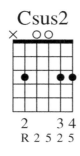

Csus2

2   3 4
R 2 5 2 5

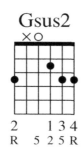

Gsus2

2   1 3 4
R   5 2 5 4

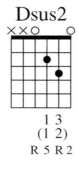

Dsus2

1 3
(1 2)
R 5 R 2

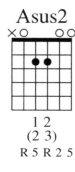

Asus2

1 2
(2 3)
R 5 R 2 5

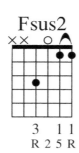

Fsus2

3   1 1
R 2 5 R

SUSPENDED FOURTH (sus4)

Csus4

3 4 1 1
R 4 5 R 4

Gsus4

3   1 4
R 5 R 4 R

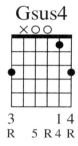

Dsus4

1 3 4
R 5 R 4

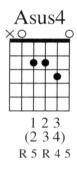

Asus4

1 2 3
(2 3 4)
R 5 R 4 5

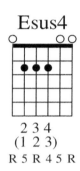

Esus4

2 3 4
(1 2 3)
R 5 R 4 5 R

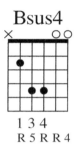

Bsus4

1 3 4
R 5 R R 4

ADD NINE

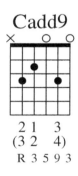

Cadd9

2 1 3
(3 2 4)
R 3 5 9 3

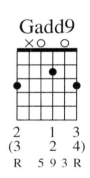

Gadd9

2 1 3
(3 2 4)
R 5 9 3 R

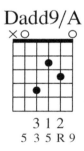

Dadd9/A

3 1 2
5 3 5 R 9

Aadd9

1 3 1 4
R 5 9 3 R

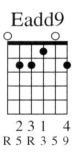

Eadd9

2 3 1 4
R 5 R 3 5 9

ADD FOUR

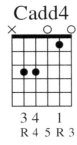

Cadd4

3 4   1
R 4 5 R 3

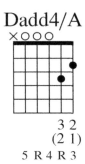

Dadd4/A

3 2
(2 1)
5 R 4 R 3

ADD NINE ADD FOUR

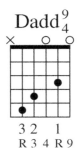

Dadd$^9_4$

3 2   1
R 3 4 R 9

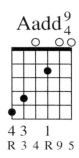

Aadd$^9_4$

4 3   1
R 3 4 R 9 5

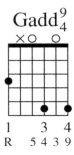

Gadd$^9_4$

1   3   4
R   5 4 3 9

SEVEN SUS FOUR

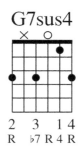

G7sus4

2   3   1 4
R ♭7 R 4 R

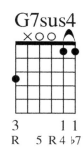

G7sus4

3   1 1
R   5 R 4 ♭7

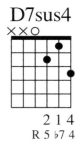

D7sus4

2 1 4
R 5 ♭7 4

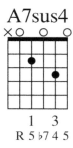

A7sus4

1   3
R 5 ♭7 4 5

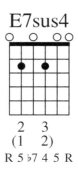

E7sus4

2   3
(1   2)
R 5 ♭7 4 5 R

SIXTH

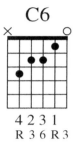

C6

4 2 3 1
R 3 6 R 3

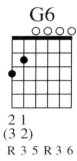

G6

2 1
(3 2)
R 3 5 R 3 6

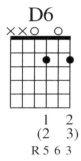

D6

1   2
(2   3)
R 5 6 3

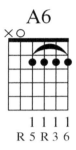

A6

1 1 1 1
R 5 R 3 6

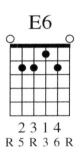

E6

2 3 1 4
R 5 R 3 6 R

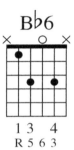

B♭6

1 3   4
R 5 6 3

MINOR SIXTH

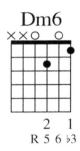

Dm6

2   1
R 5 6 ♭3

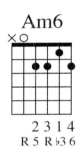

Am6

2 3 1 4
R 5 R ♭3 6

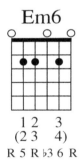

Em6

1 2   3
(2 3   4)
R 5 R ♭3 6 R

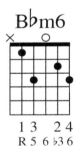

B♭m6

1 3   2 4
R 5 6 ♭3 6

NINTH

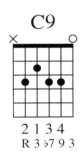

C9

2 1 3 4
R 3 ♭7 9 3

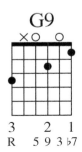

G9

3   2 1
R   5 9 3 ♭7

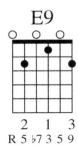

E9

2 1 3
R 5 ♭7 3 5 9

MAJOR NINTH

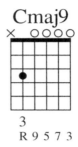

Cmaj9

3
R 9 5 7 3

Gmaj9

3   1   2
R   5 9 3 7

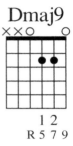

Dmaj9

1 2
R 5 7 9

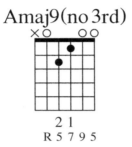

Amaj9(no 3rd)

2 1
R 5 7 9 5

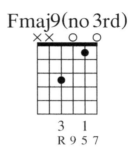

Fmaj9(no 3rd)

3   1
R 9 5 7

MISCELLANEOUS OPEN POSITION CHORDS

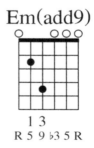

Em(add9)

1 3
R 5 9 ♭3 5 R

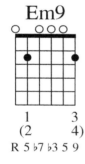

Em9

1   3
(2   4)
R 5 ♭7 ♭3 5 9

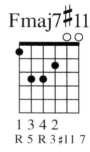

Fmaj7♯11

1 3 4 2
R 5 R 3 ♯11 7

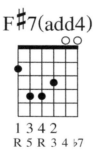

F♯7(add4)

1 3 4 2
R 5 R 3 4 ♭7

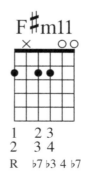

F♯m11

1   2 3
2   3 4
R   ♭7 ♭3 4 ♭7

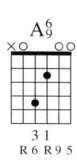

A^6_9

3 1
R 6 R 9 5

CHAPTER ONE:

First Steps in Chord Theory and Practice

So what is a chord? The formal definition of a chord changes as music itself changes, but a good practical definition would be "a bunch of notes that sound good together." Of course, "good" is a subjective term. You might tune your guitar to a collection of notes that would sound a bit sour when played along with an instrument in standard tuning, and yet you might feel that, on that guitar alone, those notes sound good together. There you go; you have yourself a good chord right there! However, it's not much of a practical chord—i.e., it doesn't work well when playing music with other people.

Let's begin with a very traditional chord so we can understand some basic concepts on how chords get their names. The most basic, traditional, textbook-approved chord is called a *triad*, which means that it is made up of three different unique notes. A triad begins with a *root note*. This is the note on which the chord is built, and it's really important in the naming of the chord. The root note can be abbreviated as "R" (or sometimes "1"), and this kind of abbreviation—slightly different from the abbreviation of intervals introduced earlier—will be referred to as the note's *function*. Every chord block diagram in this book will have a *functional analysis* shown below the fingering. (Refer back to the **Rosetta Stone for Guitar Chords** to see how the functional analysis will appear.) Keeping with the simplest way a traditional triad chord can be built, we'd add another note above the root note at a distance of either a major or minor 3rd. This note is referred to as the *3rd* of the chord. Because it is the intervallic distance of either a major or minor 3rd above the root note, it can be either a *major 3rd*, abbreviated as "3," or a *minor 3rd*, abbreviated as "♭3." Then there's another note on top of the 3rd, again at a distance of either a major or minor 3rd above the first 3rd. This note is the *5th* of the chord, and if you take the time to figure out all the permutations of intervals, you'll find that it can be a *diminished 5th* ("♭5" in chord function shorthand), a **perfect 5th** (5) or an *augmented 5th* (♯5) above the root note. This is a bit of an abstract way of constructing chords, based on properties of chords that evolved over several centuries in Western music. However, it does lead us to a checklist of possible tertiary triads, based on all of the intervals just named. Each of these chords is given a name that will be discussed throughout this chapter.

> ### A Checklist of Possible Tertiary Triads
> R + ♭3 + ♭5 = diminished chord
> R + ♭3 + 5 = minor chord
> R + ♭3 + ♯5 = minor sharp five chord, or minor augmented
> R + 3 + ♭5 = major flat five
> R + 3 + 5 = major
> R + 3 + ♯5 = augmented

Building Chords Based on Scales

There's another more practical and more musical way to look at chord construction, based on scales. You are probably familiar with the concepts and use of major and minor scales to some extent. Almost all of the music we listen to is based on seven-note scales, and almost all of the chords we hear are based on notes within a given scale at the moment that chord is heard. The notes of a chord are found in a very simple way with regard to that scale. Let's start with a C major scale played on the B string, and let's assign functional analysis numbers to each note of the scale, like this:

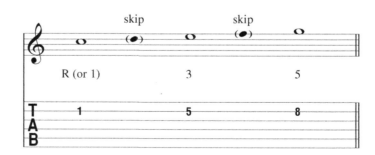

functional analysis: R (or 1)   2   3   4   5   6   7   8 or 1

Now let's begin on the first note of the scale, which we'll identify as the root (R) of the chord we are about to build, and let's simply choose notes from the scale in ascending 3rds until we have three notes. Think of this as "play a note, skip a note, play a note, skip a note, and play a note." We have a root note (C), the third note of the scale (E, a major 3rd above the root, so it can be shorthanded as "3"), and the fifth note of the scale (G, a minor 3rd above the note E and a perfect 5th above the root note C, so it can be shorthanded as "5"). This "play-a-note, skip-a-note" form of building chords is called *tertiary* construction, and this most basic three-note chord is called a *tertiary triad*. Check it out in the music figure below:

These are the three notes of a C major chord. C is the "one," root, or R; E is the 3rd or 3, and G is the 5th or 5. Remember that, although we've used the B string to find these notes, and we've written them on specific lines and spaces on a treble clef, eventually we want to be able to think of them as *any* C, *any* E, and *any* G. When we hear these three notes sounding at the same time, in almost any octave and in almost any quantity, as long as they are fairly close in pitch and volume, we'll call that sound a C major chord. You can confirm this by inspecting your open-position C major chord—the one you've probably been playing for at least a few years now. Let's take a little music-notation and note-naming detour for a moment. Let's go through this chord and see if these three notes—and only these three notes—are in the chord. Here's a diagram of an open-position C major chord, with a complete analysis of every note in the chord as well as its notation on the staff:

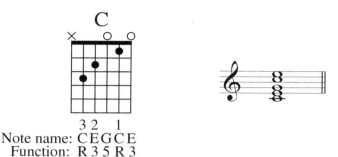

Obviously, our back-porch C major chord is really just a scattered bunch of C, E, and G notes. Let's simplify this chord in music notation and reduce it to just the lowest C, E, and G notes. Here's our simplest R–3–5 C major chord in music notation.

That's much clearer, isn't it? Notice that, when written as whole notes, the notes C, E, and G—the root, 3rd, and 5th, or R–3–5—sit in a nice vertical stack with no gaps between the notes and no notes pushed to one side. I like to call this stack of notes a **snowman chord**, because the three notes are stacked like the three big snowballs of a snowman. Snowman chords are the most basic chord shape in traditional music theory, and we're going to want to know them well.

Let's confirm the intervals between these notes. If the chord is rewritten with the notes spaced horizontally, we can bracket and identify all of the intervals between all of the notes in the chord. You should also play them along the 5th string of your guitar to confirm their linear distances.

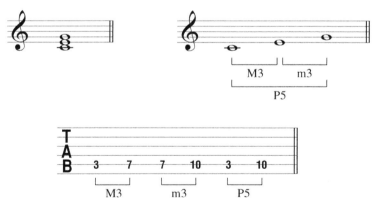

Now let's build some more snowman chords in the key of C. At this point, this is strictly paperwork—not guitar work. Pull out a piece of music manuscript paper and write out each of the following chords, snowman-style. You already have the C major chord, so continue with the chord built on the second note of the scale, D. Using the "play a note, skip a note, play a note, skip a note, and play a note" approach, you should find yourself with the notes D, F, and A for the root, 3rd, and 5th functions. Examining the intervals between these notes, I hope you notice that the distance from D to F is a *minor 3rd*—not a major 3rd as in the C major chord. The minor 3rd is shorthanded "m3." You should also see that the distance from F to A is a *major 3rd* (M3), and the distance of D to A is a perfect 5th (P5). Because of the minor 3rd or ♭3 in this chord, we call it a D minor chord (Dm), and its functional spelling is R–♭3–5.

Next in line is the note E, and its snowman chord is Em. Again, notice how the distance between the notes gives us a functional spelling of R–♭3–5.

Continuing with the chords built on F and G, you should find that they are both major, functionally spelled R–3–5, and the chord built on A is a R–♭3–5 minor.

Something curious happens when we build a snowman chord on the note B, though. The distance from B to D is a minor 3rd, so we might suspect that B will be a minor chord in the key of C. But when we stack that 5th note, F, on top of the D, we find that it's also a minor 3rd above D, and so it's a *diminished* 5th above the root note, B. The functional spelling of this chord then is R–♭3–♭5, and it's called a diminished triad, no doubt in honor of that diminished 5th. The usual symbol for "diminished" is a little circle (B°), although I prefer the suffix "dim," as in Bdim. You'll see it both ways.

Perhaps you've been strumming along as we've worked our way through these chords. You probably had no problem with basic shapes for the first six chords, but what's up with that B°? Here you are, playing the most basic chords in the most basic key of C, and here's this insect of a chord that turns your fingers into a pretzel and doesn't even sound so great when you finally figure out how to play it. Don't ignore it or pretend it doesn't exist; the diminished triad is a cool key to unlocking several universes of sound in our system of music. We'll get back to it soon.

Complete your snowman chords in the key of C by bringing them home with a final C major chord one octave higher than the starting chord. Then number them with Roman numerals: upper case for major, lower case for minor, and lower case plus "°" for our close personal friend, the B° chord. Your completed set of chords should look like this:

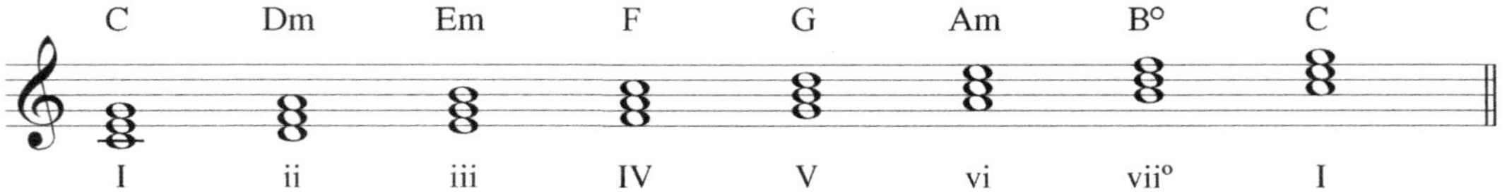

Because this system of putting a chord together is based on stacking one note atop the other at an interval of a 3rd, it is referred to as **traditional tertian harmony**. "Tertian" actually means, somewhat obliquely, "every other thing" and is based on the Latin word *tertius*. Another term for this stacking-of-3rds approach to basic chord construction is **traditional 3rds-based harmony**. We refer to the chords you just constructed as **traditional tertiary triads** (or 3rds-based triads, or triads built on 3rds, or chords built on 3rds, etc.).

Here are two exercises that every guitarist should work through:

- Create thirteen armies of snowmen. Write out and name all the basic major, minor, and diminished chords in every common major key. It's in the figure above in the key of C, and that's a good place to begin. You might continue by choosing new keys chromatically, in which case the next key would be C♯ major – or would it be D♭ major? Try both, and deide for yourself which is easier to work in. The key after that would be D major, then E♭ major, and so on. Another approach to organizing your armies of snowmen is to follow the keys through the circle of fifths and fourths, as was shown back on page 2, at the beginning of the chapter entitled **A Prelude in Musicspeak**. You will develop a much stronger sense of the correct combinations of chords and how they are named by working through an exercise like this.

- It would also be a good idea at this point in your study of chord theory to grab your guitar, a pencil, and some music paper and write out all of your basic open-position major and minor chords in standard music notation. The basic major chords in open position are C, G, D, A, and E major; the basic minor chords are Dm, Am, and Em. You'll find them just a few pages back in the section entitled **A Beginner's Collection of Chords in Open Position**. You should be able to identify the function (root, 3rd, or 5th) of each note in each of these chords, and you should be able to reduce each chord to a snowman chord on paper. You don't have to play them as snowman chords (yet); just write them out. By the way, you'll see the functional analysis in every chord diagram right there at the bottom of each block diagram, so you could suffer from the belief that since you have this book in your hands, you now somehow own this information. Not so. Close the book, sit with your guitar and some music-writing materials, and write it all out. Puzzle it out. And most importantly, listen to the quality of the notes.

Moving From Chord to Chord

Chords move. In most of the music that we listen to today, we hear a series of chords played in an even rhythmic pulsation. Whether we are creating or recreating a guitar part based on these chords, or imitating the sound of other musicians playing chords—a piano player and a drummer, or a keyboard synthesizer and a sampled rhythm track, for example—we usually generate this rhythmic pulsation by strumming the strings of the guitar. The easiest way to notate this kind of rhythm and chord changing is with a ***rhythm chart***. In a rhythm chart, a time signature (4/4, 3/4, 2/4, 6/8, etc.) is written at the beginning of the music. The music is divided into appropriate measures, or bars, with bar lines. Within each bar, the rhythm can be shown with a series of diagonal lines usually representing the beats. Chord names are written above these diagonal lines, or slashes, to indicate when to play the appropriate chord, and for how many beats. Here's a simple rhythm chart using the most common open position major and minor chords:

Open Position Major and Minor Chords

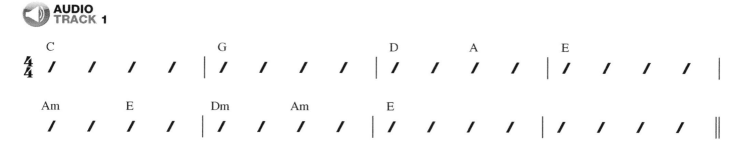

The simplest interpretation of a rhythm chart is to strum one time for each beat, but the strumming rhythm can be made simpler or more complex as the music dictates. Listen to the audio example, and you will hear the strumming in the first four bars just as it is written—once per diagonal line. The strumming rhythm becomes busier in the last four bars, but the chords still change according to the beats as written.

Technique Tip: Changing Chords

Guitarists of all levels of skill will come across chord fingerings that are challenging to play at certain tempos. Here's a way to build confidence and increase speed and accuracy in changing chords. Begin with the chord that's most challenging and pair it with a chord that's easier. As an example, we'll pair E/G# (with a partial barre of the first finger and a somewhat delicate placement of the third and fourth fingers) with an Asus2 (using only the strong first and second fingers).

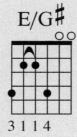

E/G♯   Asus2

3 1 1 4   1 2

Play each chord carefully and without regard for time. Take as long as you need to get a clear sound from each string in the most difficult chord, and then switch to the easier chord. Within a couple of minutes, you'll begin to feel a cadence and tempo forming—perhaps three seconds to place the fingers and play the difficult chord, and less than a second to play the easy one. Turn on a metronome now and set it to 60 beats per minute (one beat per second).

continued on next page

Technique Tip: Changing Chords, cont'd.

Play the chords like this:

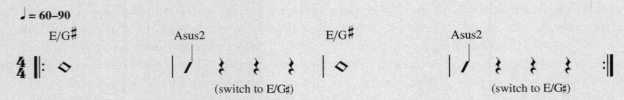

Notice that you should be holding the difficult chord for a relatively long time, then playing the easy chord briefly and giving yourself three seconds (three beats of rest) to set up your fingers for the difficult chord. Play this repetitively for about a minute at a time (about eight repetitions of the two chords at this tempo). Now increase the speed by about 15%. In this example, that would be 72 beats per minute. (A 15% increase in tempo is usually a very "human" change—just enough to feel, but not impossible to do.) Again, play about eight repetitions. You might try yet another leap of 15% in the tempo, to about 84 beats per minute. This could easily constitute a five-minute block of a day's practice; do this for several days until you can begin at the fastest tempo. Continue increasing the tempo in this way until you can play at a tempo that's about 50% faster than your starting tempo. In this example, that would be about 88 to 92 beats per minute. Now return to your original tempo, but shave a beat off of the switching time by adding a strum to the easy chord, like this:

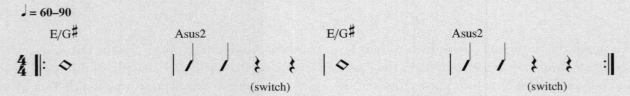

Notice that you've decreased your switching time from three seconds to two seconds. Repeat the incremental increase in tempo through the same range of numbers, then once again shave another beat off the switching time and return to the original tempo. (Your switching time is now one quarter rest or about one second.)

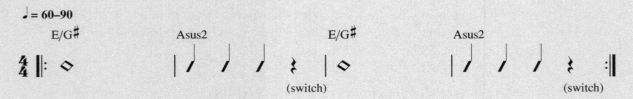

Your hands will build up a muscular memory, and within a week or two, the difficult chord will become quite playable. You'll soon be able to play it with continuous strumming. This process can be heard in miniature on the audio track.

Another important part of understanding how chords move is by appreciating that we humans seek a **tonal center** when we hear music. We might say that, in an objective sense, chords are just blobs of vibrations, but in our subjective listening world, we apply an intricate set of values to the notes in a chord. It's almost as if we are following a road or a set of instructions as one chord unfolds into another. The music begins, and a chord is formed. When another chord arrives in the music, we feel that the music has moved. Perhaps it's moved forward, moved away from what we like, or moved us deeply. But we sense motion when chords change.

If you took the time to do the functional analysis of the eight basic open chords that I discussed earlier (C, G, D, A, E, Dm, Am, and Em), you might have noticed a curious thing: a note common to two different chords will have a totally different function. As a quick example, let's examine C, Em, and G. In the C chord, the note C is the root of the chord, E is the 3rd (a major 3rd, of course), and G is the 5th (a perfect 5th, as you so well know). Yet, in the Em chord (which has two notes in common with the C chord), E is now the root, and G is the 3rd. When we change to a G chord from Em, G becomes the root, and B is the 3rd. Two things are happening here, both of which are important in understanding chord motion. First, each chord is like a little universe or atom with notes revolving around its root. We always define chord tones with respect to the root of the chord of the moment, regardless of what chord precedes or follows it. Even when one or more notes are common to two chords, we sense some kind of shift when the chords shift. Second, there's a pleasant commonality between G, Em and C. Each chord shares two notes from the previous chord, and every new note that's introduced is common to two closely related keys—specifically C major and G major. It's commonly said that there's very little harmonic motion between these chords.

There's another kind of chord motion that's essential to understanding Western harmony. This is the concept of **tension and resolution**. Throughout this book, we'll examine chords for their relative stability. What we'll find is that the choice of stable and unstable chords, and the length of time each chord sounds, is a primary building block in understanding how chords move and how we perceive tonal centers.

Here are some brief exercises to show how chords create a tonal center and how tension and resolution can help to guide that tonal center.

Etudes for Establishing a Tonal Center

If we use just the three chords we were just talking about—C, Em, and G—we can create a tonal center that feels like C major by starting and ending on the C chord and emphasizing its use. (You might try improvising some melodies in C major over this progression.)

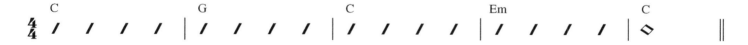

The very same chords, reordered and with a greater emphasis on the G chord, will sound as though they favor G major as a tonal center. (Again, try improvising in G major over this progression.)

When we introduce chords that sound unstable by themselves, or that introduce some musical tension between more stable chords, the sense of a tonal center can be made stronger, or even redirected to a new tonal center. The following figure mixes the three previous chords with several more active chords to lead us from C major to E minor.

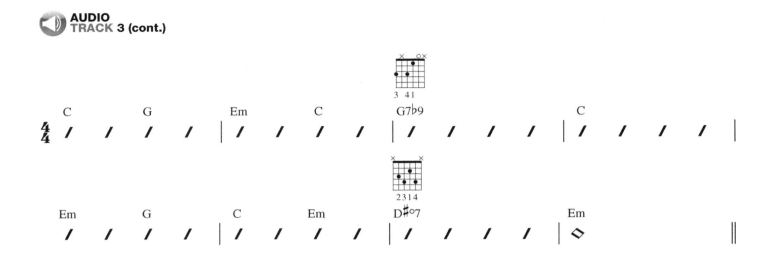

The Dilemma of Becoming a Musician, Rather than Just a Guitar Player

If you are just beginning on the path of music, you might find some of the challenges I've presented to be daunting—perhaps even annoying. This is good; there's some music that comes easily through the guitar and some that doesn't. As we continue to play the guitar, and to tackle chords on the guitar, we need to look towards what makes us better musicians—not just better guitar players. There's a vocabulary of common "guitarisms" that causes most guitarists to sound like each other—keys that are easy to play in because they favor open strings, for instance, and chords that are easy to use because they favor comfortable fingerings. Perhaps when you were naming all the chords in all of the major keys, you noticed a whole lot of chords—simple major and minor chords!—that didn't appear in **A Beginner's Collection of Chords in Open Position**. Perhaps you got a sense that the world of music is bigger than you thought. The next chapter will introduce ways to understand these myriad chords—perhaps even to give you a sense of becoming a musician.

CHAPTER TWO:

Movable Chord Shapes, Part One— The Barre Chord

What Is a Movable Chord Shape?

A movable chord shape is one that does not contain any open strings and can therefore be moved up and down on a string set while retaining the same chord **quality**. By **quality**, we mean that the structure of the chord remains the same. If we reduce the chord to its simplest snowman constuction and analyze all of the intervals within the chord, we'd have a recipe for that chord's quality. (You'll find the complete list of possible tertiary triads, along with their recipes, back at the top of page 26.) When different chords have the same quality, it means that they are all major, or all minor, or all diminished, etc. This should be easy to see when we take a simple chord fingering and move it up the neck. For example, take this chord:

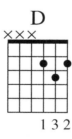

Don't strum any other strings except the three that you're pressing down. Now move your fingers up one fret, and you have an E♭ (or D♯) major chord. Ta-daaa!

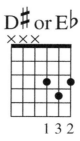

There's a movable chord shape for you. We can call this shape a "D major type of shape" or, as I like to call it, a D-type shape. Notice that, as long as we play just the three strings that are fretted, we can move this chord up and down on the three strings and it will be some kind of a major chord. It will always retain it's major quality. However, playing just three strings is not always a useful approach to playing chords on the guitar, especially for the beginner or early intermediate level of player. If you're trying this as you read along, you've probably already played this shape in a few places besides the one I've suggested, and you may have accidentally hit some open strings as well—probably the open D or A strings. Sometimes a higher shape will sound good with one or more of these open strings, and sometimes it won't. There's a lot of fun to be found in this kind of meandering, and you should feel free to explore this. But for the present moment, let's get back to exploring movable shapes. What we need is a set of shapes (or fingerings) that are relatively easy to play, that use all (or most) of the strings, and that can be moved up and down the neck while retaining their quality.

If you've been playing the guitar or a year or two, you've probably begun to play **barre chords**. Hopefully, you've been a bit successful, as the repertoire of chords to be played without the barre technique is severely limited. But if you've struggled with getting a good sound from the guitar when trying to play a barre (pronounced "bar"), hang tough and I'll show you some approaches to conquer this challenge. First, let's look at why barre chords are so useful and how they are formed.

Why Barre Chords Are Useful

If you refer back to the chord diagrams I introduced back in **A Beginner's Collection of Chords in Open Position**, you'll find that some chord roots occur quite frequently, and some occur hardly at all. We can say that some chords (like these open position chords) are very friendly to the beginning guitarist, and some are not. And if you look back to the exercise of building snowman chords at the bottom of page 28, you'll realize that if you limit yourself to just these open position chords, you miss a lot of chords from any given key. If you don't mind the limitation of always sounding like a beginning guitarist, don't bother to learn to play barre chords. But if you do mind that limitation—and I suspect you do or you wouldn't be reading this book—then read on, and get ready to play.

Barre chords are useful because they give us everything we asked for in a set of movable chord shapes:

- They're relatively easy to play and remember.
- They use all (or most) of the strings.
- They can be moved up and down the neck while retaining their quality.

On the guitar, a barre is a fingering where one finger presses down two or more strings at the same fret. The easiest barre to play is with the first finger straight across all six strings, and the easiest place to do this on the guitar is around the seventh fret. The diagram for a barre at the seventh fret, along with an illustration of what the hand looks like, is shown below.

When we first try to play a barre, we tend to put our first finger straight across the neck and pile up our other fingers atop it for added strength. The resulting sound may be six clearly ringing strings, but the resulting chord is pretty limited in its use. We need to liberate our other fingers and maximize the function of the first finger. Here's the perfect exercise to build strength in the first finger barre.

An Exercise to Get You Ready for Barre Chords

When you play more than one string at the same fret with just one finger, it is called a "barre" (pronounced "bar"). The barre is indicated in a chord diagram with an arch connecting two or more dots. You'll also see the same finger indicated with a number below all the barred strings. In the diagram at right, the first finger is pressing down the high E, B, and G strings at the third fret.

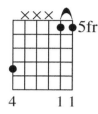

Try the shape shown at the left at fifth position. Notice that the first finger is barring the two highest strings, while the poor little pinky is all alone at the eighth fret on the low E string. In order to get this grip, you'll find it almost absolutely necessary to put your thumb well behind the back of the neck, about halfway between the first and fourth fingers. Play only the three strings that you're pressing down. When you can get a good sound from these three notes, try this sequence:

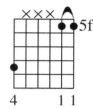 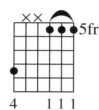 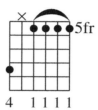 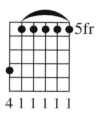

Go through this sequence slowly and carefully. Don't expect it to be instantaneously playable, and don't over-work your hand. It may take several short sessions over several days or weeks to get it. Once you can play the shapes as shown, move down to fourth, third, second, and first position as shown in the following music example.

An Exercise for Developing the Barre

Where Do Barre Chords Come From?

Barre chords are derived from open chord shapes. The first four barre chords that we'll tackle are based on the shape of the open E, Em, A, and Am chords. This will give us two different major and minor chord shapes.

Transforming an Open E Chord into a Barre Chord

Let's begin by transforming the open E chord into a barre chord. The concept is fairly simple. Visualize the guitar's nut—the piece that the strings rest on at the end of the fretboard leading to the headstock—as a straight line stopping the six strings. In a very real sense, the nut is a "zero fret," stopping the strings just as our fingers stop a string when we press them into the frets. Now re-fret a common E chord *without* using your first finger. In other words, use fingers 3, 4, and 2 on strings 5, 4, and 3, respectively. Then lay your first finger down across all the strings behind the nut. That's your barre chord shape. Slide all your fingers up one fret, so that your first finger is actually fretting the strings, and you'll be playing an E-type barre chord.

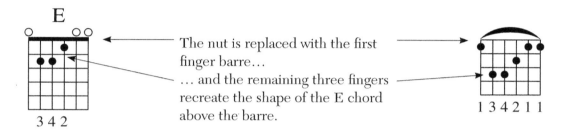

The nut is replaced with the first finger barre…
… and the remaining three fingers recreate the shape of the E chord above the barre.

Transforming the E-Type Barre Chord into an Em-Type and Am-Type

Once this concept and execution is clear, it's pretty easy to transform this E-type barre chord into an Em-type barre and an Am-type barre, as shown in Fig. 14.

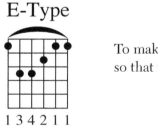

To make this shape minor, lift the second finger so that the third string rings ar the barre.

To make the Am-type shape, move the 2nd, 3rd, and 4th fingers over one string as shown.

Transforming an Open A Chord into an A Barre Chord

There's one more basic barre chord shape we need to conquer. It's based on the open A major chord. For a beginner, it's a pain-in-the-butt grip, or perhaps we should call it a pain in the *thenar eminence*—the muscle at the base of the thumb. There are three different fingerings for this shape, and they're all discussed below. I trust that you can see how, in all of these fingerings, the barred shapes relate to the open A chord.

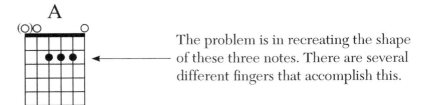

The problem is in recreating the shape of these three notes. There are several different fingers that accomplish this.

(1)1 3 3 3 1

First, tackle the dreaded "double barre."

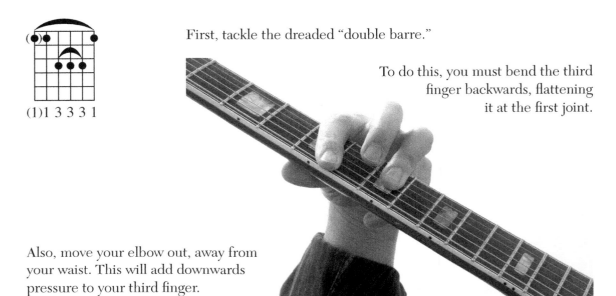

To do this, you must bend the third finger backwards, flattening it at the first joint.

Also, move your elbow out, away from your waist. This will add downwards pressure to your third finger.

The third finger might touch (and mute) the high E string. This is fine. However, the B or 2nd string **must** ring.

(1)1 4 4 4 1

Another solution is to barre with the 4th finger. I can't do this very well, but I've seen it done by James Taylor, George Harrison, Eric Clapton, and several of my students over the years.

(1)1 2 3 4 1

Yet another solution is to recreate the shape of the open A with your second, third, and fourth fingers. I use this fingering when I need the (barred) high E string to ring clearly and/or when I need to change just one of the notes held by the 2nd, 3rd, or 4th fingers.

In summary, we now have four barre chord shapes to use. We'll generalize and call them E-type and A-type barres, and here they are, including their functional analyses.

major

1 3 4 2 1 1
R 5 R 3 5 R

minor

1 3 4 1 1 1
R 5 R♭3 5 R

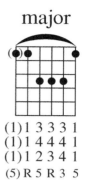

major

(1) 1 3 3 3 1
(1) 1 4 4 4 1
(1) 1 2 3 4 1
(5) R 5 R 3 5

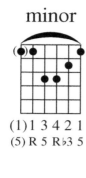

minor

(1) 1 3 4 2 1
(5) R 5 R♭3 5

Here are some points to keep in mind regarding the function of each note in each of these chords.

- **The most important note to know is the lowest root in each of these shapes.** To state the obvious: the lowest root of the E-type chords is on the low E string, and the lowest root of the A-type chords is on the A string. This means that if we can name the notes on the low E and A strings, we can play all of the major and minor chords built on those root notes. Pay attention to this, because we're going to put it to work in bit.

- **In each of these shapes, there's only one 3rd, identified as either 3 or ♭3.** It is absolutely vital that the 3rd rings. If it doesn't, you're not playing a major or minor chord; you're playing a "five" chord—a.k.a. a "power chord." We'll get to them in the next chapter. They're great chords, but you should be able to play major, minor, and "five" chords with intention.

- **In the A-type barre chords, I'm showing the barred low E string as an optional note to play by placing it in parentheses.** When most beginning guitarists are confronted with the task of playing barre chords, it's all they can do to get their index finger down and get a clear sound out of the appropriate strings. This is fine at first, but as you evolve in your musicianship, you should recognize that playing the 5th below the lowest root makes for a somewhat lopsided sound. Again, we'll work on this a little further along in the text.

Returning to the first point above—if we can name the notes on the low E and A strings, we can play all of the major and minor chords built on those root notes—it should be apparent that if we want to move on in any significant way as chord-playing guitarists, we should be able to name the notes on the low E and A strings. To help you with this task, I hereby present the following:

A Map of Notes on the Low E String

Good for finding ROOT NOTES of chords

The open string is the note E

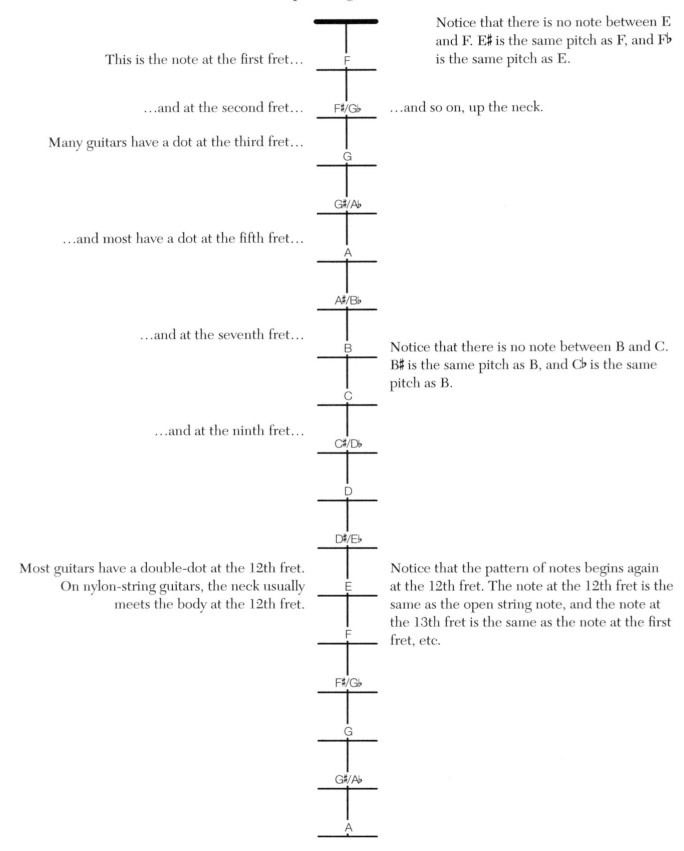

Notice that there is no note between E and F. E♯ is the same pitch as F, and F♭ is the same pitch as E.

This is the note at the first fret...

...and at the second fret...

...and so on, up the neck.

Many guitars have a dot at the third fret...

...and most have a dot at the fifth fret...

...and at the seventh fret...

Notice that there is no note between B and C. B♯ is the same pitch as B, and C♭ is the same pitch as B.

...and at the ninth fret...

Most guitars have a double-dot at the 12th fret. On nylon-string guitars, the neck usually meets the body at the 12th fret.

Notice that the pattern of notes begins again at the 12th fret. The note at the 12th fret is the same as the open string note, and the note at the 13th fret is the same as the note at the first fret, etc.

A Map of Notes on A String

Good for finding ROOT NOTES of chords

The open string is the note A

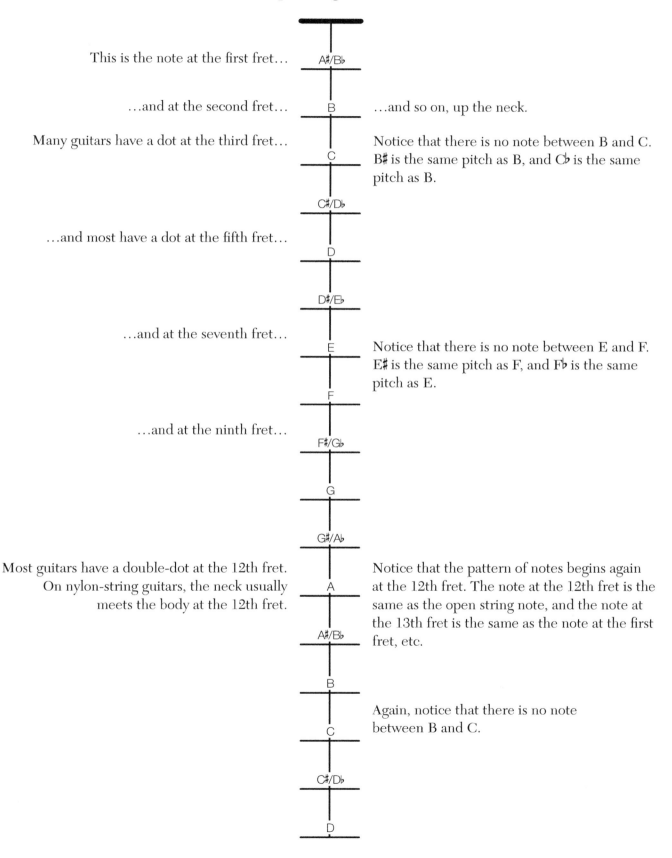

This is the note at the first fret...   A#/B♭

...and at the second fret...   B   ...and so on, up the neck.

Many guitars have a dot at the third fret...   Notice that there is no note between B and C.
B♯ is the same pitch as B, and C♭ is the same
C   pitch as B.

C#/D♭

...and most have a dot at the fifth fret...   D

D#/E♭

...and at the seventh fret...   E   Notice that there is no note between E and F.
E♯ is the same pitch as F, and F♭ is the same
F   pitch as E.

...and at the ninth fret...   F#/G♭

G

G#/A♭

Most guitars have a double-dot at the 12th fret.
On nylon-string guitars, the neck usually   A   Notice that the pattern of notes begins again
meets the body at the 12th fret.   at the 12th fret. The note at the 12th fret is the
same as the open string note, and the note at
A#/B♭   the 13th fret is the same as the note at the first
fret, etc.

B

Again, notice that there is no note
C   between B and C.

C#/D♭

D

Reality Check:

You should be able to play the barre chord shapes I've just introduced.

- You understand the idea of what a root note is, and you can identify it in the just-introduced barre chords.

- You know the notes on the low E and A strings well enough to move among them with your barre chords. (A note to instructors and motivated students: it's not too hard to come up with simple drills to strengthen note recognition, first on a single string, then on the string set. For example, you might play this sequence of major barre chords with the root on the low E string: F, F♯, G, G♯, A, A♭, G, G♭, F. Then create a similar sequence with the root on the A string. Mix the two. Move to a new area of the neck, and so forth. But don't get too caught up in exercises without playing some music as well.)

- I've observed that many guitarists, having spent most of their time playing open-position chords, tend to confuse "minor" with "sharp" or "flat." When they are playing a major barre chord and I ask them to "make it minor," they tend to move one fret lower or higher. It's important to recognize this confusion and address it. Using the barre chord shapes I've just introduced, you should clearly understand that the difference between a major and a minor chord with the same root will be found within the same position.

- Another common point of confusion among beginners is that of ***enharmonic equivalence***. It takes a while for some to get comfortable with the fact that, for example, F♯ and G♭ are the same. Acknowledging that sharps and flats rarely intermingle in music notation, especially at first, it's a good practice to play musical examples and exercises that use sharps and flats equally.

Here are some exercises for putting your barre chords to work. These are written in the form of a simple rhythm chart, which indicates only the chord name and the number of beats each chord receives. Simple charts like these should be springboards for creativity. You can play them fast or slow, in any style at all. Listen to the audio tracks, both to confirm that you are playing the correct chords and to hear the variety of styles in which they can be played.

An Exercise for E-Type and A-Type Major Barre Chords

- In this and all subsequent exercises, you should be able to identify the lowest root note of each chord.

- Play every chord as a barre chord.

- In theory, no chord in this exercise is more than three positions from the previous chord. However, you'll probably "run out of neck" at some point, and a leap of more than three positions will be necessary.

AUDIO TRACK 5

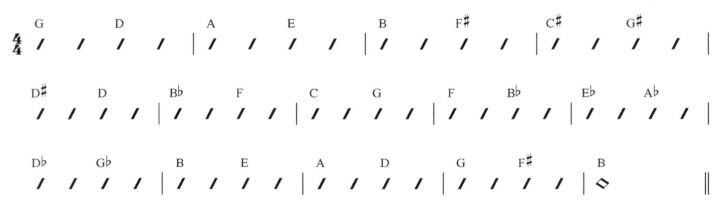

An Exercise for E-Type and A-Type Minor Barre Chords
Reminders:

- Identify the lowest root note of each chord.

- Play every chord as a barre chord.

- Keep the chords as close to each other as possible by alternating between E-type and A-type shapes. Make a large leap only when necessary.

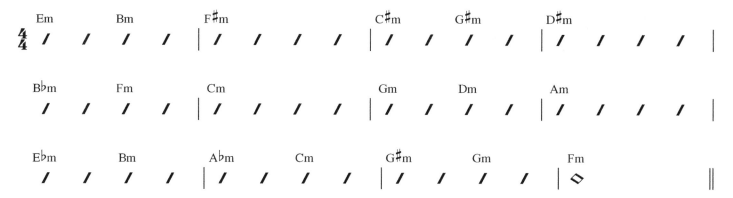

Also, feel free to write on the chart to remind yourself when you need to move or where a hard-to-remember chord is.

An Exercise for E-Type and A-Type Major and Minor Barre Chords

Perhaps you noticed that, in the last three exercises, the chord sequences had a somewhat unsettled quality. This was deliberate. I organized the chord names and locations in a mildly surprising way, with sequences that would not be found in most popular music of the moment. Now, let's reground ourselves and return to our old friend, the ***major tonality***, and use these barre chords in a slightly different way. Look back on page 28, when we were making snowman chords, yet were limited to open-position chord fingerings. You'll recall that we couldn't play all of the chords in any one major key. With the barre chords just introduced, we almost can. We need one more chord shape to get us by, and that's the diminished triad. I consider the simple diminished triad sort of a "stunt" chord at this point in our chord vocabulary. It is nearly impossible to find in any popular song, and the fingerings are annoying. But bear with me. It's worth working through for the sake of your fingers, your ears, and your brain.

Here's a gift: two movable diminished chord shapes.

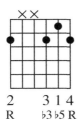

2   3 1 4
R   ♭3 ♭5 R

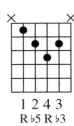

1 2 4 3
R ♭5 R ♭3

Technique Tip:

There's no way (in standard tuning, at least) to play a diminished chord using a full barre. These shapes include strings that must be muted or unplayed, or the chords will sound foul. If you're working on right-hand fingerpicking technique, this may be less of a problem, but strummers like myself will want to observe the following:

- In the case of the diminished triad with the root on the low E string, slant the second finger slightly towards the A string so that it presses the low E string and mutes the A string. Place the third finger on the G string with a little preference towards the D string. With a little attention and work, you should be able to mute the D with the tip of the third finger.

- In the case of the diminished triad with the root on the A string, place the first finger on the A string with a little preference towards the low E string. Placed correctly, the tip of the first finger can mute the low E string. The first finger can also flop over the high E string right about where the finger meets the palm of the hand, which should keep that string muted.

With these two shapes, we can now play a really nice, simple, grounded chord progression: the ***harmonized major scale***. Musically, there's nothing spectacular about this; in fact, it has a kind of first-year student quality to it. Consequently, it's amazing to me how few guitarists can play this. Become one of the few and play through these next exercises.

An Etude for Movable Chords in G Major

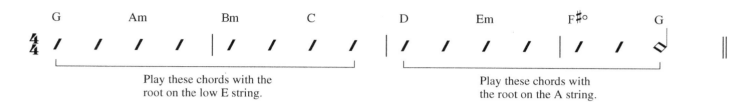

Play these chords with the root on the low E string.

Play these chords with the root on the A string.

An Etude for Movable Chords in C Major

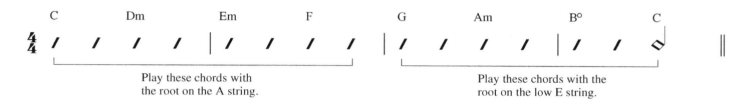

Play these chords with the root on the A string.

Play these chords with the root on the low E string.

CHAPTER THREE:

Introducing the "5" Chord

(also known as the Power chord, the "no 3rds" chord, the modal chord, or the open 5th)

The Origin of the Power Chord

There's a huge list of songs you can play using the major, minor, and (very rarely) the diminished chords we've just introduced. But there's much more that any guitarist worth his or her salt will want to know to be functional in contemporary music. A large (but moderately simply played) category of chords is the "5" chord, written as C5, F#5, Bb5, etc. When I was first learning chords and chord theory in the late 1960s, these chords revealed one of the first "disconnects" between what I played and what was described to me in general music theory. Music theory taught that the most basic chord was a triad—three different notes—which would contain a root, a major or minor 3rd, and a perfect, diminished, or augmented 5th. Remember this from the beginning of Chapter One? Well, almost as soon as I started playing guitar, I noticed the widespread use of something else that functioned just like a chord, but didn't fit the traditional definition. It was a root note and a perfect 5th, with no 3rd.

There were two musical contexts in which these chords-that-weren't-chords were used. On the electric guitar, the sound of deliberate distortion had just come into use. Guitar amps were played at or near the limit of their output, overdriving the tubes and generating thick, woolly distortion. Pedals such as the Fuzz Face became as necessary as a cable to achieve that same meltdown tone at reasonable volume as well as for their own sonic signature. What any decent guitarist noticed was that, when the distortion got pretty thick, those basic major and minor barre chords (which had done great service in the playing of rock 'n' roll through the fifties and early sixties) sounded kind of crappy. It took a decade or two to sort out exactly why all that good, thick distortion obliterated the old school triads, but the quick and practical upshot was that electric guitarists began playing only the lowest strings of barre chords—the root and the 5th, with no 3rd at all. They were great for playing thick, powerful chord-like riffs and so became known among guitarists as "power" chords.

Guitarists of the electric variety weren't the only ones using this "no 3rds" sound. Many styles of folk music employed these, and the quasi-academic term I recall for them in a "folk" context was "modal" chords. They could be heard in bluegrass music, in American and English folk songs, and in Southern blues, to name a few styles, and the cross-pollination of acoustic and electric music made this chord common currency among guitarists.

The insidious invasion of this evil chord-that-wasn't caused all manner of trouble for music transcribers. Sheet music had evolved around the piano as the primary instrument, with guitar chord names (and usually over-simplistic first-position block diagram shapes) floating above the melody line. Music that used power chords or modal chords was often plumped up with non-existent full triads. The result was sheet music that didn't sound like the song as played by the artist. How then to name this chord? I recall using a "3" with a slash through it for a while. The problem with this kind of symbol—and an important point to remember for all chord naming—is that there's no "3 with a slash through it" on a standard QWERTY keyboard. At this point in time, chords are best named with the numbers, letters, and symbols of the standard QWERTY keyboard and standard fonts. Finally, adding a "5" after the root has become the currently accepted shorthand for this kind of chord.

Playing Power Chords, Part One

Now let's play a few power chords on guitar. The most common shapes for these chords are shown below. Can you see how these shapes are found within the shapes of the barre chords we just covered?

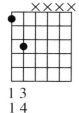

1 3
1 4
R 5

This is the simplest fingering…

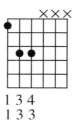

1 3 4
1 3 3
R 5 R

…and this is a fuller sounding fingering…

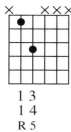

1 3
1 4
R 5

Here is the two-fingered grip with the root on the A string…

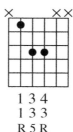

1 3 4
1 3 3
R 5 R

…and the fuller sounding fingering with the root on the A string.

Remember, the most important note in these (or any) chords is the root note—the note that names the chord. In all of the shapes shown, the root note is being played by the first finger. If you can name the note that the first finger is playing, you can name the chord. The charts on pages 40 and 41 are great for finding root notes on the low E and A strings. The next couple of exercises will help you with this in concept and execution if you haven't gotten it yet.

Technique Tip:

Some "five"-chord positions will sound good with open strings ringing (and we'll explore that cool sound in a bit), but some will sound like doggie doo-doo. To deaden unwanted strings when the root is on the low E string, allow your first finger to drape across the treble strings, almost as if you're playing a barre, but without pressing down—except at your fingertip, of course. When the root is on the A string, you can also allow your first finger to drape over and deaden the two higher open strings, but also extend the tip of your finger just enough to touch the open low E string.

To build up your confidence in playing "five" chords, try the next exercise.

"Five" Chord Etude

AUDIO TRACK 10

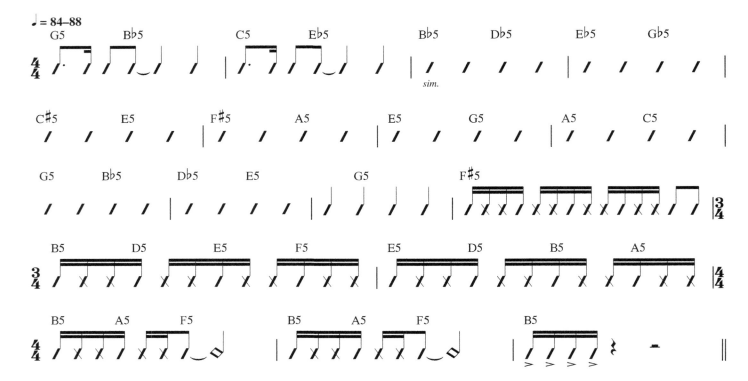

Reminders:

- Identify the lowest root note of each chord.
- Play every chord as a "five" chord—no majors or minors, and no open strings.
- Keep the chords as close to each other as possible by alternating between E-root and A-root shapes. Make a large leap only when necessary.
- Feel free to write on the chart to remind yourself when you need to move, or where a hard-to-remember chord is.

Open "Five" Chords

While we're looking at "five" chords, let's return for a moment to our open chords and see how they can be modified to sound as "five" chords. The strategy is simple: know where the 3rd is in either the major or minor chord shape, and don't play it. You can do this in one of three ways, and you'll see each of these in the shapes to come:

- Mute the string that has the 3rd on it.
- Play another note (usually the 5th) instead of the 3rd on a given string.
- Don't play the string with the 3rd at all.

Examine each of the following open chord shapes carefully and see if you can identify all the notes in each chord. Sure, you can just read the analysis at the bottom of the chord, but see if you can name the notes and analyze them without looking at the diagrams. Be sure that you can see how the 3rd was taken out of the chord. Most importantly, play the chords correctly and see if you can hear the quality of the missing 3rd. Can you switch back and forth between an open "five" chord and its major or minor counterpart and hear the 3rd coming and going?

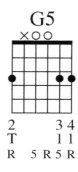

G5

2   3 4
T   1 1
R 5 R 5 R

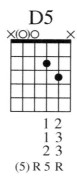

D5

1 2
1 3
2 3
(5) R 5 R

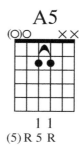

A5

1 1
(5) R 5 R

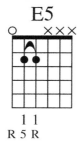

E5

1 1
R 5 R

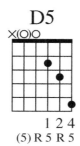

D5

1 2 4
(5) R 5 R 5

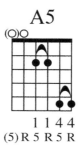

A5

1 1 4 4
(5) R 5 R 5 R

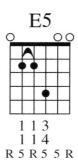

E5

1 1 3
1 1 4
R 5 R 5 5 R

Technique Tips:

- To mute the A string in the G5 chord, touch it lightly with your second finger or your thumb, depending on which is fretting the low E string.

- To mute the low E string in the first D5 chord, try using your thumb. The thumb can also mute the low E string in the first A5.

- To mute the high E string in the first D5 chord, use either your first or second finger.

- The second D5 and A5 chords may seem like a stretch. Now's the time to work on them—note that you're keeping your fingers within a four-fret range, which should be a natural range for most hands. The trick is to pay attention to your thumb; keep it behind the neck, towards the center of your palm, and in line behind your second finger. The unsounded strings are simply not played or, in some cases, might be muted with the right/picking hand.

You might also puzzle through these challenges:

- Why is there no open C5? Can you make up a C5 fingering?

- Can you make up fingerings for any other open "five" chords that aren't given here?

An Introduction to Inversions and "Slash" Chords Through the "Five" Chord

When we *invert* a chord, we play it with a note other than the root as the lowest note. Inversions really come to life when we apply them to triads, which we'll do in the next chapter, but let's preview the concept with "five" chords. Remember that the "five" chord consists of just two notes: a root note and a perfect 5th. We can double these notes in different octaves, but remember that, as long as the sound can be reverted to just the two notes in question, it's a "five" chord. Since there are only two different notes in a "five" chord, there's going to be only two possible notes as the lowest note in the chord: the root or the 5th.

To show an inversion of a chord, a slash is used. Look back to the first chords in **A Beginner's Collection of Chords in Open Position**. Notice that the first and second chords are both named "C" because the note C—the root of the chord—is the lowest note sounded. In the third chord, the note E sounds as the lowest note. This is reflected in the name: C/E. This is usually spoken as "C over E" and it means, literally, that a C chord is played over the note E. In traditional chord theory, this is often spoken as "C with an E in the bass." I refrain from using the term "bass" because, as guitar players, we don't know what the bass players are up to. Hopefully they can read and play the note to the right of the slash, but they may be less literate than you.

Now check out the following and see how a simple two-note E5 chord can blossom and travel all over the neck.

Recipes for Power Chord Inversions

Step One: Begin with this simple, open-position E5:

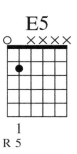

Step Two: Leapfrog the low E up an octave, over the B, making B the lowest of the two notes. These two specific notes can be played in two places on the guitar. There's no single common name for this inversion, by the way. It could be called E5/B ("E five over B") or it could be called B4 (a B plus E, the note a fourth above), the latter being fairly rare and not likely to be universally understood. In our current context, we'll call it E5/B.

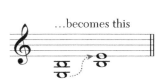
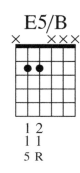
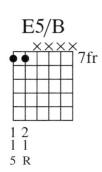

Step Three: Moving on, leapfrog the B up an octave, over the E. We're back to the root-plus-5th E5 from **Step One**, but an octave higher than where we started. These two notes can be played quite easily at several points on the neck.

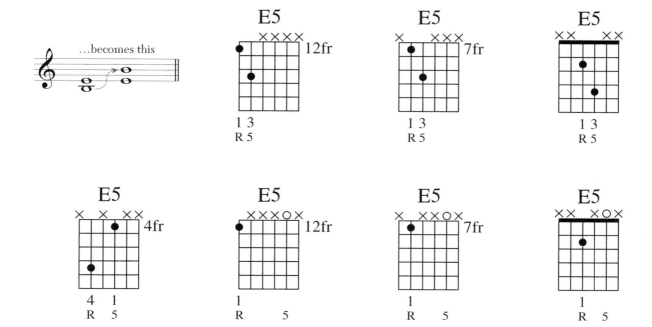

Step Four: Leapfrog the E up an octave, over the B. We're back to an E5/B, like the one we created in **Step Two**, but an octave higher. These two notes can be played on adjacent strings in five different places on the guitar. There are some possible ways of playing this E5/B using non-adjacent strings, but I'll leave it to you, gentle and aspiring guitarist, to find them. Notice, by the way, as we move into the guitar's upper register, that these pairs of notes feel less like a chord in the usual sense.

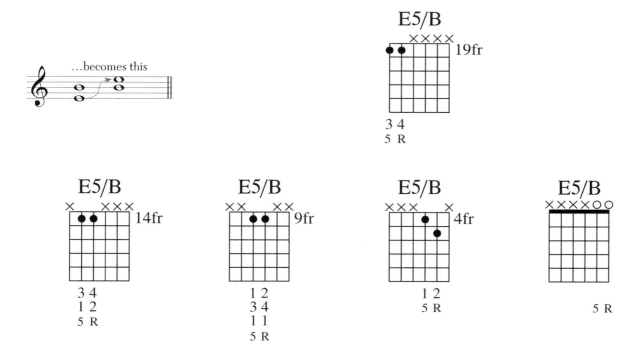

Step Five: Another leapfrog, and we're back to an E5 two octaves above our starting chord. Many electric guitars will have access to the nineteenth-position shape, and most guitars of any build will accommodate the fourteenth-position shape. If your guitar has 24 frets, try using that low E on fret 24 for a shape. Essay question: Do any of these feel at all like a chord to you?

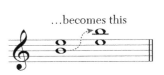

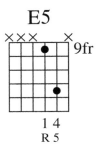

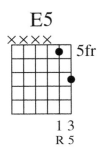

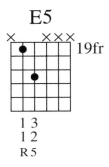

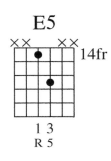

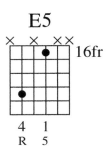

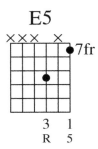

Technique Tips:

If you find yourself struggling with playing some of these upper-position shapes, consider your posture and how you hold the guitar. Stand or sit with a straight back and use your strap to support the guitar, raising it to where you can reach notes in twelfth position (and higher) without bending your wrist excessively. Strict classical guitarists who refuse to use a strap should be sure to raise the guitar on their leg by using a footstool of the proper height. The lower the neck and body of the guitar, the more your wrist will curl to reach notes in higher positions, and the more you will be tempted to grab the neck like a baseball bat, curling the fingers into a fist.

Also note that some of the notes played on non-adjacent strings require either very attentive muting of unplayed strings or alternative picking techniques, such as hybrid picking or finger picking, discussed on page 61.

There's a very important and interesting phenomenon about how we humans perceive music. The phenomenon has no formal name of which I'm aware, but it can be described like this: We humans tend to favor a tonal center in our music. Once a tonal center is established, we tend to "fill in the blanks" with any sound that follows, employing a persistence of memory that favors the maintenance of that tonal center. If a tonal center changes, we have a strong response to that change.

We can demonstrate (and experience) this phenomenon fairly easily using "five" chords. You'll recall that a "five" chord has no 3rd; it is neither major nor minor. Yet a sequence of "five" chords will tend to sound "right" when a major or minor tonal center is maintained. In the following example, the chords are all within the key of B♭ major. A B♭ major chord is never played, yet the use of the D5/A and the G5 fill in almost all of the notes of a B♭ major scale; the E♭5/B♭ in the third measure really seals the case.

An Etude for "Five" Chords with Inversions in B♭ Major

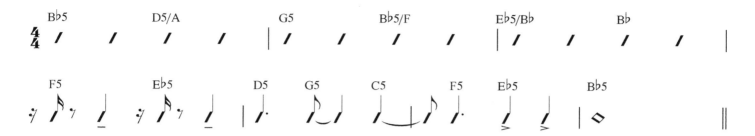

In this next example, the chords are all within the key of B♭ minor, and the same phenomenon occurs. By the time the B♭5 in the third measure is sounded, the progression is decidedly minor. You can test this persistence of memory by either fleshing out the chords with "inappropriate" 3rds or by swapping a minor-derived chord with a major-derived chord. For example, plump up the final B♭5 in the previous example with a B♭ minor. Sounds a little odd, doesn't it? Likewise, toss in a B♭ major at the end of the following example. Surprisingly bright, eh? Another test: swap out, say, the D5 in measure 5 of the preceding figure with a D♭5. Hmmm…. A little out of place, don't you think?

An Etude for "Five" Chords with Inversions in B♭ Minor

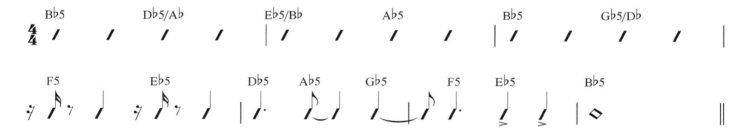

Let's do a little more exploring with open 5ths. First, let's construct a harmonized major scale with open 5ths, just like we did with full major and minor triads in the previous chapter. After the work of learning the miserable diminished triad, this will be a piece of cake. We'll begin with a G major scale with the root on the low E string and use the root-5th-octave (R–5–8) voicing of the five chord.

An Etude in G Major: Scalar Harmonization in Fifths and Octaves • Strings 4–5–6 and 3–4–5

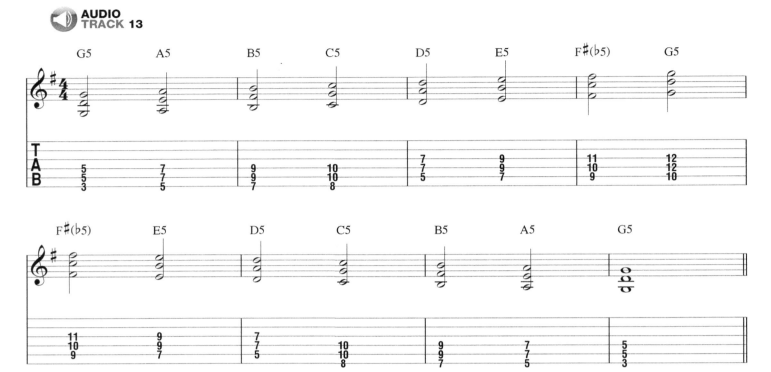

Notice that I've chosen to make a leap from the starting string set to the next highest string set at the halfway point, moving from the incomplete IV chord (C5) to the incomplete V chord (D5). Also notice that zany F#(♭5). It's an incomplete diminished triad. Outside of some metal, it doesn't show up in a lot of contemporary popular music (at least it hasn't yet) so I just made up a name for it. In this context, I think it makes good sense.

Here's another major scale in parallel 5ths using the R–5–8 voicing. The only thing to be aware of here is the shift in the shape of the chord because of the tuning between the G and B strings.

An Etude in C Major: Scalar Harmonization in Fifths and Octaves • Strings 3–4–5 and 2–3–4

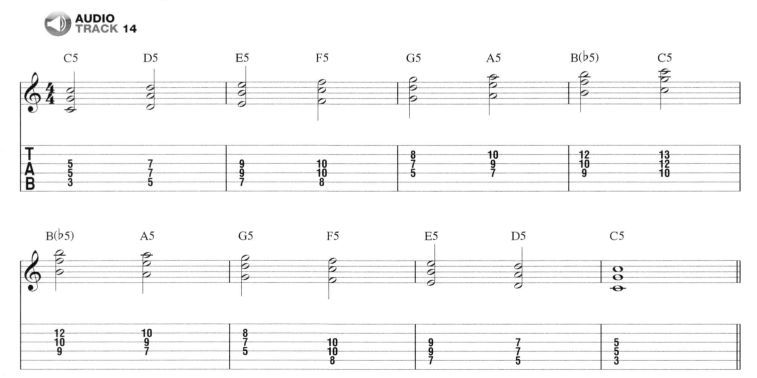

Here's a variation: In the next figure, we stay on string set 2–3–4, first using the R–5–8 voicing, then shifting to the 5–R–5 voicing. With gobs of distortion, you'll notice that this generates a "ghost bass" playing the notes shown in the second staff.

An Etude in F Major: Scalar Harmonization in Fifths and Octaves, with Inversions • Strings 2–3–4

AUDIO TRACK 15

Here's another variation that will lead us into another topic about open 5ths. Here we're playing parallel 4ths (inverted 5ths) without an added octave, and we're using shapes that move across the neck rather than up and down. Notice here that the "melody notes"—the scale notes—are supported with the 4th voiced below the root. If you place a 4th above the root, it feels unresolved. Try it, perhaps by harmonizing a C major scale with a 4th above (or a 5th below) the scale note and see what you get.

An Etude in E♭ Major: Scalar Harmonization in Fourths

AUDIO TRACK 16

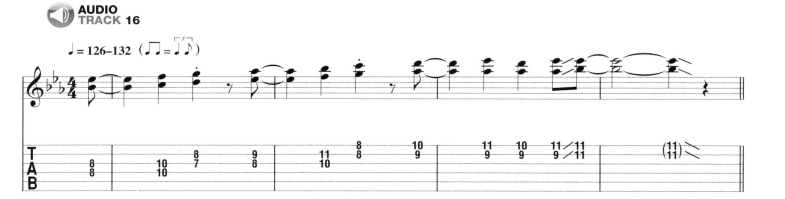

What the previous example hints at is that open 5ths and 4ths can function as chords or as harmonized melody notes. In the lower octave-and-a-half of the guitar, and particularly with open strings, these note groups feel very chord-like. But the higher we move on the neck (and also depending on the tone of the guitar), the more they begin to feel like intervals that are somewhat ambiguous as to what chord they are a part of. (Notice that above, I chose not to give each interval a chord name. It begins with E♭5/B♭, but the "chords" move so quickly that they function more like a harmonized melody, and the unwieldy long names crowd the page.) In fact, open 5ths and 4ths can take on aspects of both a chord and a harmonized melody. Let's explore this a bit.

Using Open 5ths and 4ths as Harmonized Melody Notes

First, we'll play some open 5ths and 4ths along with several open strings functioning as a ***drone***—a continuously ringing sound. The resulting sound is almost like a standard chord progression, but a little more grounded. The drone strings keep the chords from moving too far from the drone's home key. It's a sound that's common in traditional folk music from all over the world and was particularly common in popular music of the late sixties and early seventies by artists like Joni Mitchell, Crosby, Stills, Nash and Young, and Nick Drake. Jazz-based musicians such as Pat Metheny and Ralph Towner (Paul Winter Consort, Oregon) have gotten good mileage from this sound as well. Check it out.

An Etude for 5ths and 4ths with Drone Strings in E Major

 **AUDIO TRACK 17**

This audio track uses two chord shapes, as shown below. I leave it to you to decipher at what frets they are being played. Also note that many of the chord names would be more complex if the drone notes were added to the naming process.

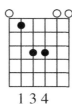

1 3 4

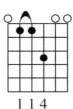

1 1 4

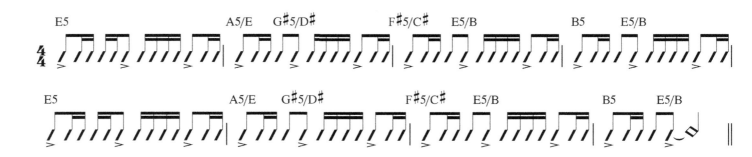

Now we'll explore the concept of open 5ths as a harmonized melody. Here's "Greensleeves" harmonized in 4ths and 5ths in a jazz-flavored environment. Don't worry about the chord names shown above the primary guitar part; if you can play them, absolutely do so, but if they elude you, read about them in later chapters.

Greensleeves: A Melody Harmonized in Fifths, Fourths and Octaves

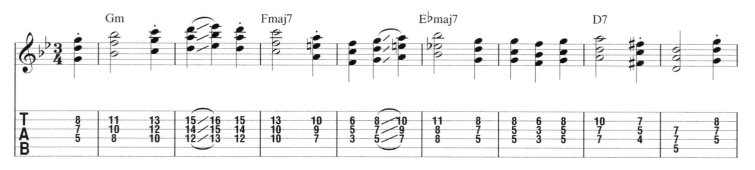

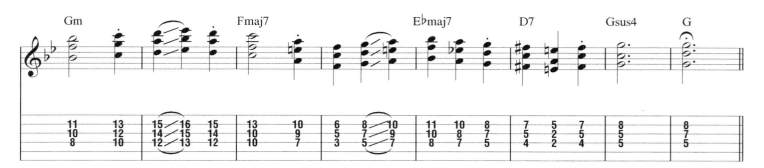

Other Intervals That Can Function as Chords

To wrap up this chapter, let's look at other intervals that function as chords. Here's a classic rock 'n' roll rhythm figure that alternates between an open 5th, a major 6th, and a minor 7th. It's usually notated as you see it here: G5, G6, G7, G6 etc. although the G6 and G7 are rather incomplete. (We'll explore full "six" and "seven" chords in Chapters Five and Six.)

A Rock 'n' Roll Rhythm Using Incomplete Chords

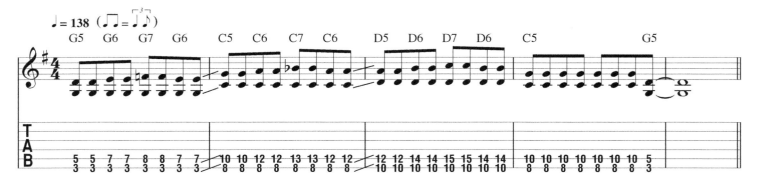

The next example is a mix of open 5ths and open major and minor 6ths. With moderate distortion and a little too much reverb, it takes us to a classic eighties power ballad sound. But remember not to stigmatize or ghettoize any of these chords. Just because I present them in some clearly defined style (like an eighties power ballad) doesn't mean that they are stuck in that style. They might be waiting for you to liberate them.

More Intervals Implying Complete Chords

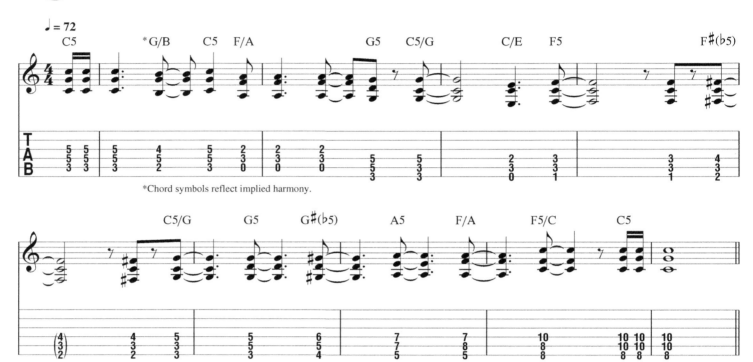

*Chord symbols reflect implied harmony.

As with open 5ths and 4ths, we can move simple two-note open 6ths (and their inversions, close 3rds) to the higher strings and get a very useful harmonized melodic sound. These harmonized melodic intervals usually accompany a standard full chord progression, but in the following example, I've placed them against a steady single bass note. It's kind of a melody and kind of a chord progression at the same time.

Still More Intervals Implying Complete Chords

*Chord symbols reflect implied harmony; bass pedals on A.

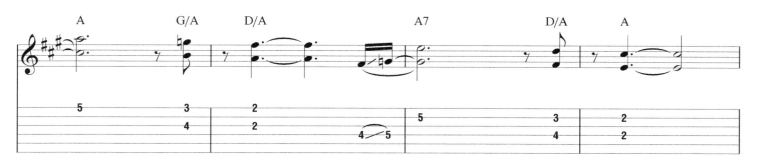

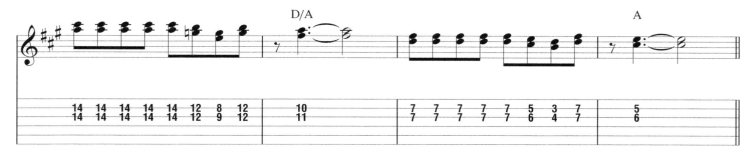

CHAPTER FOUR:

Movable Chords, Part Two— Playing Triads

Introducing the "Little Self-Contained Chord Shape" on Three Adjacent Strings.

We've covered quite a lot of practical chords so far, but we've only begun to scratch the surface of what chords are all about. To further explore even the most basic chords, we need to return to our snowman chords in tertian or 3rds-based harmony, introduced in Chapter 1. Specifically, you'll want to review the exercise on p. 28. And I must emphasize that it will be vital in your growth as a guitarist to be able to play chords using less than six strings. Most chord-playing guitarists discover how to mute one or two strings in order to play better-sounding chords, as we've seen in many of the previously introduced chords. What we now need to focus on is the ability to play any set of *three* strings without playing other strings. Very often, we'll be able to mute unwanted strings with a combination of left-hand muting and right-hand discrimination, but you should become familiar with a couple of other techniques to help you control which strings you do and don't play.

First, consider finger-style playing, using the thumb and the first three fingers without a pick at all. Generally, the thumb will play the lowest string, and the three fingers (in any combination) will play whatever higher strings need to be played. Many guitarists who use finger-style playing in conjunction with plectrum picking will "palm" the pick while using the fingers. My own approach is to hold the pick between my first and second fingers, as illustrated on the following page. I remember developing confidence in this approach when I first started playing jazz and bossa nova tunes and wanted to alternate between dark, mellow chords, and strong single note lines.

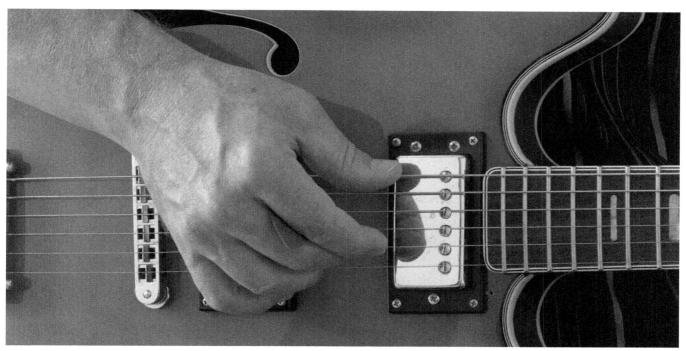

Playing with the fingers while keeping the pick available.

Another useful approach is referred to as "hybrid picking." In this technique, the thumb and first finger grip the pick in a relatively traditional manner, but the second and third fingers play strings as well. You can see my right hand grip for hybrid picking below. In both finger-style playing and hybrid picking, the fourth finger can get involved as well. Personally, I don't use my fourth finger much; the music I play hasn't required it, and I haven't practiced it, so I won't comment on it further. But it's a powerful possibility that you should explore if it calls to you.

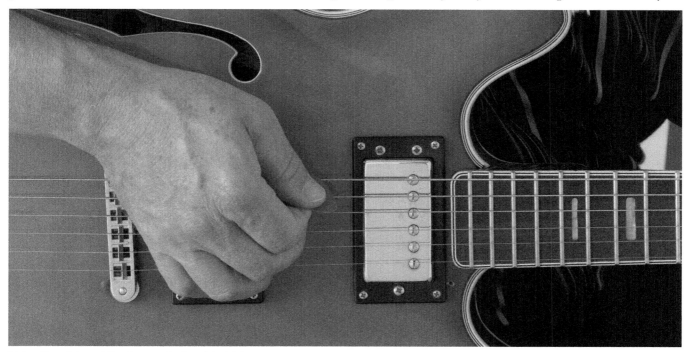

Using the pick and the fingers for hybrid picking.

Technique Tip:

A useful aphorism to guide your work on the guitar is this: A guitarist becomes more than a beginner when he or she can play more than one string at a time, but less than six.

Harmonizing the Major Scale

Now let's return to the snowmen. Back at the beginning of Chapter One, you wrote out a set of snowman chords in the key of C major. Perhaps you wrote them out in all of the major keys, as I suggested in the exercise on p. 28. It shouldn't hurt your brain too badly to recall them in the key of G major, like this:

If it didn't occur to you already, I'm going to make it explicit: you should be able to play these snowman chords on the guitar. These are chords in their most basic forms, laid out as a keyboard player might first learn them or as they might be introduced in a first-year music theory course. The first way we'll play these chords will be on string set 4–5–6. The root (R) of each chord will be on the sixth string, the 3rd (3 or ♭3) will be on the fifth string, and the 5th (5 or ♭5) will be on the fourth string. In a very real way, what you will be playing is a G major scale from G to G on the sixth string, from B to B on the 3rd string, and from D to D on the fourth string.

Some guitarists, having never dealt with any of these shapes, nor having ever played a major scale on one string, should take the time to play a G major scale on the sixth string, at the very least. Eager players will want to play all major scales on all strings, first limiting themselves to one string at a time, one finger at a time, then exploring the many possible combinations of fingers on a single string. But that's a topic for another book. In the meantime, here's a G major scale, ascending and descending, harmonized snowman-style on string set 4–5–6 in standard music notation and tablature:

Etude for Snowman Chords in G Major • Scalar Root Motion • Strings 4–5–6

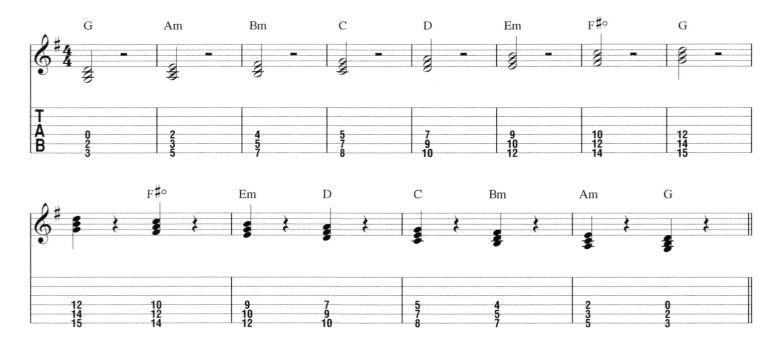

Technique Tips:

The opening G major chord can be fingered with any two fingers that you like. In all of the other chords, the fourth finger plays the root (R), the 3rds are handled by either the third (3) or second (♭3) finger, and the first finger plays the 5th (5 or ♭5). I like to think of the diminished triad as a minor chord with a flatted 5th (R–♭3–♭5), so I assign the second finger to the ♭3 and stretch the first finger to reach the ♭5. It also bears mentioning that some guitarists, even those with more years of playing than fingers on their hands, may have never played these shapes in this manner. Many guitarists avoid the use of the wimpy fourth finger on the hunky fat strings, probably because they have not addressed the fundamental technique of bringing the thumb behind the neck rather than wrapping it around the neck. Many of these same guitarists also sound bland and dull. And if you already think me worth burning at the stake, I'll add fuel to the fire and confess to another bout of tutorial sadism. The last four bars of this figure are much harder to play than the first eight. Other things being equal, descending figures are almost always harder to play than ascending figures, and I've doubled the speed of the changes in the second half as well.

If you are playing a traditional nylon-stringed classical guitar or a steel-stringed guitar with the neck-body joint at the twelfth fret, you might find the shapes in the highest positions (the F♯° and G chords in bars 7 and 8) quite difficult, even if your thumb is positioned properly throughout the rest of the exercise.

Some guitarists use the "thumb over" technique to address this structural obstacle. Lay your thumb across the neck from the top, and play the note D on the D string with the side of your thumb at the 12th fret. You first finger plays the note B on the A string, 14th fret; and your second finger plays the note G on the low E string, 15th fret.

Photos of this hand position are shown below. This is a more advanced technique, and these exercises are opportunities to practice it.

When the previous example is digested, you'll want to move on to playing snowman chords in all 13 common major keys, on all the string sets. String set 3–4–5 is a relatively simple matter, since the shapes are identical to those of string set 4–5–6. String sets 2–3–4 and 1–2–3 present unique shapes because of the pesky standard tuning of the guitar with that major 3rd between the G and B strings. Here are a few examples of how to go about this, each presented with a slightly different execution:

Etude for Snowman Chords in C Major • Scalar Root Motion • Strings 3–4–5

Etude for Snowman Chords in F Major • Scalar Root Motion • Strings 2–3–4

Etude for Snowman Chords in B♭ Major • Scalar Root Motion • Strings 1–2–3

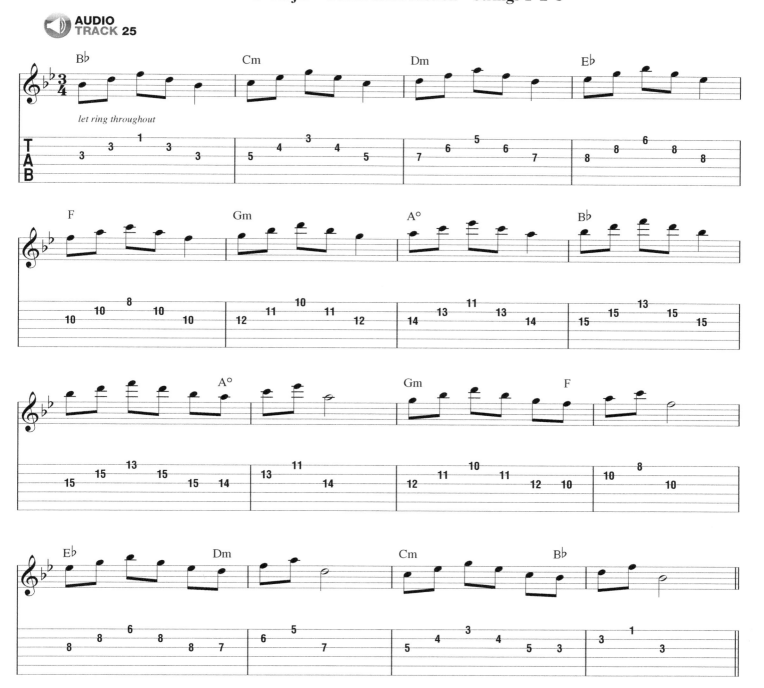

As mentioned earlier, it might prove physically impossible to play the entire harmonized scale on a single string set. We might also find ourselves in need of shifting from one string set to another in the middle of passages. We might begin very high on the neck, or we might seek a different tone for a set of chords, or we might have just broken a string mid-phrase. The following example shows one alternate approach.

Etude for Snowman Chords in E Major • Scalar Root Motion • Shifting String Sets

Harmonizing the Harmonic Minor Scale

So far, all of the music examples have contained notes within the major scale. Apart from the modes of the major scale, which we'll visit in Chapter 5, there are several hundred other possible scales in our equal-tempered system. But in practical terms, we'll only need to know one more scale to complete our collection of traditional triads: the ***harmonic minor scale***. In the Western classical tradition, this scale evolved partly as a way of creating a traditional dissonant-consonant cadence. But this scale also evolved, in our culture and others, simply because it has a unique sound. Here's a C harmonic minor scale played on the fifth string, then harmonized with snowman chords.

C Harmonic Minor

This is a really juicy scale, and you can get a lot from it. For now, try to savor the peculiar dark and tangy flavor of the chords as they move along. Notice the Roman numerals that identify the chords—lower case for minor, lower case plus ""°"" for diminished, upper case for major, and upper case plus ""+"" for augmented. Also notice how each chord is defined with relation to the major scale:

- The chord type is altered to match the notes of the harmonic minor scale. What was a major chord built on the first note of the major scale is now a minor chord; what was minor on the second note of the major scale is now diminished, etc.

- The identification of the root note of the chord is altered to match the scale. Specifically, the 3rd and sixth chords in the sequence are identified with a flat before their Roman numerals (♭III and ♭VI) to indicate how their root notes vary from the major scale.

Pay special attention to the E♭+ (augmented) chord in bars 3 and 13 of the harmonized scale. We constructed this chord back in Chapter One by stacking notes a major 3rd apart, but at that time it was just a kind of structural curiosity—something you could do with notes, but without a musical context. Now we can hang with it as part of the relatively common harmonic minor scale. The functional spelling of the augmented chord is R–3–♯5, but it contains a fascinating quality that gives it a kind of an Alice in Wonderland personality. In musical notation, we can reveal this personality by performing a couple of leapfrog moves and employing some enharmonic spellings.

E♭+, root position: Here's the E♭+ chord as we constructed it in the C harmonic minor scale. Notice that it clearly fits our basic snowman construction: it's a tertiary triad. Analytically, it is constructed of two major 3rds.

Now, let's leapfrog the lowest note (E♭) up to the top.

E♭+, first inversion: Here's E♭+ in first inversion. Analytically, it's constructed of a major 3rd and a diminished 4th. Now a diminished 4th is a pretty kinky interval in our musical system. It doesn't sound like a cold, strong 4th; it sounds like a major 3rd.

So what happens if we rewrite the first-inversion E♭+ chord with a major 3rd on top instead of a diminished 4th?

G+, root position: Wow! Our first-inversion E♭+, rewritten with a D♯ instead of an E♭, looks like a root-position, snowman G+—and it is.

What happens if we leapfrog the lowest note of G+?

G+, first inversion: Here's G+ in first inversion. Like the E♭+ above, it's constructed of a major 3rd and a diminished 4th. Can we transform that diminished 4th into a major 3rd and get another root position augmented chord from it? Yes, but we are going to enter a strange realm of enharmonic equivalents.

B+, root position: If we maintain the low B and D♯, the only way we can push the top snowball note (G) down to create a snowman stack is to rename it F double-sharp (F𝄪). So be it. Remember that an augmented chord can be thought of as a major chord with a raised (or sharped 5th), and if you consider that we're trying to create a B+ chord here, you could calculate backwards: B major is spelled B–D♯–F♯ (R–3–5), and if you want to raise or sharp the 5, you have to add a sharp to the already-sharp F♯ to make it F𝄪.

C♭+, root position: There's another snowball spelling for this chord. Rather than spell the top note with a double-sharp, we can change the bottom two. If we maintain G on top, we can rename D♯ as E♭ and B as…C♭! Again, some backwards thinking might be in order: C major is spelled C–E–G (R–3–5), so C♭ major must be spelled C♭–E♭–G♭ (R–3–5). Since C♭+ requires a sharped 5, G♭ gets hoisted up to G natural.

In short, E♭+ = G+ = B+/C♭+. If you haven't spent a lot of time with music notation, the very thoughts of F double-sharps and C flats might cause smoke to waft from your ears. Fortunately, there's a much easier way to see this quality. Here are the notes of this chord in a chromatic circle:

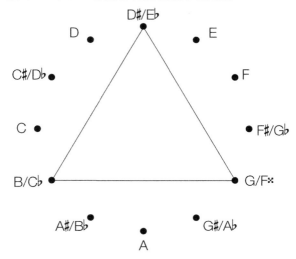

An augmented chord is an equilateral triangle! The chromatic circle shows that the intervals between the three notes are all major 3rds. Because the intervals are equidistant, any one of the three notes in the augmented triad could be the root. This is a ***symmetrical chord***, and the symmetry is obvious when we draw it out in a chromatic circle. Perhaps this is a kind of theory of musical relativity, which points to another curiosity of the harmonic minor scale: If Eb+ = G+ = B+/Cb+, then in all harmonic minor scales, bIII+ = V+ = VII+. This means that on the fifth and seventh notes of the scale, two different chords can be constructed. Do I smell brain cells burning, or are you just glad to be studying chord theory?

Constructing Tertiary Triads with a Chart

By harmonizing the major and the harmonic minor scales, we've touched upon the four basic traditional tertiary triads: major, minor, augmented, and diminished. At the beginning of Chapter One, brief mention was made of another way of building chords: creating a chart or list of all possible combinations of notes that fit the definition of "tertiary triad." That chart appeared at the top of p. 26. Let's review this approach in a more complete manner. In the chart below, each possible triad will be shown by analysis and a practical example built on the note C. With this chart, we'll have touched upon every possible tertiary triad in the Western equal-tempered system of music, including two that don't appear in either the major or harmonic minor scales.

	Root	Third	Fifth	Resulting chord, with comments	Music notation and circle chart
Analysis	R	b3	b5	° (diminished)	
Example	C	Eb	Gb	C°	
				This chord is found in both the major and harmonic minor scales.	
Analysis	R	b3	5	minor	
Example	C	Eb	G	Cm	
				This chord is found in both the major and harmonic minor scales.	
Analysis	R	b3	#5	??? (minor sharp five?)	
Example	C	Eb	G#	Cm#5	
				This chord is not found in either the major or harmonic minor scale, but will prove useful later on. See comments that follow in the text.	

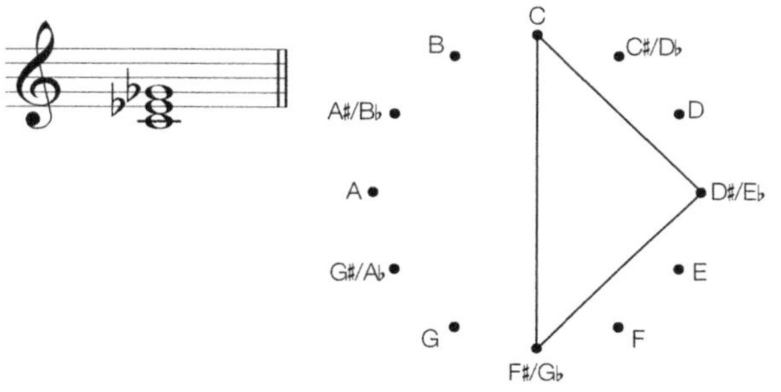

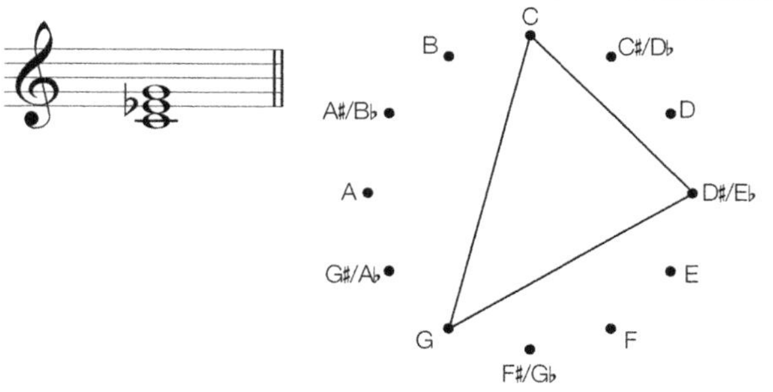

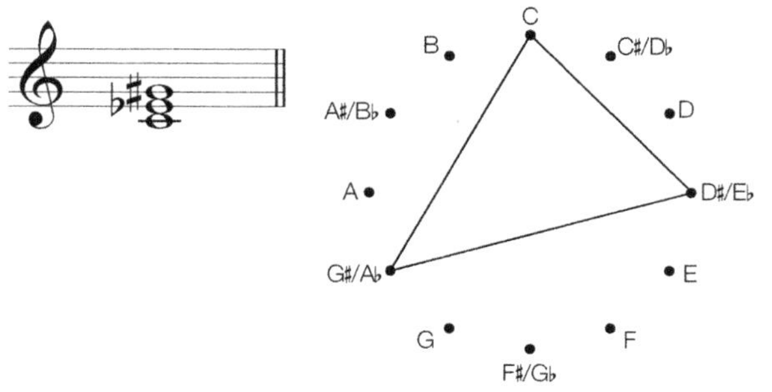

Analysis	R	3	♭5	??? (major flat five?)
Example	R	3	♭5	??? This chord is not found in either the major or harmonic minor scale, but will prove useful later on. See comments that follow in the text.
Analysis	R	3	5	major
Example	C	E	G	C This chord is found in both the major and harmonic minor scales.
Analysis	R	3	♯5	augmented
Example	C	E	G♯	C+ This chord is found in the harmonic minor scale.

Let's discuss the two curiosities of this chart. First, there's the "minor sharp five" chord in row three. It's a perfectly legitimate tertiary triad on its own, but in terms of practical usage, it's usually retagged as a major chord in inversion. You can see this by using a couple of circle charts, side by side:

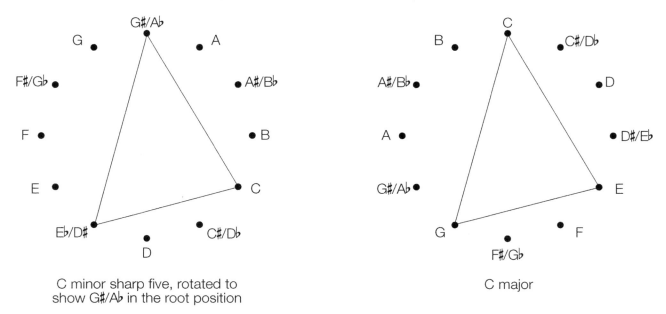

C minor sharp five, rotated to show G♯/A♭ in the root position

C major

In the figure on the left, the "minor sharp five" chord has been rotated so that G♯/A♭ is in the root position at the top of the circle. If you compare it to the figure on the right (a C major triad), you can see that the shape is a simple major triad. This might also be clearer if you rename the G♯ as A♭. While C–E♭–G♯ seems to be an exotic "minor sharp five" triad, A♭–C–E♭ (the same notes renamed and reordered) is a simple A♭ major triad. In most music, it will be named by its major triad name rather than its "minor sharp five" name. For practicality's sake, set the "minor sharp five" triad aside for now.

The second curiosity that our chart created is the "major flat five" chord. This little sonority has remained under the rocks because there's no traditional scale that includes a major 3rd and a flatted 5th. You might try playing this chord a bit and see if it leads you somewhere. (Chords do move, remember?) But for practicality, set this chord aside as well.

Inversions of Tertiary Triads

Remember how we inverted the "five" chord dyads in Chapter Three? We want to do the same thing with our traditional triads, and we want to hear and play them in some of their more common musical settings. Putting aside the two oddball triads (the "minor sharp five" and the "major flat five"), let's work on inversions of these four chord types. As with any approach to manipulating chords, we can create variations in a number of different ways.

One simple way is to use the leapfrog approach that we used with dyads. As we do this, it's important to remember that there are two ways of moving on the neck of a guitar: *laterally*, or across the neck within a small range of frets, and *linearly*, or up and down the neck within a small group of strings.

Let's begin with a C major chord in the snowman friendly root position and travel laterally across the neck to create different inversions of the chord. Here's a C major chord in root position on the three lowest strings:

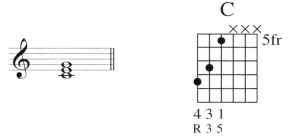

Now let's leapfrog the note C up an octave while keeping the notes E and G on the third and fourth strings. It should be clear that the up-an-octave C will be on the G or third string, and with a bit of finger-shifting, you should arrive at a first inversion C major chord. Notice that the chord is named C/E to indicate that it is a C major chord, and E is the lowest note played. Here it is:

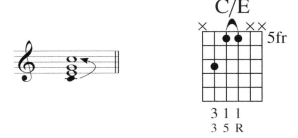

Now leapfrog the low E note up an octave while keeping the notes G and C on the fourth and third strings. Again, the highest note is found on the next free string—the B or second string—and the second inversion C major chord is named, written, and played like this:

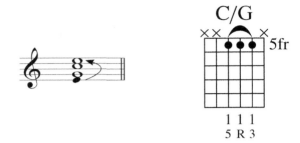

This is a really useful and important shape on the standard-tuned guitar, by the way: a second-inversion major chord across the second, third, and fourth strings in the same fret. It's played here with a first-finger barre, but any finger can barre it, or it can be portioned out among two or three fingers. Remember the double-barre chord back in Chapter Two? This voicing is just a fragment of that big double barre.

With one string left, we can do another leapfrog move and create a root-position C major chord one octave above the one with which we began. Here it is:

Here us the same approach applied to minor, augmented, and diminished triads across the neck. I've chosen Cm, C+, and C° to illustrate these shapes, but any serious guitarist will want to work through chords in all keys to get to know these shapes well. I've indicated some of the alternate names of the augmented triads, but not all. You're welcome to complete their synonymous naming.

Inversions of C minor Across the Neck

Inversions of C+ Across the Neck

Cm

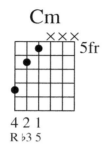

4 2 1
R ♭3 5

C+

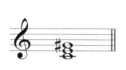
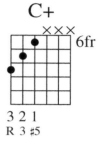

3 2 1
R 3 ♯5

Cm/E♭

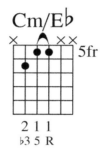

2 1 1
♭3 5 R

C+/E (or E+)

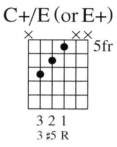

3 2 1
3 ♯5 R

Cm/G

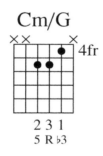

2 3 1
5 R ♭3

C+/G♯ (or G♯+ or A♭+)

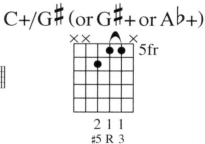

2 1 1
♯5 R 3

Cm

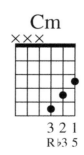

3 2 1
R ♭3 5

C+

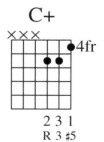

2 3 1
R 3 ♯5

Inversions of C° Across the Neck

C°

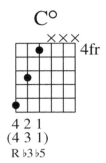

4 2 1
(4 3 1)
R ♭3 ♭5

C°/E♭

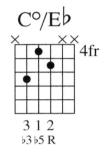

3 1 2
♭3 ♭5 R

C°/G♭

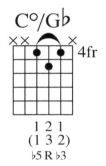

1 2 1
(1 3 2)
♭5 R ♭3

C°

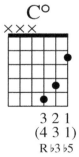

3 2 1
(4 3 1)
R ♭3 ♭5

Now let's apply the leapfrog approach, but travel linearly, or on single string sets. To make room on our necks, we'll drop to chords with their roots in the lower frets. This can be a much more challenging way to play these chords, because it requires visualizing each new shape with no fretboard reference to the previous shape other than the distance between notes. There are no common note locations, even though two of the three pitches are identical. Also note that the higher positions of these chords may not be playable on all guitars. Whenever necessary, move an inversion to a higher string set to complete the series.

Inversions of A♭ major on String Set 4-5-6   **Inversions of D♭ major on String Set 3-4-5**

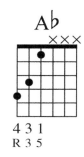
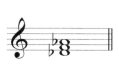
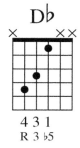

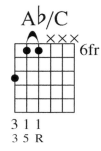

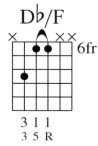

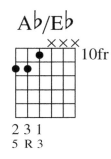

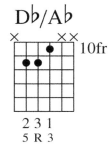

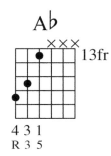

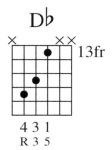

Inversions of F major on String Set 2-3-4

Inversions of B♭ major on String Set 1-2-3

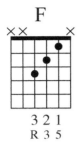

F

3 2 1
R 3 5

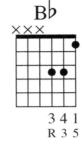

B♭

3 4 1
R 3 5

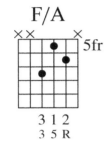

F/A

5fr

3 1 2
3 5 R

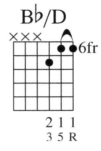

B♭/D

6fr

2 1 1
3 5 R

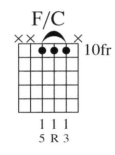

F/C

10fr

1 1 1
5 R 3

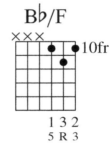

B♭/F

10fr

1 3 2
5 R 3

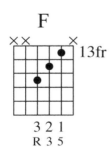

F

13fr

3 2 1
R 3 5

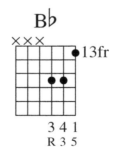

B♭

13fr

3 4 1
R 3 5

Inversions of G♯ minor on String Set 4-5-6

G♯m

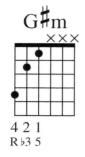

4 2 1
R ♭3 5

G♯m/B

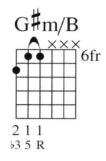

6fr

2 1 1
♭3 5 R

G♯m/D♯

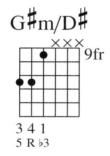

9fr

3 4 1
5 R ♭3

G♯m

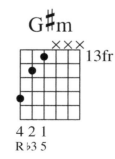

13fr

4 2 1
R ♭3 5

Inversions of C♯ minor on String Set 3-4-5

C♯m

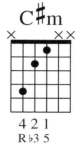

4 2 1
R ♭3 5

C♯m/E

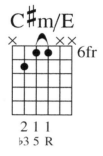

6fr

2 1 1
♭3 5 R

C♯m/G♯

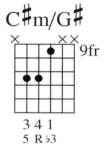

9fr

3 4 1
5 R ♭3

C♯m

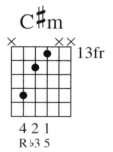

13fr

4 2 1
R ♭3 5

Inversions of F minor on String Set 2-3-4

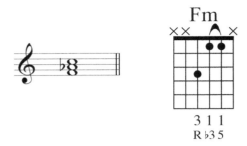

Fm

3 1 1
R ♭3 5

Fm/A♭

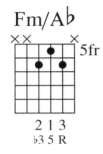5fr

2 1 3
♭3 5 R

Fm/C

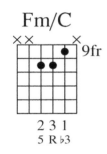9fr

2 3 1
5 R ♭3

Fm

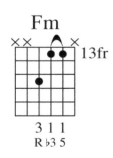13fr

3 1 1
R ♭3 5

Inversions of B♭ minor on String Set 1-2-3

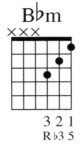

B♭m

3 2 1
R ♭3 5

B♭m/D♭

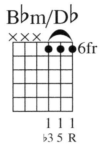6fr

1 1 1
♭3 5 R

B♭m/F

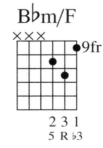9fr

2 3 1
5 R ♭3

B♭m

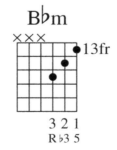13fr

3 2 1
R ♭3 5

Inversions of G+ on String Set 4-5-6

Inversions of C+ on String Set 3-4-5

G+

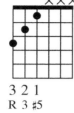

3 2 1
R 3 #5

C+

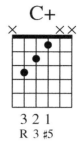

3 2 1
R 3 #5

G+/B (or B+)

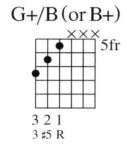

3 2 1
3 #5 R

C+/E (or E+)

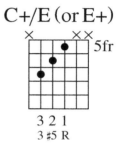

3 2 1
3 #5 R

G+/D♯ (or E♭+)

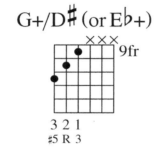

3 2 1
#5 R 3

C+/G♯ (or A♭+)

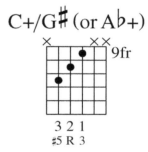

3 2 1
#5 R 3

G+

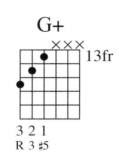

3 2 1
R 3 #5

C+

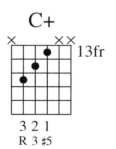

3 2 1
R 3 #5

Inversions of E+ on String Set 2-3-4

Inversions of A+ on String Set 1-2-3

E+

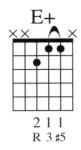

2 1 1
R 3 ♯5

A+

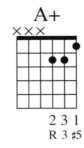

2 3 1
R 3 ♯5

E+/G♯ (or A♭+)

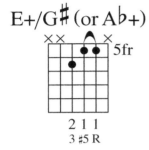

5fr

2 1 1
3 ♯5 R

A+/C♯ (or D♭+)

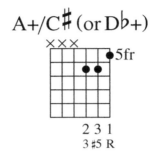

5fr

2 3 1
3 ♯5 R

E+/C (or C+)

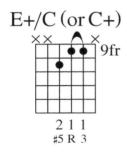

9fr

2 1 1
♯5 R 3

A+/E♯ (or F+)

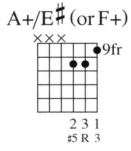

9fr

2 3 1
♯5 R 3

E+

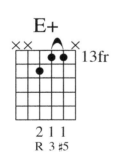

13fr

2 1 1
R 3 ♯5

A+

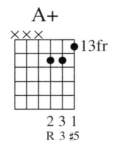

13fr

2 3 1
R 3 ♯5

Inversions of A° on String Set 4-5-6

Inversions of D° on String Set 3-4-5

A°

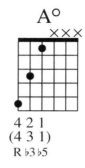

4 2 1
(4 3 1)
R♭3♭5

D°

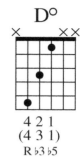

4 2 1
(4 3 1)
R♭3♭5

A°/C

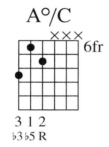
6fr

3 1 2
♭3♭5 R

D°/F

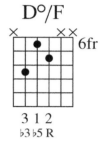
6fr

3 1 2
♭3♭5 R

A°/E♭

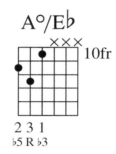
10fr

2 3 1
♭5 R ♭3

D°/A♭

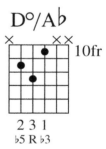
10fr

2 3 1
♭5 R ♭3

A°

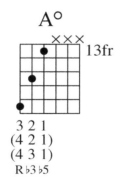
13fr

3 2 1
(4 2 1)
(4 3 1)
R♭3♭5

D°

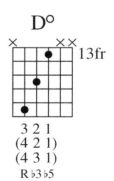
13fr

3 2 1
(4 2 1)
(4 3 1)
R♭3♭5

Inversions of F#° on String Set 2-3-4

Inversions of B° on String Set 1-2-3

F#°
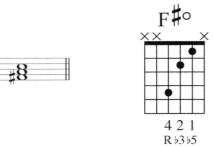

B°

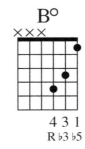

4 2 1
R ♭3 ♭5

4 3 1
R ♭3 ♭5

F#°/A

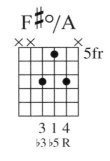

B°/D

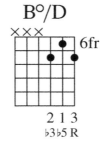

3 1 4
♭3 ♭5 R

2 1 3
♭3 ♭5 R

F#°/C

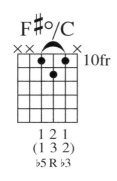

B°/F

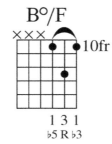

1 2 1
(1 3 2)
♭5 R ♭3

1 3 1
♭5 R ♭3

F#°

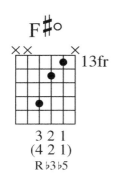

B°

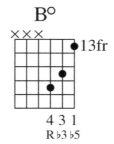

3 2 1
(4 2 1)
R ♭3 ♭5

4 3 1
R ♭3 ♭5

These two approaches—organizing inversions laterally across the fretboard and linearly on string sets—are very organized, but not very musical. Remember, chords move, and when we hear that motion, we get a far better sense of the quality of the chord than when we deal with it as a static "object." Once we experience the sound of a chord in motion, we might return to the more analytical organization of lateral and linear fingerings where technical and informational challenges command our attention.

Traditional Voice-Leading of Tertiary Triads

A practical and musical way of understanding chord inversions from chord motion is to use *traditional voice leading*. Let's imagine we're singing in a trio, and we want to sing a standard I–IV–I–V–I progression. One way to move from one chord to the next would be in parallel motion, as demonstrated below. As you can see and hear, this has a big, clunky sound—it's fairly easy to play, but it's difficult to sing, and if the chords had to change quickly, it would get very clumsy very fast.

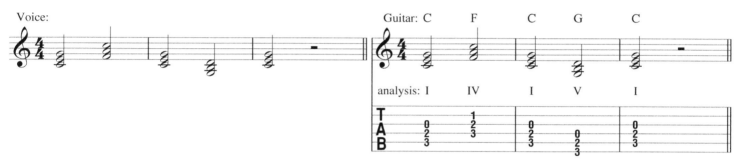

A much easier way to sing and play this progression is to use traditional voice leading, demonstrated here.

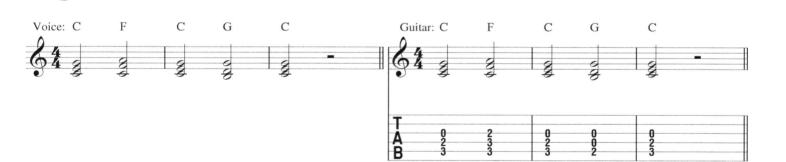

Here's the premise of traditional voice leading: music can be built on interwoven melodies that move in relatively small steps. As these melodies move forward simultaneously in time, chords are created. It would be fair to say that, historically, chords evolved from the practice of voice leading, which evolved from the interweaving of melodies. Once a set of common chords was established, they became a currency of their own, and voice leading was often employed to bring those chords to life.

Consider a G major chord moving to an E minor chord. The three notes of each chord, voiced in root position, can move in parallel motion, as in Fig. A below. Or the notes common to both chords can be held and root position voicing can be kept, as in Fig. B. This leaves a rather clumsy third note dropping from a high D to a low E. It doesn't sound too smooth. It's crossing over the range of the other two notes, and it's making a big leap in pitch. A better solution is to allow the D to rise to an E. The root position G major changes to a first-inversion E minor, and the result is much smoother, as in Fig. C.

Fig. C demonstrates three good rules of traditional voice leading:

1) Move the individual notes—the voices—as little as possible.

2) Don't cross voices.

3) Keep the notes within an octave of each other, with the occasional exception of the lowest octave on guitar.

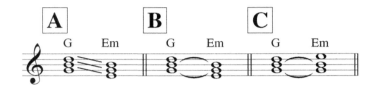

The rules of voice leading and traditional counterpoint can be painfully daunting and complex, especially to a non-singing, keyboard-illiterate guitarist. Even the most accomplished of guitarists can find four-part voice-leading to be difficult. Yet smooth voice leading can make for beautiful music on the guitar, and a practical under-standing of it is essential to arranging parts for keyboards, horns, strings, and voices.

Fortunately, there's a very simple way to visualize traditional voice leading without working through all the rules. It's a method introduced by Joseph Schillinger; my high school music teacher, Thom Gorden introduced this approach to me, and I've used it ever since. Thank you, Mr. Gorden! Visualize the three notes of a triad as points on a circle.

R

Using our previous example of G major moving to E minor, we could begin with the note G, recognizing that it is a note that's common to both chords. In the circle diagram, this would be shown as an arrow from R (G, the root of G major) to 3 (G, the 3rd of E minor):

5   3

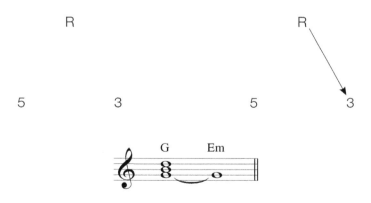

The note B is also common to both chords. This would be shown as an arrow from 3 (B, the 3rd of G major) to 5 (B, the 3rd of E minor):

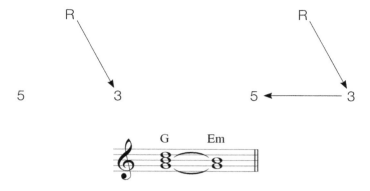

This leaves D, the 5th of the G chord, with only one place to go—to the root of the Em chord.

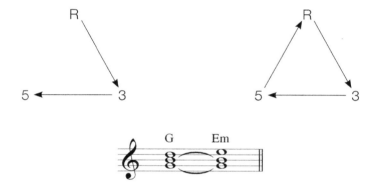

And the easiest way to get there is to move up by a major second, as we saw previously.

What if we have a chord change with motion in the opposite direction? What if the root moves to the 5th, the 5th to the 3rd, and the 3rd to the root? Schillinger's circle still works beautifully. Below, we can see how a G major chord moves to a C major chord, where G—the root of the G major chord—is common to the 5th of the C major chord (shown in the diagram with the arrow from R to 5). The other two notes move as little as possible, and we have nice, smooth traditional voice leading.

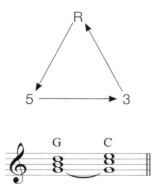

What if we have a chord change with one note in common, but other notes from a distant key? For example, how might we deal with a G major chord moving to an E♭ major chord? The Schillinger circle still works.

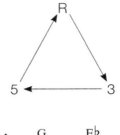

What if we have a chord change with no notes in common? If the roots of the two chords are close by, sometimes parallel motion is fine, as demonstrated here, where a G major chord moves to an A minor chord. (Notice that parallel motion appears as no motion on a Schillinger circle.)

If we want to create motion opposite the root motion, we just move any one note from the first chord down to the second chord, observe and notate its change, and plug in the values for the other two notes.

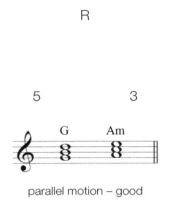

parallel motion – good

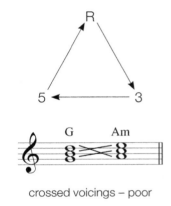

crossed voicings – poor

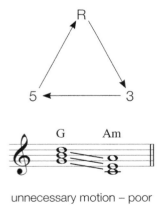

unnecessary motion – poor

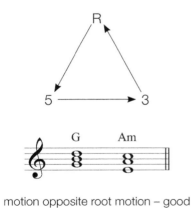

motion opposite root motion – good

Once we begin to employ traditional voice leading, it's essential to understand and use all three inversions of tertiary triads. ***Root position*** is the standard term for the order of notes in a chord when the root is in the lowest position. A chord with the 3rd as the lowest note isn't called "third position;" it's called ***first inversion***. Likewise, with the 5th as the lowest note in the chord, it's not called "fifth position" but ***second inversion***.

The common chord symbol for showing a chord inversion is the slash—the forward-leaning diagonal line found on any QWERTY keyboard. We first encountered the slash symbol (/) on page 50 when discussing "five" chords. Now it will be used to show either of the two notes besides the root in any tertiary triad. For example, a C major chord can be played with C as the lowest note, and its chord name would be written as "C." But if we wanted E to be the lowest note, we would indicate this as "C/E." If G was to be the lowest note, it would be written "C/G."

Chord inversions can be shown using an ***inversion formula***. While I've never seen these formulas used elsewhere, I have used them myself for some time and find them easy to understand and apply. Here's how they work: If we want to show any major chord in root position, we can symbolize it as "X." If it is to be played in first inversion—that's, with the 3rd of the chord as the lowest note—it would be symbolized as X/3, meaning that X is the major chord, and the chord's major 3rd (3) is played as the lowest note. Second inversion of a major triad, where the 5th of the chord is the lowest note, is symbolized as X/5. Minor triads can be shown as Xm, and their inversions can be symbolized as Xm/♭3, where ♭3 indicates the flatted or minor 3rd of the chord, and Xm/5. Diminished triad inversions can be symbolized as X°/♭3 and X°/♭5. Augmented chords, as we discovered earlier in this chapter, are more easily named by whatever note is lowest in the voicing, but if inversions need to be considered, the augmented triad's inversions are symbolized as X+/3 and X+/♯5. Slash chords are spoken as "X over Y," meaning that chord X has the note Y as its lowest note; some musicians say "X with a Y in the bass" or "X with Y as the lowest note."

Now let's return to basic chord progressions and how these inversions appear when traditional voice leading is employed. If we stay within a given major key—that is, if we play diatonically—there are really only three different paths a chord sequence can follow and six ways to read those sequences. Check it out.

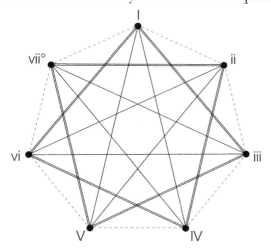

One path to follow is stepwise, around the outside of the hexatonic circle. There are no notes common to these adjacent chords, so this path is shown with a dotted line. We can follow this path clockwise or counter-clockwise. In musicspeak, the clockwise sequence would be called ***root motion by ascending seconds***, and it reads:

$$I - ii - iii - IV - V - vi - vii\,° - I$$

The counterclockwise sequence would be called ***root motion by descending seconds***, and it reads:

$$I - vii\,° - vi - V - IV - iii - ii - I$$

If we explore diatonic chord changes with one note in common, we follow the path shown with one solid line. Clockwise, this path would be called ***root motion by 4ths***, and it reads:

$$I – IV – vii° – iii – vi – ii – V – I$$

Notice the appearance of the long-lived ii–V–I cadence and, by extension, the iii–vi–ii–V–I progression as part of this sequence.

Reading counterclockwise, we create a path called ***root motion by 5ths***. The sequence reads like this:

$$I – V – ii – vi – iii – vii° – IV – I$$

Finally, we can follow the diatonic changes with two notes in common, shown by the path with two solid lines. Moving clockwise, this path would be called ***root motion by ascending 3rds***, and it reads like this:

$$I – iii – V – vii° – ii – IV – vi – I$$

Following this path counterclockwise, we have the sequence known as ***root motion by descending 3rds***. It reads like this:

$$I – vi – IV – ii – vii° – V – iii – I$$

One thing I discovered in my own study of chords was that these six fundamental sequences were never discussed much and never showed up in guitar chord books. It's as if no one saw the 600-pound gorilla sitting in the living room. Maybe nobody wanted to practice them. Or maybe, once someone discovered them, they felt the sequences were so obvious and simple that they weren't worth mentioning. Who knows? My own experience was quite different. First of all, it seemed clear to me that these complete sequences were fundamental. Similarly, it seemed easy to visualize them in a circular image. When I played through these sequences, I found all kinds of fascinating sounds, challenging technical problems to solve, and seductive patterns to play. We've already played the outermost sequences—root motion by ascending and descending seconds—whenever we harmonized scales earlier in this chapter. Of course, we only played them in root position (or snowman voicings, if you will). If we return to the basic voice leading we were discussing, we can apply it to these six sequences and develop a very complete understanding and practical skill of tertiary triads in all their inversions.

Let's begin with the maximum amount of voice leading: two notes out of the three in each chord remaining the same, found in root motion by ascending 3rds (following the double line clockwise around the hexatonic circle) and root motion by descending 3rds (following the double line counterclockwise around the hexatonic circle). First, let's listen to these two sequences played by a trio of fuzz guitars. In this example, notes common to two adjacent chords are held. All notes are held as long as possible, except right in the middle, where I chose to jump from the second-inversion C major down to a first-inversion C major. I did this to cover as many different inversions of the chords as possible, although it still doesn't cover them all in one exercise. (More on that in a minute.) The score has been reduced to a single line of music notation and tab.

Etude for Fuzz Guitar Trio • Voice Leading in Ascending and Descending 3rds

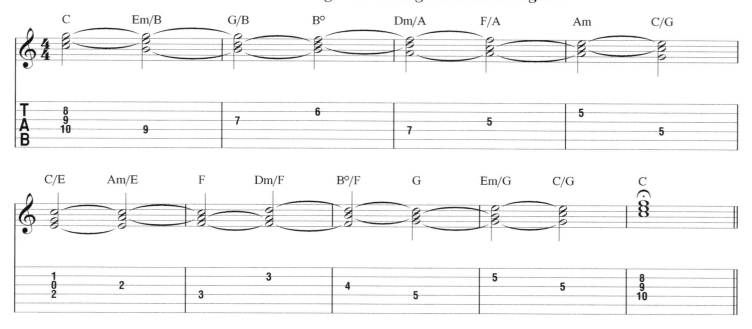

What you can hear is a relatively stable sound that evolves slowly downwards (root motion by ascending 3rds), leaps downwards to a lower inversion of the home chord, evolves slowly upwards (root motion by ascending 3rds), then concludes with another leap upwards to end where it began. An intelligent guitarist will play through these shapes as individual chords and will perhaps play each voice in the progression, one at a time. With multi-track recoding devices so cheap and plentiful, it would be a small matter to recreate this example on your own. (Try another key or a different progression while you're at it.) Each manifestation—the blocked chords, the sound of the fuzz guitar trio, and the act of being one voice among three—will have its own feel and experience. Allow it to soak into your ears and fingers as well as your head.

If you examine the chords by the inversions, you'll see that the I chord (C major) appears in all three inversions because I added the leap in the middle. All of the other chords appear in only two of their three inversions. When I first began to meditate upon this sequence, I wanted to find a way to play all the chords in all their inversions in a single etude. I also liked the sound of playing the chords as ringing arpeggios, so I created the etudes that follow. As you can see and hear, I chose to leap to a harmonically distant (but musically and physically close) new key whenever the sequence completes a cycle. This ensures that all the chord types are played in all their inversions. The etude is presented in both a block chord version and an arpeggiated one. Two guitars play two examples as a single etude on Track 32.

AUDIO TRACK 32

Etude for Voice Leading • Root Motion by 3rds •
Tertiary Triads • String Set 4-5-6 • First Guitar: Block Chords

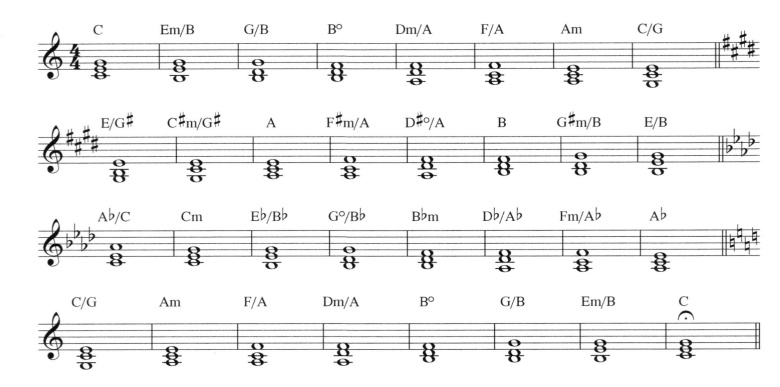

Technique Tips:

- Play the block chords using finger technique, causing all notes to ring simultaneously.

- The rolling, ringing arpeggios can be played using right hand finger technique or with a flat pick.

- The arpeggios are deliberately written to lead to the note that will change in each subsequent chord. For example, the pattern of the first measure is established by playing the root note twice, then playing the R–3–5 pattern repetitively so that the first note of the second measure drops down to the 5th of the Em chord, establishing the Em as a second inversion voicing (5–R–b3). The arpeggio patterns will flow easily if you pay attention to the starting and ending arpeggios in each key.

- I employed a really annoying left-hand technique to make the transitions from chord to chord as smooth as possible. If you follow the fingerings shown, you will see that the fingers often "roll" through chord shapes, replacing one note at a time so that when the next chord arrives, one finger is free to move to the one note that changes between chords. You don't have to play it this way; you can change chords in single grip-like moves, and if you do it fast enough, it will probably sound quite smooth. But you might try my rolling fingering as well.

AUDIO
TRACK 32, (cont.)

Etude for Voice-Leading • Root Motion by 3rds •
Tertiary Triads • String Set 2-3-4 • Second Guitar: Ringing Arpeggios

AUDIO
TRACK 32 (cont.)

To keep our fingers and brains healthy and happy, it's only fair to present a similar etude with root motion in 4ths and 5ths. Here's the same approach as the previous etude, but with changes appropriate to the new root motion.

**Etude for Voice-Leading • Root Motion by 4ths and 5ths •
String Set 3-4-5 • First Guitar: Block Chords**

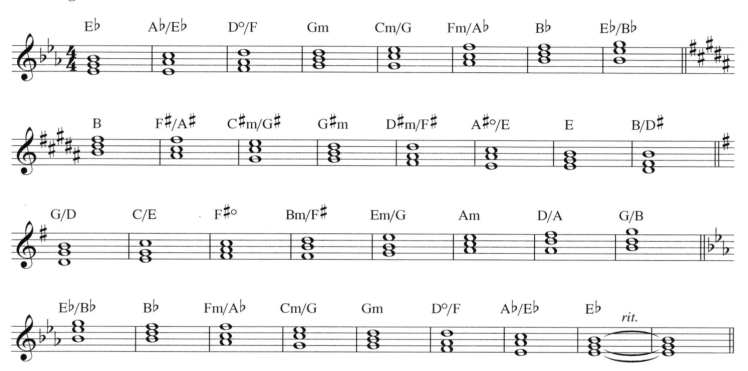

Technique Tips:

- I dispensed with the technique of "rolling fingers" that was used in the previous etude. You might try to use this technique to understand why it doesn't work very well in this etude.

- If your guitar doesn't allow access to the highest frets necessary in this etude, you should take the initiative to transpose it to a lower key.

AUDIO TRACK 33 (cont.)

**Etude for Voice-Leading • Root Motion by 4ths and 5ths •
String Set 1-2-3 • Second Guitar: Ringing Arpeggios**

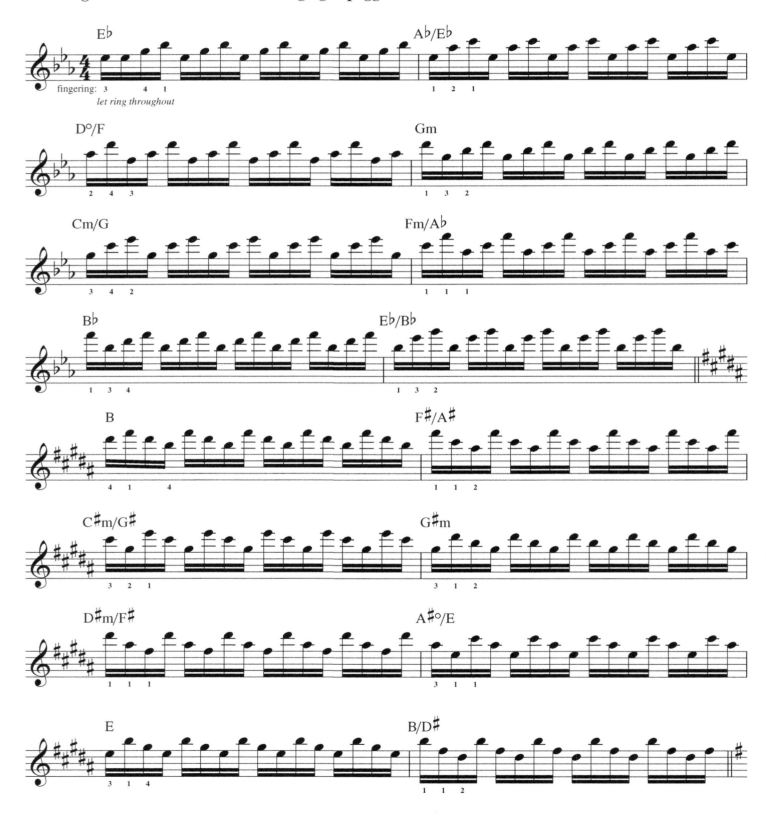

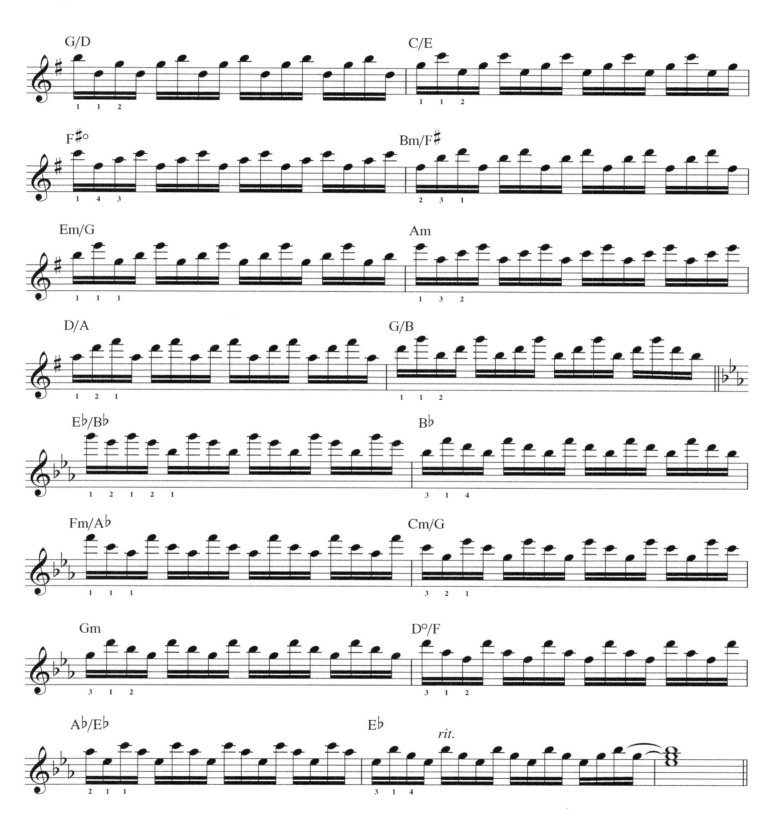

In terms of our basic tertiary triads and our traditional musical tonalities, the other area we should explore is the sound of the *harmonic minor tonality*. There's one simple-as-dirt solution to creating etudes similar to the two just presented: use the same root motion and chord patterns, but transpose each major key into its parallel harmonic minor. You are welcome to do this. On the other hand, you might want to move through the six tonal centers not yet touched upon in the previous etudes, as I have done in the next two etudes.

AUDIO TRACK 34

Etude for Voice Leading • Root Motion by 3rds • String Set 3-4-5 •
First Guitar: Block Chords

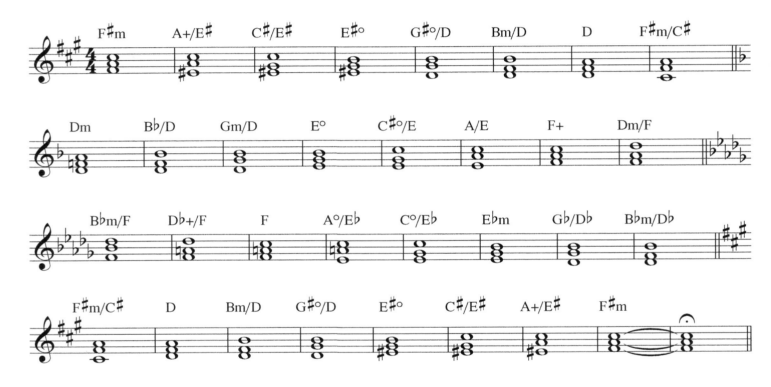

**Etude for Voice Leading • Root Motion by 3rds • String Set 1-2-3 •
Second Guitar: Ringing Arpegigos**

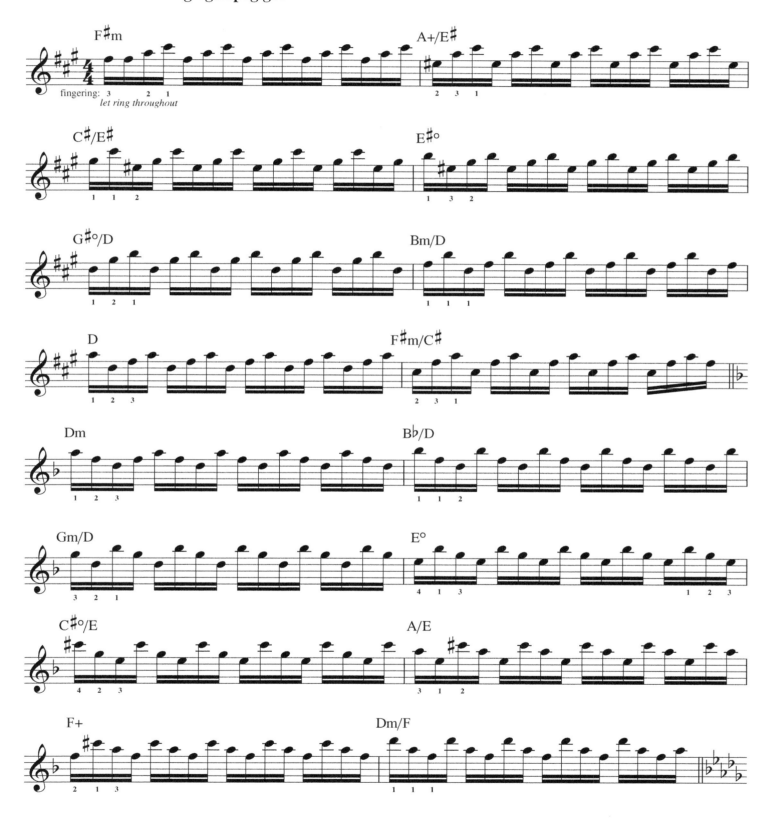

AUDIO TRACK 35

Etude for Voice Leading • Root Motion by 4ths and 5ths •
String Set 4-5-6 • First Guitar: Block Chords

AUDIO
TRACK 35 (cont.)

Etude for Voice Leading • Root Motion by 4ths and 5ths •
String Set 2-3-4 • Second Guitar: Ringing Arpeggios

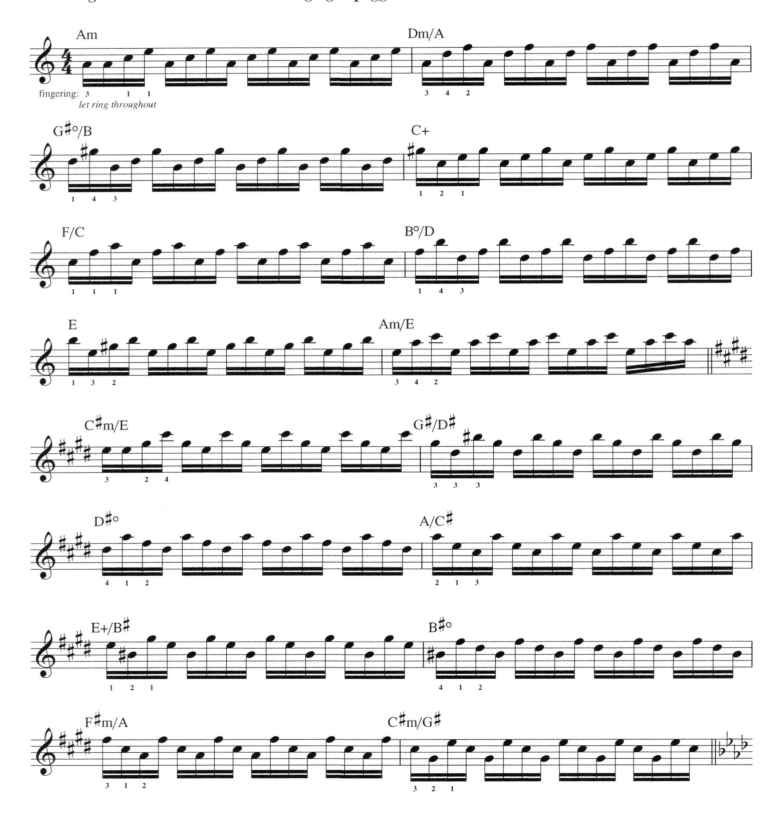

AUDIO
TRACK 35 (cont.)

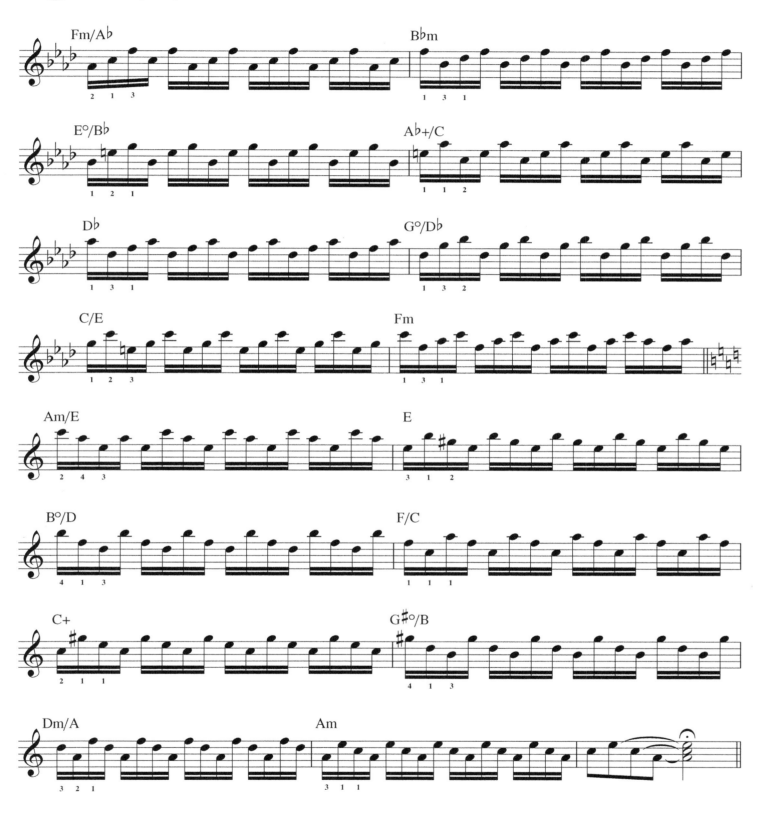

Open Voicings

So far, all of the chord voicings you just played have been constructed with the notes as close to each other as possible. Whether in *root position* (the snowman stack), *first inversion* (with the 3rd as the lowest note), or *second inversion* (with the 5th as the lowest note), the notes were as close as they could be, and only the three notes necessary to define the chord were used – there was no doubling of notes in different octaves. But if you look back to the exercise on page 28, where you notated many of your simple open-position chords on guitar, you hopefully noticed that many of these chords had "skips" in their voicing. For an example (which I'm sure you've already written out), here is an open-position D major chord as it is played on the guitar:

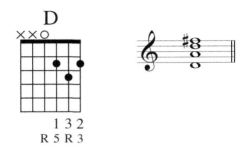

It should be obvious, especially after the workout of close-voiced chords in the previous etudes, that there's a gap between the low root (D, played on the open D string) and the fifth (A, played on the G string). Now check out what happens when we eliminate the doubled D note on the B string:

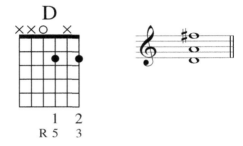

We have a wide-open D major chord. It has all the snowballs of a D major snowman – a root (D), a 3rd (F♯), and a 5th (A) – but in a curiously open order. The musical term for a chord voiced in this way is an ***open voicing*** of the chord. There's a very simple process to find all the voicings of a chord, including the close voicings of the earlier etudes, the open voicings we are about to explore, and the numerous voicings possible with chords that have four or more notes in them. With a pencil and paper, and without thinking of the note names as any kind of chord, but only as members of a set, it should take no more than a minute to see that there are six permutations of the three members of the set. Here's a chart for a D major chord, showing the note names, their functions, and the resulting notation and proper name of the chord voicing.

Note names	Funciton	Notation and Voicing Name	
D F♯ A	R 3 5		Root position, close voicing
F♯ A D	3 5 R		First inversion, close voicing

A D F♯	5 R 3		Second inversion, close voicing
D A F♯	R 5 3		Root position, open voicing
F♯ D A	3 R 5		First inversion, open voicing
A F♯ D	5 3 R		Second inversion, open voicing

The three open voicings shown above can be applied to any three-note chord. They're not just abstract constructions or textbook knowledge, either.

They prove really useful on the guitar. First, they sound really fresh. Most beginner-to-intermediate guitarists play the usual barre and movable shapes—sometimes the close voicings we've just studied—but few play these open voicings. Second, they work wonderfully when using distortion on the electric guitar. Close-voiced chords can sound like undifferentiated static with certain distorted tones. The highly accentuated overtones of each note within the chord tend to scrape against each other, and the smallest tuning discrepancy will cause octaves to sound like a cheap gas engine in need of a tune-up. By placing the notes in an open voicing, chords become clearer. I first noticed this when I learned to play "Sunshine of Your Love" by Cream. If I played the opening chords of the main riff (D–D–C–D) using a standard E-type barre chord shape with my Univox Superfuzz, the chord lost its punch. It got better when I limited myself to the lower strings, and I recognized the notes F♯ and E (in the D and C chords, respectively) as kind of important in getting the sound I wanted. After years of playing, I finally discovered that by eliminating the high D and C notes on the D string, the chord sounded right.

You can hear these three voicings of a D major chord on Track 36.

 **AUDIO TRACK 36**

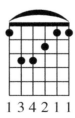
1 3 4 2 1 1

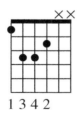
1 3 4 2

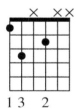
1 3   2

Technique Tip – The Chord Study Toolkit

Any time we run into a new chord, whether a new voicing of an old favorite or some rare and exotic new species, it behooves us to put it through its paces with this chord-study tool kit:

- Play the chord type in all its diatonic variations through at least the major and harmonic minor scales with root motion in ascending and descending scale steps. (This is one of the three paths of the diatonic circle, traveled in two directions.)
- Play all of the chords discovered in the first step above in all of their inversions laterally across the neck.
- Play all of the chords discovered in the first step above in all of their inversions linearly up and down the neck on specific string sets.
- Play all of the chords discovered in the first step above in all of their inversions through at least the major and harmonic minor scales with root motion in ascending and descending 3rds and ascending and descending fourths. (These are the other two paths of the diatonic circle, traveled in both directions.)
- Consider what makes up the chord and create a chart to see if any other chords of that type exist beyond the major and harmonic minor tonalities.

Without further ado, here's the open-voiced tertiary triad laid bare. First, we'll look at root motion stepwise, ascending and descending through the key of G major, played with a simple block approach.

AUDIO TRACK 37

Open-Voiced Chords in G Major

Technique Tip:

It becomes ever more critical to play only the notes indicated. I played this audio track using my fingers, and I can't imagine using a pick alone. The unwanted strings can produce chords that may be interesting and fun; set aside time to explore them. But also work on playing only the notes asked for. Also, some contemplation of these shapes will reveal alternate fingerings and string sets. Try them for sure, because they will show up eventually anyway, whether in this book or in the real world.

Here's a somewhat more interesting approach to the problem at hand—a fingerpicking pattern. Note the steady rhythm of the thumb that alternates between the root and the 5th of each chord.

AUDIO
TRACK 38

Open-Voiced Chords in B♭ Major

Working with clean guitar tones is always good for ensuring strong technique and allowing you to hear the notes of each chord clearly and distinctly. However, it's really important to have some fun with chord exercises, too. The next etude is a real basher—an opportunity to flail on the skinny strings a bit with a healthy gob of distortion.

AUDIO
TRACK 39

Open-Voiced Chords in E Major

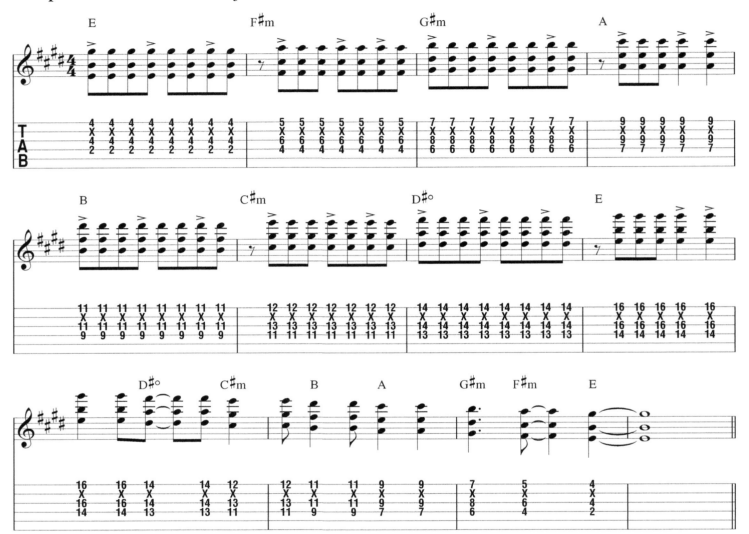

Technique Tip:

E major is a forgiving key on the guitar, and in the previous etude, it would have been very easy to rely on this forgiveness and wallop strings that are not notated. For example, you could cause the open B and low E strings to drone away throughout the study, and you might fancy yourself the most skilled git-fiddler on your block. However, these added notes tend to smidge the crispness of the chords. The open A string is the most blatantly unwanted note; it will simply turn most of these chords into crap. Try to flail and wallop with control and avoid the unwanted strings by muting as needed with the fretting hand and limiting the strings that you strum, as in the audio example.

For the dual goals of brevity and creativity, I've chosen to shift ever so slightly from the strictly sequential approach in chord motion for the next etude. Like many of the previous etudes, this is a two-part study with one guitar focusing on the higher strings in block form and the second on the lower strings in ringing arpeggios. But I've mixed sequences of root motion by ascending and descending 3rds, with leaps to two distant harmonic minor keys. A thorough sifting of all the voicings will uncover all of the major food groups: major, minor, augmented, and diminished triads, in all inversions, all in open voicings. I'll leave the analysis of root motion to you—and also the curious case of bar 15, where E+ transforms to A♭+.

**Etude for Voice-Leading • Root Motion Mostly by Thirds •
String Sets 1-3-4 and 1-3-5 • First Guitar: Block Chords**

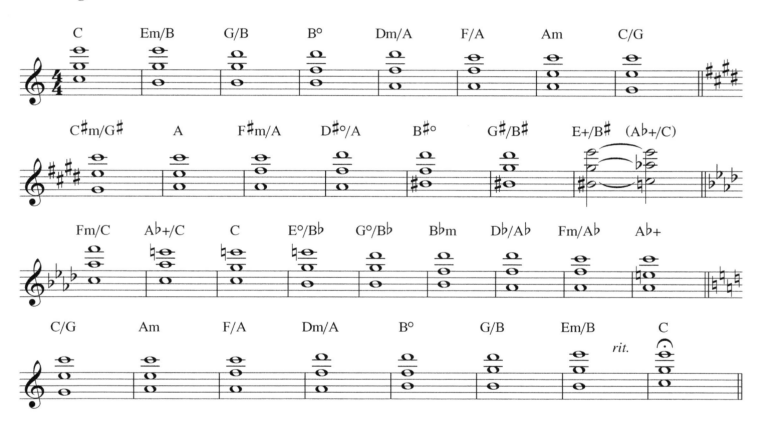

AUDIO
TRACK 40 (cont.)

Etude for Voice-Leading • Root Motion Mostly by Thirds •
String Set 3-5-6 • Second Guitar: Ringing Arpeggios

A Suspension of Tertiary Belief:
A Brief Introduction to the Curious Sus2 and Sus4 Chords

There's another kind of chord to group in with our tertiary triads—the so-called ***suspended chord***. The term "suspension" comes from traditional Western theory, where every note in a piece of music was identified as either a chord tone (a root note, 3rd, or 5th) or a non-chord tone. If it was a non-chord tone, it was labeled according to its relation to the current, previous, or following chord and how it would move from one to the other. Numerous terms were used—among them *anticipation*, *neighbor tone*, *escape tone*, and several types of *suspensions*. But of all the terms used, only suspended (abbreviated as "sus" and pronounced "suss") became a generalized term added to our chord lexicon. A sus chord is one in which the major or minor 3rd of the chord has been replaced with either the major second (sus2) or perfect 4th (sus4) above the root. (Very rarely, the augmented 4th (sus♯4) or the minor second (sus♭2) are used.) In other words, a sus chord has no major or minor 3rd, but it has three notes in it. It's a ***non-tertiary triad***, and although we might say that its major or minor quality has been suspended, we should also recognize it as chord on its own. Just like power chords and other dyads functioning as chords, sus2 and sus4 chords have managed to work their way into common chord use simply because they fit our needs as a chord type.

Let's inspect some common open-position sus2 and sus4 chords to see what they're made of and then build some of our own.

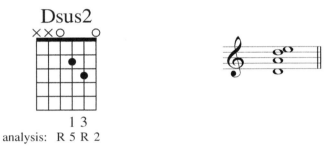

Here's a Dsus2 chord with all the notes in the chord as they sound on the guitar. You can see that the analysis of the chord reads R–5–R–2. Let's assume that the chord comes from some kind of D scale; we don't know if it's major or minor, do we? Building on the first five notes of the scale and distilling the chord down to its essence, we arrive at the notes shown below:

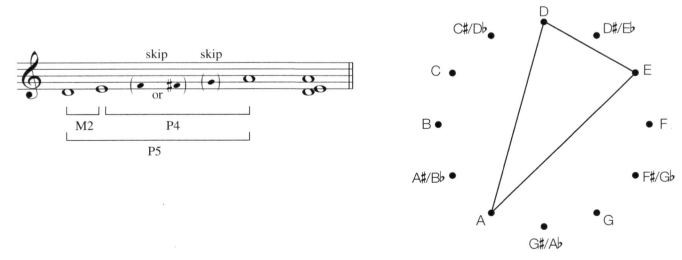

The tidy pattern of "play-skip-play-skip-play" has been broken, and the snowman's abdomen has tumbled sideways. The chord is built from the first, second, and fifth notes of the scale. A similar fate befalls the snowman of a Dsus4 chord:

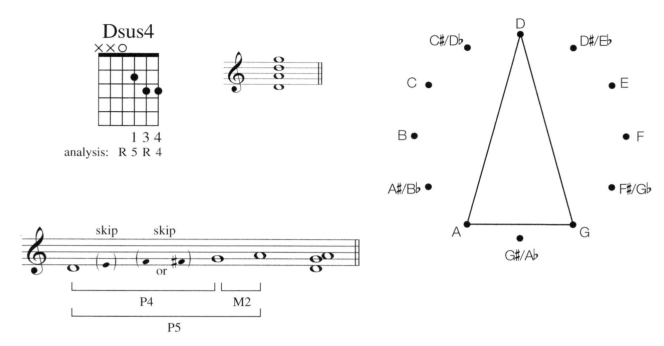

Again, "play-skip-play-skip-play" has been abandoned. Using the first, fourth, and fifth notes from the scale (which, again, could be either major or minor), we get a snowman with a bit of gas in its belly, which has risen and bumped the snowman's head sideways. Notice the remarkable similarity in shape between Dsus2 and Dus4, as revealed in the circle diagrams. Could these two chord types—sus2 and sus4—be a single chord type? We shall see…

The same peculiarities are revealed in the chords Asus2 and Asus4, as shown below. (Astute observers of chord construction will notice that Dsus2 and Asus4 have the same three notes in them.):

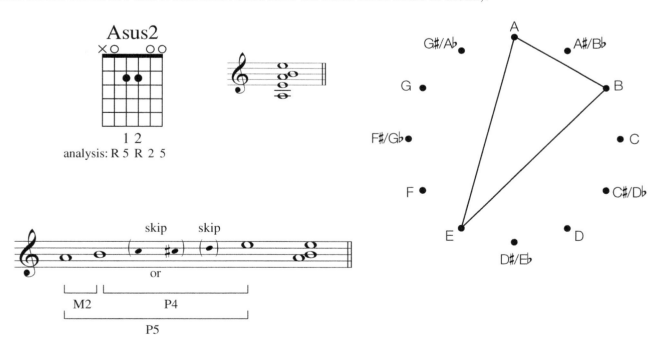

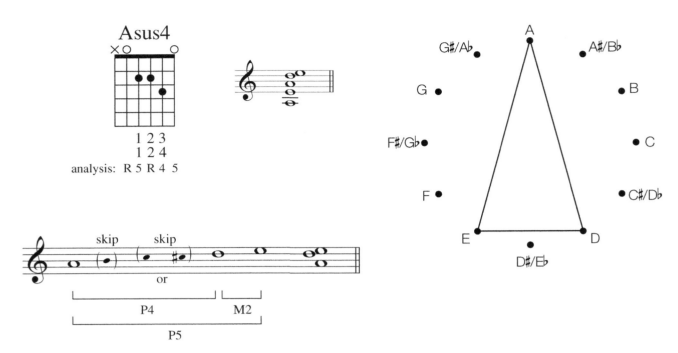

Just like all of the chords we've studied so far, we have a root note upon which the chord is built, and we assume that a scale rises from that root note. In these cases, the scale is somewhat ambiguous; it could be major or minor. That major-minor ambiguity is *usually* clarified in the context of the chord progression, since sus2 and sus4 chords are *usually* played before, after, or between unambiguous major or minor chords.

Here's a typical chord progression using sus2 and sus4 chords. You'll notice a sound clearly associated with Beatles-era pop, folk, and folk-rock, which has been carried on through various guitar-friendly pop styles to the present. Notice how each sus2 and sus4 chord is a variation on an adjacent major or minor chord.

AUDIO TRACK 41

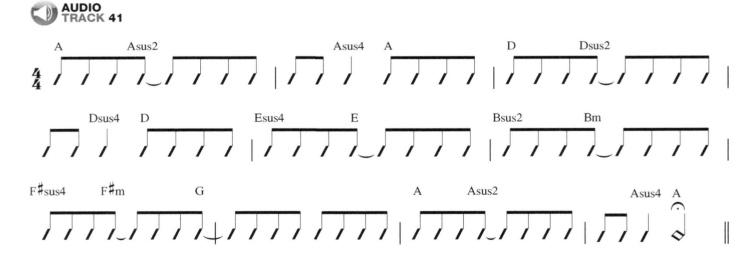

Interestingly, not all diatonic sus2 and sus4 chords will work in common chord progressions. Let's examine the wobbly snowman chords based on the sus2 construction (R–2–5) in the key of E major:

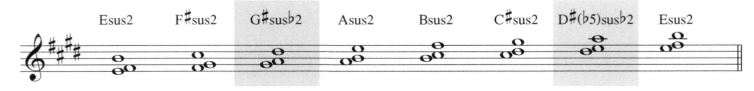

The majority of these chords—the "plain" sus2 chords—sound rather pleasant on their own because two strong intervals (a perfect 4th and a perfect 5th) seem to balance the mild dissonance of the major second. The two problematic chords indicated with shaded boxes around them—G#sus♭2 and D#(♭5)sus♭2—have a rather unsettled quality about them. First, let's look at G#sus♭2:

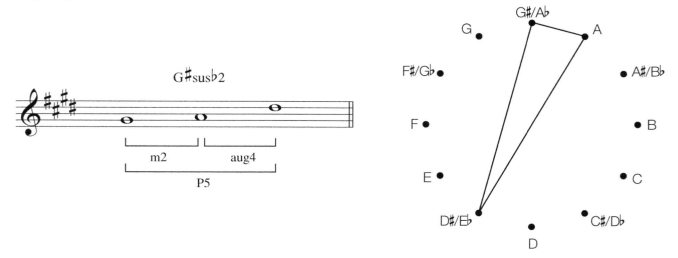

The G# and A notes rub together in a minor second, and the A and D# sit an ambiguous augmented 4th apart. The perfect 5th from G# to D# doesn't seem to reconcile this dissonance and ambiguity. This could be a lovely chord in the right context, but it's a rare one.

Equally rare is the D#(♭5)sus♭2:

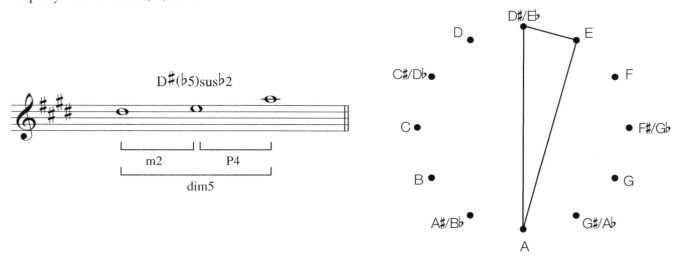

It's got that grinding minor second (D#–E) and an ambiguous diminished 5th (D#–A). Neither interval seems tamed by the relatively consonant perfect fourth (E–A). If we fit these two chord types (sus♭2 and ♭5sus♭2) into a logical musical pattern, they can sound okay, but they are somewhat exotic for practical purposes.

A look at diatonic sus4 chords reveals similar rule-dodging. Here are the high-waisted snowman chords based on the sus4 construction (R–4–5) in the key of D major:

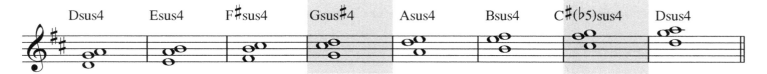

Just like the sus2 chords, the "plain" sus4 chords sound rather pleasant on their own because they contain the same intervals as the plain sus2 chords: strong perfect 4ths and perfect 5ths that balance the mild dissonance of the major second. The two problematic chords—Gsus♯4 and C♯♭5sus4—have that same unsettled quality as the peculiar sus♭2 and ♭5sus♭2 chords. Here's Gsus♯4:

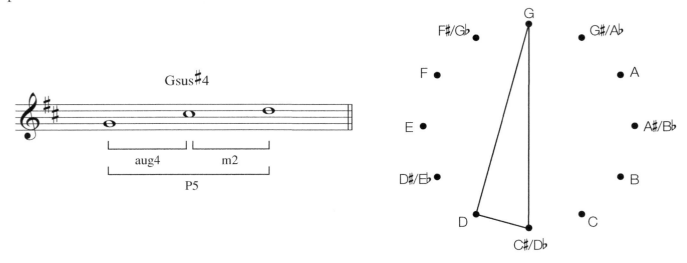

The G and C♯ notes sit an ambiguous augmented 4th apart, while the C♯ and D notes rub together in a minor second. The perfect 4th from G to D doesn't seem capable of keeping the peace. It's a nice chord in the right hands, but those hands are rare.

Equally rare is the C♯(♭5)sus4:

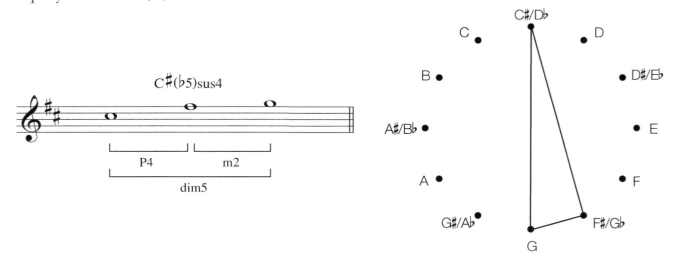

Neither the fractious minor second between F♯ and G nor the ambiguous diminished 5th (C♯ and G) seem reined in by the perfect fourth (C♯–F♯). Remember, there's nothing wrong with these chords, and they'll sound fine if used properly. They are simply rare in current practical use. But astute observers of shape and sound will recognize the remarkable similarity between all of these chords.

Normally, when we run into a new chord, whether a new voicing of an old favorite or some rare and exotic new species, it behooves us to put it through its paces with our chord-study tool kit. These five steps were introduced on p. 104.

Technique Tip:

- Play the chord type in all its diatonic variations through at least the major and harmonic minor scales with root motion in ascending and descending scale steps. (This is one of the three paths of the diatonic circle, shown on p. 87, traveled in two directions.)

- Play all of the chords discovered in the first step above in all of their inversions laterally across the neck.

- Play all of the chords discovered in the first step above in all of their inversions linearly up and down the neck on specific string sets.

- Play all of the chords discovered in the first step above in all of their inversions through at least the major and harmonic minor scales with root motion in ascending and descending 3rds and ascending and descending fourths. (These are the other two paths of the diatonic circle, traveled in both directions.)

- Consider what makes up the chord and create a chart to see if any other chords of that type exist beyond the major and harmonic minor tonalities.

As we put these to work with some brief etudes, we'll discover some more curiosities about these peculiar sus2 and sus4 chords. First, I offer a brief study for sus2 and sus4 chords using root positions and close voicing in ascending and descending scale steps through A major (ascending) and A harmonic minor (descending) with a final traditional resolution to A major at the end. The fingerings are challenging, but the sound is inviting. As with many of the earlier etudes, this is organized as a duet where one guitar plays the block chord voicings while a second guitar plays the ringing arpeggios. I placed the root position close voicings in block form on the higher strings because the seconds sound a bit muddy on most guitars when played in block form on the lower strings.

Etude for Sus2 and Sus4 Chords • First Guitar: Block Chords

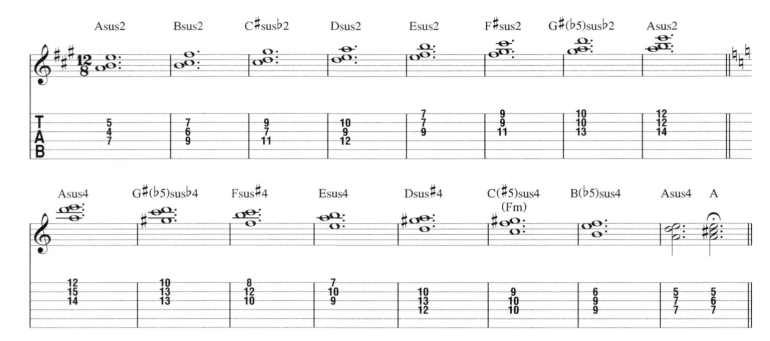

AUDIO TRACK **42**

Etude for Sus2 and Sus4 Chords • Second Guitar: Ringing Arpeggios

So what do you think of that C(♯5)sus4 in the previous etude? Can you see that the notes C–F–G♯, spelled enharmonically as C–F–A♭ are actually a second inversion Fm chord? That's why Fm appears in the music in parentheses. Sus chords are strange creatures indeed. In fact, apart from the plain sus2 and sus4 chords, I am going to let the stranger ones go their own way for now. At the end of this section, I'll offer a chart to show what we will and won't use in the world of sus chords.

But let's take a little time to explore the plain sus2 and sus4 chords in all their inversions, laterally across the neck. This will help solve the mystery of the doubly-named sus chords we discovered when we first began looking at these beautiful creatures.

Let's compare inversions of Esus2 and Bsus4 while playing them across the neck.

Inversions of Esus2 Across the Neck

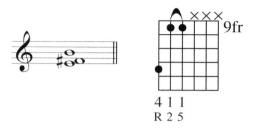

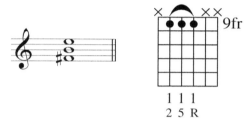

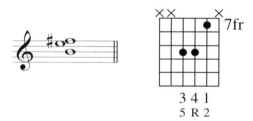

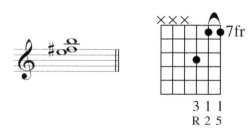

Inversions of Bsus4 Across the Neck

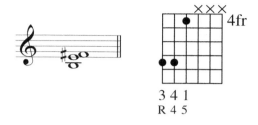

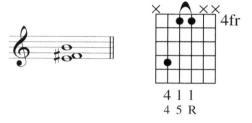

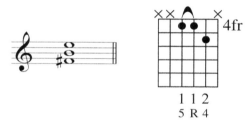

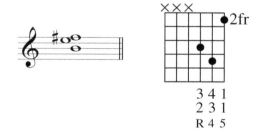

I deliberately chose these two chords—Esus2 and Bsus4—because, if you hadn't noticed by now, they're the same set of notes. Check it out: Esus2 is E–F♯–B, and Bsus4 is B–E–F♯—the same three notes in a different order. You can see it in the music notation: The first voicing of Esus2 (in the left column above) is the same as the second voicing of Bsus4 (in the right column). The second voicing of Esus4 is the same as the third voicing of Bsus4. The third voicing of Esus2 is the same as the fourth voicing of Bsus4. And the fourth voicing of Esus2 is the same as the second voicing of Bsus4, only one octave higher. You might ask yourself, "Well, if E can be a root in this three-note chord, and B can be a root, might F♯ also be a root?" To paraphrase an old Bugs Bunny cartoon, "It might, rabbit. It might." We'll meet up with it later as a quintal/quartal chord.

To confirm that we really know and feel the plain sus2 and sus4 chords, and to further see their commonality, let's leapfrog through the inversions of some more sus2 and sus4 chords and see how they can be played on various string sets.

Inversions of Asus2 on String Set 4-5-6 | **Inversions of Dsus2 on String Set 3-4-5**

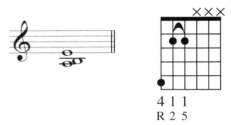

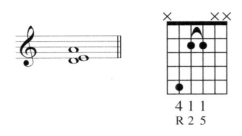

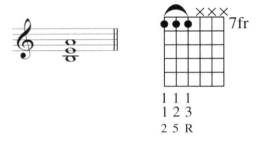

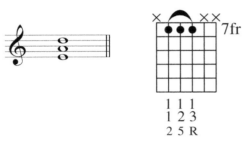

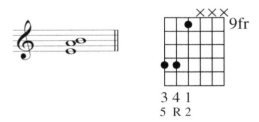

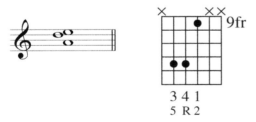

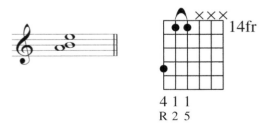

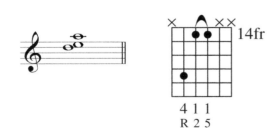

Inversions of Gsus2 on String Set 2-3-4

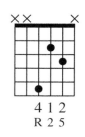

4 1 2
R 2 5

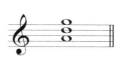
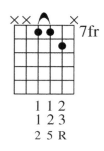

7fr

1 1 2
1 2 3
2 5 R

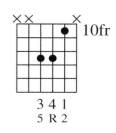

10fr

3 4 1
5 R 2

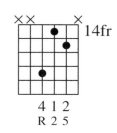

14fr

4 1 2
R 2 5

Inversions of B♭sus2 on String Set 1-2-3

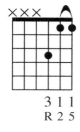

3 1 1
R 2 5

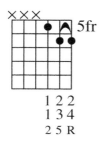

5fr

1 2 2
1 3 4
2 5 R

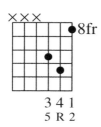

8fr

3 4 1
5 R 2

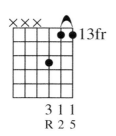

13fr

3 1 1
R 2 5

Inversions of Asus4 on String Set 4-5-6

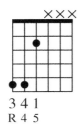

3 4 1
R 4 5

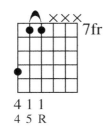

7fr

4 1 1
4 5 R

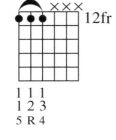

12fr

1 1 1
1 2 3
5 R 4

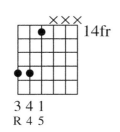

14fr

3 4 1
R 4 5

Inversions of Dsus4 on String Set 3-4-5

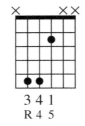

3 4 1
R 4 5

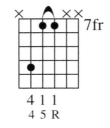

7fr

4 1 1
4 5 R

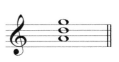
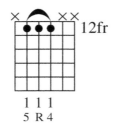

12fr

1 1 1
5 R 4

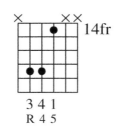

14fr

3 4 1
R 4 5

Inversions of Gsus4 on String Set 2-3-4

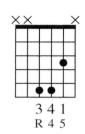

3 4 1
R 4 5

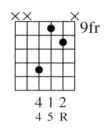

9fr

4 1 2
4 5 R

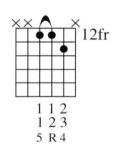

12fr

1 1 2
1 2 3
5 R 4

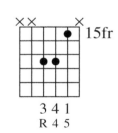

15fr

3 4 1
R 4 5

Inversions of B♭sus4 on String Set 1-2-3

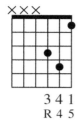

3 4 1
R 4 5

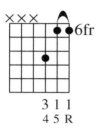

6fr

3 1 1
4 5 R

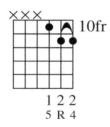

10fr

1 2 2
5 R 4

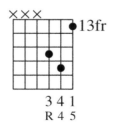

13fr

3 4 1
R 4 5

With a chord as simple and yet as ambiguous as this, how do we know what shape to use if, for example, a Dsus2 has the same set of notes as an Asus4? Or if we're playing a chord that we're sure is some kind of sus chord, which name do we give it? There are three solutions that come to mind:

1. **Chords move.** Sus2 and sus4 chords are commonly played before or after simple major or minor chords and will share the same root note. That common root note will name the chord.

2. **The complete voicing of the sus2 or sus4 chord across four or five strings on the guitar will ensure that one or more notes will be doubled or even tripled in different octaves.** The note used more than once will almost certainly be the root of the chord.

3. **When a musical situation occurs outside of the first two solutions above, it doesn't matter what you call the chord as long as your identification of it is clear to the other musicians with which you'll communicate.** One of the best ways to communicate musically ambiguous information is to write it down in standard music notation.

Think of the major 2nd above the root as being below the 3rd of the chord, and think of the perfect 4th as being above the 3rd of the chord. If you know your major and minor chord shapes on all string sets and in all inversions, you can scramble your fingers to create sus2 and sus4 chords based on those shapes. Let's return to the open-position Asus2 and Asus4 that we began with in this chapter to show the complete approach to transforming a major or minor chord into a sus2 or sus4 chord.

Creating Sus2 and Sus4 Chords from Major and Minor Chords

In an open-position A major chord, you should be able to identify the root (R), 3rd (3), and 5th (5) of the chord, like this.

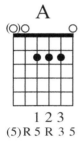

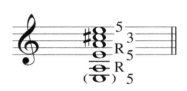

To create an Asus2 chord, you need to replace (or suspend) the 3rd with the second note of the scale from which A major is made. That would be the note B. Conveniently, the note B is the open string on which the 3rd (C♯) is played. So by lifting the finger that plays the note C♯, the note B rings instead. The 3rd has been suspended with the 2nd just below it.

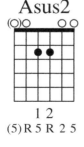

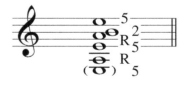

To create an Asus4 chord, you need to replace (or suspend) the 3rd with the fourth note of the scale from which A major is made. That would be the note D. D is a minor second, or one fret, above C♯. So by moving the finger that plays the note C♯ up one fret, we get D. The 3rd has been suspended with the 4th just above it.

Asus4

1 2 3
(5) R 5 R 4 5

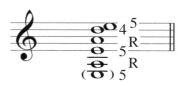

It doesn't matter if the chord is major or minor—the second and fourth notes in major and minor scales are the same. So you can also suspend a minor chord in the same way. If you begin with an Am, lift the finger that plays the note C (the ♭3 or minor 3rd of the chord) and replace it (or suspend it) with the note B just below it to create an Asus2. To create Asus4, place your fourth finger on the note D on the B string—the note just above C. Voila! The minor 3rd has been suspended with the 4th just above it.

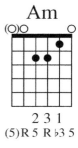

Am

2 3 1
(5) R 5 R ♭3 5

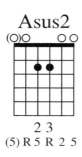

Asus2

2 3
(5) R 5 R 2 5

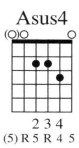

Asus4

2 3 4
(5) R 5 R 4 5

Here's another brief etude to help you understand sus2 and sus4 chords.

AUDIO TRACK 43

Etude for Sus2 and Sus4 Chords

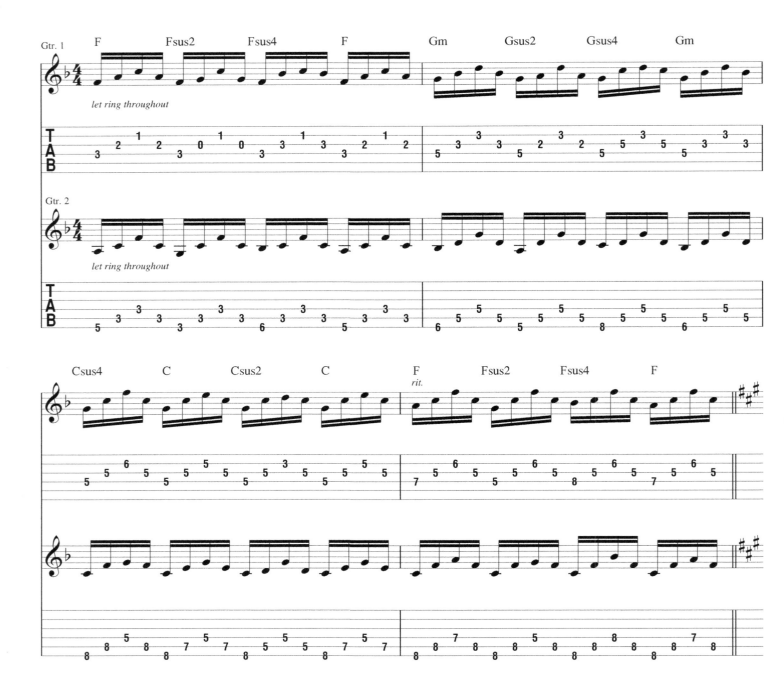

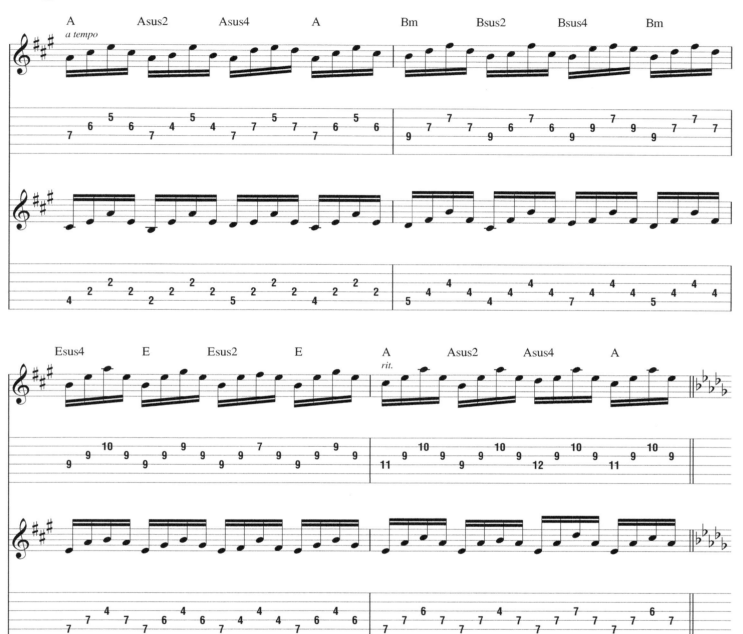

A few practical movable shapes are in order as well. These are your go-to chord shapes, based on the practical, movable major shapes from the previous chapter.

Based on the E-type barre chord

major

```
1 3 4 2 1 1
R 5 R 3 5 R
```

sus4

```
1 3 3 3 1 1
    2 3 4
R 5 R 4 5 R
```

Based on the A-type barre chord

major

```
(1)1 3 3 3 1
(5)R 5 R 3 5
```

sus2

```
(1)1 3 4 1 1
(5)R 5 R 2 5
```

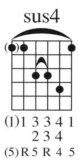

sus4

```
(1)1 3 3 4 1
     2 3 4
(5)R 5 R 4 5
```

Based on the C-type barre chord

major

```
(1)4 3 1 2 1
 3 R 3 5 R 3
```

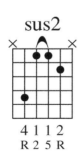

sus2

```
4 1 1 2
R 2 5 R
```

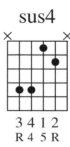

sus4

```
3 4 1 2
R 4 5 R
```

Based on the G-type barre chord

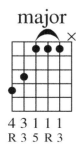

major

```
4 3 1 1 1
R 3 5 R 3
```

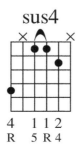

sus4

```
4   1 1 2
R   5 R 4
```

Another Kind of Chord Construction: Quintal and Quartal Chords

So far, this discussion of sus2 and sus4 chords has revolved around the idea of recognizing and naming them as variations on tertiary triads. This disregards the observation that sus2 and sus4 chords can be constructed in a way that's as coherent and consistent as tertiary construction. This form of construction can be identified as *quintal* or *quartal construction*, based on the intervals of a 5th (quintal) or a 4th (quartal). Instead of stacking the chord notes in 3rds, snowman-style, they are stacked in succesive 5ths or 4ths. Let's take a Csus2 chord and see how it can be reconfigured in these ways.

Begin with the three notes of a Csus2 on just the third, fourth, and fifth strings, like this:

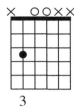

Now move from a close voicing to an open voicing by transposing the middle note up one octave, like this. Notice the change in fingering to accommodate the new voicing.

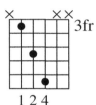

In this voicing, it can be seen that the notes are a perfect 5th apart: C up to G is a perfect 5th, and G up to D is a perfect 5th. If you recall from Chapter Three, the open 5th is a strong and stable interval, and the sound of this pair of open 5ths should strike you as similarly strong and stable. Consider this the basic *quintal chord*. Unfortunately, our current system of chord naming doesn't have a name for this simple construction, except to shoehorn it into a tertiary-based name like Csus2—or is it Gsus4?

If we return to our original voicing of Csus2 and leapfrog the C from the bottom of the chord to the top, we can see the construction built on 4ths.

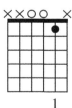

In this voicing, it can be seen that the notes are a perfect 4th apart: D up to G is a perfect 4th, and G up to C is a perfect 4th. The sound of successive 4ths is certainly different than the sound of successive 5ths, and if we were to think of this chord as being built upwards from the note D, it would want to have an identity much different than an inversion of the quintal chord built from C. Consider this the basic *quartal chord*. Again, our current system of chord naming can't identify this chord except as a variation on a tertiary construction.

By shuffling the note names of this particular chord as if they are members of a set, we'll get six different arragements of this set of notes:

1. CDG: the construction we identified as Csus2
2. CGD: the fundamental quintal construction
3. DGC: the fundamental quartal construction
4. DCG: an unusual construction of a 7th (D to C) and a 5th (C to G)
5. GCD: a construction we'd probably identify as Gsus4
6. GDC: another unusual construction of a 5th (G to D) and a 7th (D to C)

Constructing chords on 5ths and 4ths is not some bizarre intellectual activity. They appear regularly in popular music. Dave Matthews' "Satellite" opens with a quintal chord, and Andy Summers opens "Every Breath You Take" with a quintal chord. They have been used extensively in jazz, most prominently by McCoy Tyner in the late 1950s and then by virtually every jazz keyboard player thereafter. Classical and so-called "serious" composers have used quartal and quintal voicings since the beginning of the twentieth century. And if we go back to music before the common practice period—before, say, 1600—we would find quintal and quartal harmonies in moderately common use.

Quintal and quartal chords are a rich area of harmony that every guitarist should explore. You might try applying the Chord Study Toolkit (see p. 104) to them. Perhaps some clever mind will create a way of easily naming these chords on a QWERTY keyboard, and they will become as much a part of our chordal vocabulary as our tertiary triads currently are. In the meantime, I'll continue to identify them as they arise from the practical and conventional chordal vocabulary of the past century.

CHAPTER FIVE:
Seventh Chords

Snowmen with Four Body Parts

So far, we've done an exhaustive amount of work with a relatively limited set of chords. To summarize, we've worked with dyads (two-note intervals that often function as chords), tertiary triads (three-note chords built from the interval of a 3rd), and sus chords (chords derived from tertiary triads). We've taken these chords and arranged their notes in all inversions, in close and open voicing, and put them through their paces with sequences and progressions. We even took a brief detour, thanks to sus chords, to identify quintal and quartal triads—three-note chords built on 5ths and 4ths.

In standard music theory, the next step in chord complexity is to consider the so-called "seventh" chords—four-note chords consisting of a tertiary triad plus another tertiary leap up from the 5th. When dealing with the chord in snowman form, this new note is some kind of a 7th scale note above the root, which is where we get the generic name of "seventh."

Unlike many of the tertiary triads we tackled in Chapters Two and Four, most of these seventh chords are really difficult to play on the guitar when presented in close voicing. This is a critical point in your understanding of chord theory and its practice on the guitar, because now we have this lovely stack of four snowballs on paper that most keyboard players will comfortably whiz through but which you will have to rearrange in order to play on the guitar. You need to come to grips with the fact that some chords exist in certain forms in theory and on a keyboard, but may never be played that way on the guitar. You need to be able to extract the theory and apply it in a practical way to the guitar, which we'll do in a little bit. But first, let's get a grip on the theory behind seventh chords by analyzing the diatonic tertiary seventh chords of C major and C harmonic minor.

Naming and Dissecting Seventh Chords in the Major Tonality

Introducing the Major Seventh Chord

Tertiary seventh chords are built in the same way as tertiary triads. Working in the key of C major and using the "play a note, skip a note" snowman approach to chord construction, we begin with notes C, E, and G, and then add a B on top.

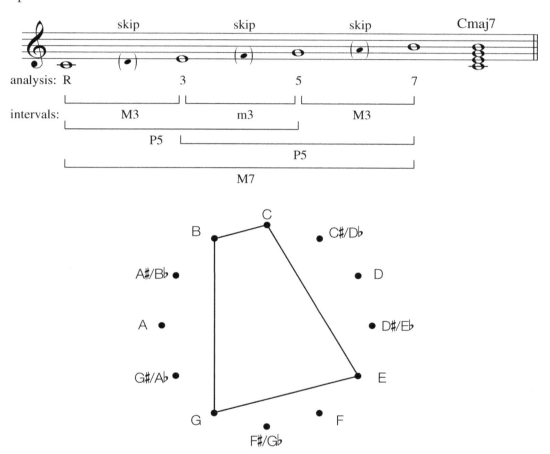

Here we sit with a root note (C), a major 3rd above the root (E), a perfect 5th above the root (G), and a major seventh above the root (B). You should recognize that the R–3–5 construction is a C major triad along with a major 7th placed like an extra snowball on top. We call this chord "C major seven" (written Cmaj7), not because it's a C *major* chord with a sweet diatonic 7th on top, but because it's a C major chord with a *major* 7th on top. Just as a C major chord is written "C" where the "nothing" that follows the root name indicates that the chord is major, so Cmaj7 is written with "nothing" after the root name, but with maj7 tacked on to indicate a major seventh added to the major triad.

Besides looking at Cmaj7 as a C major triad with a major seventh added, there are two other note groupings to be aware of—two important yet often-overlooked components in the practical use of seventh chords. First, you'll notice in the collection of intervals that there are two sets of perfect 5ths: C–G and E–B. Harkening back to Chapter Two, it would be silly not to recognize these as two perfect 5th dyads—two loud and proud power chords: C5 and E5. So a major seventh chord is not just a major triad with a seventh added on top; it's also an interlocked pair of "five" chords a major 3rd apart. Second, look at the notes E, G, and B—the upper three notes of the chord. This is an E minor triad, which means that another way to look at a major seventh chord is as a different triad (a minor triad a major 3rd above the named root) with the root added a major 3rd below the minor triad. We'll explore these aspects, and what they mean to our feeling, perception, and playing of this chord, as we continue through this chapter.

Introducing the Minor Seventh Chord

Let's continue with seventh chords in the major tonality by examining the seventh chord built on the note D within the C major scale.

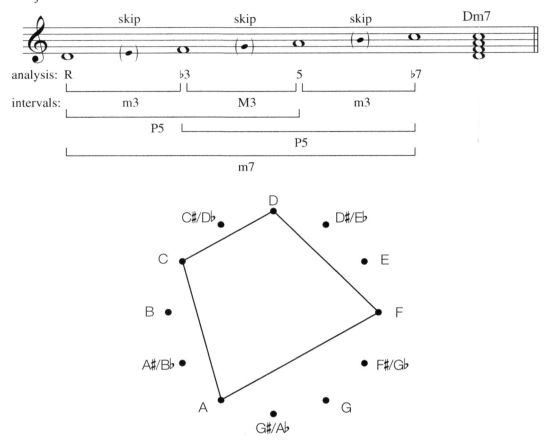

Referring to the music and diagrams above, we can see that the root is D, the minor 3rd (♭3) above the root is F, the perfect 5th (5) above the root is A, and the minor 7th (♭7) above the root is C. Again, recognize the simple R–♭3–5 construction of the D minor triad along with a minor 7th (C) placed on top. We call this chord "D minor seven" (written Dm7) because it's a D *minor* chord with a minor or ♭7th added. The ♭7th interval gets special treatment in our world of chord names. It gets preferential treatment, like the major triad, by having no additional tags added. When I name chord notes aloud, I often refer to this note as the "plain seven."

Like the Cmaj7 chord, there are two other groups of notes to be aware of within our root position, close-voiced Dm7 chord. First, you'll notice the two sets of perfect 5ths: D–A and F–C. Just like the major seventh chord, we have two open 5ths: D5 and F5. So a minor seventh chord is not just a minor triad with a minor 7th added on top, but also an interlocked pair of "five" chords a minor 3rd apart. Second, the notes F–A–C should hit you in the face as an F major triad. A minor seventh chord is also a different triad (a major triad a minor 3rd above the named root) with the root added a minor 3rd below the major triad.

Here's the chord built on the note E within the C major scale.

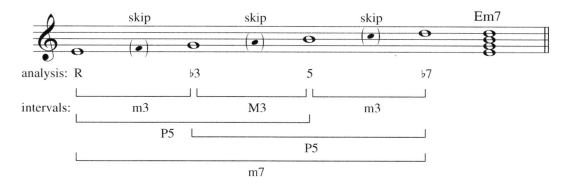

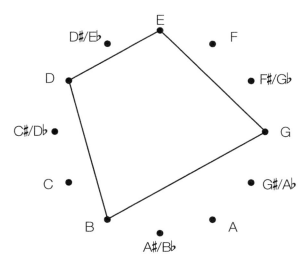

This is an Em7 chord. We can see that the root is E, the minor 3rd (♭3) above the root is G, the perfect 5th (5) above the root is B, and the minor 7th (♭7) above the root is D. Just as with the Dm7 chord, you should recognize the simple R–♭3–5 construction of the E minor triad along with a minor 7th (D) placed on top. Notice that the analysis of the chord and the intervals shown are all the same as the Dm7, so we now have two minor seventh chords so far in the key of C major.

Just as we found the two open 5ths and the major triad within Dm7, so we have an E5 and a G5 interlocked within Em7, as well as a G major triad along with the root added a minor 3rd below.

Here's the chord built on the note F within the C major scale.

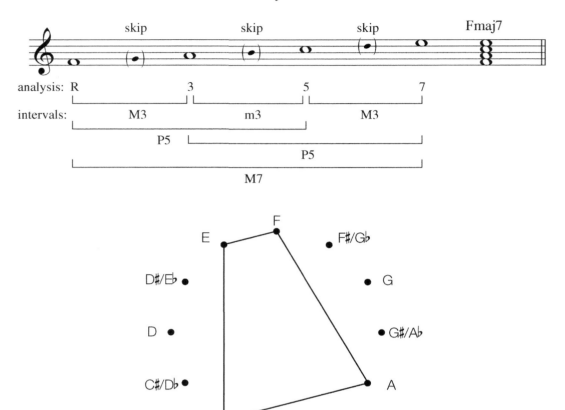

A quick back-and-forth scan between this chord and the Cmaj7 chord should verify that here's another major seventh chord—specifically, Fmaj7. There's the root note (F), a major 3rd above the root (A), a perfect 5th above the root (C), and a major 7th above the root (E). You should recognize that the R–3–5 construction is an F major triad along with a major seventh (E) placed like an extra snowball on top.

Be sure that you can see the interlocked open 5ths: F5 and A5, as well as the A minor triad floating above the root note F.

Introducing the "Plain" or Dominant Seventh Chord

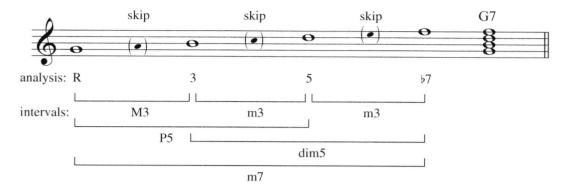

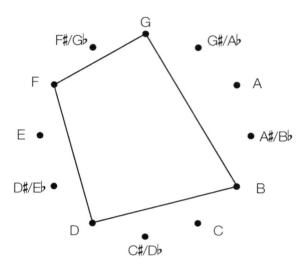

The chord built on the note G within the C major scale will really kick the hornet's nest of chord theory and naming. As you can see, we have here a G major chord—the root (G), major 3rd above the root (B), and perfect 5th above the root (D), but with a *minor 7th* (F) on top. Our two major chords so far—Cmaj7 and Fmaj7—both had *major* 7ths on top. We call this chord G7—a major chord with a minor or ♭7th on top. Remember that the major triad (G) gets nothing after its root name, and the minor or flatted seventh also gets nothing before its identification. Thus, the chord is named G7. A plain G major chord with a "plain" 7 added.

In traditional Western music theory, this kind of chord was often called the ***dominant*** chord. It was considered the most dissonant and unstable of all chords and, historically, it was the first chord to have the 7th added to it. So while most of the fancy-pants rich European people's music from 1650 to 1875 consisted of tertiary triads, the one crazy four-note chord allowed into the party was the dominant seventh chord. That plain 7th shook up European composers for two or three centuries.

Notice that, unlike all of the seventh chords so far, there's only one open perfect 5th within the G7 chord: the notes G and D. The other 5th is a diminished 5th or ♭5—B and F. There's one strong, proud open 5th dyad: G5. Then there's that grating, fighting-itself B(♭5) dyad. Also notice that the triad that lives above the note G is a diminished triad: B°. Of course, B° contains the flatted 5th, and as you should recall, the interval of the flatted 5th is the evil *diabolus in musica*—the unstable and ambiguous interval of Satan, as medieval musicians may have called it. Whether you recognize this interval as evil and Satanic, a little edgy, or flat out cool, it's important to see it as a vital part of the dominant seventh chord. If you want to understand music that maintains the credibility of traditional Western harmony, you'll want to get a real feel for the dominant seventh chord and all of its family members. You'll want to contain its slippery devilish tension and be able to lead that tension around, as if on a leash. In the same light, if you understand the horns that this sound sprouts, you can let it off its leash and let it romp free from any historical constrictions.

Now on to the completion of the seventh chords built upon the C major scale. Here's the seventh chord built upon the note A within the C major scale:

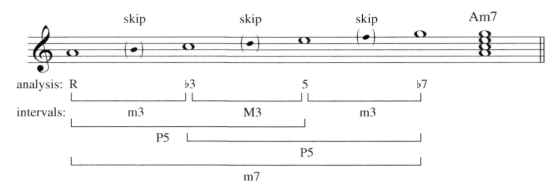

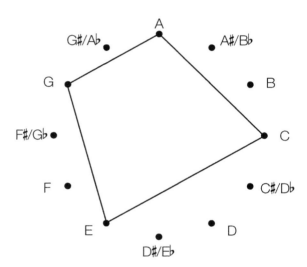

A return to normalcy! With a root (A), a minor 3rd (♭3) above the root (C), a perfect 5th (5) above the root (E) and a minor 7th (♭7) above the root (G), we return to the familiar minor seventh chord. Be sure to identify the simple R–♭3–5 construction of the A minor triad along with the minor 7th (G) placed on top. Also dig the interlocked open 5ths—A5 and C5—and the C major triad above the root note A. We call this chord "A minor seven" (written Am7) because it's an A *minor* chord with a (minor or flatted) seventh added. Notice that the analysis of the chord and the intervals shown are the same as the Dm7 and Em7, so we now have three of this chord type in the key of C major—three different minor seventh chords.

Introducing the Minor Seven Flat Five Chord

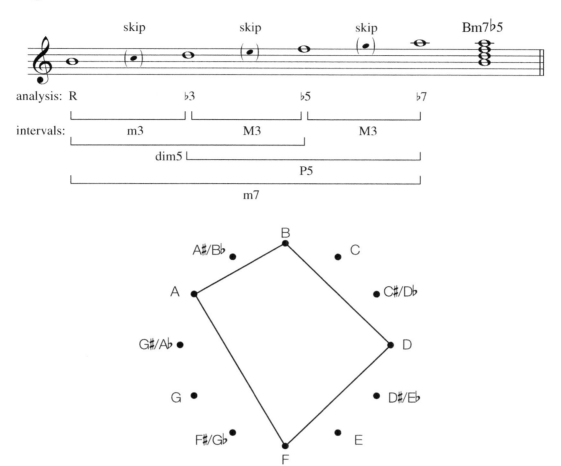

Strange things always seem to happen in the major scale when we reach the seventh note, and so it is when we build a seventh chord on the note B within the key of C. If G7 seemed like a cartload of chaos for such a plain-named sound, our next chord dumps the cart out and runs away with some chaos of its own. The root is B, the minor 3rd is D, the diminished 5th is F, and the minor 7th is A. We call this chord Bm7♭5, read "B minor seven flat five." The first craziness about this chord is that every note in the chord is identified in the name. Check it out: B = root, m = ♭3 (D), 7 (plain or ♭7) =A, and ♭5 = F. Chord names are supposed to be a kind of shorthand, but this one is a flourish of long-handed explicitness. And here's more craziness: although it sits as happy as a clam within the major scale, and although it can be found in lots of music in every conceivable style, it's the first chord that many guitarists shy away from. "It's one of those weird half-demolished flatted pretzel chords!" they scream. Indeed, it's an unstable knot of notes—there's no perfect-5th backbone attached to the root to prop it up. Instead, it's built upon the spine of the devil—the diminished 5th. A perfect 5th (D and A) sits above, almost begging the chord to tip over into some kind of D minor. You did notice the D minor triad atop the root note of B, didn't you?

Of all the chords we've covered so far, this is the second that creates a kind of unsteadiness that does not take well to "campfire strumming." The first was the diminished triad, which you know well from the last chapter. By "campfire strumming," I refer to the kind of strumming where one chord is held (and strummed, sometimes vigorously, sometimes lazily) for a moderately long period of time without regard for change to another chord. Since the m7♭5 chord is built upon the diminished triad, we should recognize the commonality of the diminished 5th above the root of each of these chords that creates this sense of unrest. Notice also that we passed right by the diminished triad within the plain or dominant seventh chord just two chords earlier—specifically G7—and any guitarist worth his or her salt will know that plain seventh chords are just fine for campfire strumming. We can say that the diminished triad within the plain seventh chord is tamed by the perfect 5th of the root-5th team, but the minor seven flat five lacks this upright root-5th spine, and so it just doesn't stand up around the campfire.

Naming and Dissecting Seventh Chords in the Harmonic Minor Tonality

Some of the stranger seventh chords will be uncovered in the harmonic minor tonality. Using C harmonic minor as our demonstration key, let's build some four-note snowman chords and see what we get.

Introducing the Minor Major Seventh chord

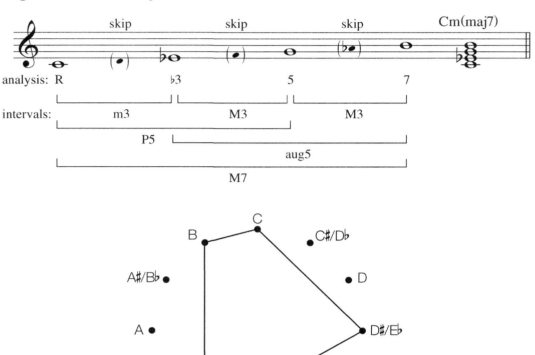

The home or "one" chord in C harmonic minor is built on the root note C, with a minor 3rd above the root (E♭), a perfect 5th above the root (G), and, staying strictly within the scale, a *major* 7th above the root (B). You should recognize that the R–♭3–5 construction is a minor triad along with a major 7th placed like an extra snowball on top. We call this chord "C minor major seven"—written Cm(maj7). There's no deep mystery—except for the sound. We'll play this chord in several ways later in this chapter, but our analytical antenna should begin to quiver when we look at the other bits of what makes up this chord. First, although there's a firm perfect 5th between the root (C) and the 5th (G), there's that woozy augmented 5th between the minor 3rd (E♭) and the major seventh (B). Cm(maj7) can be thought of as a C5 dyad plus an E♭(♯5) dyad. The triad that lives above the root note is the augmented triad of E♭–G–B, so we can also think of the minor major seventh chord as an augmented triad with another note added a minor 3rd below the triad's root name. The sound is a bit unsteady, and in most music involving seventh chords in a minor tonality, the min(maj7) chord will be used as a passing chord between other, more stable chords.

Now let's move on to the chord built on the second note of the C harmonic minor scale.

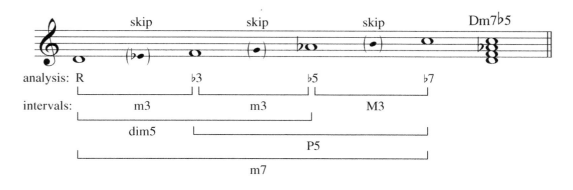

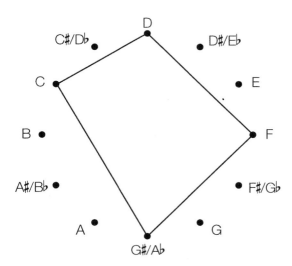

This is a Dm7♭5. It's a diminished triad (D–F–A♭, or R–♭3–♭5) with a ♭7th on top. There are no surprises, other than those already introduced with the minor seven flat five chord found in the major key.

Introducing the Major Seven Sharp Five Chord

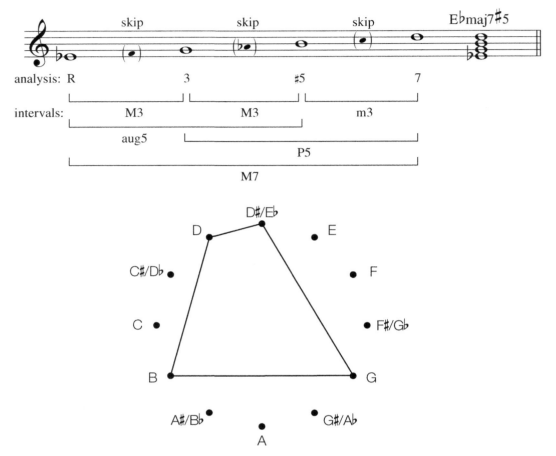

The chord built on the third note of the C harmonic minor scale is another one with a name that confounds the logical mind. The founding triad is Eb+, and a major seventh (D) is added on top. But the apparent name, Eb+(maj7), is never used. Instead it gets the somewhat bass-ackward title of Ebmaj7#5. The two dyads are an Eb(#5), along with a more stable G5 dyad. Notice that lurking within this seemingly thorny chord is a major triad—G major, spelled G–B–D. It will often be useful to think of the maj7#5 chord as a major triad with a slightly peculiar note placed a major 3rd below the major triad's root, abstractly written as X/b6.

Compared to the previous three chords, the chord built on the note F within the C harmonic minor scale provides some stability.

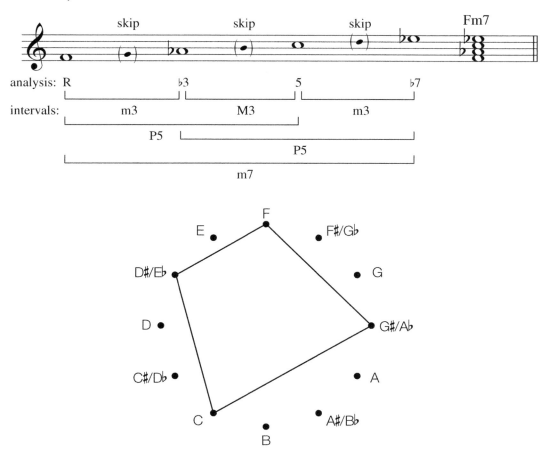

It's Fm7, a type of chord found in abundance in the major scale. The root is F, the minor 3rd (♭3) above the root is A♭, the perfect 5th (5) above the root is C, and the minor 7th (♭7) above the root is E♭. Here's the simple R–♭3–5 construction of the F minor triad along with a minor seventh (E♭) placed on top. Remember, the name Fm7 comes from the F minor chord with a minor or ♭7th added. The ♭7th gets special treatment in our world of chord names by having no additional tags added. I like to call it the "plain seven."

Here's the chord that gives the harmonic minor scale its traditional juiciness. It's built from the fifth note of the scale.

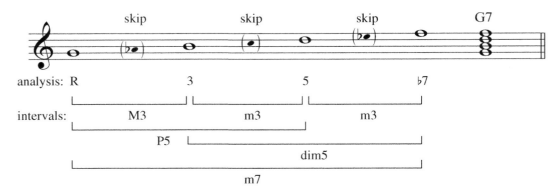

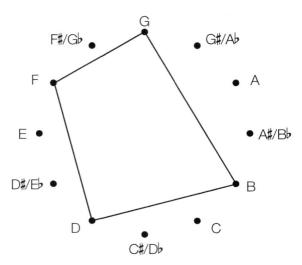

It's our friend the dominant seventh chord, specifically G7—a major triad (G–B–D) with a minor 7th added. In the common practice period of Western harmony (1650–1850), so much hoopla was associated with the resolution of the leading tone—the seventh note of the major scale, in this case B—to the tonic note (in this case, C) that the minor scale was altered to add this note. If we were using the C natural minor scale, the G chord would be a minor seventh, with a B♭ instead of a B. The power of the plain seventh chord will be summoned, worshipped, tamed, and altered as we continue through this book.

The chord built on the sixth note of the harmonic minor scale is also familiar.

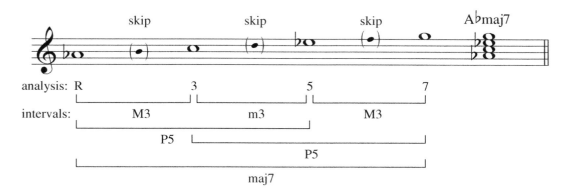

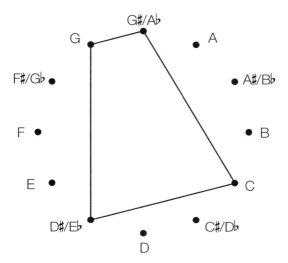

It's an A♭maj7. There's the root note (A♭), a major 3rd above the root (C), a perfect 5th above the root (E♭), and a major 7th above the root (G). You should recognize that the R–3–5 construction is an A♭ major triad along with a major seventh (G) placed like an extra snowball on top.

Be sure that you can also see the interlocked open 5ths: A♭5 and E♭5, as well as the C minor triad floating above the root note A♭.

Introducing the Diminished Seventh Chord

By now, you should come to expect strange things on the seventh degree of any scale with a traditional leading tone (M7) involved. The harmonic minor scale delivers a haunted house of strangeness. Here it comes…

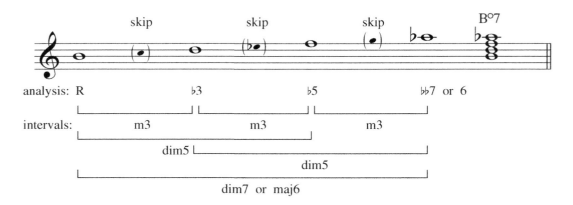

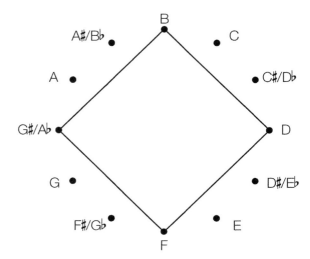

We begin with a diminished triad: B–D–F or R–♭3–♭5. Then, because the B is raised in the harmonic minor scale, the next note—the 7th—is a whole new kind of seventh: a *diminished 7th*. Think about it for a moment (and play it on your guitar, of course): B up to A♯ would be a major 7th, and B up to A♮ would be a minor 7th, so B to A♭ would be a diminished seventh. Since A♭ can also be named G♯, it's not too hard to think of that diminished seventh as a major 6th. Because of that curious diminished 7th and the confusion of naming it two different ways (A♭ or G♯), the fundamental structure of this chord can be lost. Break it down by playing it on a single string, arpeggio-like, measure the intervals, count the frets—do whatever it takes to realize that this chord is a stack of minor 3rds, with a distance of another minor 3rd from the diminished seventh up to the root. The absolutely ambiguous structure of this chord can be difficult to recognize or explain in our traditional system of music notation and note naming. But one look at the circle diagram reveals its symmetric ambiguity. It's a square! It has four equal sides!

The diminished seventh chord gets a perfectly ambiguous name, of course. It's a diminished triad, but with an odd diminished 7th planted on top. Remember that a diminished triad with a minor 7th added was named a "minor seven flat five." So the diminished seventh chord could be called a "diminished seven flat five." But it's not. The diminished 7th note could be renamed as a major 6th, and the diminished seventh chord could be called a "diminished sixth" chord—a name I happen to like. But it's not. It's called a diminished seventh. Get used to it, as I have. (It's also occasionally called "fully diminished," whereas a m7♭5 chord is sometimes called a "half diminished.")

Notice that, unlike all of the seventh chords so far, there are no open 5ths in the diminished seventh chord. Using some enharmonic equivalents (or just looking at the circle diagram), it reveals itself as a swarm of diminished 5ths: B and F, D and A♭, F and C♭, and G♯ and D. It's a group of four minor 3rds, or two ♭5 dyads. In the devil-and-angel world of traditional Western harmony, it is the tongue-kiss of Satan and the most unsympathetic to campfire strumming. Consider it the slipperiest of all seventh chords, but also in many ways the most useful. It can function like a trap door to tonal ambiguity or a hidden stairway to alternate universes.

Open-Position Seventh Chords

Another good way to get to know seventh chords is to look at the open-position chords you already know and analyze the notes in the chord. Even if you rarely venture past the fourth or fifth fret on your guitar, your understanding of the notes in a chord and how they function will help you use the chords you know more effectively and find the occasional new chord more quickly. Here are some common open-position seventh chords along with their simpler triadic parents to help you recognize the important notes in each chord.

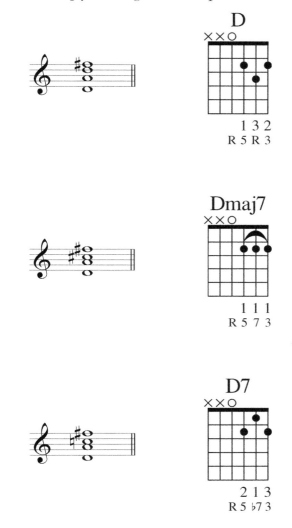

A simple D major chord provides a good example of how the major seventh resides just below the root of the chord. In this case, there's a high root note on the B string at the third fret. D major becomes Dmaj7 by dropping the high root down one fret. Drop the same note one more fret and you have D7.

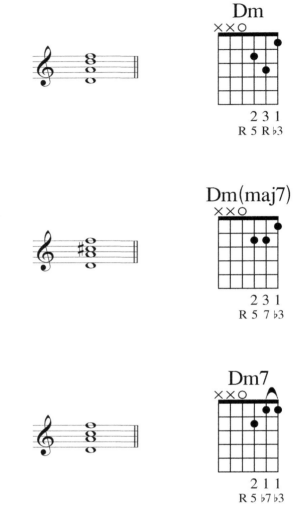

D minor provides a similar example of how a simple triad can be transformed into several different seventh chords. Just as with the D major chord, the high root is dropped one fret to create Dm(maj7), then another fret for Dm7.

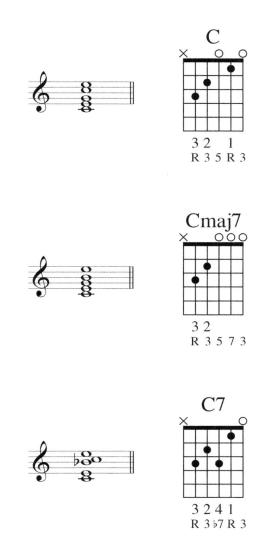

The open-position C major chord is a good place to stretch your application of chord theory on the guitar as well as understand the limitations of open-position chords. Transforming the C major chord to Cmaj7 is a simple matter of recognizing the note C on the B string and lifting your first finger to allow the open B (the major 7th) to ring. Compare the 5–R–3 voicing of the chord on strings 3–2–1 to the voicing on the D major chord. Now, if you only had another fret below the open B string, you could create a C7 chord! Ah, but you don't, so the solution is to recognize the note that creates a C7 chord, Bb, and play that note on a different string. Even a beginner, unfamiliar with naming notes on the guitar, should recognize that the G string tunes to a unison with the B string at the fourth fret; therefore, the fourth fret note on the G string is a B, and the third fret note is a Bb. Since you don't want a major 7th (B♮) and a flatted 7th (Bb) in the same chord, return to a standard C major chord and add your fourth finger on the G string as shown. Now the cleverest of all my readers may gasp. "Where's the 5th? There's a doubling of roots and 3rds, and the sophisticated 7th has covered the only extant 5th!" Welcome to the wild and wacky world of seventh chords, children. Very often, complex chords are pared down to accommodate either practical fingerings, limitations of the guitar's tuning, or even musical taste. We'll explore this rude loss of notes in many chord fingerings later in this book.

The open-position C major chord is also a good example of why open-position chords alone can be limiting: there's no commonly used open-position C minor chord, so there's no commonly used open-position Cm(maj7) or Cm7. They will need to be constructed from barre chords.

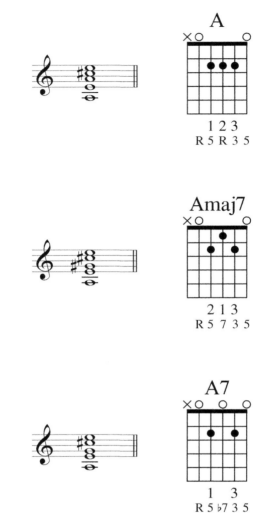

Let's explore the A major chord as a final example of how to add the major and minor sevenths to a basic chord.

The traditional open position A major chord accommodates the major 7th and ♭7th quite easily. Notice that, just like the D major and C major chords, there's a 5–R–3 voicing on three adjacent strings (in this case, strings 4–3–2) to accommodate the doubled root, which can then descend to the major 7th or flatted 7th. On the next page is another voicing of A major to work with:

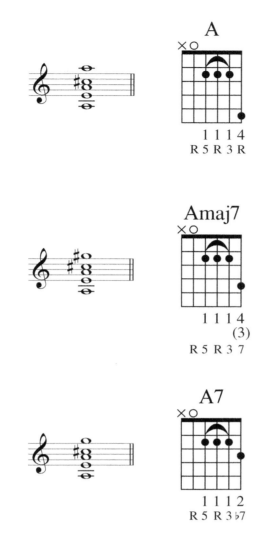

This voicing of A major places a high root on top, which is perfect for transforming into various sevenths. (I first picked up this unusual voicing of A major from watching John Lennon in the Beatles' movie *Let It Be*. John uses this voicing in "I've Got a Feeling.") It's good to compare the voicings of the seventh chords here with the previous example. With the seventh on top like this, it really jumps out—almost like an added melody note atop the chord. I like to think of this as the "bright" seventh voicing and the other voicings we've played as somewhat "darker" voicings.

Deriving Seventh Chords from Basic Movable Triad Shapes

In addition to understanding seventh chords in open position, it's good to examine a movable triad shape and see how the seventh figures into that shape. If we return to one of the basic movable triad shapes introduced in Chapter Four, we can often find fingerings of the various seventh chords derived from that triad by adding the seventh to the shape. A more complete guide to movable seventh chord fingerings follows shortly (p. 169), but this process can help you understand why those fingerings work and how to create fingerings of your own without this book (or any reference book) in front of you.

Let's begin with an E-type barre chord, played as A major at the fifth fret.

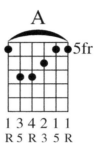

By recognizing the two higher roots in this chord shape, we can see that there are two locations where a seventh can be added. Let's start with the ♭7th. Think of this added note not only as a minor 7th above the root, but also as a major second below the root. Consider the root note A, played on the D string at the seventh fret with the fourth finger. By dropping this note down two frets, we can turn it into a ♭7. That can be easily done by simply lifting the fourth finger and being sure that the string rings from the barre of the first finger.

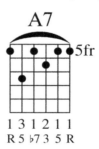

Ironically, if you begin with the same basic E-type barre chord, you'll have a difficult time adding a major seventh to the shape. Following the logic of the previous example, you could end up with something like this:

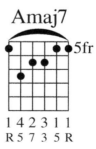

But yeow! What a difficult fingering to grab! The high root clashes with the major 7th in the middle as well. However, understanding where that major 7th is and why it doesn't work so well in this particular barre chord will lead you to a better understanding of why most guitarists use this shape:

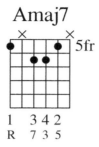

That understanding will probably generate a stronger memory of the chord shape as well. Keep this in mind as you continue to acquaint yourself with various seventh chords.

All Possible Closed-Voicing Seventh Chords in Root Position

Back in Chapter Four, I introduced a chart to generate and crosscheck all the possible tertiary triads. We can create a similar chart for all of our tertiary seventh chords. Let's bring back all six of the tertiary triads—the traditional major, minor, augmented, and diminished triads plus the oddball R–3–♭5 and R–♭3–♯5 and mate them with all of the possible sevenths we've come across. (In the practical system of chord construction and naming, the interval of a diminished 7th never occurs other than as part of the diminished seventh chord. I invite you to see what kinds of chords arrive when you add diminished sevenths to these triads. You may meet up with them later in this book.) Chords that have been introduced already in the major and harmonic minor scales will be so noted, and there will be no need to repeat their constructions, but the curious new chords that appear will be addressed.

Basic triad: Diminished	Added seventh: diminished seven	Resulting chord type: diminished 7th Resulting analysis notation: R–♭3–♭5–♭♭7	This chord is found within the harmonic minor scale as vii°.
Triad analysis notation: R–♭3–♭5	Analysis notation: ♭♭7	Resulting analysis notation: R–♭3–♭5–♭♭7	
Example: C°	Example: B♭♭ Reminder: this will be the only time that we'll use the diminished 7th interval.	Example: C°7	

Basic triad: Diminished	Added seventh: flat seven	Resulting chord type: minor seven flat five	This chord is found within the major scale as vii7♭5 and harmonic minor scale as ii7♭5.
Triad analysis notation: R–♭3–♭5	Analysis notation: ♭7	Resulting analysis notation: R–♭3–♭5–♭7	
Example: C°	Example: B♭	Example: Cm7♭5	

Basic triad: Diminished	Added seventh: major seven	Resulting chord type: diminished major seven	This chord is found within the **diminished scale**. A discussion of this scale is in the text following this chart.
Triad analysis notation: R–♭3–♭5	Analysis notation: 7	Resulting analysis notation: R–♭3–♭5–7	
Example: C°	Example: B	Example: C°(maj7), Cm7♭5 This is a really cool chord that we'll meet up with later as a 7♯9 without a root. It's a shame it shows up so rarely in traditional chord use. Note that the ♭3–♭5–7 in the key of C is E♭–G♭–B. This can be respelled as D♯–F♯–B, which is a first inversion B major triad, so this chord would probably be called B/C, or, abstractly, X/♭2.	

Basic triad: Minor	Added seventh: flat seven	Resulting chord type: minor seven	Found within the major scale as ii7, iii7, and vi7, and harmonic minor scale as iv.
Triad analysis notation: R–♭3–5	Analysis notation: ♭7	Resulting analysis notation: R–♭3–5–♭7	
Example: Cm	Example: B♭	Example: Cm7	

Basic triad: Minor	Added seventh: major seven	Resulting chord type: minor major seven	This chord is found within the harmonic minor scale as i(maj7).
Triad analysis notation: R–♭3–5	Analysis notation: 7	Resulting analysis notation: R–♭3–5–7	
Example: Cm	Example: B	Example: Cm(maj7)	

Basic triad: Minor sharp five	Added seventh: flat seven	Resulting chord type: minor seven sharp five	The #5 can be enharmonically renamed as a b6, which will make the chord diatonic to the major scale. However, it would retain the "sharp five" name, as iii7#5 and vi7#5.
Triad analysis notation: R–b3–#5	Analysis notation: b7	Resulting analysis notation: R–b3–#5–b7	Cm7#5 C, B, C#/Db, A#/Bb, D, A, D#/Eb, G#/Ab, E, G, F, F#/Gb
Example: Cm(#5) This is one of the two odd triads that are not part of the traditional tertiary triads.	Example: Bb	Example: Cm7(#5) Here's a beautiful sounding chord that's rarely seen in traditional chord naming. It could be renamed as Abadd9/C or Ebsus4/C.	
Basic triad: Minor sharp five	Added seventh: major seven	Resulting chord type: minor major seven sharp five	The #5 can be enharmonically renamed as a b6, which will make the chord diatonic to the harmonic minor scale. However, it would retain the "sharp five" name, as i(maj7)#5.
Triad analysis notation: R–b3–#5	Analysis notation: 7	Resulting analysis notation: R–b3–#5–7	Cm(maj7)#5 C, B, C#/Db, A#/Bb, D, A, D#/Eb, G#/Ab, E, G, F, F#/Gb
Example: Cm(#5)	Example: B	Example: Cm(maj7#5) This curiosity could be renamed Abm/C or Abadd#9/C. Abstractly this could be symbolized as Xm/3.	

Basic triad: Major flat five	Added seventh: flat seven	Resulting chord type: seven flat five	This chord is found within the **diminished scale** and the **whole tone scale**. A discussion of this scale can be found in the text following this chart.
Triad analysis notation: R–3–♭5	Analysis notation: ♭7	Resulting analysis notation: R–3–♭5–♭7	
Example: C(♭5) This is the other of the two oddballs of the traditional tertiary triad clan, but notice how it is a part of two relatively common seventh chords.	Example: B♭	Example: C7♭5 Although this chord is derived from an "oddball" triad, it's quite a common chord in the traditional jazz world. Its symmetrical structure allows it to be renamed as F♯7♭5.	
Basic triad: Major flat five	Added seventh: major seven	Resulting chord type: major seven flat five	The ♭5 is more commonly enharmonically renamed as ♯11, and the chord is found in the major scale as the IVmaj7♯11
Triad analysis notation: R–3–♭5	Analysis notation: 7	Resulting analysis notation: R–3–♭5–7	
Example: C(♭5) This is the other of the two oddballs of the traditional tertiary triad clan, but notice how it is a part of two relatively common seventh chords.	Example: B	Example: Cmaj7♭5 Here's another chord that, although derived from an "oddball" triad, is quite a common sound in the traditional jazz world. However, it will be renamed Cmaj7♯11 later on.	

Basic triad: Major	Added seventh: flat seven	Resulting chord type: seven, or dominant seven	This chord is found in both the major and the harmonic minor scale as V7.
Triad analysis notation: R–3–5	Analysis notation: ♭7	Resulting analysis notation: R–3–5–♭7	
Example: C	Example: B♭	Example: C7	

Basic triad: Major	Added seventh: major seven	Resulting chord type: major seven	This chord is found in the major scale as Imaj7 and IVmaj7 and in the harmonic minor scale as ♭VImaj7
Triad analysis notation: R–3–5	Analysis notation: 7	Resulting analysis notation: R–3–5–7	
Example: C	Example: B	Example: Cmaj7	

Basic triad: Augmented	Added seventh: flat seven	Resulting chord type: seven sharp five	As named and analyzed, this chord is found in the **whole tone** scale. If the ♯5 is enharmonically renamed as a ♭6, this chord can be found in the harmonic minor scale as V7♯5. If the 3rd of the basic triad is enharmonically renamed as a ♭4, it can be found in the harmonic minor scale as VII7♯5.
Triad analysis notation: R–3–♯5	Analysis notation: ♭7	Resulting analysis notation: R–3–♯5–♭7	
Example: C+	Example: B♭	Example: C7♯5	

Basic triad: Augmented	Added seventh: major seven	Resulting chord type: major seven sharp five	This chord is found within the harmonic minor scale as ♭IIImaj7♯5.
Triad analysis notation: R–3–♯5	Analysis notation: 7	Resulting analysis notation: R–3–♯5–7	
Example: C+	Example: B	Example: Cmaj7♯5	

Basic triad: Suspended second or sus two	Added seventh: flat seven	Resulting chord type: seven sus two	This chord can be found in the major scale as ii7sus2, iii7sus2, and vi7sus2, and in the harmonic minor scale as iv7sus2.
			C7sus2
Triad analysis notation: R–2–5	Analysis notation: ♭7	Resulting analysis notation: R–2–5–♭7	
Example: Csus2	Example: B♭	Example: C7sus2	
		This is a somewhat uncommon name, although we'll see how it is used in a bit. It's more commonly named either C9 (and would be considered an "incomplete" 9 chord because of the missing 3rd) or Gm/C, because in the key of C, the 2–5–♭7 would be the notes D–G–B♭, which is a second-inversion Gm chord. Its abstract name would then be X/4.	
Basic triad: Suspended second or sus two	Added seventh: major seven	Resulting chord type: major seven sus two	This chord can be found in the major scale as Imaj7sus2 and IVmaj7sus2 and in the harmonic minor scale as imaj7sus2.
			Cmaj7sus2
Triad analysis notation: R–2–5	Analysis notation: 7	Resulting analysis notation: R–2–5–7	
Example: Csus2	Example: B	Example: Cmaj7sus2	
		Here's another uncommon name, only from lack of use. Just as with C7sus2, this chord would probably be named Cmaj9 or Cm9maj7 (and be considered incomplete because of the lack of any kind of 3rd) or G/C (because the 2–5–7 would be the notes D–G–B, a second-inversion G chord). Its abstract name would then be Xm/4.	

Basic triad: Suspended fourth or sus four	Added seventh: flat seven	Resulting chord type: seven sus four	This chord can be found in the major scale as ii7sus4, iii7sus4, V7sus4, and vi7sus4, and in the harmonic minor scale as iv7sus4 and V7sus4. It can be reanalyzed as a quintal/quartal chord.
Triad analysis notation: R–4–5	**Analysis notation:** ♭7	**Resulting analysis notation:** R–4–5–♭7	
Example: Csus4	**Example:** B♭	**Example:** C7sus4	
Basic triad: Suspended fourth or sus four	Added seventh: major seven	Resulting chord type: major seven sus four	This chord is almost never used as named. It can be found in the major scale as Imaj7sus4. It can be reanalyzed as a quintal/quartal chord.
Triad analysis notation: R–4–5	**Analysis notation:** 7	**Resulting analysis notation:** R–4–5–7	
Example: Csus4	**Example:** B	**Example:** Cmaj7sus4	

To summarize one observation from this chart: we now have seventeen different seventh chords, most of which are considered common chords in the popular music of the past century. Here's the list, grouped by scales and with commentary on how often they are used:

Seventh Chords from the Major and Harmonic Minor Scales

1. Major seventh, written maj7: extremely common and essential to know

2. Minor seventh, written m7: extremely common and essential to know

3. Seven, written 7: extremely common and essential to know

4. Minor seven flat five, written m7♭5, also commonly named "half-diminished: extremely common and essential to know

5. Seven sus two, written 7sus2: common and essential to know

6. Seven sus four, written 7sus4: common and essential to know

7. Major seven sus two, written maj7sus2: This is an uncommon name for a common chord. See comments in previous chart.

8. Major seven flat five, written maj7♭5, or preferably enharmonically respelled and renamed as major seven sharp eleven, written maj7#11: common in jazz and sophisticated pop music—very good to know

9. Minor seven sharp five, written m7#5: can be revoiced, rewritten, and renamed Xsus4/2 or Xsus2/4—good to know in all its names

10. Major seven sus four, written maj7sus4: rarely used as named

Seventh Chords from the Harmonic Minor Scale

11. Minor major seventh, written m(maj7): extremely common and essential to know

12. Diminished seventh, written °7: extremely common and essential to know

13. Seven sharp five (with enharmonic respelling), written 7#5: common in jazz and sophisticated pop music—very good to know

14. Major seven sharp five, written maj7#5: somewhat uncommon, but worth knowing

15. Minor major seven sharp five, written m(maj7)#5: not used as named—would probably be renamed as a 7#9 chord, without the root.

Seventh Chord from the Diminished and Whole Tone Scales

16. Seven flat five, written 7♭5: common in jazz and sophisticated pop music—very good to know

Seventh Chords Exclusively from the Diminished Scale

17. Diminished major seventh, written °(maj7) or X/♭2: not used as named—would probably be renamed as a 7#9 chord.

Two new scales have made their appearance in this discussion of seventh chords: the ***diminished scale*** and the ***whole tone scale***. Both of these scales are symmetrical scales, which means that they are constructed of simple repetitions of intervals and consist of an even number of notes. The whole tone scale consists of six different notes, each of which is separated from its neighbor by the interval of a "whole tone," or major 2nd. The diminished scale consists of eight different notes with an intervallic pattern of M2–m2–M2–m2, etc. Here are circle charts to compare these scales with the major and minor scales we've been using so far:

A Comparison of Scales

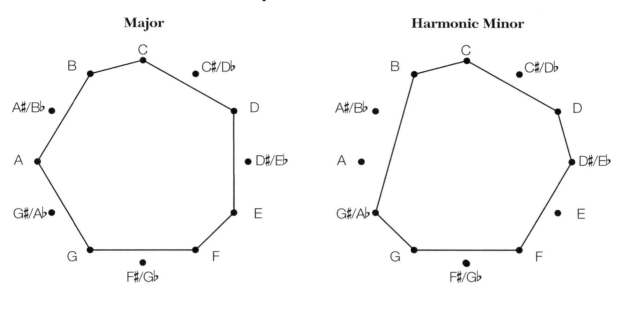

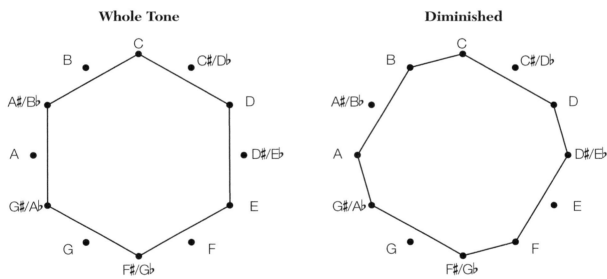

Lots of interesting and unusual chords can be found in the whole tone and diminished scales, as well as unusual combinations of many traditional chords. For practical purposes, we can think of these two scales as temporary ambiguous tonalities from which some unusual chords can be constructed.

Let's return to the practical problem of playing all the seventh chords we just uncovered. What we just did—all that paper analysis of all the seventh chords—was easy. Understanding seventh chords on the guitar is harder, for at least two good reasons:

1. They are almost never played in basic R–3–5–7 (root position, close voicing) form. We'll explore the probable, possible, and painful (if not impossible) voicings of seventh chords next.

2. As seen in the commentary, some of these chords are far more common that others. We'll discuss their use later in this chapter.

First, let's work on voicings of seventh chords. As I just mentioned, seventh chords are almost never played in close voicing in root position. It would be worth your while to try to play them this way on your own and really experience firsthand why most of the root-position close voicings are so difficult, but I'll toss you a bone and point out their terrors to you with a few examples. Let's try to build the three most common and stable seventh chords (major seven, minor seven, and dominant seven) in root position on each string set, as shown in the following figures.

Possible, Probable and Painful Fingerings for Seventh Chords in Close Voicing—Major Seventh Chords

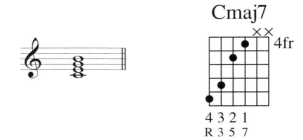

Cmaj7: POSSIBLE in higher positions, PAINFUL for many in lower positions because of the stretch between the second and third fingers.

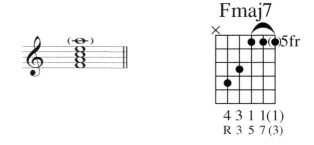

Fmaj7: PROBABLE—a fundamental shape, especially with the doubled 3rd on the first string.

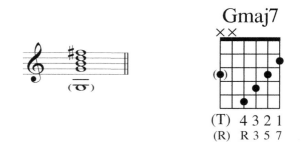

Gmaj7: PROBABLE—a fundamental shape. Try doubling the root with the thumb on the sixth string.

Possible, Probable and Painful Fingerings for
Seventh Chords in Close Voicing—Minor Seventh Chords

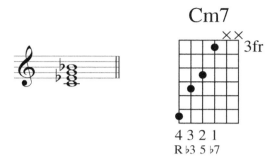

Cm7: PAINFUL for all but the most experienced guitarists.

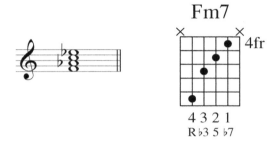

Fm7: PAINFIL for most—POSSIBLE for some in the higher positions.

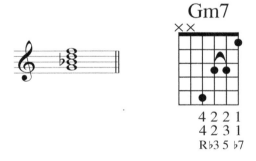

Gm7: PAINFUL for the majority of the guitar population.

Possible, Probable and Painful Fingerings for Seventh Chords in Close Voicing—Dominant Seventh Chords

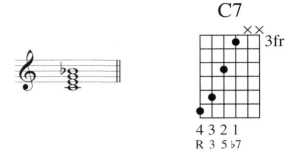

C7: PAINFUL for all but the most experienced guitarists.

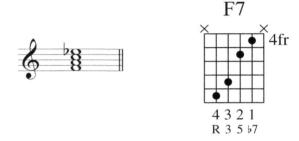

F7: PAINFUL for many in the lower positions because of the stretch between the second and third fingers—POSSIBLE in the higher positions.

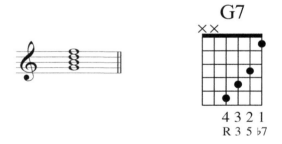

G7: POSSIBLE in lower positions and PROBABLE in higher positions.

Back in Chapter Three, I introduced the idea of using permutations of a set to consider all possible voicings of a chord type. With triads, it was rather simple to see the six permutations of the set:

R—3—5 (root position, close voicing)
R—5—3 (root position, open voicing)
3—R—5 (first inversion, open voicing)
3—5—R (first inversion, close voicing)
5—R—3 (second inversion, close voicing)
5—3—R (second inversion, open voicing)

With seventh chords (a set with four members: R, 3, 5, and 7), the number of permutations becomes much greater. It's an excellent exercise to sit with a pencil and paper and discover all of the permutations on your own (and that exercise has some powerful applications in and of itself), but that's for another time and place. Instead, here's another gift: all the permutations of the set of seventh chords, with no doubling of notes. Notice that the concept of "open" and "close" voicings becomes quite clumsy now, and I will abandon it for these chords; although, I will add the limitation that no interval between any two notes of a seventh chord will be greater than a major 7th.

All Permutations of the Set of Seventh Chords, Demonstrated with C Major Seventh

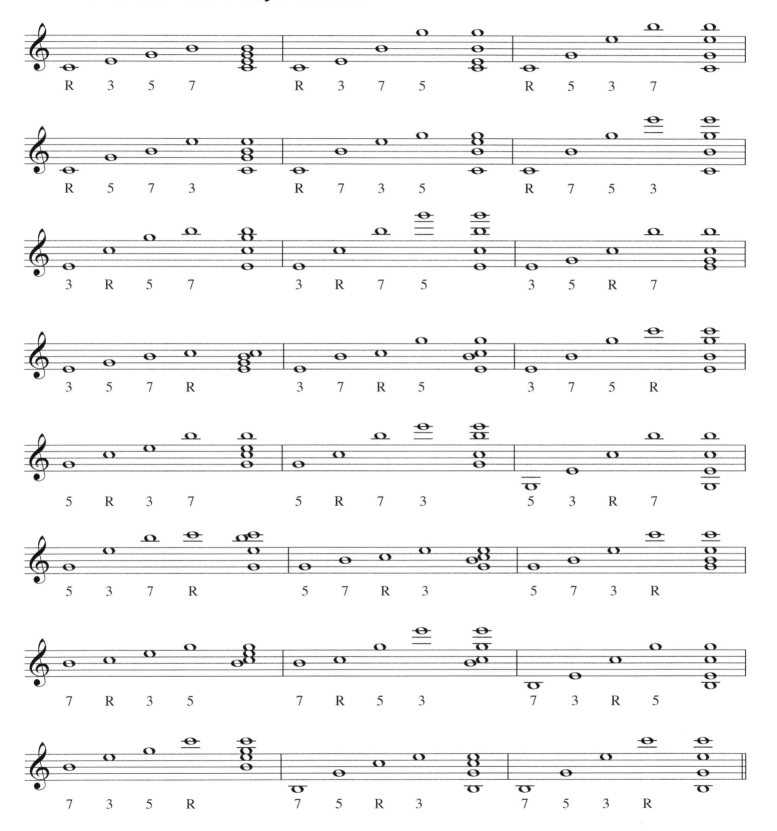

One practical use of this list would be to attempt to play all of the voicings shown. This will stretch your ears and your fingers and cause you to consider what is possible for you, possible for others, and impossible on the guitar. Another practical use would be to choose any one of the seventeen seventh chords from the previous list and modify the notes of the Cmaj7 chord to fit the new chord. For example, if you wanted to get a real feel for "minor major seven sharp five" chords, modify the spelling of the C major seventh (C–E–G–B, or R–3–5–7) to C–E♭–G♯–B, or R–♭3–♯5–7 and apply it to the list of Cmaj7 permutations. Of course, once you're on a path like that, you'll want to explore the chord in all possible keys. (Just a suggestion.)

Practical Fingerings for Seventh Chords

A couple of pages back, I introduced a list of seventeen possible seventh chords. The following pages are filled with practical, movable fingerings for these chords along with further commentary on the fingerings and voicings. Here are some guidelines to consider as you check them out:

- The root or 5th usually sounds best as the lowest note in the chord.

- Things can get murky with the 3rd as the lowest note. If there's a perfect 5th above the 3rd (a major 3rd and a major 7th, or a minor 3rd and a minor 7th), they will tend to team up and make the chord sound a little lopsided, as if the 3rd is the root of the chord. If you are playing with other musicians, playing the 3rd as the lowest note may interfere with another musician playing the root or the 3rd in the same range. Remember: generally avoid close intervals—2nds and 3rds—in the lowest octave of the guitar.

- If the 7 is played as the lowest note, the chord will be named as a slash chord, symbolized as X/Y. Slash chords were discussed in Chapters Three and Four.

- As you play each chord, try to identify the triad above the root of the chord. For example, if you are playing a Cmaj7 chord, find the Em triad above the root note C. What inversion is it? Is it complete, or has a note been dropped?

- If you are learning a chord type for the first time, choose just one or two fingerings to use. You should have a practical application for the chord—a song or an etude—and you should try to play it from memory at least once a day.

- If you are attempting to work on these chord shapes and you can't find the root note on the appropriate string, then you might be in over your head. You'll have a tough time identifying an A♭7♭5 if you can't find the note A♭ on your guitar.

- Five previously identified seventh chords are omitted from the following fingerings:

  → Major Seven Sus Two: This is an uncommon name, and the chord will be considered an incomplete major ninth chord. It will be addressed in Chapter Seven.

  → Major Seven Flat Five: This chord is better renamed as major seven sharp eleven, and so will be addressed in Chapter Seven.

  → Major Seven Sus Four: This chord is so rarely used that it will not be addressed.

  → Minor Major Seven Sharp Five: This name is clumsy and long, and the chord can be more easily renamed as a seven sharp nine chord, which will be addressed in Chapter Seven.

  → Diminished Major Seven: This is an unused name for a chord that can be easily written as a slash chord (X/♭2) or as a seven sharp nine chord without the root. For example, C°(maj7) can be seen as A♭7♯9 without an A♭.

These five rogues will only get parenthetical mention as we move forward.

Practical Fingerings of Movable Seventh Chords – Major Seven

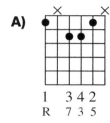

```
1   3 4 2
R   7 3 5
```

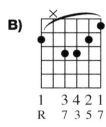

```
1   3 4 2 1
R   7 3 5 7
```

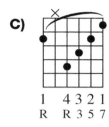

```
1   4 3 2 1
R   R 3 5 7
```

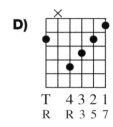

```
T   4 3 2 1
R   R 3 5 7
```

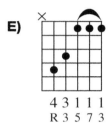

```
4 3 1 1 1
R 3 5 7 3
```

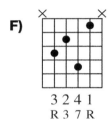

```
3 2 4 1
R 3 7 R
```

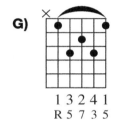

```
1 3 2 4 1
R 5 7 3 5
```

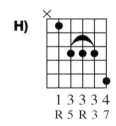

```
1 3 3 3 4
R 5 R 3 7
```

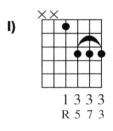

```
1 3 3 3
R 5 7 3
```

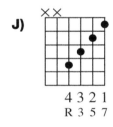

```
4 3 2 1
R 3 5 7
```

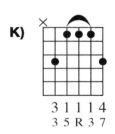

```
3 1 1 1 4
3 5 R 3 7
```

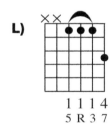

```
1 1 1 4
5 R 3 7
```

A) The most common mistake beginners make with this fingering is to allow the first finger to flop over and fret the third string. Unconsciously adding a perfect 4th to a major seventh chord is punishable by fines of up to $50 per occurrence, and possible banishment from future gigs.

B) and C) This is a useful "stunt" fingering" when you want to bring out the major 7th on top while having the low root note on the sixth string. Arch the first finger a bit, and you'll find that it can angle over to the lower fret on the first string.

F) This is a delicate sound. The major 7th and the high root will be very abrasive if your tuning and technique are not spot on.

G) Avoid lobbing the first finger onto the sixth string. This voicing already has two 5ths in it. Another 5th could have it expelled for excessive drinking.

K) Although this has the 3rd in the bass, you might be able to use it when playing solo or when you're higher on the neck.

Practical Fingerings of Movable Seventh Chords – Minor Seven

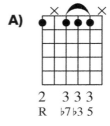

A)

```
2   3 3 3
R   b7 b3 5
```

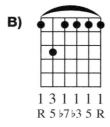

B)

```
1 3 1 1 1 1
R 5 b7 b3 5 R
```

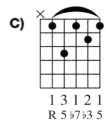

C)

```
1 3 1 2 1
R 5 b7 b3 5
```

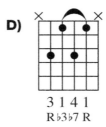

D)

```
3 1 4 1
R b3 b7 R
```

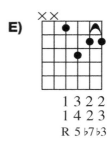

E)

```
1 3 2 2
1 4 2 3
R 5 b7 b3
```

With the root anywhere other than in the bass, m7 chords tend to sound like major 6 chords. Sixth chords are discussed in Chapter 6.

Practical Fingerings of Movable Seventh Chords – Plain or Dominant Seven

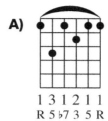

A)

1 3 1 2 1 1
R 5 ♭7 3 5 R

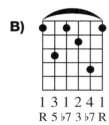

B)

1 3 1 2 4 1
R 5 ♭7 3 ♭7 R

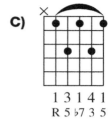

C)

1 3 1 4 1
R 5 ♭7 3 5

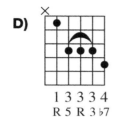

D)

1 3 3 3 4
R 5 R 3 ♭7

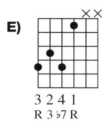

E)

3 2 4 1
R 3 ♭7 R

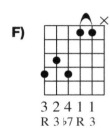

F)

3 2 4 1 1
R 3 ♭7 R 3

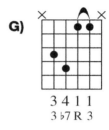

G)

3 4 1 1
3 ♭7 R 3

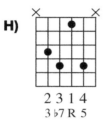

H)

2 3 1 4
3 ♭7 R 5

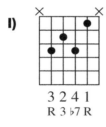

I)

3 2 4 1
R 3 ♭7 R

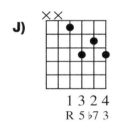

J)

1 3 2 4
R 5 ♭7 3

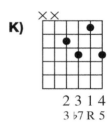

K)

2 3 1 4
3 ♭7 R 5

E and F) A little stretchy, but good above third position.

G, H, and K) The "lopsided" quality of placing the 3rd in the bass works well with dominant seventh chords.

Practical Fingerings of Movable Seventh Chords –
Minor Seven Flat Five or Half-Diminished

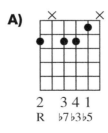

A)

2   3 4 1
R   ♭7♭3♭5

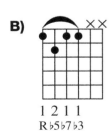

B)

1 2 1 1
R ♭5♭7 ♭3

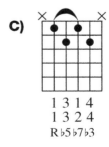

C)

1 3 1 4
1 3 2 4
R ♭5♭7♭3

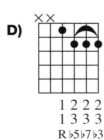

D)

1 2 2 2
1 3 3 3
R ♭5♭7♭3

With the root anywhere other than in the bass, m7♭5 chords tend to sound like m6 chords. This is discussed in Chapter 6.

Practical Fingerings of Movable Seventh Chords – Diminished Seven

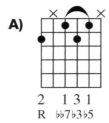

A)

2   1 3 1
R ♭♭7♭3♭5

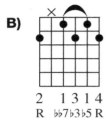

B)

2   1 3 1 4
R ♭♭7♭3♭5 R

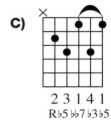

C)

2 3 1 4 1
R♭5 ♭♭7 ♭3♭5

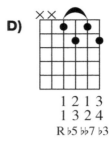

D)

1 2 1 3
1 3 2 4
R ♭5 ♭♭7 ♭3

A through D) Because of the symmetric structure of the diminished seventh chord, any note in the chord could be the root. Here's a very good mental exercise to get to know diminished seventh chords:

1. Play one of the fingerings first with the root as the lowest note. Name and give the analysis of all the other notes in the fingering. The simplest enharmonic names are encouraged.

2. Move the fingering up so that the ♭3rd is the lowest note. Name and give the analysis of all the other notes in the fingering.

3. Continue with the ♭5th and the ♭♭7th as the lowest notes. Open the windows to clear the room of brain smoke after you're done.

Practical Fingerings of Movable Seventh Chords – Minor Major Seven

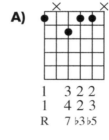

A)

1   3 2 2
1   4 2 3
R   7 ♭3♭5

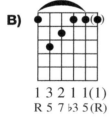

B)

1 3 2 1 1(1)
R 5 7 ♭3 5(R)

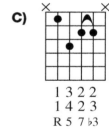

C)

1 3 2 2
1 4 2 3
R 5 7 ♭3

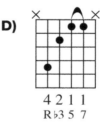

D)

4 2 1 1
R♭3 5 7

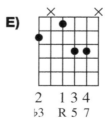

E)

2   1 3 4
♭3   R 5 7

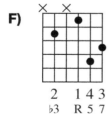

F)

2   1 4 3
♭3   R 5 7

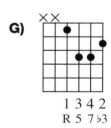

G)

1 3 4 2
R 5 7 ♭3

B) It's very difficult to mute the first string when barring the other strings like this.

E and F) Here are two voicings with the 3rd as the lowest note.

Practical Fingerings of Movable Seventh Chords – Seven Flat Five

A)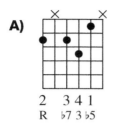

2   3 4 1
R   ♭7 3 ♭5

B)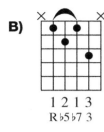

1 2 1 3
R ♭5 ♭7 3

C)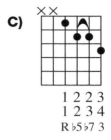

1 2 2 3
1 2 3 4
R ♭5 ♭7 3

D)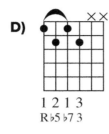

1 2 1 3
R ♭5 ♭7 3

E)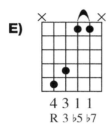

4 3 1 1
R 3 ♭5 ♭7

Because of the symmetrical structure of the seven flat five chord, the root of one named chord is the ♭5th of another; the 3rd of one is the ♭7th of that other chord; the ♭5th of one is the R of that other chord; and the ♭7th of one is the 3rd of that other chord. For example, C7♭5 = F♯7♭5. The same exercise that was presented for diminished seventh chords can be applied to seven flat five chords, like this:

1. Play one of the fingerings with the root as the lowest note. Name and give the analysis of all the other notes in the fingering. The simplest enharmonic names are encouraged.

2. Move the fingering up so that the ♭5th is the lowest note. Name and give the analysis of all the other notes in the fingering.

3. Another twist is to hold a single fingering while naming and analyzing the chord in two ways. For example, play an A♭7♭5 and name and analyze the chord first as A♭7♭5, then as D7♭5. After you're done, wipe the sides of your cheeks where the melted brain tissue has dribbled out of your ears.

Practical Fingerings of Movable Seventh Chords – Seven Sharp Five

A)
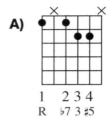

1   2 3 4
R   ♭7 3 ♯5

B)
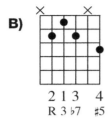

2 1 3   4
R 3 ♭7   ♯5

C)
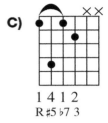

1 4 1 2
R ♯5 ♭7 3

D)
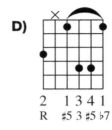

2   1 3 4 1
R   ♯5 3 ♯5 ♭7

E)
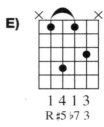

1 4 1 3
R ♯5 ♭7 3

F)
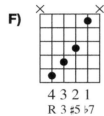

4 3 2 1
R 3 ♯5 ♭7

G)
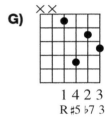

1 4 2 3
R ♯5 ♭7 3

H)
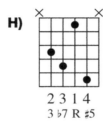

2 3 1 4
3 ♭7 R ♯5

I)
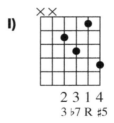

2 3 1 4
3 ♭7 R ♯5

J)
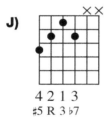

4 2 1 3
♯5 R 3 ♭7

K)
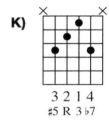

3 2 1 4
♯5 R 3 ♭7

L)
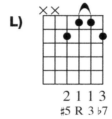

2 1 1 3
♯5 R 3 ♭7

Practical Fingerings of Movable Seventh Chords – Major Seven Sharp Five

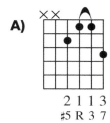

A)

2 1 1 3
♯5 R 3 7

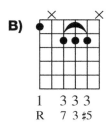

B)

1   3 3 3
R   7 3 ♯5

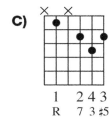

C)

1   2 4 3
R   7 3 ♯5

D)

3 2 2 1
4 2 3 1
R 3 ♯5 7

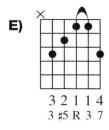

E)

3 2 1 1 4
3 ♯5 R 3 7

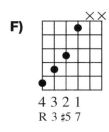

F)

4 3 2 1
R 3 ♯5 7

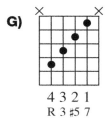

G)

4 3 2 1
R 3 ♯5 7

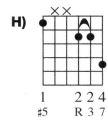

H)

1   2 2 4
♯5   R 3 7

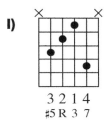

I)

3 2 1 4
♯5 R 3 7

Practical Fingerings of Movable Seventh Chords – Minor Seven Sharp Five

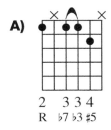

A)

2   3 3 4
R   ♭7 ♭3 ♯5

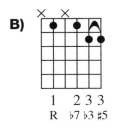

B)

1   2 3 3
R   ♭7 ♭3 ♯5

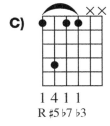

C)

1 4 1 1
R ♯5 ♭7 ♭3

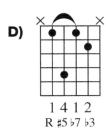

D)

1 4 1 2
R ♯5 ♭7 ♭3

The ♭3, ♯5, and ♭7 have a strong and stable nature to them. For example, in a Cm7♯5, the ♭3 is E♭, the ♯5 is G♯(or A♭), and the ♭7 is B♭. This can be rearranged as A♭–E♭–B♭, which is a series of perfect 5ths. These notes tend to "overwhelm" the root note in many potential voicings, causing the chord to sound like an A♭add2/C, an E♭sus4/C, or an A♭ quintal or B♭ quartal chord with a C added. These other chords will be discussed soon, and this is why so few voicings are shown here.

Practical Fingerings of Movable Seventh Chords – Seven Sus Two

A)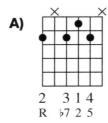

2 3 1 4
R b7 2 5

B)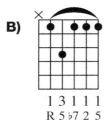

1 3 1 1 1
R 5 b7 2 5

C)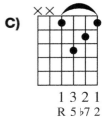

1 3 2 1
R 5 b7 2

Seven sus two chords may also be named as incomplete nine chords or as minor chords with a non-triadic "slash" note in the bottom. For example, C7sus2 may be named as an incomplete C9 (incomplete because it has no 3rd) or as a Gm/C.

Practical Fingerings of Movable Seventh Chords – Seven Sus Four

A)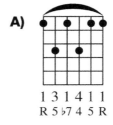

1 3 1 4 1 1
R 5 b7 4 5 R

B)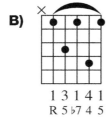

1 3 1 4 1
R 5 b7 4 5

C)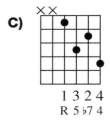

1 3 2 4
R 5 b7 4

D)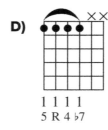

1 1 1 1
5 R 4 b7

E)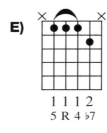

1 1 1 2
5 R 4 b7

F)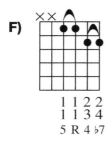

1 1 2 2
1 1 3 4
5 R 4 b7

D), E), and F) These three fingerings show this chord as a four-note quartal chord.

Seventh Chords as Slash Chords

Just as triads are often notated as slash chords to indicate an inversion, so seventh chords can be notated. The more notes in a chord, the more critical it is to indicate the voicing of that chord. As we've already seen, one way of looking at seventh chords is as if they are a different triad with an added root or bass note. For example, Cmaj7 can be seen as an Em triad with a C as the lowest note. Cmaj7 could be written as Em/C if the music called for it.

So when does the music call for it? When should we name a chord by its "seven" name, and when should we name it with a slash? Here are a couple of examples.

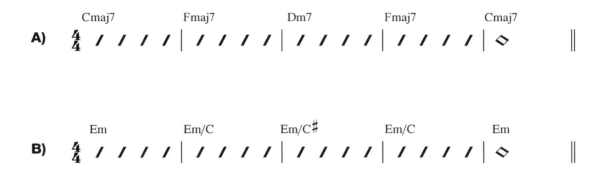

In Example A, the chord progression is clearly built around the key of C, and Cmaj7 feels very much like home. Calling it Em/C would only confuse things. On the other hand, the progression in Example B clearly sits with Em as the home. The Em triad is a kind of drone, under which the notes B, C, and C♯ move. This is made clear by the slash names. In this context, it would be equally confusing to name the Em/C as Cmaj7. (Clever intermediate guitarists will also know how Em/C♯ could be renamed as a seventh chord.)

Remember the list of seventeen possible seventh chords found earlier in this chapter? Recalling that list, we can examine each chord and consider a possible renaming of every seventh chord as a slash chord, where the upper triad is identified separately from the root.

Type of Seventh chord Practical Example	Voicing as Slash Chord Formula Practical Example
Major Seventh Cmaj7	Xm/♭6 Em/C
Minor Seven Cm7	X/6 E♭/C
Seven C7	Not used. Naming the chord as Xdim/♭6 is unknown. Keep it in mind for an April Fools prank.
Minor Seven Flat Five Cm7♭5	Xm/6 E♭m/C
Seven Sus Two C7sus2	Xm/4 Gm/C
Seven Sus Four C7sus4	No alternate slash name. The upper triad of 4–5–♭7 is not a named triad.
Major Seven Sus Two Cmaj7sus2	X/4 G/C As mentioned earlier, this is the more common name for this chord type.
Minor Seven Sharp Five Cm7♯5	Xsus4/6 E♭sus4/C

Minor Major Seven Cm(maj7)	Xaug/6 E♭aug/C
Seven Sharp Five C7#5	No alternate slash name. The upper triad of 3–#5–♭7 is not a simply-named triad.
Major Seven Sharp Five Cmaj7#5	X/♭6 E/C
Seven Flat Five C7♭5	No alternate slash name. The upper triad of 3–♭5–♭7 is not a simply-named triad.
Minor Major Seven Sharp Five Cm(maj7)#5	**Preferred name:** Xm/M3 A♭m/C If you were to use this chord at all, it would probably be renamed in this way.
Diminished Major Seven Cdim(maj7)	**Preferred name:** X/♭2 B/C If you were to use this chord at all, it would be renamed in this way.
The following seventh chords are not shown in this chart: • The major seven flat five chord will be identified as a major seven sharp eleven chord hereafter. • The major seven sus four chord is not shown, as it is so rarely used. • No diminished seventh chord is shown, as the diminished triad (which is the upper triad of the diminished seventh chord) is so rarely used.	

When the chord is voiced with the seventh as the lowest note, it often changes the name of the chord. In most instances, the chord reverts to its triadic name with the seventh shown as a slash note. Here's another chart to clarify this naming concept.

Type of Seventh chord Practical Example	Voicing as Slash Chord Formula Practical Example
Major Seventh Cmaj7	X/7 C/B
Minor Seven Cm7	Xm/♭7 Cm/B♭
Dominant Seven C7	X/♭7 C/B♭
Minor Seven Flat Five Cm7♭5	Xm7♭5/♭7 Cm7♭5/B♭ Although the basic tertiary triad is a diminished triad, the use of the diminished triad is so rare that naming the chord as Xdim/♭7 is unused.
Seven Sus Two C7sus2	Xsus2/♭7 Csus2/B♭
Seven Sus Four C7sus4	Xsus4/♭7 Csus4/B♭

Major Seven Sus Two Cmaj7sus2	Xsus2/7 Csus2/B Notwithstanding earlier comments about the major seven sus two chord as a kind of rogue name, we'll see that this voicing is essential for certain Disney-empire confessional teen ballads. Listen to the beginning of Audio Track 52 for an example of this.
Minor Seven Sharp Five Cm7♯5	Xm♯5/♭7 Cm♯5/B♭ **Preferred name:** A♭/B♭ Because the minor sharp five triad can be renamed as a first inversion major triad (Cm♯5 = A♭/C), the minor sharp five with the seven as the lowest note would be renamed as well.
Minor Major Seven Cm(maj7)	Xm/7 Cm/B
Seven Sharp Five C7♯5	Xaug/♭7 Caug/B♭
Major Seven Sharp Five Cmaj7♯5	Xaug/7 Caug/B
Seven Flat Five C7♭5	X7♭5/♭7 There's no common name for the "major flat five" triad, so the full seventh-chord name is given along with the 7th as the lowest note.

The following seventh chords are not shown in this chart:

- The major seven flat five chord will be identified as a major seven sharp eleven chord hereafter.

- The major seven sus four chord is not shown, as it is so rarely used.

- No diminished seventh chord is shown, as the symmetrical structure of the chord allows any note in the chord to be the root or lowest note.

- The minor major seven sharp five and the diminished major seventh chords are not shown because of their ambiguous structure and probable renaming.

As Long as We're on the Topic of Slash Chords...

It would be useful to bring up the concept that any chord can be decorated from below with a slash note. Generally, slash chords will function in three ways:

1. As an indication of a specific voicing of a chord.

2. As an indication of a bass line moving beneath one or more chords.

3. As an indication of a single low note (sometimes called a "pedal tone") beneath more than one chord.

We've had a few examples of slash chords functioning as indicators of specific chord voicings. Let's look at some examples of the other two functions mentioned above. First, check out the bass line that moves beneath this progression:

AUDIO TRACK 44

Slash Chords as a Moving Bass Line

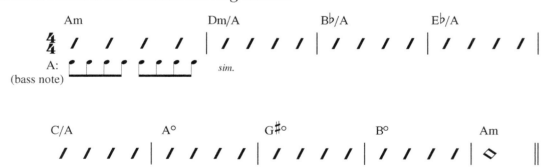

In the figure above, focus first on the underlying chord progression: A, Dm, A, F#m, E, A. A good beginning guitarist would want to play these chords first and perhaps deliberately avoid the lower strings so as not to interfere with the moving bass line. Intermediate players would begin to handle the bass line as part of the progression, and advanced players would be able to revoice the chords several ways, in perhaps two different octaves.

Now see how slash chords can indicate a stable bass line that holds an edgy progression together:

AUDIO TRACK 45

Slash Chords: A Stable Bass Beneath Moving Chords

In both of the above examples, it would be possible to rename many of the slash chords as seventh chords, but it would obscure the intention of the music. Try it.

As I wrote a moment earlier, *any* chord can be decorated from below with a slash note, and that means that any chord can coexist with any slash note. A good exercise is to choose a triad and check out all eleven possible chromatic notes that could be slash notes. (Remember that the root, one of the twelve chromatic notes, is assumed to be the lowest note in the chord, so it doesn't count as a slash note.) Here's an example, with commentary, using C major as the triad:

C/Db: This has come up before, and we'll meet it again in Chapter Seven, as an incomplete 7♯9 chord.

C/D: Another chord that we'll see in Chapter Seven. This is very common and useful.

C/Eb: A bit bi-tonal. It's a shy one, but it could show up some day.

C/E: The first inversion of C major. Obviously this is very common and useful.

C/F: Renamed Fmaj9, it is common and useful with either name. Look for it in Chapter Seven.

C/F♯: Watch out for the minor ninth from F♯ to G—not bi-tonal, but shy.

C/G: The second inversion of C major. Obviously this is very common and useful.

C/Ab: It could be Abmaj7♯5, which we've discussed earlier in this chapter. With either name, it is somewhat common. Be prepared for it.

C/A: Renamed Am7, it is extremely common and useful with either name.

C/Bb: An inversion of C7, but it could be renamed Bbmaj13♯11; it is common and useful with either name.

C/B: An inversion of Cmaj7. This is very common and useful.

Working through this list of slash chords, a beginner would begin to become an intermediate guitarist. An intermediate guitarist will have played many of these and would consider all the other triads with all eleven slash notes. An advanced guitarist will use these chords regularly and hear potential uses for some of the odder ones.

Inversions, Voicings, Harmonized Scales and Etudes for Seventh chords

I mentioned earlier that there are twenty-four possible voicings of any four-note chord and demonstrated it with a Cmaj7 chord. I also noted that many of these voicings are unplayable on a single guitar. So the study of inversions and voicings of four-note chords becomes a somewhat limited project. However, if we refer back to our tool kit of chord study, we can create a few instructive etudes using seventh chords. Once again, here's the tool kit.

Technique Tip: The Chord Study Toolkit

Any time we run into a new chord, whether a new voicing of an old favorite or some rare and exotic new species, it behooves us to put it through its paces with a chord-study tool kit.

- Play the chord type in all its diatonic variations through at least the major and harmonic minor scales with root motion in ascending and descending scale steps. (This is one of the three paths of the diatonic circle, traveled in two directions.)

- Play the chord type in all its inversions laterally across the neck.

- Play the chord type in all its inversions linearly up and down the neck on specific string sets.

- Play the chord type in all its diatonic variations through at least the major and harmonic minor scales with root motion in ascending and descending 3rds and ascending and descending fourths. (These are the other two paths of the diatonic circle, traveled in both directions.)

- Consider what makes up the chord and create a chart to see if any other chords of that type exist beyond the major and harmonic minor tonalities.

Here are three simple etudes for seventh chords diatonic to the major tonality with root motion mostly in ascending and descending scale steps. There's almost no voice leading used, and most of the chords are in root position.

This first etude uses chord shapes with roots on the low E and A strings and plays through two different keys.

AUDIO TRACK 46

Diatonic Seventh Chords in the Keys of G Major and B♭ Major

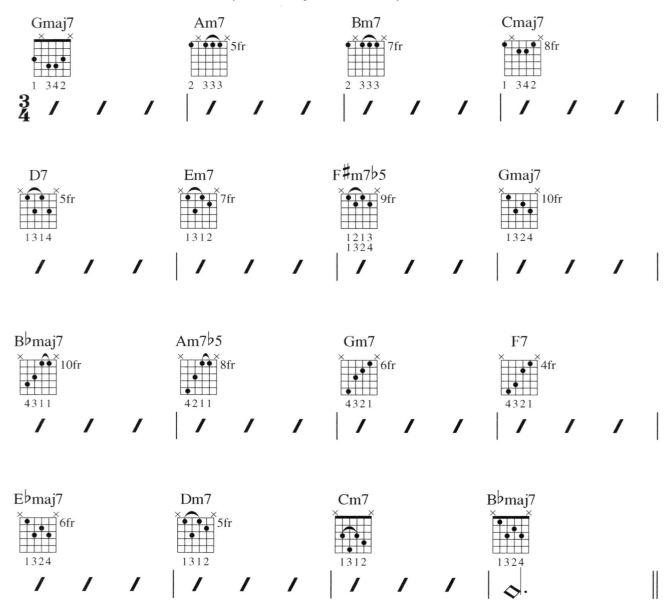

This etude begins with roots on the A string, then shifts to second inversion voicings (the 5th as the lowest note) with a good old-fashioned V7–Imaj7 ending.

Diatonic Seventh Chords in C Major

This third etude uses root notes on the D string but follows a different scalar approach to playing all the chords in a given key.

 AUDIO TRACK 48

Diatonic Seventh Chords in A♭ Major

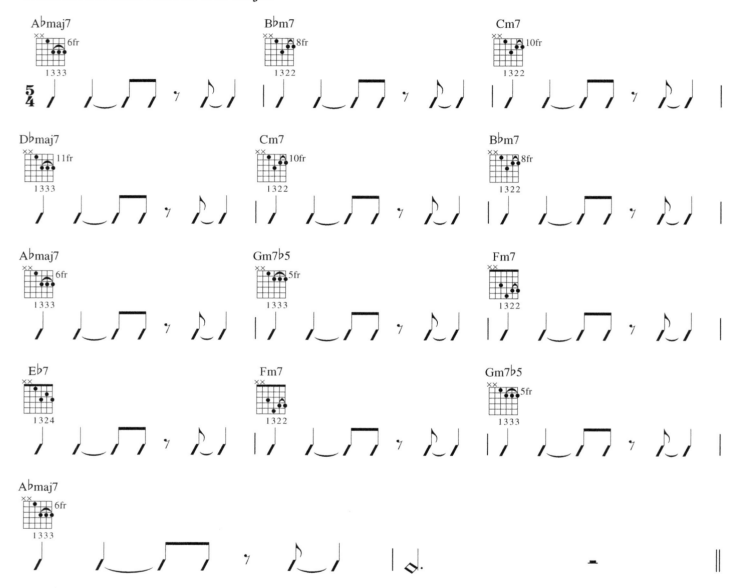

Some interesting things happen if you consider using proper voice leading with seventh chords. You should recall this chart (the diatonic circle) from the previous chapter:

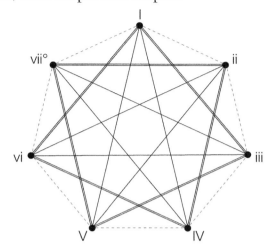

Remember that this chart shows all the possible single-interval sequences in a seven-note scale. The dotted line shows root motion in ascending or descending stepwise motion; the single solid line shows root motion in ascending or descending fourths; and the double solid line shows root motion in ascending or descending thirds. Refer back to p. 87 to review this concept. Since a seventh chord has four different notes in it, and a seven-note scale has only seven different notes, any two chords within that scale will have at least one note in common. Specifically, root motion by seconds (the dotted-line path on the chart above) will have one note in common.

For example, consider root motion by ascending seconds in the key of C major. Begin with a Cmaj7 written in four-note snowman form (root position, close voicing) and next to it, a Dm7 in the same form:

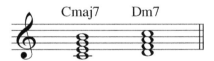

It's easy to see that both chords share the note C, and for the purposes of traditional voice leading, we can rewrite the Dm7 with C as the lowest note (Dm/C), tying the two C notes together to indicate their commonality:

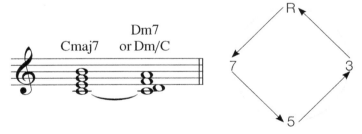

I would invite you to take the time to write out the remainder of the sequence of ascending seconds using proper voice leading. The circle diagram of voice leading should help you, too. Putting the circle diagram into a series of written instructions, it would read as follows.

In a sequence of root motion by ascending seconds:

- The root (R) of the first chord will move to the 7th (7) of the second chord. (In this case, the note remains the same, but the function of the note changes from root to 7th).

- The 7th of the first chord will move to the 5th (5) of the second chord.

- The 5th of the first chord will move to the 3rd (3) of the second chord.

- The 3rd of the first chord will move to the R of the second chord.

The voice leading diagram sums this up much more clearly, I think. Once you work this out in snowman form, you will see that this sequence creates a stepwise descending pattern of notes, with one note common to every succeeding chord. Read the music backwards, from right to left, and reverse the direction of the arrows in the voice leading diagram, to see what happens with root motion by descending diatonic 2nds: the chord tones ascend.

Now consider root motion by ascending diatonic 4ths: specifically Cmaj7 to Fmaj7.

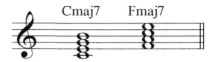

You can see that both chords share the notes C and E, and when we drop them down an octave, the two remaining notes also create a downward motion.

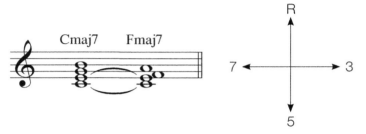

The two-headed arrows in the voice-leading diagram show that the root moves to the fifth and the fifth moves to the root, while the seventh moves to the third and the third moves to the seventh. As a series of written instructions, the two-headed arrows in the voice-leading diagram would read as follows:
- The root of Cmaj7 (the note C) becomes the fifth of Fmaj7 by remaining as a C.
- The fifth of Cmaj7 (the note G) moves to F, the root of F maj7.
- The seventh of Cmaj7 (the note B) moves to A, becoming the third of Fmaj7
- The third of Cmaj7 (the note E) becomes the seventh of Fmaj7 by remaining as an E.

It's amusing to notice that the same pattern applies when reading the voice-leading circle "backwards" to generate motion by descending fourths. Consider Cmaj7 to G7:

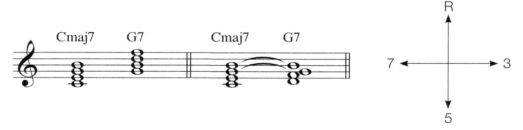

Again, the root moves to the fifth and the fifth moves to the root, while the seventh moves to the third and the third moves to the seventh. But as a series of specific written instructions, the two-headed arrows in the voice-leading diagram would read as follows:
- The root of Cmaj7 (the note C) becomes the fifth of G7 by moving to the note D.
- The fifth of Cmaj7 (the note G) becomes the root of G7 by remaining as a G.
- The seventh of Cmaj7 (the note B) becomes the third of G7 by remaining as a B.
- The third of Cmaj7 (the note E) becomes the seventh of G7 by moving to the note F.

Finally, let's look at root motion by ascending 3rds using Cmaj7 to Em7.

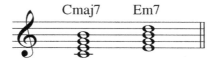

Even with the two chords written in root position and close voicing, the shared notes align with no octave displacement. It's a small matter to drop the note D down an octave, creating a voice-leading pattern like this:

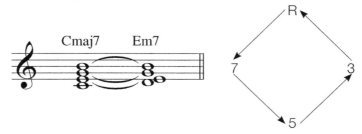

It's almost motionless; when seventh chords move with root motion in ascending diatonic 3rds, three notes remain the same, and one rises by a diatonic second. Follow it backwards (and reverse the direction of the arrows in the voice leading diagram) to work out root motion by descending diatonic 3rds.

To summarize, when using voice leading with diatonic seventh chord sequences:

- Root motion by ascending or descending 2nds will generate chord voicings with one note shared between adjacent chords.

- Root motion by ascending or descending 4ths will generate chord voicings with two notes shared between adjacent chords.

- Root motion by ascending or descending 3rds will generate chord voicings with three notes shared between adjacent chords.

Here's an amended chart of all possible chord motion reflecting these commonalities:

- One line shows one note in common (sequences of 2nds).

- Two lines show two notes in common (sequences of 4ths).

- And three lines shows three notes in common (sequences of 3rds)

We'll also show the chords with their appropriate 7ths added in parentheses.

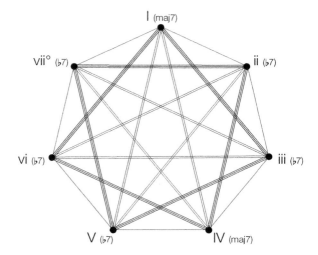

As I demonstrated earlier, these lovely snowmen with four body segments are great on paper, but have almost no practical application on the guitar. The fingerings are too difficult. However, if we begin with one of the more practical voicings of a seventh chord, we can find some really pleasant and unusual sequences of voicings and fingerings. Here's an example of root motion by ascending and descending 2nds.

 AUDIO TRACK 49

Diatonic Seventh Chords in B♭ Major and G Major with Voice-Leading

Notice that this progression is exactly the same as the three presented just a few pages earlier (Audio Tracks 46, 47, and 48). The difference in the sound when voice leading is added changes the quality of the progression quite a bit, though, doesn't it?

At this point, I could introduce etudes for properly voice-led seventh chords in major tonalities with root motion in ascending and descending 4ths, where each chord would share two voices, and with root motion in ascending and descending 3rds, where each chord would share three voices. In fact, I would recommend any intermediate or advanced guitarist to work these out for themselves. But I am going to skip over such etudes, primarily because they introduce quite a few difficult chord fingerings. The focus of this book is on useable chord theory. I've given you the theory and one practical example using voice leading; I leave the ball in your court to compose more.

Let's move on to the harmonic minor tonality. So far, I've used the harmonic minor as a way of introducing some of the chords not found in the major tonality. However, when we harmonize the harmonic minor scale with seventh chords, that raised seventh note of the scale can really stretch the seams of harmonic stability. You'll recall from Chapter Four that it creates an augmented triad in steps 3, 5, and 7 of the scale. When we build diatonic seventh chords from the harmonic minor scale, this triad appears as the ♭3–5–7 of the root or "one" chord of the scale, and as the R–3–♯5 of the chord built on the third step of the scale. When we harmonize a scale, we expect to hear these steps as strong and stable chords. When they're not, it sounds a little strange.

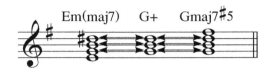

The figure above shows the G augmented triad lurking within these chords in the E harmonic minor scale. It's important to know that the harmonic minor scale was developed among composers at a time when the only seventh chord in common use was the dominant seventh, and the most common sequence of chords used at the end of a section of music was V7–I or V7–i. In the minor keys, composers altered the scale to create that V7 chord so that the V would have that extra juice of the tritone to bring the V–i sequence to a satisfying conclusion. They didn't alter the scale to create a complicated set of unsettled seventh chords! Still, the unsettled quality of the harmonic minor is well worth wrapping your ears and fingers around. The next etude is an edgy and aggressive take on the harmonic minor tonality that moves through three different harmonic minor tonal centers using sequences of root motion in ascending 2nds, descending 4ths, and descending 3rds.

Diatonic Seventh Chords in G Harmonic Minor, C♯ Harmonic Minor, and B♭ Harmonic Minor

AUDIO
TRACK **50** CONTINUED

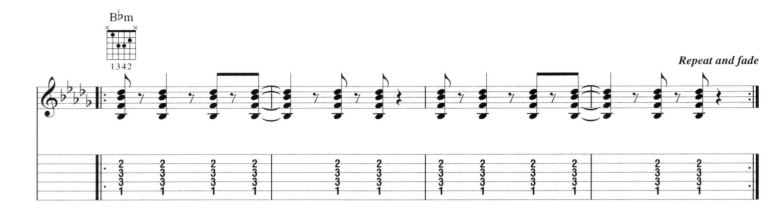

The Strength and Sizzle of the Dominant Seventh chord

Throughout this chapter, I've referred to the traditional function of the dominant seventh chord. This chord occurs within the major and the harmonic minor tonalities as the tertiary seventh chord built upon the fifth note of the scale, usually abbreviated V7. To be clear, here it is in the keys of C major and C harmonic minor:

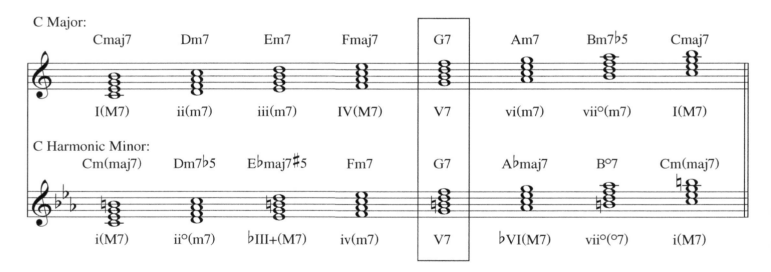

Remember that the natural minor scale was altered to become the harmonic minor scale specifically to accommodate that V7 chord. As you just saw, in the keys of C major and C harmonic minor, the dominant seventh chord would be G7. In the keys of E major and E harmonic minor, the dominant seventh would be B7. In the keys of A♭ major and A♭ harmonic minor, the dominant seventh chord would be E♭7, and so on.

What gives the dominant seventh chord so much power? A better question to ask would be, "*Who* gave the dominant seventh chord so much power?" because in fact, it was the music written by white male European composers between about 1650 and 1900 that gave the dominant seventh chord its dominant role in music. The motor driving music of this era was the perceived dissonance of the V7 chord moving to the consonance of the I or i chord. A basic and small sequence of chords like this is referred to as a ***cadence***; V7–I and V7–i are the two most basic cadences of traditional Western harmony. The crux of these cadences is the resolution of the dissonant tritone to a consonant 3rd or 6th. The following example demonstrates some simple ways to play and hear this sound on the guitar.

AUDIO TRACK 51

V-I Cadences in C Major and C Minor

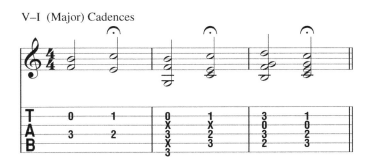

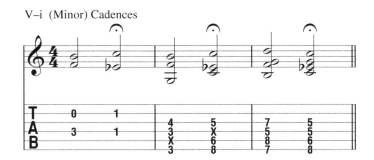

As Western music progressed through the late eighteenth and nineteenth centuries, the V7 chord was the first to become more and more elaborate and to appear in all sorts of surprising ways. Numerous alterations to the chord were introduced, and virtually any consonant chord in a given tonality might be preceded by its own V7. Traditional music theory texts are filled with the study of cadences, their classification, and the correct voice leading to be employed.

We guitar players tend to dodge the bullet of playing examples from traditional music theory for several practical reasons:

- The music was originally written on keyboard instruments. These cadences are easy to play on keyboards, but often extremely difficult on a single guitar.

- The ascendancy of guitar as a popular instrument in the early twentieth century was simultaneous with the ascendancy of music that either minimized the "proper" use of V7–I cadences (jazz) or didn't use such cadences at all (most music from the rest of the world, including blues).

- When, in the early-to-mid twentieth century, the guitar did play a V7–I cadence, it was functioning as a rhythm instrument where subtleties of voice leading were not emphasized.

Refer back to any of the chord sequences I've used so far, and you'll see that several of them had something like a V7–I cadence in them. Specifically:

Sequences based on root motion by ascending fourths have ended in V-I, V-i, V7-I(maj7) or V7-i(maj7)

Sequences based on root motion by ascending seconds have ended in vii°–i, vii°(m7)–I(maj7), vii°–I, or vii (°7)–i(maj7). Remember that the V7 chord has a vii° triad as its upper three notes, and all of these forms of the vii chord can be experienced as V7 or extended V7 chords without the root.

Whenever you played or listened to these sequences, I'll bet you got a sense of that traditionally satisfying harmonic resolution that classicists have been using for centuries. Whenever a chord is used to lead to another in a dissonant-consonant kind of sound like this, the first chord is identified as a ***functioning dominant*** chord. On the other hand, when you played or listened to the other sequences, you probably experienced a different sensation—a kind of floating-around-home sensation.

Consider also how often you listen to music that uses the plain or dominant seventh chord without any traditional resolution to a major or minor chord a 4th up. For example, blues progressions often string together seventh chords with no traditional resolution. (Blues has its own set of resolutions that are sometimes as ornate as any traditional classical composition.) A plain seventh chord in this context will sound as much like "home" as a simple triad would in another context.

Many forms of music rest on a chord or sound that can be described as a plain seventh chord with no motion to another chord at all. Dance music since the mid-1960s has used continuous seventh chords with perhaps no change in the chord at all. The seventh chord is the "home" chord. Other cultures, especially those with drone-based music, might also maintain a single chord-like sound that would be analyzed as a plain or dominant seventh chord, but with no need to move anywhere.

Let's conclude this chapter with examples of these three scenarios. First, we'll encounter a traditional use of the dominant seventh chord and its functioning siblings to create a chain of dissonant-consonant cadences. Watch how these chords allow the music to leap from key to key, as indicated by the analysis that appears below the music notation.

Dominant or Plain Seventh Chords as Portals to New Keys

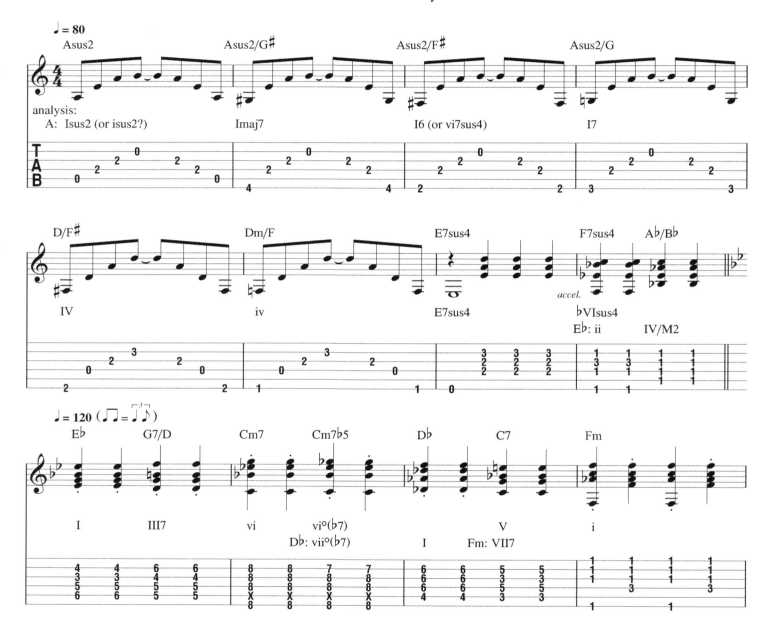

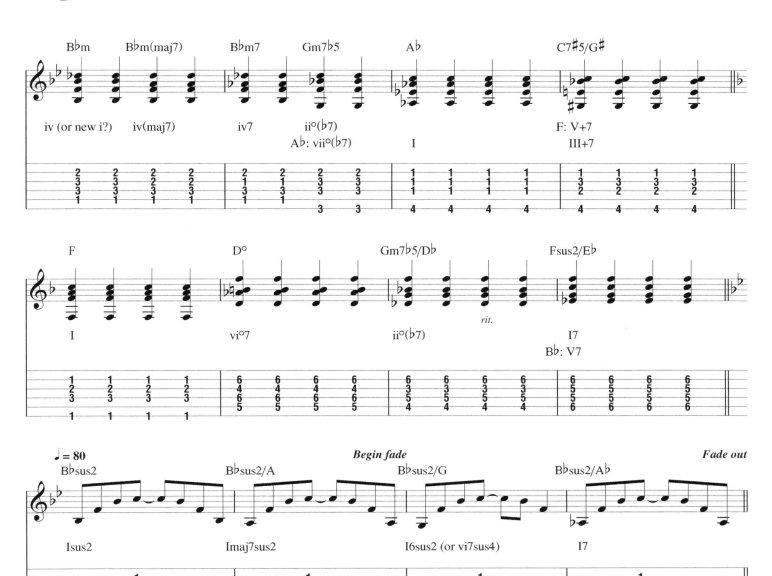

Next is an example of a traditional 12-bar blues progression consisting entirely of seventh and minor seven flat five chords. In this context, there's never a sense that the seventh chords need to "resolve" to major or minor triads.

AUDIO TRACK 53   **Dominant or Plain Seventh Chords in the Blues**

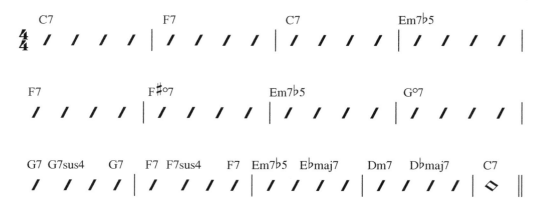

Finally, listen to the next audio track, a typical "one-chord groove" based on a C7 chord. There's no need for a chart or an analysis—it's all based on a C7.

AUDIO TRACK 54   **A One-Chord Groove on a Dominant or Plain Seventh Chord**

Modes: What They Are and How to Establish Them

In music, a *mode* is a collection of notes that, when ordered into a scale (usually of seven different notes), appears to be the same as a common major or altered minor scale. What sets the mode apart from its parent scale is that some note other than the root note of the parent scale is treated like the root note of the mode. Historically, modes of the major scale have been given Greek names, and when notes are altered, they are added to the name. A very simple way of visualizing a mode is to use circle diagrams where the root note is placed at the top (12:00) position of the circle. For example, here's a C major scale shown on a circle diagram:

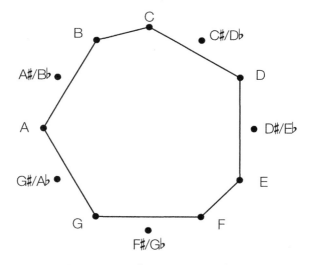

C major, or the Ionian mode

Now let's use the same note but rotate the circle so that the note D occupies the top spot.

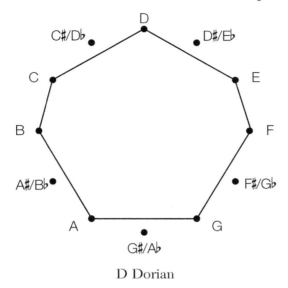

D Dorian

This is the D Dorian mode—the second mode of C major. It is the same set of notes but clearly a different shape when we view it this way. Another rotation of the circle shows E Phrygian:

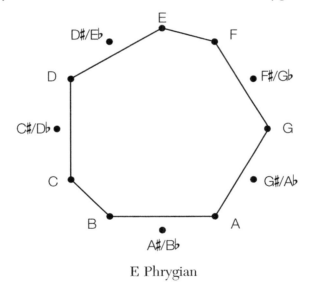

E Phrygian

The remaining modes of C major can be seen by continuing to rotate the circle, like this:

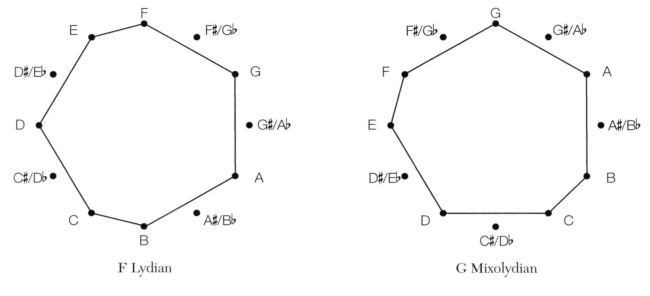

F Lydian   G Mixolydian

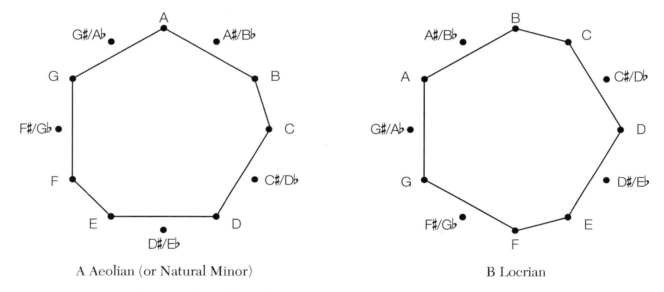

A Aeolian (or Natural Minor)   B Locrian

It's important to understand that, although each mode is made up of the same set of notes, each mode has a unique sound and subjective feel. In terms of use, the major (Ionian) and the natural minor (Aeolian) are the most common. The Dorian, Lydian, and Mixolydian modes are also very common. The Phrygian mode is less common in Western culture, but is often used in the music of Persia and Moorish Spain. The Locrian mode is the only mode with no perfect 5th above the root, and so it feels rather unstable and is rarely used.

Chords have a great influence on establishing a mode, and here are several steps that help to do this:

- Put the new mode into the air. If you've been playing in C major for five or ten minutes, playing a D minor chord won't feel much like a new mode—it'll feel like a chord that wants to change and go back to a C major chord, either directly or through a few other C major-friendly chords. In order to put it "into the air," allow a little silence to go by; ten to thirty seconds is a fair pause.

- Establish a rhythm that places the home chord of the new mode on a strong beat or gives more time to the new home chord than to other chords.

- Minimize or avoid the tritone notes of the parent scale. If you are establishing D Dorian as the new mode, the combination of B and F should be tiptoed around.

- Play the trump card: the dominant seventh chord of the new mode. In the case of D Dorian, this would be an A7. This *temporarily* introduces a note outside of the scale (in this case, C♯), but it pushes all the musical chips to the D minor side of the table.

Here are some brief musical examples demonstrating all of the modes of the major scale. To make things a little more interesting, I've moved to the key of E major. Every progression is built around a simple scale-like melody that helps to emphasize the given mode.

AUDIO TRACK 51   **Ionian Mode (or Major Scale)**

AUDIO TRACK 51 (cont.)   **Dorian Mode**

Phrygian Mode

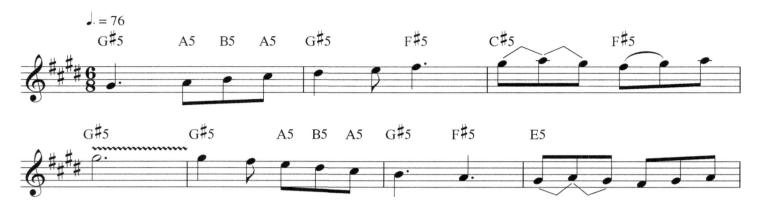

Lydian Mode

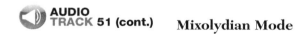

Mixolydian Mode

Aeolian Mode (or Natural Minor Scale)

Locrian Mode

CHAPTER SIX:

The "Color" Notes

Introducing 6, add9, and add4 Chords

So far, we've covered three broad categories of chords:

- **Dyads:** Two notes that work together as chords, covered in Chapter Three. The most common dyad is the open 5th or "power chord," spelled R–5, but we also included its inversion (5–R), its altered form (R–♭5 or R–♯4), and other dyads based on R–3 and R–6 combinations.

- **Triads:** Three notes that work together as chords, covered in Chapters One, Two and Four. Most of them were tertiary triads—three-note chords with the notes spaced apart in intervals of 3rds—and generically spelled R–3–5. We also included "sus" chords in our three-note chord explorations. The sus2 chord is generically spelled R–2–5, and the sus4 chord is generically spelled R–4–5.

- **Tertiary seventh chords:** Four notes that work together as chords, with the notes spaced apart in intervals of 3rds. These were covered in Chapter Five and can be generically spelled R–3–5–7.

Now it's time to consider another group of four-note chords: those with added "color" notes. Consider the other possible notes besides a 7th that can be added to a R–3–5 triad: 2, 4, and 6. When the 6th is added, it gets preferential treatment, like the dominant 7th, and is simply added to the chord name. When the 2 or the 4 are added to a chord, they are identified as "add2" and "add4."

Adding the 6th to Chords in the Major Tonality

Major Sixth Chords

Let's begin with a look at sixth chords by working with a C major triad within a normal C major scale. Here's the triad:

And here's a portion of the C major scale showing the three notes of the C major chord plus the sixth note above C (the note A) that we'll add to the chord, along with the resulting chord in its most compact snowman-like form.

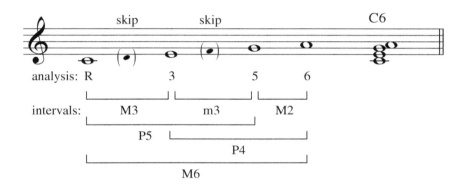

Just as with seventh chords, it's important to understand all the relationships that are shown between the notes of this chord. It should be clear that this chord consists of a root note (C), a major 3rd above the root (E), a perfect 5th above the root (G), and a major 6th above the root (A). Notice that the 6th nestles in next to the 5th in the interval of a major 2nd. With all of the work previously done with sus2, sus4, and seventh chords, you should recall that a major 2nd (and its inversion, the minor 7th) is a moderately stable interval when paired with other stable notes. In the C6 chord, there's a stable triad to begin with, and the added 6th (A) pairs up nicely with the 3rd (E) for a perfect 4th.

Like the seventh chords, a chord with an added 6th can be seen (and heard!) as a pair of dyads. Specifically, our C6 has a C5 dyad (the notes C and G) and, in the close voicing we're looking at now, an inverted A5 dyad (E and A). But unlike the seventh chords, there's no additional triad lurking within the upper three notes. E, G, and A don't form any kind of traditional triad no matter how they are scrambled and reassembled. So nope, there's no extra triad here. No way. Uh uh.

Sheep! Lemming! Of course there's another triad! I even pointed it out in the last chapter, and the A5 dyad should have been the giveaway clue. Take a look at the notes C, E, and A. Roll them around. Try all their permutations. At some point, I would pray that a light bulb would illuminate your labor and you'd see that C, E, and A could be reassembled as A–C–E, which is an A minor chord. Now what chord from Chapter Five contained a C major triad and an A minor triad? Yes, it's an Am7 chord! C6 has the exact same notes in it as Am7. This can also be seen quite easily when we put the circle diagrams of the two chords next to each other without rotating the circle for the Am7 chord so that C remains at the top:

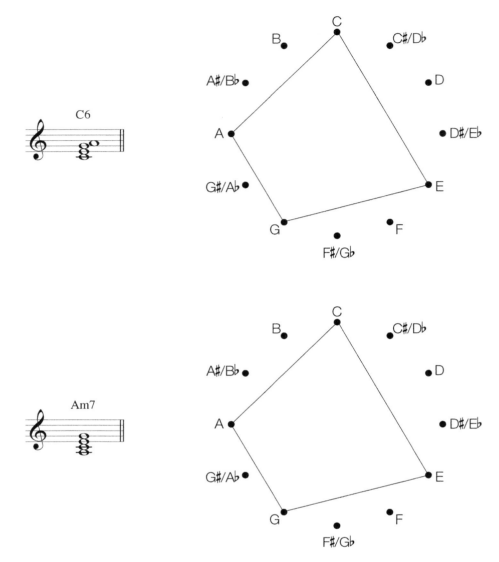

The difference between the two is in the voicing. Place the 6th in the bottom of a major chord and it sounds like a minor seventh chord—e.g. C6 with A as the lowest note sounds more like Am7. So another way to see and hear the 6th is as a downward extension of a tertiary triad. Remember that adding a 7th to a chord is like an upper extension of the chord—another 3rd placed atop a stack of 3rds. Think of the 6th, then, as another 3rd slipped in *below* a stack of 3rds, but usually voiced up an octave.

When it was made clear that C6 was also Am7, perhaps you got a sneaking suspicion that all sixth chords will prove to be inversions or re-voicings of seventh chords. It will be a good suspicion to follow. As we look at the remainder of sixth chords, I'll point out their secret double-identities as seventh chords.

Minor Sixth Chords

Let's continue by adding a 6th to Dm, the triad built on the second note of the C major scale.

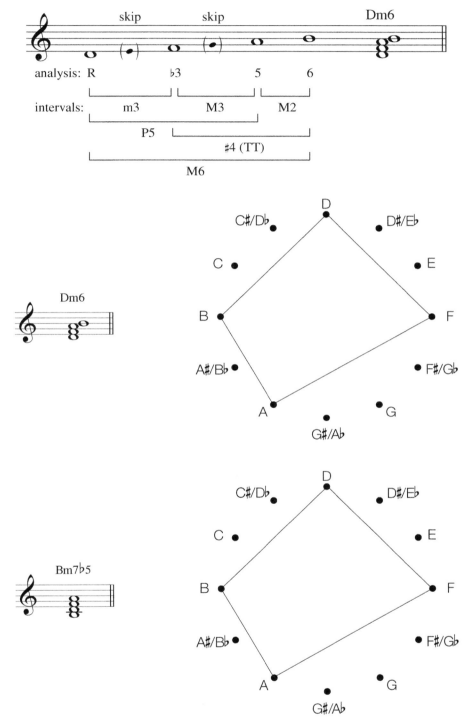

This chord consists of a root note (D), a minor 3rd above the root (F), a perfect 5th above the root (A), and a major 6th above the root (B); it's called Dm6 ("D minor sixth" or "D minor six"). Notice that the 6th (B) nestles in next to the 5th in the interval of a major 2nd. With an augmented 4th between the 6th and the minor 3rd, your analytical antennae should be alerting you that this chord might be a bit edgy, and in fact it does have a nice bite to it. As you can see above, a Dm6 is also a Bm7b5, and the qualities of Bm7b5 are here as well. However, they become a bit diluted because the name Dm6 implies D as the root note and therefore a voicing that probably places D as the lowest note in the voicing of the chord. This gives the chord some stability, and in fact a minor sixth chord can function well as an ending chord for music in a minor key or as a continuous chord for rhythmic music. I'm thinking specifically of "Brick House" by the Commodores, which grooves on an Am6 for the verses.

Minor Flat Sixth

Moving to the third note of the C major scale, we can build a sixth chord on the note E, like this:

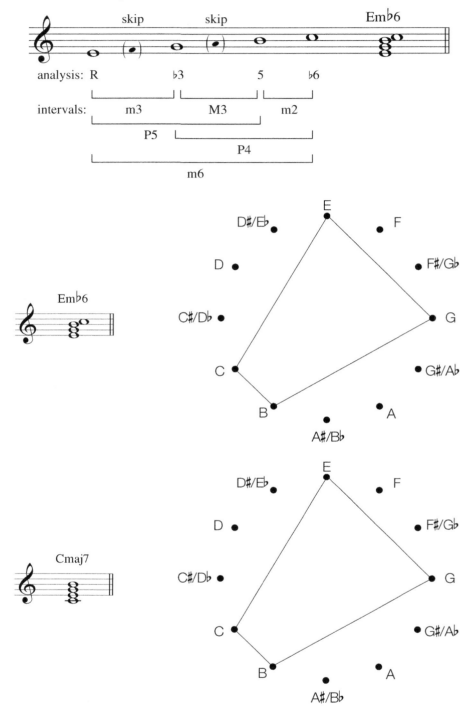

The Em♭6 chord consists of the root (E), a minor 3rd above the root (G), a perfect 5th above the root (B), and a minor 6th above the root (C). Notice that the interval of a minor 6th is indicated by "♭6" in the chord name. This chord's alter ego is Cmaj7, and as Em♭6, it seems to have a hard time asserting itself as a minor triad with an added note. The 3rd and the flat 6th seem to want to team up as a perfect 5th and become the 5th and root of the alternate major seventh chord. Voicing this chord is tricky; if you place the flat sixth more than an octave above the 5th, it becomes a minor 9, which is a very dissonant interval. If you place the 5th too high above the root, it doesn't bond as a strong R–5 dyad, and the 3rd and 6th become the stronger R–5 team. If Em♭6 is preceded by a B7 (a V–i cadence), it gains some credence as a stable minor chord. It also works well as a chord with a chromatic melody passing through it, as in Em–Em♭6–Em6–Em♭6, for example.

The sixth chord built on the fourth note of the major scale is an F6:

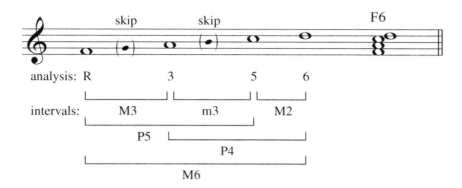

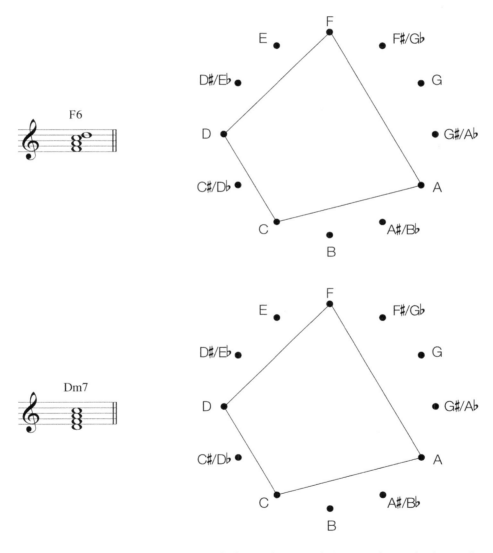

Like C6, F6 consists of a root note (F), a major 3rd above the root (A), a perfect 5th above the root (C), and a major 6th above the root (D). The 6th and 5th lie a major 2nd apart, and the added 6th feels moderately stable when paired with the stable F major triad. The 6th and the 3rd are a perfect 4th apart, which lends more stability. F6 is a closeted Dm7, as you can see in the circle diagram above, and when it functions as F6, it provides a relatively stable sound.

Here's G6, the sixth chord built on the 3rd note of the C major scale:

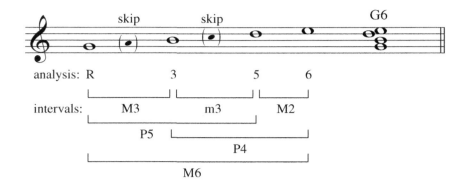

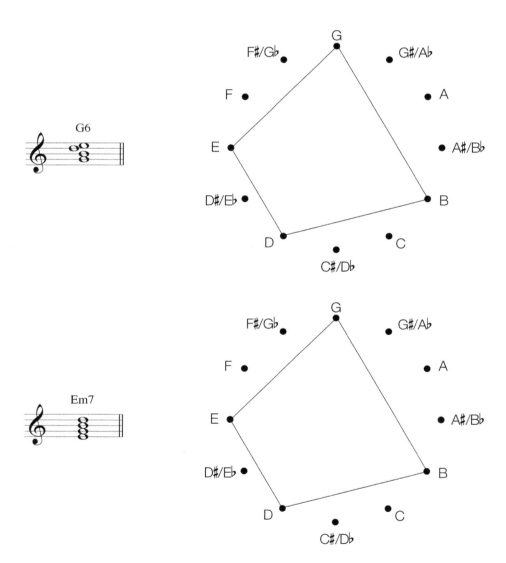

Like C6 and F6, G6 is another clean and clear major sixth chord. Its structure is the same as C6 and F6: a root (G) with a major 3rd above (B), a perfect 5th above (D), and a major 6th above (E). Again, just as with C6 and F6, it feels stable and sweet when its voicing and function allow it to sound as G6.

Moving to the sixth note of the C major scale, we can build an Am♭6 like this:

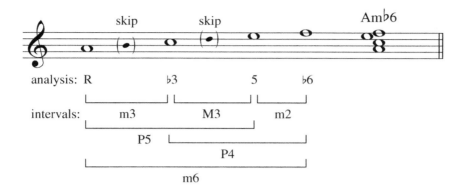

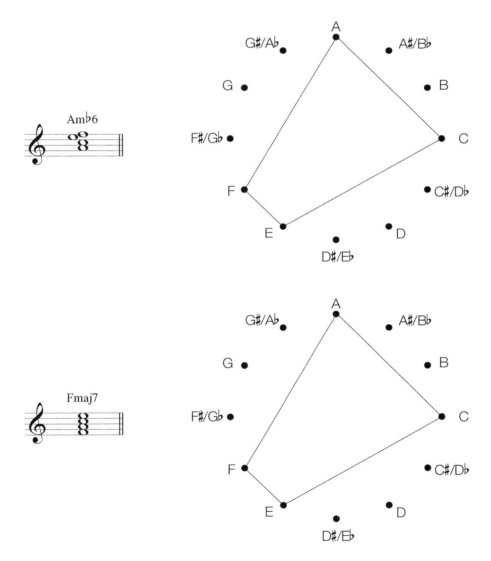

Am♭6 consists of the root (A), a minor 3rd above the root (C), a perfect 5th above the root (E), and a minor 6th above the root (F). Notice that the interval of a minor 6th is indicated by "♭6" in the chord name. This chord's alter ego is Fmaj7, and just like Em♭6, it seems to have a hard time asserting itself as a minor triad with an added note. It suffers the same problems, of course: a strong 3rd and 6th and a dissonance between the 5th and 6th that draws our attention away from the root as the "home" of the chord. Precede it by an E7, and it gains some stability.

A Fool's Chord

The seventh note of the major scale always packs a punch, and building a diatonic sixth chord on the note B within C major does not fail to disappoint. Here it is:

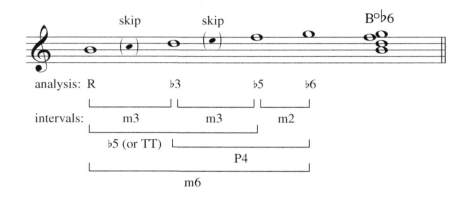

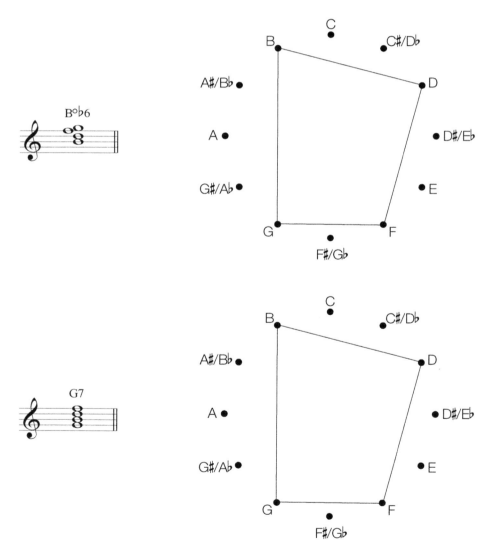

This chord is never used as named. B°♭6 is a chord for April Fools. Review its analysis and intervals, and then simply recognize that it is an inversion of G7. It has no R–P5 spine, and G7 is used so frequently as G7/B, there's no use in crowding the chord dictionary with B°♭6, except on April 1st.

Adding the 6th to Chords in the Harmonic Minor Tonality

By now, you should have a clear grasp of the process of building and analyzing chords in both the major and harmonic minor tonalities. Rather than repeat a complete analysis and commentary on every chord with an added 6th in the harmonic minor, I'll comment on them as necessary, using C harmonic minor as our example:

Cm♭6: An ambiguous home chord that can be easily replaced with its alter ego, A♭maj7. Preceded by G7, it gains some stability. See earlier comments about the minor flat six chord (specifically Em♭6) in C major.

D°6: Now here's a chord to slap on the back and invite into your house! Using enharmonic spellings, D°6 is the same as the symmetrical diminished seventh chord that was introduced in the previous chapter. Let's recall B°7 from the C harmonic minor scale and compare it, note for note, with D°6:

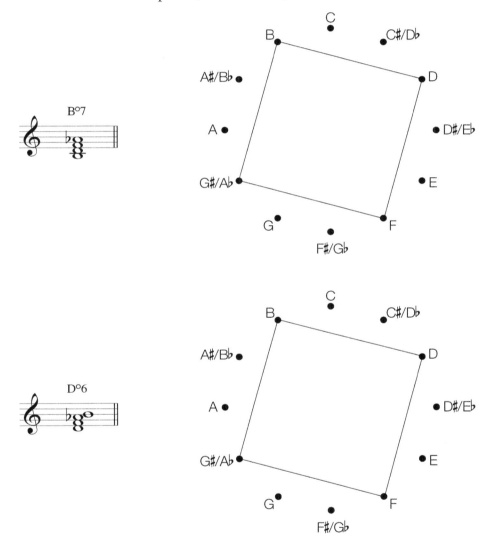

Clearly, the notes of the two chords are identical; D°6 is the first inversion of B°7. Because the chord is totally symmetrical, you can be sure that the other two notes in the chord (F and A♭/G♯) can function as root notes, and the chord can be named with all of those note names—either as a diminished seventh chord or as a diminished sixth chord. Here's a complete illustration of this musical curiosity.

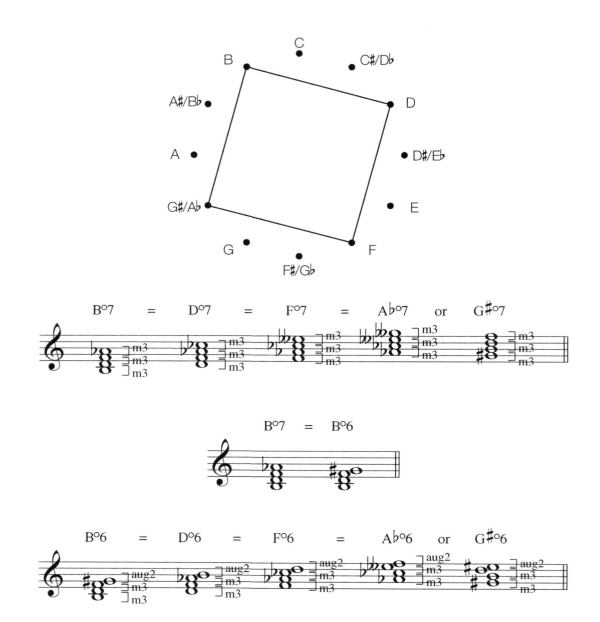

As you can see in the first line of music above, we can name the four notes as a stack of minor 3rds (a diminished triad plus a diminished 7th above the root). Using enharmonic note names, this gives us the chord names B°7, D°7, F°7, A♭°7, and G♯°7. In the second line of music, the diminished 7th interval (B–A♭) is renamed as a major 6th (B–G♯), demonstrating that B°7 can also be named B°6. In the third line of music, B°6 is analyzed as two minor 3rds (a diminished triad) plus a major 6th above the root. Using enharmonic names, this gives us the chord names B°6, D°6, F°6, A♭°6, and G♯°6. The overwhelming problem of the °7/°6 chord is that it has a symmetrical structure in a non-symmetrical musical language. No matter how their notes are named, most °7/°6 chords require peculiar spellings to fit into the traditional system of tertiary triads. The practical approach at this writing is to be totally fluid in your note-naming and interval identification. I accept that, historically, the °7 name will show up on most music, but I also believe that the °6 suffix is often more practical. My immediate hope is that it will be used more in the future; my greater hope is that a system of note naming will evolve to acknowledge both tonality and dodecaphonic symmetry.

E♭+6: Another ambiguous chord that can be replaced with its alter ego, Cm(maj7). Try voicing this with the 6th immediately above the augmented 5th. It sounds moderately dissonant with the 6th a ♭9th above the augmented 5th, and it sounds more like Cm(maj7) with the 6th below the augmented 5th.

Fm6: See comments on the minor sixth chord in the major tonality. Briefly, Fm6 is the same set of notes as Dm7♭5, but the perfect 5th of the root (F) and 3rd (C) gives the chord enough stability to function as an ending chord in a minor cadence or as a rhythmic groove chord.

G(♭6): A rarely used chord name. The dissonance of the P5 and ♭6 presents a problem. It will be more commonly named as E♭m(maj7).

A♭6: Pleasant and stable, A♭6 can be renamed as Fm7 based on the voicing.

B♭6: As we have seen in previous chord names, the b6 suffix presents problems under the best of circumstances. In this case, refer back to the preceding section on seventh chords. Is that a spider on your shoulder?

Sixth Chords in Open Position

As with all new and unusual chord types, a very good way to get to know chords with added 6ths is to play them in open position. Whether or not you ever venture past the lower positions, your understanding of the notes in a chord and how they function will help you use the chords you know more effectively and find the occasional new chord more quickly. Here are some common open-position sixth chords along with their simpler triadic parents to help you recognize the important notes in each chord.

E

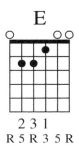

2 3 1
R 5 R 3 5 R

E6

2 3 1 4
R 5 R 3 6 R

A simple open E major chord provides a good example of how the major 6th can be found a major 2nd above the chord's perfect 5th. In this case, there are two 5ths—two B notes—in this voicing of the chord. We'll focus on the higher 5th, the open B string. By adding the fourth finger to the B string to play the note C♯, a major 6th is added to the chord, turning E into E6. Notice the bright, sunny quality the 6th adds to the major chord. In contrast, a lower 6th can be added on the A string, like this:

E6

4 2 1
R 6 R 3 5 R

This seems to have a huskier, thicker quality than the first voicing, don't you think? Take some time to play only the 5th and 6th within each of these voicings. Listen to the two notes simultaneously to get a feel for them. Alone, without their supporting notes, they can sound a little harsh, but in the context of the complete chord, they sit quite nicely. Another good exercise is to identify the minor chord that lurks within the major sixth chord. In the case of E6, it is a C#m, so search for the root, 3rd, and 5th of C#m in these E6 chords. The above voicing makes a nice C#m7 chord, by the way—especially when you omit the low E string.

A

 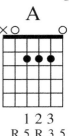

1 2 3
R 5 R 3 5

An open position A major chord is rich with possible 6ths. Remember, the 6th is a major 2nd, or two frets, above the chord's 5th. In an A major chord, the 5th is E, and we can begin with the open high E string as a likely place to add a 6th. The simplest fingering for this is to barre across the four highest strings in the second fret, adding an F# to the chord. As with the E chord above, the addition of the high 6th adds a bright, sunny quality to the chord, like this:

A6

1 1 1 1
R 5 R 3 6

A chiming, middle-voiced 6th can be made by raising the note E on the D string up two frets to an F#, like this:

A6

 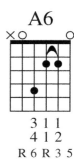

3 1 1
4 1 2
R 6 R 3 5

A low F# can also be added on the low E string, as shown below. Be careful when you use this, though, because:
- It basically sounds like F#m7.
- It can muddy things up if you're playing with another musician whose instrument is in this range (keyboards, another guitarist, a bassist, etc.).
- Depending on the sound of your guitar, it can muddy up your own sound because of the proximity of the low F# and A notes.

A6, A/F#
or F#m7

 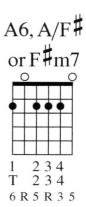

1   2 3 4
T   2 3 4
6 R 5 R 3 5

Let's add some 6ths to an open D major chord.

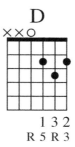

We might begin by raising the 5th (the note A) on the G string by two frets, like this:

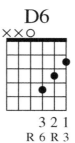

The problem with this voicing is that it covers the only available 5th, unless we play the open A string below the root. It could work under the right circumstances, but here's another approach: remove the high D from the chord and replace it with the open B string, like this:

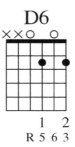

Finally, try adding a low 6th on the A string. Again, be careful when placing the 6th as the lowest note in the chord because it will sound like the root of the chord's alternate identity as a minor seventh chord—in this case, it sounds like Bm7. Here are two possible fingerings for this approach:

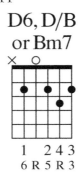

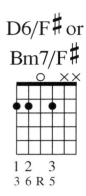

D6/F♯ or

Bm7/F♯

1 2   3
3 6 R 5

Now try these fingerings for G6 and C6. In each chord voicing, be sure to identify the function of each note.

G6

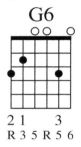

2 1   3
R 3 5 R 5 6

G6

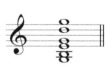

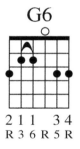

2 1 1   3 4
R 3 6 R 5 R

C6

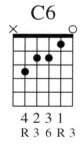

4 2 3 1
R 3 6 R 3

C6

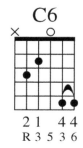

2 1   4 4
R 3 5 3 6

Moving on to minor chords with added 6ths, we can begin with Em6 as a good starting point. Remember that the minor sixth chord has the same kind of 6th (a major 6th above the root of the chord) as a major sixth chord, so we can add the note C♯ to the open Em chord in the same places where we added them in the E major chord, like this:

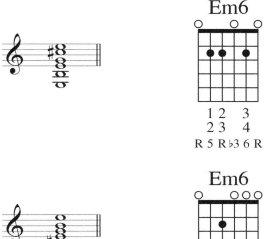

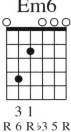

The second voicing above, with the lower sixth on the A string, is a good place to explore the sound of the dreaded m7♭5 chord; in this case, it's C♯m7♭5. Simply avoid playing the low E, and the thorniest of all the seventh chords in the major tonality will purr like a kitten in your lap.

Here are 6ths added to an Am chord. The first voicing highlights the piquant sound of the tritone (C and F♯), the second voicing smoothly buries the 6th in the middle, and the third teeters darkly downward towards F♯m7♭5.

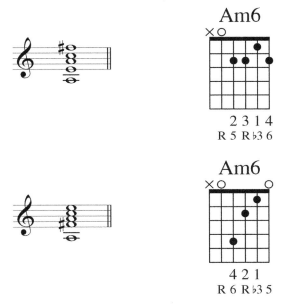

Am6, Am/F#
or F#m7b5

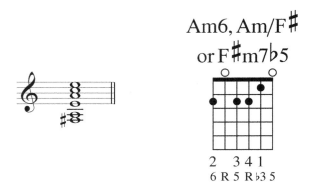

Let's add some 6ths to an open D minor chord, with observations similar to D6. We might begin by raising the 5th (the note A) on the G string by two frets, like this:

Dm6

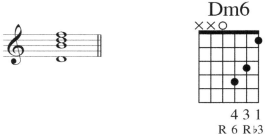

The problem with this voicing is that it covers the only available 5th, which makes the chord sound a little too unstable—like a B° in first inversion. You can add the open A string below the root, but that too is a bit unstable. Try removing the high D from the chord and replacing it with the open B string, like this:

Dm6

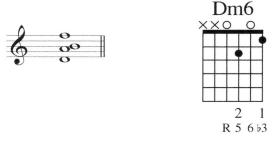

Finally, try adding a low 6th on the A string. As always, this will tend to sound like the root of the chord's alternate identity—a minor seven flat five chord (in this case, Bm7b5). Here's a fingering for this approach:

Dm6, Dm/B
or Bm7b5

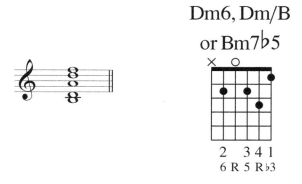

All Possible Closed-Voicing Sixth Chords in Root Position

In addition to the diatonic 6ths that can be added in the major and minor tonalities, it is possible to create "synthetic" sixth chords by calling up a chart, as we've done earlier with triads and seventh chords. Back in Chapter Four, I introduced a chart to generate and crosscheck all the possible tertiary triads, and in Chapter Five, these triads were mated with all the possible sevenths. Remember, we have six tertiary triads: the traditional major, minor, augmented, and diminished triads plus the oddball R–3–$\flat$5 and R–$\flat$3–$\sharp$5 (actually an inverted major triad). Then we have the two unusual three-note chords that are quintal/quartal, but named as if they were derived from tertiary triads: the sus2 and sus4 chords. We can pair these eight three-note chords with the two kinds of 6ths that our chord system uses: the major 6th, indicated with a 6, and the minor 6th, indicated with a $\flat$6. We will come across those inevitable curious chords that weren't discovered earlier in this chapter, and they will be indicated with clever comments.

Because many sixth chords are actually inversions of some other seventh chord, the synonymous seventh chord name will be given whenever possible.

Basic triad	Added sixth	Resulting chord	Music notation, circle chart synonymous seventh chord and commentary
Basic triad: Diminished	**Added sixth:** flat sixth	**Resulting chord type:** diminished flat sixth	
Triad analysis notation: R–$\flat$3–$\flat$5	**Analysis notation:** $\flat$6	**Resulting analysis notation:** R–$\flat$3–$\flat$5–$\flat$6	
Example: C°	**Example:** A$\flat$	**Example:** C$\flat$6	Better named as A$\flat$7/C, which would be the V chord in the major and harmonic minor scales.

Basic triad: Diminished	Added sixth: sixth	Resulting chord type: Diminished sixth	
Triad analysis notation: R–♭3–♭5	**Analysis notation:** 6	**Resulting analysis notation:** R–♭3–♭5–6	
Example: C°	**Example:** A	**Example:** C°6	

Equivalent to C°7. With enharmonic spellings, this chord can be found in the harmonic minor scale as the ii°6, iv°6, ♭vi°7, and vii°7.

Diminished seventh and diminished sixth are different names for the same chord, because the diminished 7th (♭♭7) is enharmonic to the major 6th (6). Understanding this is an excellent way to spell and understand the symmetrical diminished seventh chord.

Basic triad: Minor	Added sixth: flat sixth	Resulting chord type: minor flat six	
Triad analysis notation: R–♭3–5	Analysis notation: ♭6	Resulting analysis notation: R–♭3–5–♭6	
Example: Cm	Example: A♭	Example: Cm♭6	

Equivalent to A♭maj7/C. This chord is found in the major scale as iii♭6 and vi♭6 and in the harmonic minor scale as I♭6.

Basic triad: Minor	Added sixth: sixth	Resulting chord type: minor sixth
Triad analysis notation: R–♭3–5	Analysis notation: 6	Resulting analysis notation: R–♭3–5–6
Example: Cm	Example: A	Example: Cm6

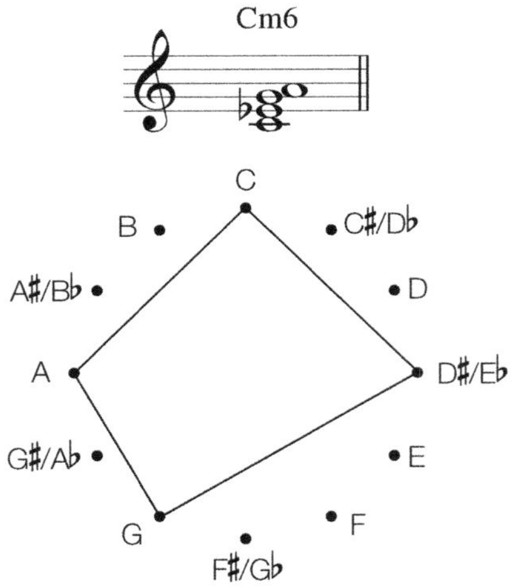

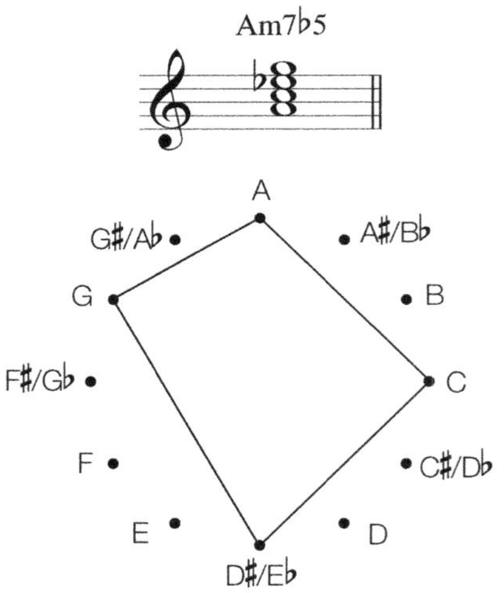

Cm6

Am7♭5

Equivalent to Am7♭5/C. This chord can be found in the major scale as ii6 and in the harmonic minor scale as iv6.

Added sixth: flat sixth (♭6)

You wouldn't want to add a ♭6 to a chord with a ♯5 in it, because a ♭6 and a ♯5 are the same note! Try writing a chord chart with Cm♯5(♭6) when April 1st comes around.

Basic triad: Minor sharp five	Added sixth: sixth	Resulting chord type: minor six sharp five	
Triad analysis notation: R–♭3–♯5	**Analysis notation:** 6	**Resulting analysis notation:** R–♭3–♯5–6	
Example: Cm♯5 This is one of the two oddballs of the traditional tertiary triad clan.	**Example:** A	**Example:** Cm6♯5	

Cm6♯5

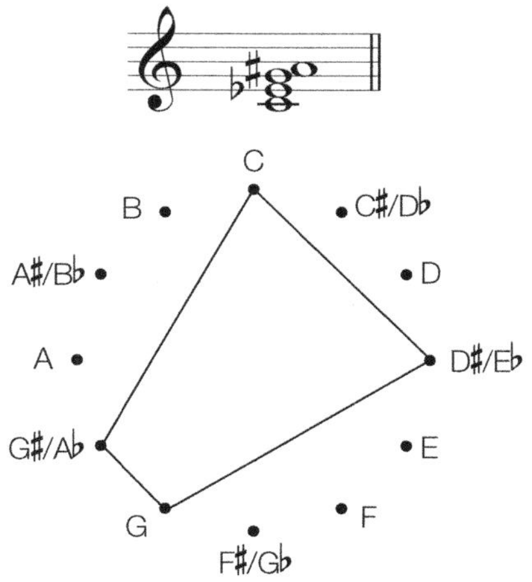

A♭/A

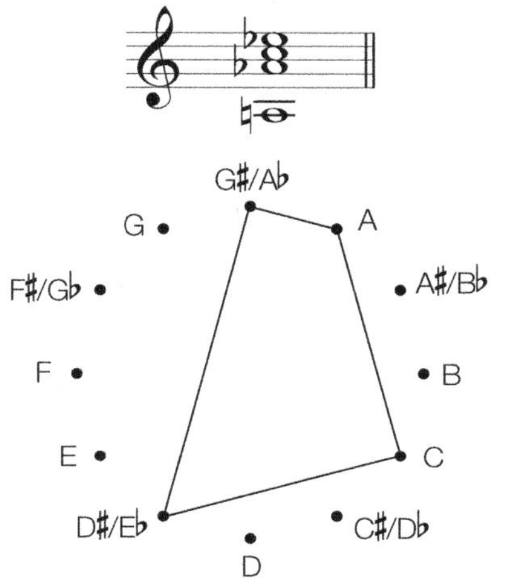

Renaming this as a seventh chord, A°maj7/C is possible but unlikely. It would be more likely revoiced and renamed as A♭/A or an incomplete F7♯9. This chord is found exclusively in the diminished scale.

Basic triad: Major flat five	Added sixth: flat sixth	Resulting chord type: flat sixth flat five	
Triad analysis notation: R–3–♭5	**Analysis notation:** ♭6	**Resulting analysis notation:** R–3–♭5–♭6	
Example: C(♭5) This is the other of the two oddballs of the traditional tertiary triad clan.	**Example:** A♭	**Example:** C(♭6)♭5	
			This chord would more commonly be named as a seven sharp five—specifically, C(♭6)♭5 would be renamed A♭7♯5/C, and is found in the harmonic minor scale as V7♯5.

Basic triad: Major flat five	Added sixth: sixth	Resulting chord type: six flat five
Triad analysis notation: R–3–♭5	Analysis notation: 6	Resulting analysis notation: R–3–♭5–6
Example: C(♭5) This is the other of the two oddballs of the traditional tertiary triad clan.	Example: A	Example: C6♭5

Much better named Am6/C or F#m7♭5/C. As an inversion of the minor sixth chord, it is found in the major scale as ii6 and in the harmonic minor scale as iv6. As an inversion of the minor seven flat five chord, it is found in the major scale as vii7♭5 and in the harmonic minor scale as ii7♭5.

Basic triad: Major	Added sixth: flat sixth	Resulting chord type: add flat six
Triad analysis notation: R–3–5	Analysis notation: ♭6	Resulting analysis notation: R–3–5–♭6
Example: C	Example: A♭	Example: C(♭6)

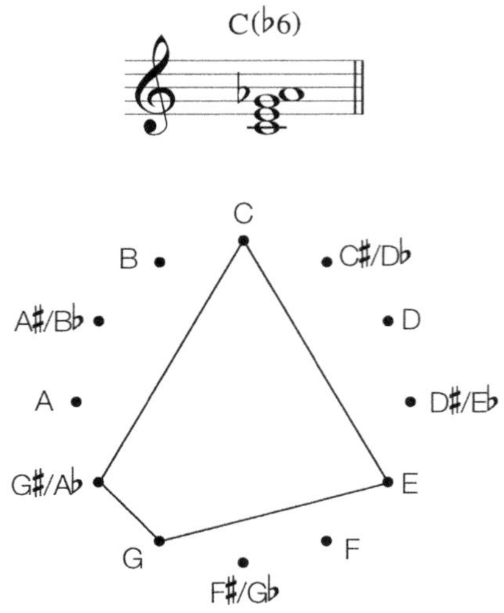

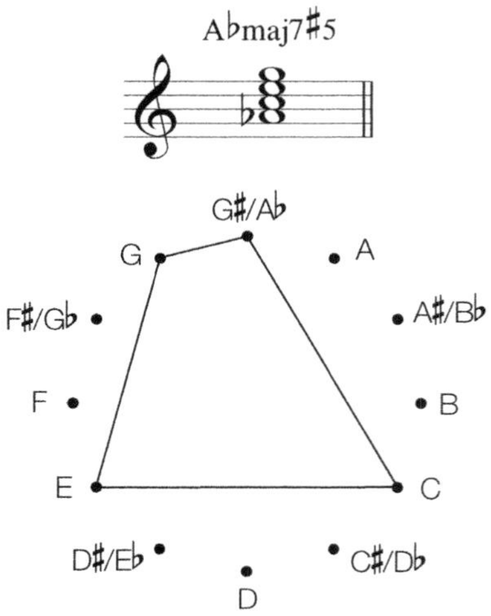

C(♭6)

Abmaj7#5

Equivalent to Abmaj7#5/C. It is found in the harmonic minor scale as III#5.

Basic triad: Major	Added sixth: sixth	Resulting chord type: sixth	C6
Triad analysis notation: R–3–5	Analysis notation: 6	Resulting analysis notation: R–3–5–6	
Example: C	Example: A	Example: C6	Am7
			Equivalent to Am7/C. It is found in the major scale as I6, IV6, and V6 and in the harmonic minor scale as ♭VI6.
	Added sixth: flat sixth (♭6) As I pointed out earlier in this chart, you wouldn't want to add a ♭6 to a chord with a ♯5 in it, because a ♭6 and a ♯5 are the same note. Save C+♭6 for the day when you put salt in the sugar bowl.		

230 COMPREHENSIVE CHORD THEORY FOR GUITAR

Basic triad: Augmented	Added sixth: sixth	Resulting chord type: Augmented sixth or sixth sharp five	
Triad analysis notation: R–3–♯5	Analysis notation: 6	Resulting analysis notation: R–3–♯5–6	
Example: C+	Example: A	Example: C+6 or C6♯5	

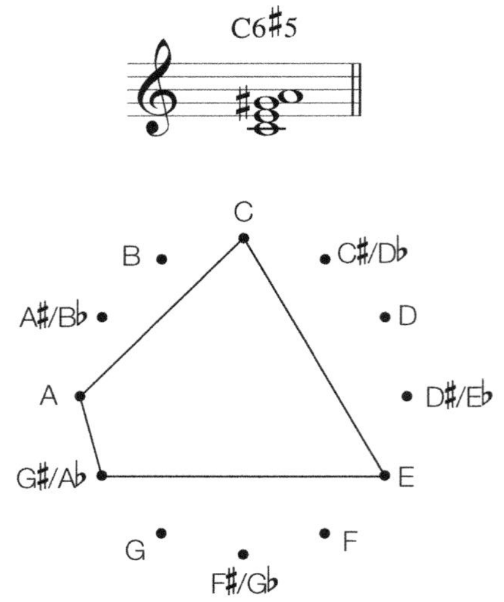

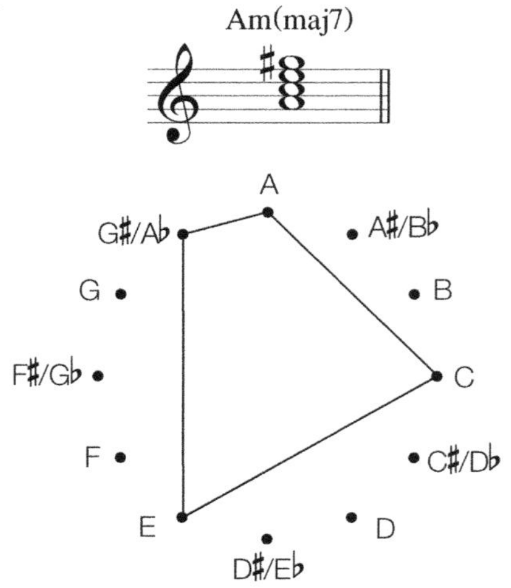

C6♯5

Am(maj7)

Better named Am(maj7)/C. Renamed, it is found in the harmonic minor scale as i(maj7)/♭3.

Basic triad: Suspended second or sus two	Added sixth: flat sixth	Resulting chord type: flat six sus two
Triad analysis notation: R–2–5	Analysis notation: ♭6	Resulting analysis notation: R–2–5–♭6
Example: Csus2	Example: A♭	Example: C(♭6)sus2

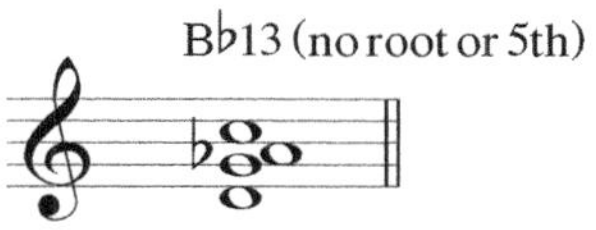

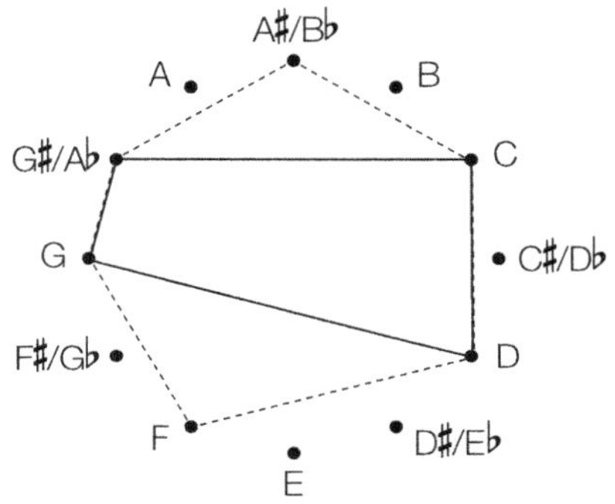

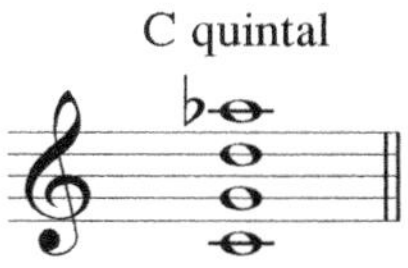

C(♭6)sus2

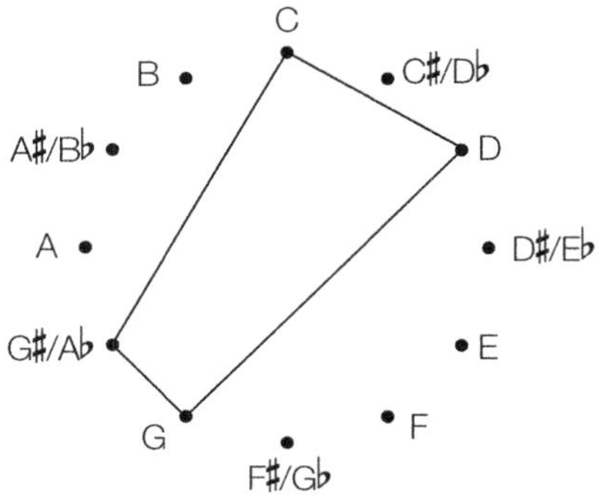

B♭13 (no root or 5th)

C quintal

Possibly renamed as D7♭5sus4 and voiced as D(♭5)sus4/C, but better named B♭13 (no root)/C.

This is an uncommon name for an incomplete 13 chord. Specifically, C(♭6)sus2 has all of the juicy notes of a B♭13—3, 7, 9, and 13—without the root, B♭ or the 5th, F. This is also a quintal/quartal chord (C–G–D–A♭), which has no name in our current system of chord naming. Named as a flat six sus two chord, it can be found in the major scale as iii♭6sus2 and vi♭6sus2 and in the harmonic minor scale as I♭6sus2 and V♭6sus2.

Basic triad: Suspended second or sus two	Added sixth: sixth	Resulting chord type: sixth sus two
Triad analysis notation: R–2–5	**Analysis notation:** 6	**Resulting analysis notation:** R–2–5–6
Example: Csus2	**Example:** A	**Example:** C6sus2

C6sus2

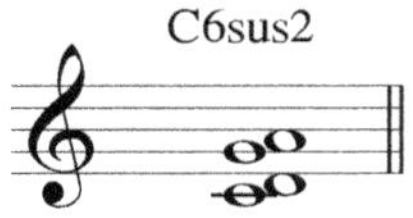

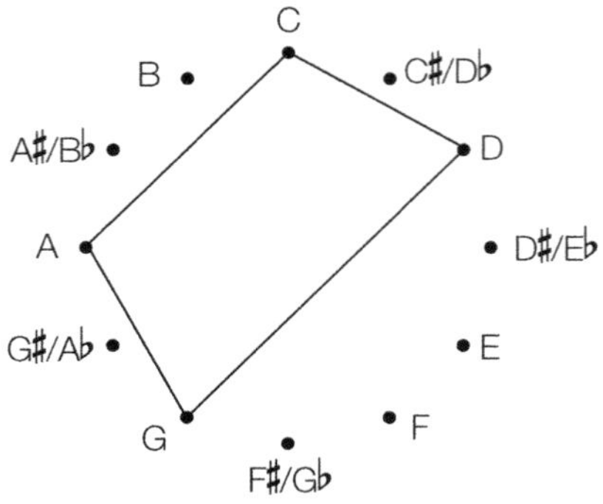

C quintal

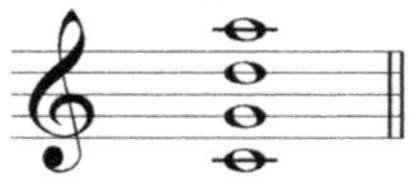

Possibly renamed as D7sus4 and voiced as Dsus4/C. It can be renamed as C6/9, although "sus2" tells the musician to leave the 3rd out. Note that it is also a quintal/quartal chord (C–G–D–A), which has no name in our current system of chord naming. As a sixth sus two chord, it can be found in the major scale as I6sus2, ii6sus2, IV6sus2, and V6sus2. It can be found in the harmonic minor scale as iv6sus2.

Basic triad: Suspended fourth or sus four	Added sixth: flat sixth	Resulting chord type: flat six sus four	
Triad analysis notation: R–4–5	Analysis notation: ♭6	Resulting analysis notation: R–4–5–♭6	
Example: Csus4	Example: A♭	Example: C(♭6)sus4	No synonymous seventh chord. It could be Fm(add9)/C or, less probably, an incomplete A♭maj13. It can be found in the major scale as iii♭6sus4 and vi♭6sus4 and in the harmonic minor scale as I♭6sus4 and V♭6sus4.

Basic triad: Suspended fourth or sus four	Added sixth: sixth	Resulting chord type: sixth sus four
Triad analysis notation: R–4–5	Analysis notation: 6	Resulting analysis notation: R–4–5–6
Example: Csus4	Example: A	Example: C6sus4

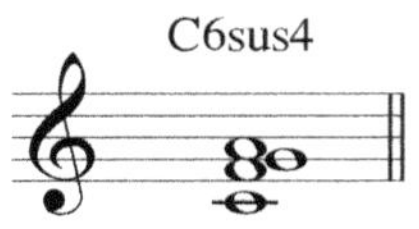

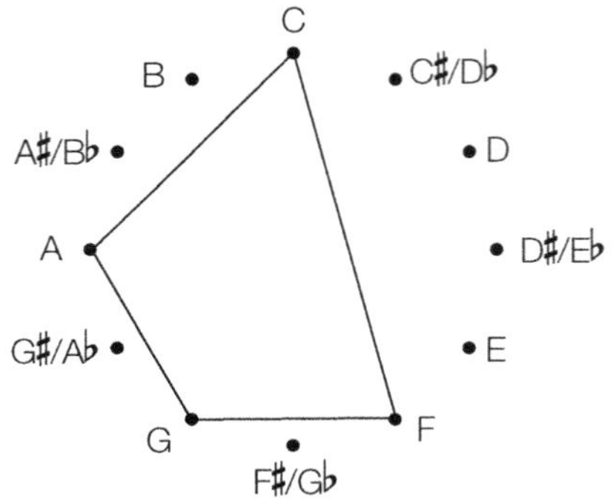

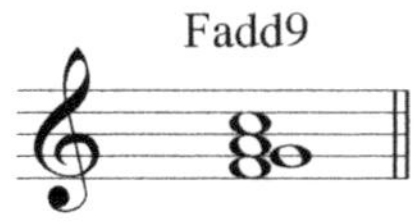

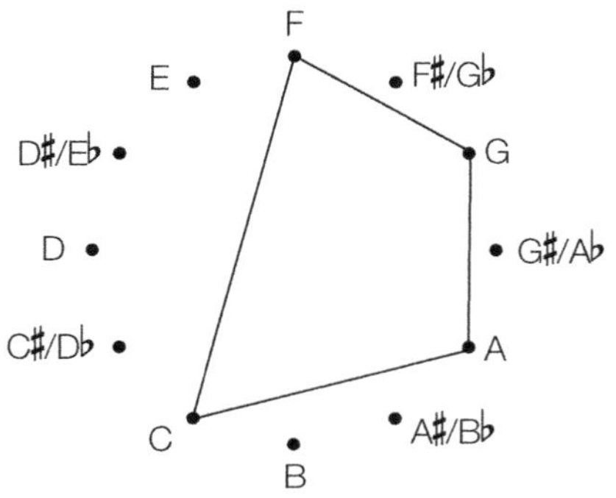

C6sus4

Fadd9

Equivalent to Am7#5. C6sus4 is a perfectly acceptable name, but because of the major triad (F–A–C) hidden in its midst, it would probably be renamed as Fadd9/C. Named as a sixth sus four chord, it can be found in the major scale as I6sus4, ii6sus4, and IV6sus4.

The previous chart revealed fourteen different sixth chords, most of which are not considered common chords in the popular music of the past century. Here's the list, grouped by scales, and with commentary on how often they are used:

Sixth Chords from the Major and Harmonic Minor Scales

1. Major sixth, written 6: extremely common and essential to know
2. Minor sixth, written m6: extremely common and essential to know
3. Minor flat sixth, written m♭6: common and essential to know
4. Six flat five, written 6♭5: not used as named

5. Flat six sus two, written (♭6)sus2: an uncommon name for a common quintal/quartal chord—a good chord to know by whatever name(s) you choose to give it

6. Six sus two, written 6sus2: an uncommon name for a common quintal/quartal chord—a good chord to know by whatever name(s) you choose to give it

7. Flat six sus four, written (♭6)sus4: not a common name—would probably be renamed as m(add9)/5

8. Six sus four, written 6sus4: not a common name—would probably be renamed as m(add9)/5

9. Diminished flat sixth, written °♭6—never used as named

Sixth Chords from the Harmonic Minor Scale

10. Add flat sixth, written add♭6: moderately common and good to know

11. Diminished sixth, written °6: not as common a name as the synonymous diminished seventh chord, but an extremely common chord, and essential to know

12. Augmented sixth or six sharp five, written 6♯5: not used as named

13. Flat six flat five, written (♭6)♭5: not used as named

Sixth Chords Exclusively from the Diminished Scale

14. Minor sixth sharp five, written m6♯5: not used as named

We can summarize the use of the added 6th with the following points:

- Adding a major 6th above the root works well with major and minor triads and is a commonly accepted sound on the guitar, in traditional harmony, and in traditional chord naming. Remember that when the 6th is voiced below the root, the chord sounds more like some kind of seventh chord. For example, G6 with the 6th (E) below the root sounds like Em7.

- Adding a major 6th above the root of an augmented triad is extremely rare in traditional chord naming.

- Adding a major 6th above the root of a diminished triad is the same as adding a diminished 7th.

- A minor 6th (or ♭6) is rarely added to a major or minor triad, but a good guitarist should understand its naming and use as a color note. It can't be added to an augmented triad, as a ♭6 is enharmonic to a ♯5. A diminished triad with a ♭6 sounds and functions so strongly as a dominant seventh chord in first inversion that the name "diminished flat six" is never used.

- Adding major or minor 6ths to sus2 or sus4 chords results in chords that would be given different names in traditional chord naming.

Now that we've covered all this theoretical discussion of sixth chords, let's consider their fingerings on the guitar. Except for a few guitar-centric fingerings, it's extremely unlikely that you'll ever play a sixth chord in close voicing on the guitar. Instead, let's consider some "utility" fingerings of sixth chords—movable fingerings for the more common ones. Here are some guidelines to consider as you check them out:

- The root, 3rd, or 5th will work best as lowest notes in the chord.

- If the 6th is the lowest note for any length of time, the chord sounds (and probably functions) like some kind of seventh chord and should be so named. However, the 6th may sound as the lowest note as part of a rhythmic pattern—e.g. C–C6–C–C6. The 6th may also sound as the lowest note in a descending bass line, but would probably be shown as a slash chord—e.g. C–C/B♭–C/A–C/G.

- As you explore sixth chords, try to unveil their alter egos as seventh chords. For example, if you come across an Am6, can you understand it as F♯m7♭5 as well?

- If you are learning sixth chords for the first time, choose just one or two fingerings to use at first. You should have a practical application for the chord—a song or an etude—and you should try to play it from memory every day.

- If you are attempting to work on sixth chords and you can't find the root note on the appropriate string, then you are probably in over your head. You'll have a tough time playing an Abmb6 if you can't find the note A♭ on your guitar.

Practical Fingerings for Movable Sixth Chords
Major Sixth

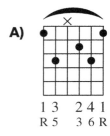

A)

1 3 2 4 1
R 5 3 6 R

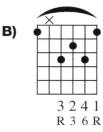

B)

3 2 4 1
R 3 6 R

A) and B) A common beginner's mistake is to play the strings that are indicated with an X. If you barre carefully and arch the first finger upwards, you can avoid these notes.

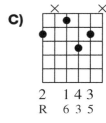

C)

2 1 4 3
R 6 3 5

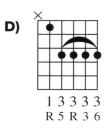

D)

1 3 3 3 3
R 5 R 3 6

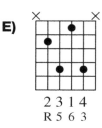

E)

2 3 1 4
R 5 6 3

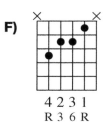

F)

4 2 3 1
R 3 6 R

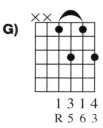

G)

1 3 1 4
R 5 6 3

D) Beginners often play this when they intend to play a major chord without the 6th.

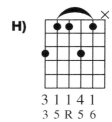

H)

3 1 1 4 1
3 5 R 5 6

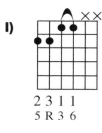

I)

2 3 1 1
5 R 3 6

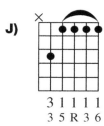

J)

3 1 1 1 1
3 5 R 3 6

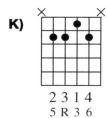

K)

2 3 1 4
5 R 3 6

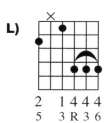

L)

2 1 4 4 4
5 3 R 3 6

H) Avoid the high E string, as barring on this string adds a (pleasant but unasked-for) 9th to the chord.

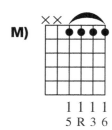

M)

1 1 1 1
5 R 3 6

M) One of the great simple fingerings of guitar chording.

Practical Fingerings for Movable Sixth Chords
Minor Sixth

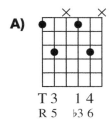

A)
T 3 1 4
R 5 ♭3 6

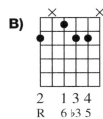

B)
2 1 3 4
R 6 ♭3 5

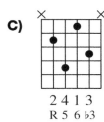

C)
2 4 1 3
R 5 6 ♭3

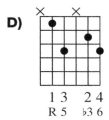

D)
1 3 2 4
R 5 ♭3 6

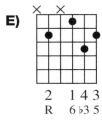

E)
2 1 4 3
R 6 ♭3 5

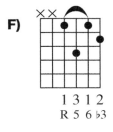

F)
1 3 1 2
R 5 6 ♭3

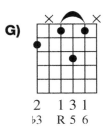

G)
2 1 3 1
♭3 R 5 6

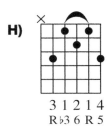

H)
3 1 2 1 4
R ♭3 6 R 5

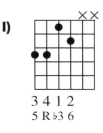

I)
3 4 1 2
5 R ♭3 6

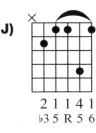

J)
2 1 1 4 1
♭3 5 R 5 6

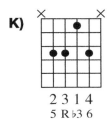

K)
2 3 1 4
5 R ♭3 6

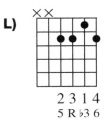

L)
2 3 1 4
5 R ♭3 6

Major Flat Sixth

The major flat sixth chord will more commonly be named as an inversion of a major seven sharp five. For example, C(♭6) is probably better named A♭maj7♯5/C. Still, here are three fingerings for this chord in root position.

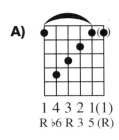

A)
1 4 3 2 1(1)
R ♭6 R 3 5 (R)

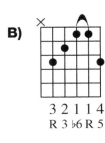

B)
3 2 1 1 4
R 3 ♭6 R 5

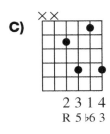

C)
2 3 1 4
R 5 ♭6 3

Practical Fingerings for Movable Sixth Chords
Minor Flat Sixth

The major flat sixth chord will more commonly be named as an inversion of a major seventh chord. For example, Cm♭6 is probably better named A♭maj7/C. But here are three fingerings for this chord in root position.

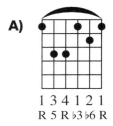

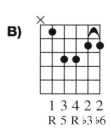

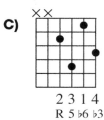

A) 1 3 4 1 2 1
    R 5 R ♭3 ♭6 R

B) 1 3 4 2 2
    R 5 R ♭3 ♭6

C) 2 3 1 4
    R 5 ♭6 ♭3

A Harmonized Scale and Two Etudes for Sixth Chords

As we've seen throughout our exploration of the various sixth chords, most of them are more commonly renamed because of their similarity to an inversion of some kind of seventh chord. Rather than attempt to build complete studies for every type of these peculiar sixth chords, I would recommend that you review the seventh chord etudes from the previous chapter and re-identify the chords as sixth chords.

The first thing to re-emphasize—and to play—is the ambiguity of the major sixth chord as an alter ego of a minor seventh chord. Beginning with a major triad and an added 6th, we've seen that it has the same set of notes as a minor seventh chord with the 6th as the root. If the 6th is the lowest note in the voicing of the chord, it will almost certainly be named that minor seventh chord. If the root of the major triad is the lowest note in the voicing, it will almost certainly receive the "sixth" name. But if the 3rd or the 5th is the lowest note, it might swing either way.

Here are two etudes to demonstrate this ambiguity. The first one begins as a D major scale ascending from the root (D) up to the 4th (G), harmonized in diatonic sixth chords. A diminished seventh/diminished sixth chord is added at the tritone (G♯). The scale then resumes at the 5th (A) but switches to D harmonic minor and descends to the root. The moderately unstable minor flat six chord changes to a major sixth to end the study. The ambiguity of the sixth chord can be seen in the naming of the chords in the two guitar parts: Gtr. 1 plays chords named as seventh chords, while Gtr. 2 plays chords named as sixth chords.

Etude for Sixth Chords

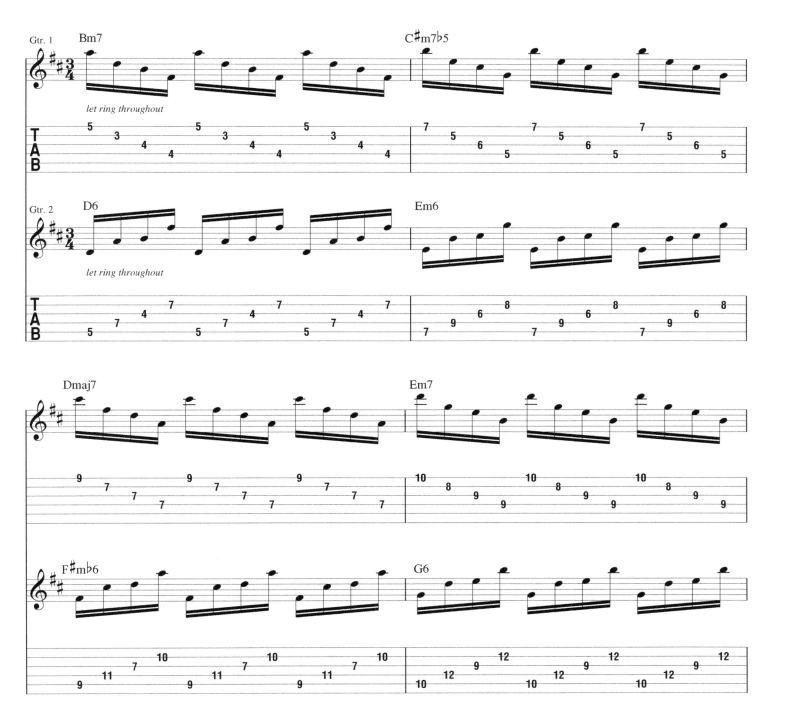

AUDIO
TRACK 56 (cont.)

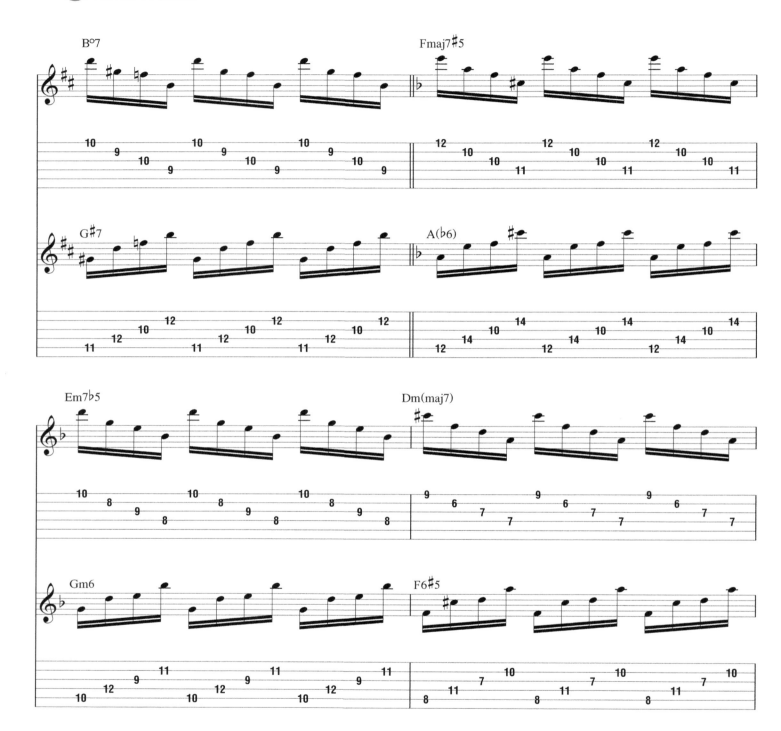

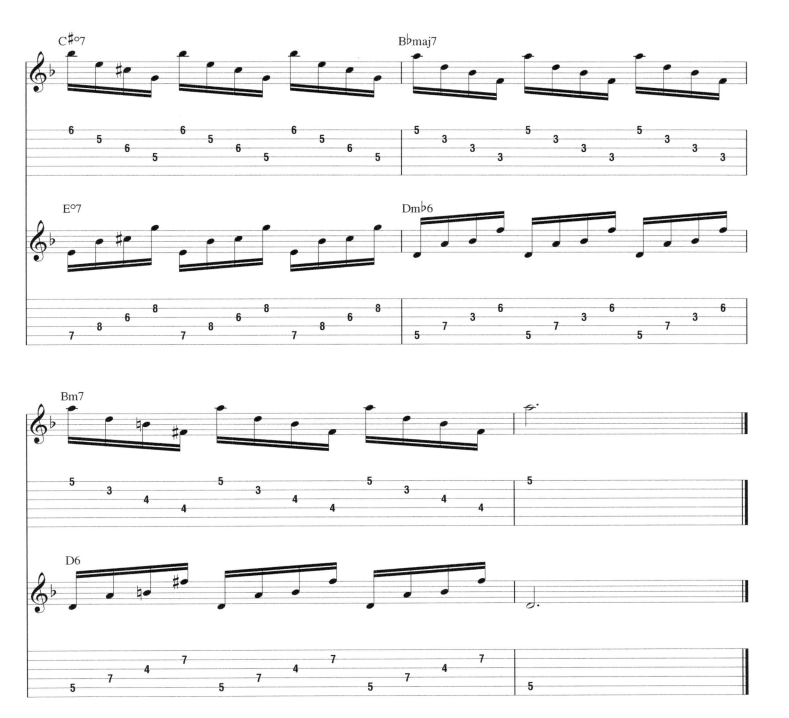

The second etude follows a very simple pattern of root notes while maintaining good voice leading. The root note pattern could be stated as "up a minor 3rd, up a minor 3rd, up a minor 3rd, and up a major 3rd." When traditional voice leading is applied (as shown in the Schillinger circle in the Technique Tip that follows), this interesting barber pole of a musical pattern allows you to play all the inversions of the sixth chord in a chromatically rising pattern for as far up the neck as you care to travel. Presented this way, the first and third chords seem to be clear major triads with 6ths added, but the second and fourth are ambiguous. Incidentally, this progression can also be played backwards, moving down the neck chromatically. Don't just think it has to be fingerpicked, either; strumming, arpeggio picking, and block-style techniques all work well.

AUDIO TRACK 57

Etude for Sixth Chords

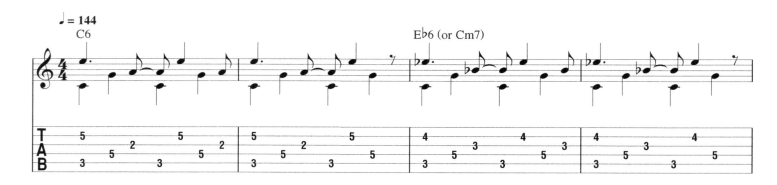

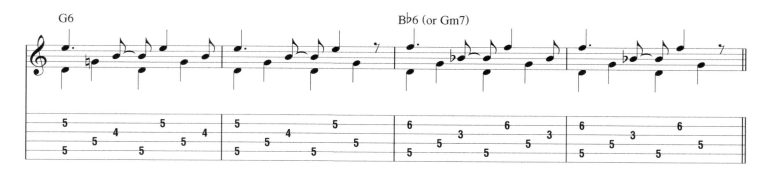

AUDIO TRACK **57 (cont.)**

Technique Tip:

This simple progression and voice leading approach can be used with almost any four-note chord. For example, any sixth chord will work equally well in the above exercise—just alter the appropriate note(s). Similarly, swap the 6th for a 7th in the Schillinger circle and you have a pattern for seventh chords. We'll use this pattern again for add9 and add4 chords.

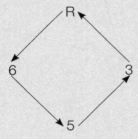

Adding the 2nd or the 9th to Chords in the Major Tonality

When we add the 2nd or the 9th to a chord, we encounter a new curiosity in our chord-naming system, because they are two different names for adding the same note. The added 2nd is called "add two" and abbreviated with "add2" suffixed to the chord name; the added 9th is called "add nine" and abbreviated with "add9" suffixed to the chord name. Let's examine a C major chord, first with an "add2." All we are doing is adding the second note of the scale from which the C major chord is traditionally derived.

Major Add Two and Add Nine

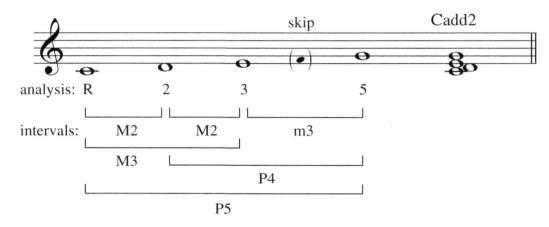

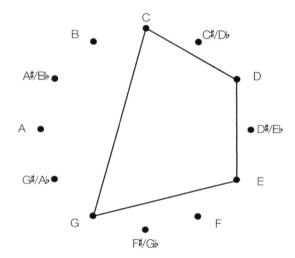

Using the same system, here's how we'd find the ninth note from the scale.

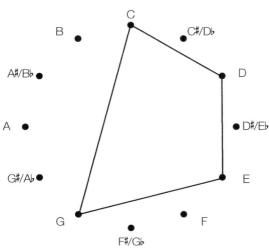

Obviously, the added note is the same in both examples—the note D. As an "add two," the note usually sounds just above the root. As an "add nine," the note sounds at least over an octave above the root. Compare these chords to the sus2 and sus4 chords discussed earlier, and note that when we add the 2nd or 9th to a chord, the 3rd remains. Also keep in mind that if this note were sounded below the root, the chord would get a "slash" name; in this case we'd call it C/D. So—three different names for the same chord, depending on where the new note is placed.

Take a look at the intervals in these chords. Although it appears as if they are somewhat different, any good music theory student will untangle the wider intervals of the Cadd9 and see that they become the same as the Cadd2. (Cadd9's P5 from G to D inverts to Cadd2's P4 of D to G, etc.) Whichever way you choose to look at it, notice the pair of power dyads: C5 and G5, the same pair that was found within Csus2. There's a lot of strength and stability in this chord without the 3rd, and the 3rd can almost be considered an added note that defines the parent tonality—in this case, major.

For the sake of brevity, we'll continue through the chords of the C major scale by examining only the add two voicings, and not the add nine voicings. Remember that "add9" is a way of telling you the desired voicing of the chord: the second note above the root of the chord is to be added an octave higher—a 9th above the root. Let's continue with the add2 chord built on the note D within the C major scale.

Minor Add Two

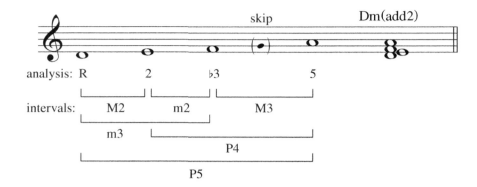

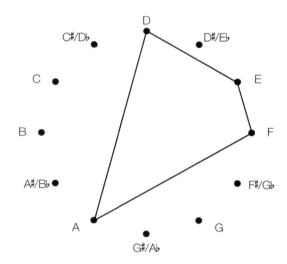

As with Cadd2, there are two strong dyads in this chord: D5 and A5. The minor 3rd above the root (F) gives this chord a delicate quality—the distance of a minor 2nd between it and the added 2nd is like a Christmas ornament. Voiced as an add9 chord, it gains a heartier sound.

Minor Add Flat Two

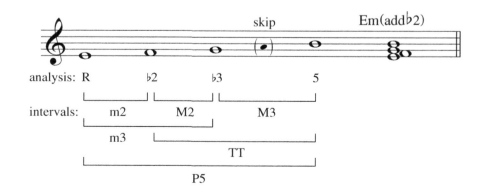

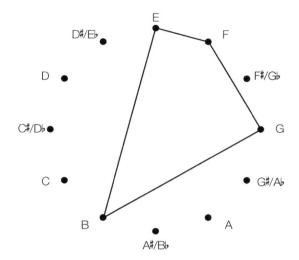

Emadd♭2 is a thorny chord. The added ♭2 rubs against both the root note and the ♭3rd. In traditional harmony, this chord sounds like an incomplete G13 and resolves beautifully to any stable C major chord. It would probably be named as such; "minor add flat two" is an almost unused name in the kingdom of chordom.

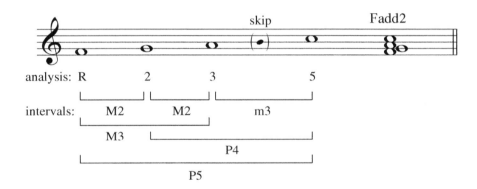

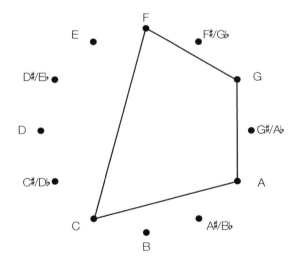

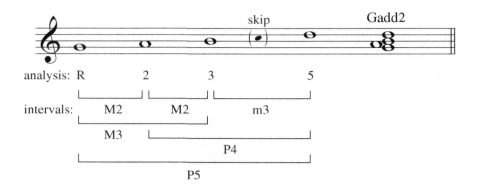

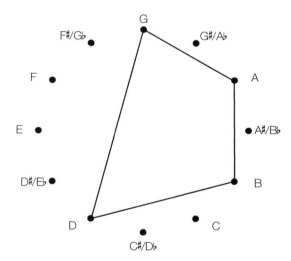

Fadd2 and Gadd2 bring no surprises to the party. They are identical in construction to Cadd2 and provide the same strength and stability. Be sure to identify the strong dyads in each chord and notice how the 3rd adds its major identity to each chord.

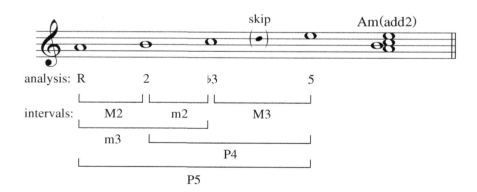

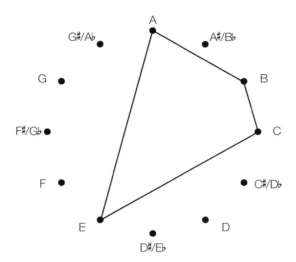

Like Dmadd2, Amadd2 contains two strong dyads—A5 and E5—and a delicate minor 3rd (C).

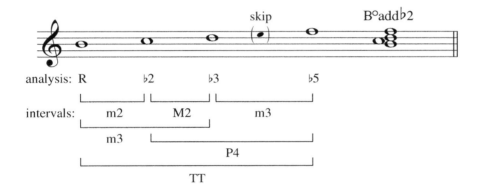

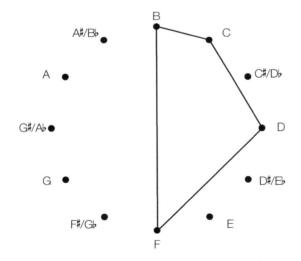

The diminished triad is a weak tertiary chord to begin with. The added ♭2 serves to topple this chord further by mating with the chord's ♭5 in a strong F5 dyad. This makes the chord sound so much like some kind of F chord (Fmaj13♯11, perhaps?) that you'll probably never see a °♭2 chord in a traditional guitar chord chart.

Adding the 2nd or the 9th to Chords in the Harmonic Minor Tonality

Most of the add two (or add nine) chords that were found in the major tonality are also found in the harmonic minor tonality. Rather than repeat myself unnecessarily, I'll simply comment on them and add full analyses for the newcomers, using C harmonic minor as the example key.

Cm(add2): A pleasantly delicate chord, as we discovered in the major tonality.

D°add♭2: As noted in the major tonality, this is a weak chord, and a name you'll probably never see.

Augmented Add Two

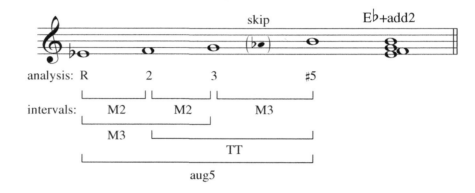

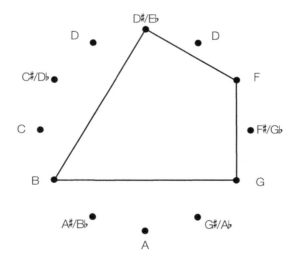

Eb+add2: An augmented triad is an ambiguous affair to start; the added 2nd manages to color this ambiguity nicely without tipping its hand. Because of the symmetrical structure of the augmented triad, this chord can be renamed as G7♯5 (the most common name) and B+add♯4.

Fm(add2): Pleasantly delicate.

Diminished Add Two

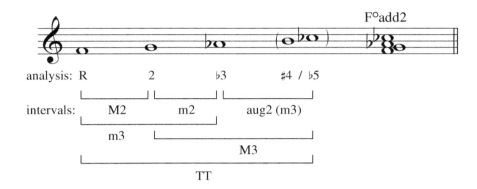

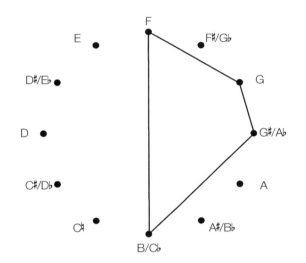

F°add2: Remember, F diminished can be found within the C harmonic minor scale by using B♮ as C♭. Adding the diatonic second (G) to this chord creates F°add2. This tense little knot of notes is virtually a cluster of four adjacent scale notes. Does it have any musical value? Try playing this little cadence:

Add Flat Two

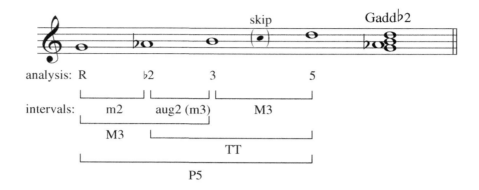

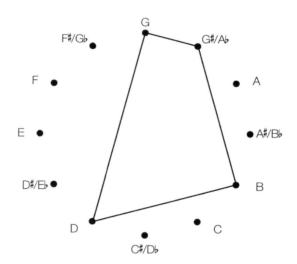

G(add♭2): This would stick out like a sore thumb in the major tonality. In a harmonic minor setting, it fits in nicely. Note the diminished triad formed by the ♭2 (A♭/G♯), 3 (B), and 5 (D). So G(add♭2) could be another name for G♯°maj7, couldn't it? The flat two will be quite welcome when we pair it with a ♭7 and rename it as a ♭9 in the next chapter.

Add Sharp Two

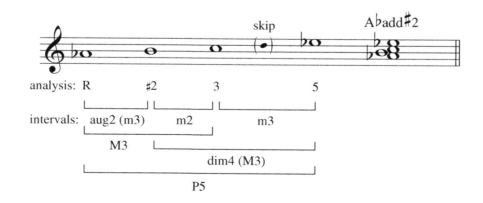

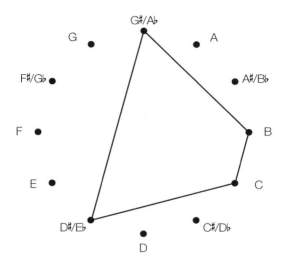

A♭add♯2: Here's a true curiosity. A ♯2 is enharmonic to a ♭3, so this chord seems to sound both major and minor. The ♯2 will be quite a welcome sound when we pair it with a ♭7 and rename it as ♯9 in the next chapter. For now, let's accept it as part of the curious world of the harmonic minor tonality.

The more thorough among you may look to the A♭° triad in C harmonic minor and attempt to add a second of some kind. I would invite them to celebrate the Roman festival of Hilaria when they're done.

B°add♭2: As mentioned above, this is a name you'll probably never see.

Add2 and Add9 Chords in Open Position

As with all new and unusual chord types, a very good way to get to know chords with added 2nds and 9ths is to play them in open position. This sound has been very common in popular music from the mid-1960s to the present (the second decade of the twenty-first century); any alert beginner will want to know these sounds.

An open C major chord is a great place to begin our understanding of the add2 and add9 sounds. Let's begin by adding the second note from C major to the C chord, like this:

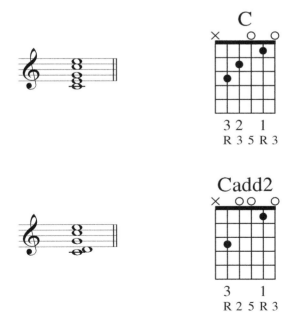

By lifting the second finger from this common shape, the note D (the open D string) is added to the chord. As long as the high E string rings, the chord is Cadd2, not Csus2. C major is also a good chord to understand how the added 2nd can be moved up an octave to become an added 9th, like this:

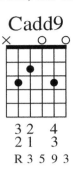

Instead of using the low open D string, we've jumped to the B string to add the color note. Be sure to see that in both of these examples, you can still find the root, 3rd, and 5th after the color note is added to the chord. Here's another useful open position fingering of Cadd9:

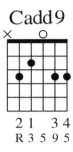

Although this fingering covers the high 3rd (E) with the 5th (G), there's still a 3rd on the D string. Here are some more fingerings for open-position major chords with add9 color notes.

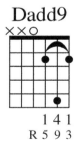

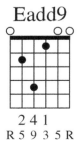

In previous chapters, I've added charts at this point to explore all the possible combinations of a new note with all of the appropriate tertiary triads. While this is possible with the color notes just introduced (add2, add♭2, add♯2, add9, add♭9, and add♯9), it reveals little. Let's move on.

Common and Uncommon Add2 and Add9 Chords—Practical Fingerings

The color notes we've identified as "add2" and "add9" are almost always added to major and minor triads. They can be successfully added to augmented and diminished triads as well. It is rare to find them added to the unusual tertiary triads we've mentioned earlier—the 1–3–♭5 and 1–♭3–♯5 constructions—so we'll bypass them. By the same token, a 2nd can't be added to a sus two triad, since the sus two already has the two in it. Add a 2nd to a sus four triad, and you have a quintal/quartal chord, which is dealt with in one of three ways in current practice:

- It is given a longish name to identify all the notes, as if it were a variation on a tertiary triad, like Cadd2sus4 or Csus2sus4.

- It is twisted back and renamed as some extended tertiary chord. Cadd2sus4 might be renamed C11 or G11 or F6/9 or Dm11—all depending on the voicing and what other chords surround it.

- It is simply identified as a quintal/quartal chord, with an apology that our chord-naming system doesn't name such chords comfortably.

As with any four-note chord, there are twenty-four possible different voicings for each add2/add9 chord, including voicings we'd name as "slash" chords but not including doubling of notes. Exploring these voicings is a great side project but not a practical one for utilitarian fingerings on the guitar. Instead, we'll move forward with an offering of practical fingerings for add2 and add9 chords. As you play these suggested shapes (and perhaps create some of your own), keep these guidelines in mind:

- Any note (including the add2/add9 color note) can work well as the lowest note in the chord. If any note other than the root is the lowest note, the chord will be given a "slash" name. However, if the 2nd is added as the lowest note, the chord is no longer given the "add two" suffix. For example, a C major triad with a D as the lowest note is named C/D—not Cadd2/D. Chords with the 2nd as the lowest note will not be shown in the following section.

- If the new color note is in the lower part of the chord's voicing, but not the lowest note in the chord, it will be named add2; if it is at least an octave above the lowest note in the chord, it will be named add9.

- As you play each chord, identify each note within the chord using the analysis below the fingering. Isolate the color note from the basic chord and listen carefully to how that note colors the chord.

- Begin with just one or two fingerings for a given chord and try to play them from memory every day. Play a song or an etude using the chords.

- If you are unsure of naming notes on the guitar, this kind of structured work may not be for you.

Practical Fingerings of Movable Add2 and Add9 Chords
Major

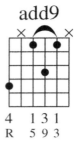
add9

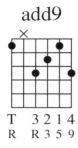
add9

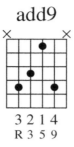
add9

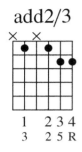
add2/3

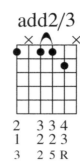
add2/3

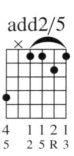
add2/5

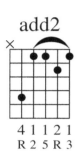
add2

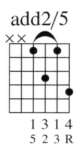
add2/5

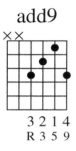
add9

Minor

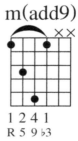
m(add9)

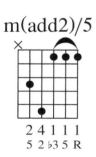
m(add2)/5

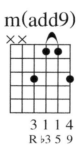
m(add9)

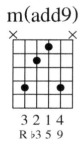
m(add9)

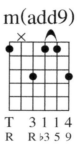
m(add9)

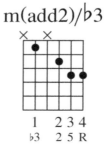
m(add2)/♭3

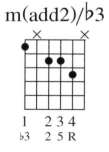
m(add2)/♭3

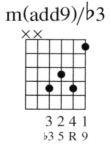
m(add9)/♭3

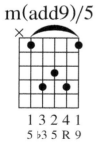
m(add9)/5

Augmented

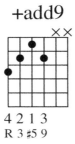

+add9

4 2 1 3
R 3 ♯5 9

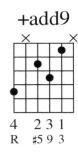

+add9

4   2 3 1
R   ♯5 9 3

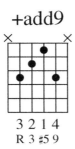

+add9

3 2 1 4
R 3 ♯5 9

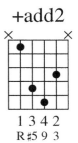

+add2

1 3 4 2
R ♯5 9 3

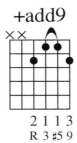

+add9

2 1 1 3
R 3 ♯5 9

Diminished

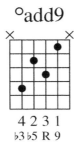

°add9

4 2 3 1
♭3 ♭5 R 9

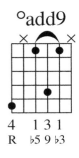

°add9

4   1 3 1
R   ♭5 9 ♭3

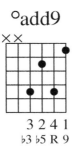

°add9

3 2 4 1
♭3 ♭5 R 9

Inversions, Voicings, Harmonized Scales, and Etudes for Add2 and Add9 Chords

Any of the just-introduced practical fingerings of the add2 and add9 chords can be further explored using our Tool Kit of chord exploration.

Chord Study Tool Kit:

Any time we run into a new chord, whether a new voicing of an old favorite or some rare and exotic new species, it behooves us to put it through its paces with this chord-study tool kit.

- Play the chord type in all its diatonic variations through at least the major and harmonic minor scales with root motion in ascending and descending scale steps. (This is one of the three paths of the diatonic circle, traveled in two directions.)

- Play all of the chords discovered in the first step above in all of their inversions laterally across the neck. (We've ruled this out, as twenty-four inversions of add2 chords aren't practical.)

- Play all of the chords discovered in the first step above in all of their inversions linearly up and down the neck on specific string sets. (Also largely ruled out, though one linear study follows.)

- Play all of the chords discovered in the first step above in all of their inversions through at least the major and harmonic minor scales with root motion in ascending and descending 3rds and ascending and descending fourths. (These are the other two paths of the diatonic circle, traveled in both directions.)

- Consider what makes up the chord and create a chart to see if any other chords of that type exist beyond the major and harmonic minor tonalities.

Let's take the first shape from the previous figure and play it specifically as an Aadd9, like this:

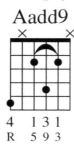

We get some truly challenging fingerings when we move this shape diatonically through A major. If your guitar isn't built to give access to all the fingerings shown, you'll do well to transpose them to a higher string set.

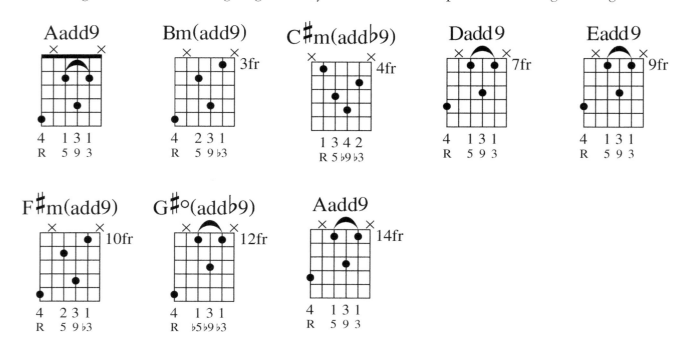

The harmonic minor tonality provides equally severe challenges to the fretting hand.

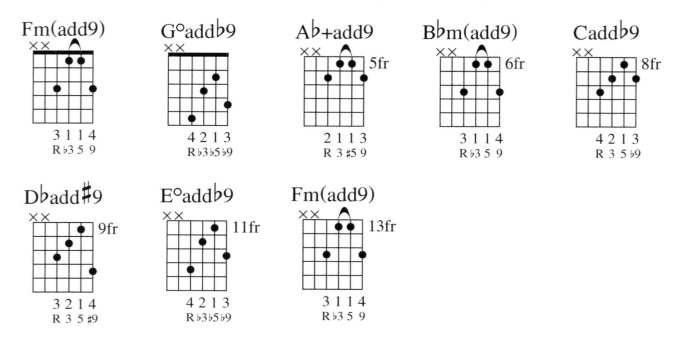

Try beginning with a specific voicing and moving each note upwards on the starting string set, like this:

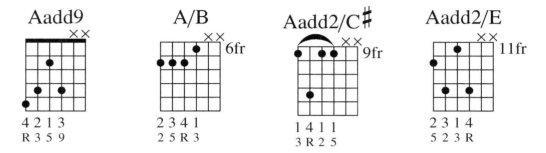

There's a problem hidden in the construction of the add two chord, and it's the reason why these chords are so difficult to play in a wide range of voicings—particularly in a close voicing. If we isolate the root, 2nd, and 3rd of the chord from the 5th, we have a new kind of non-tertiary triad, called a ***cluster chord***. A cluster chord is a group of three or more adjacent notes that cannot be reduced to a tertiary relationship. The notes can be derived from a relatively traditional scale, like the major or harmonic minor scales—in which case they would be called a *diatonic cluster*—or they can be taken from the chromatic scale—in which case they would be called a *chromatic cluster*. It's possible to construct a few special close cluster voicings around an open string, but movable close cluster chords are highly improbable creatures on a guitar in standard tuning. Still, some fingerings are possible, even when proper voice leading creates some monstrous stretches. When you examine the voice leading of add two chords, you'll find an interesting phenomenon exists: whether you move by root motion in 2nds, 3rds, 4ths, or 5ths, there are always two notes in common between chords. Cluster chords and add two chords are worth further study on your own; here are two etudes to get you started.

First, try this etude for add2, add9, and slash chords (with the 2nd in the bass) with root motion in descending 2nds in the key of C major. Notice that the last note resolves the chord to its traditional resting place as a C major triad with a doubled root. Gtr. 1 plays the chords as ringing arpeggios, while Gtr. 2 strums the chords.

Etude for Add2, Add9 and /2 Chords • Root Motion in Descending Seconds

*Gtr. 2 strums chords in steady eighth notes.

AUDIO
TRACK 58 (concluded)

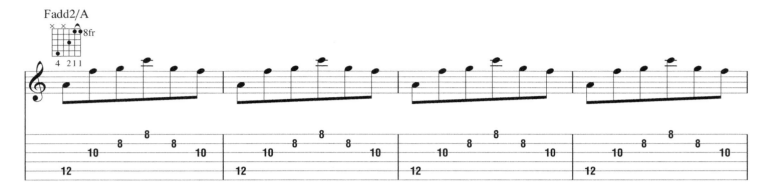

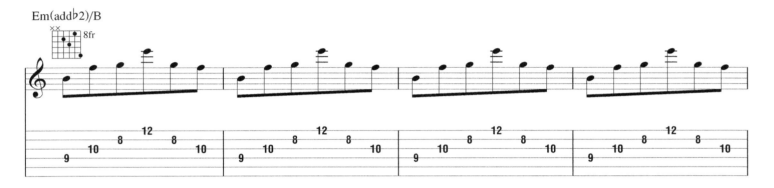

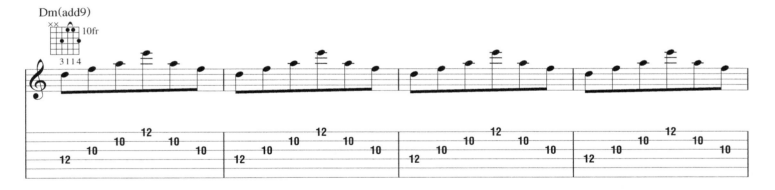

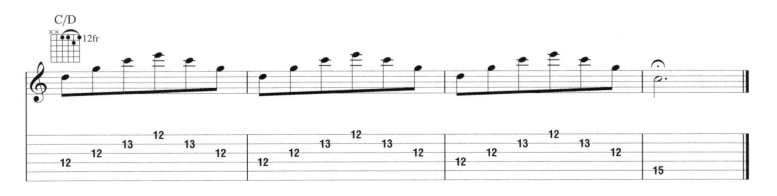

Next is an etude with root motion in descending 3rds. A with the previous etude, Gtr. 1 plays the chords as ringing arpeggios, while Gtr. 2 strums the chords. The problem of holding two notes in common to each adjacent chord has been cleverly bypassed by transposing one of the two common notes up or down an octave in each subsequent chord. For example, in the first change from Cadd2/E to Am(add9), the two notes common to both chords are C and E. However, the C is dropped an octave from the first chord to the second, dodging a knot of wicked fretting. (Okay, it's really not so clever. Take a look at the two Schillinger circles below, and the voice leading choices will be clear.)

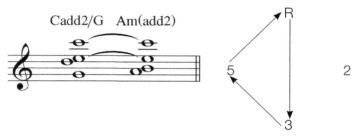

Voice leading if common notes are held.

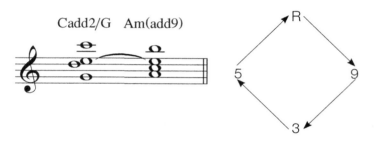

Voice leading around the Schillinger circle.

AUDIO TRACK 59

Etude for Add2, Add9 and /2 Chords • Root Motion in Descending Thirds

*Gtr. 2 strums chords in steady eighth notes.

Here's a brief introduction to a technique that often allows for much easier fingerings of these chords. The strategy behind the approach is to release one note at the beginning of an arpeggio pattern in order to play another note later in the pattern. It creates the illusion of a single chord, even though the fingering is more like two chords being played in tandem. On a guitar with no effects added to the audio signal, the first note would obviously drop out when it is released to add the later note, but by adding a delay-based effect, the first note can be repeated as part of the delay pattern, and the full chord will sound at one time. I first picked up this trick (without the delay) when I saw Andy Summers of the Police play his signature arpeggios in "Every Breath You Take." Here's an example of this technique in action, using add2 chords. On the audio track, you'll hear the example played twice—once with a relatively dry sound, and once with a single-repeat delay added.

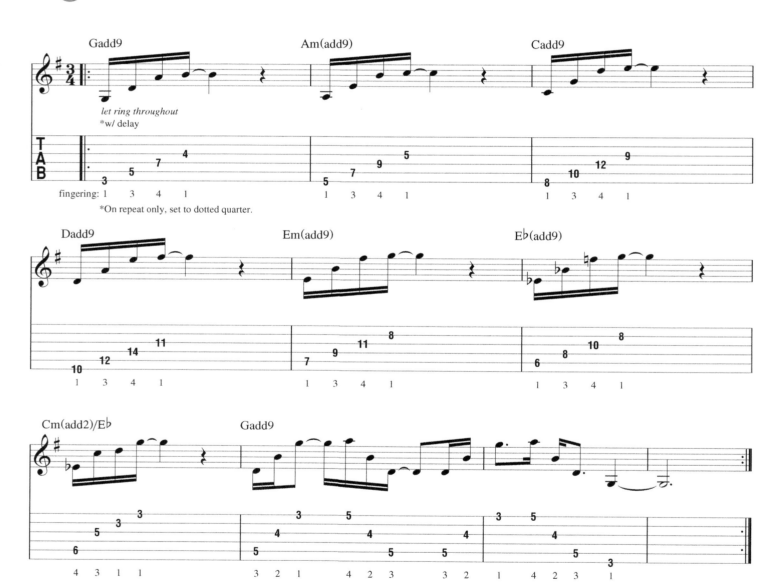

Adding the 4th to Chords in the Major Tonality

Traditional tertiary triads with an added 4th are rare and delicate creatures. When you build, play, and listen to chords with this added note, you'll understand why it's a somewhat limited (but often quite beautiful) color note. Let's begin with a C major chord. Just as the add2, add9, and slash chords add the 2nd note above the root of the chord, the add4 note is found by adding the 4th note above the root of the chord.

Major Add Four

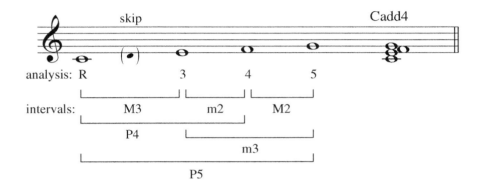

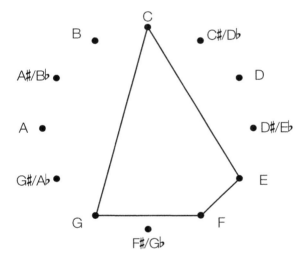

Remember that, unlike the sus2 and sus4 chords discussed in Chapter Four, the 3rd remains when a chord receives the "add" suffix. Also keep in mind that if this note is sounded as the lowest note in the chord, the chord will be given a "slash" name; in the example above we'd call it C/F, if the F was played an octave lower.

Take a look at the intervals in this chord. First and foremost, there are two power dyads: C5 and F5, the same pair that was found within Csus4. There's a lot of strength in this chord without the 3rd, and it can easily favor F as the root note, as we shall see when we invert it. Just like the add2 chord, the 3rd can almost be considered an added note that defines the parent tonality—in this case, major. The minor 2nd between the chord's major 3rd (E) and added 4th (F) is the delicate interval that limits this chord's traditional use. When we look at different inversions of this chord, we'll see that when the 4th (F) is sounded directly above the 3rd (E), it functions well as the intended color note, but if it is placed a minor 9th above the 3rd, it sounds inappropriately dissonant for traditional use. And if it is sounded below the 3rd, it might begin to sound like the root of a fancy F major chord; perhaps Fmaj9(no 3rd). Look for these qualities as you build, play, and listen to the major chord with the add4 color note.

Minor Add Four

Let's continue through the other chords of the C major scale. Here's a Dm with an added 4th, named Dm(add4).

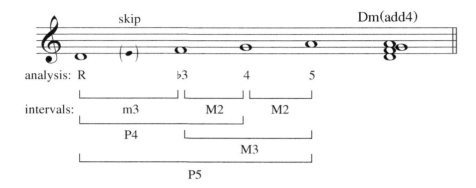

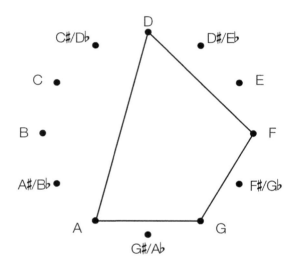

As with Cadd4, there are two strong dyads in this chord: D5 and G5. The added 4th (G) doesn't create as much trouble in the minor triad as it does in the major, because it's a major 2nd away from the chord's 3rd (F).

The next add four chord in C major is Em(add4).

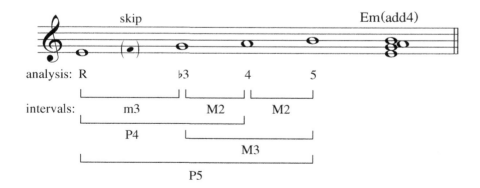

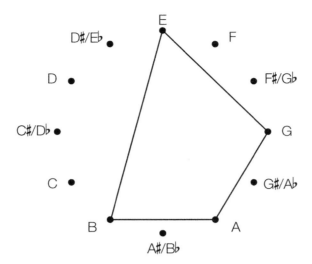

Em(add4) has the same structure as Dm(add4). There are two strong dyads—E5 and A5—and a minor 3rd (G) that sits a major 2nd below the added 4th (A).

Major Add Sharp Four

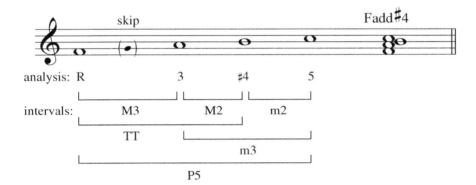

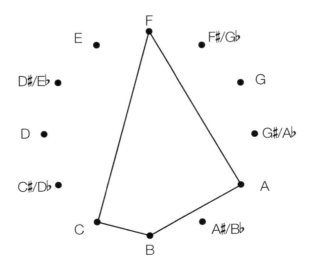

Fadd♯4 is a surprisingly attractive sound, given the tritone between the root (F) and the ♯4 (B), as well as the minor 2nd between the ♯4 (B) and the 5 (C). It stands tall with one strong dyad (F5) along with the F/B tritone. Be careful of voicing it with the ♯4 as the lowest note; it will probably catch the ear as an incomplete G9 chord.

Here is the add 4 chord built on the note G in the key of C.

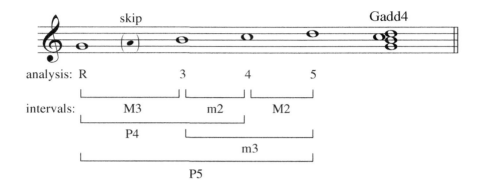

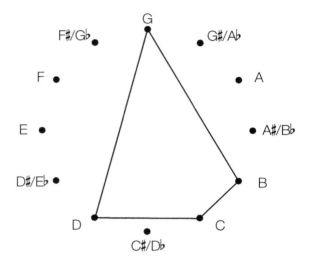

Gadd4 is structured just like Cadd4. Be sure to identify the two strong dyads as well as the quality of the added 4th.

Next up is the add4 chord built on the note A in the key of C

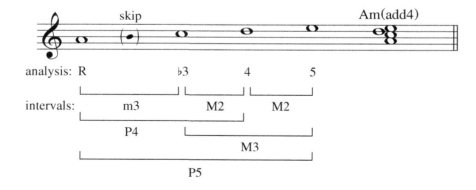

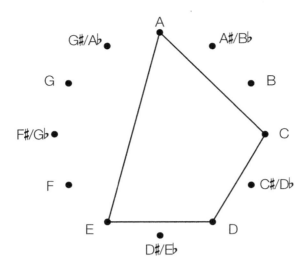

Am(add4) is identical in structure to Dm(add4).

Diminished Add Four

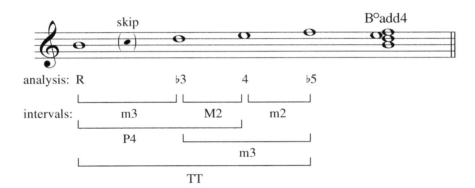

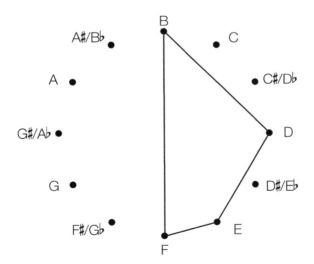

The diminished triad is a weak tertiary chord to begin with. Although you might guess that the added 4th (E) could work with the root (B) to create an E5 dyad, it doesn't quite fall that way. Instead, it seems that this chord wants to be heard as an incomplete G13 (without a G). You'll probably never see a °add4 chord in a traditional guitar chord chart.

Adding the 4th to Chords in the Harmonic Minor Tonality

Many of the add4 chords that were found in the major tonality are also found in the harmonic minor tonality. Rather than repeat myself unnecessarily, I'll add analysis, diagrams, and commentary on just the new specimens, using C harmonic minor as the example key.

Cm(add4): A pleasantly delicate chord, as we discovered in the major tonality.

D°add4: As noted in the major tonality, this is a weak chord and a name you'll probably never see in any traditional chord chart.

Augmented Add Four

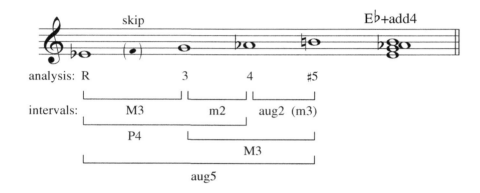

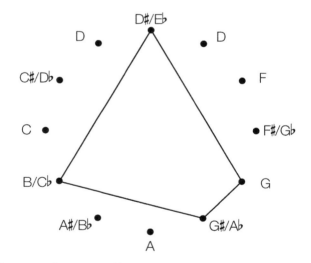

E♭+add4: An augmented triad is an ambiguous affair to start; the added 4th feels out of place in most traditional chord sequences. This is another name you'll probably never see in any traditional chord chart. It is much easier to identify this sound as an inversion of a minor major seventh chord. Specifically, E♭+add4 can be enharmonically renamed as A♭m(maj7)/E♭.

Minor Add Sharp Four

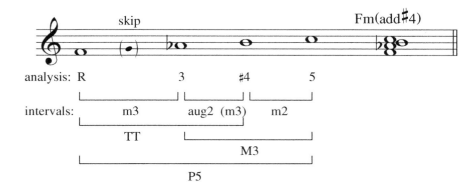

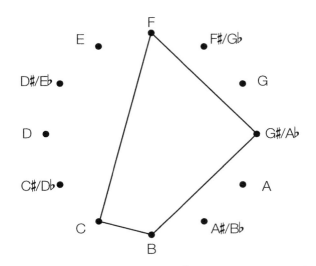

Fm(add♯4): This is worth working out on paper; the added ♯4 (B) creates an F diminished triad (F–A♭–B). The perfect 5th (C) then sounds like an intruder in conventional harmony. Here's another name you'll probably not come across in traditional chord charts.

G(add4): A chord type common to the major tonality. No surprises.

A♭(add♯4): Compare this to F(add♯4) in C major.

B°add4: As mentioned above, this is a name you'll probably never see.

Add Four Chords in Open Position

As with all new and unusual chord types, a very good way to get to know chords with added 4ths is to play them in open position. The sound of the added 4th is somewhat rare, but can be found occasionally in open position shapes; any alert beginner will want to know these sounds.

An open C major chord is good for understanding the add4 sound. Let's begin by adding the 4th note from C major to the common C chord:

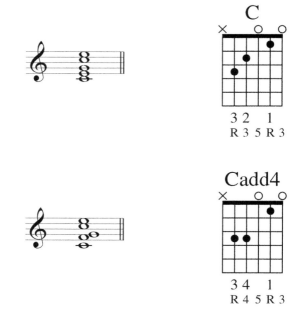

By adding the fourth finger to the D string in this common shape, the note F is added to the chord. As long as the high E string rings, the chord is Cadd4 and not Csus4. C major is also a good chord to understand how dissonant the added 4th sounds when it is moved up an octave, like this:

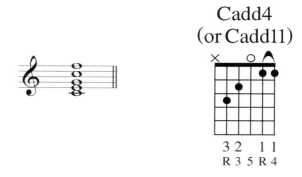

Notice that the name of this chord might be Cadd11. As a prelude to eleventh chords, discussed in the next chapter, you might take the time to think through the C major scale in two octaves to see how the 4th note of C major might be identified as the 11th. At the moment though, it's a rather academic exercise, because if you play this voicing of Cadd4, you'll hear the dissonance of the high F (high E string, first fret) against the E (D string, second fret). This kind of dissonance is rarely heard in most musical settings.

Here are some more fingerings for open-position major chords with add4 color notes.

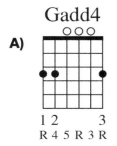

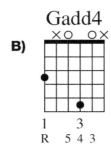

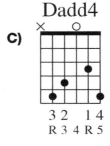

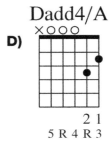

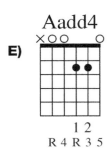

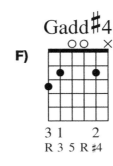

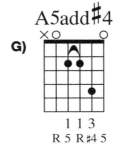

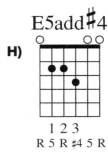

B) This is a kind of "stunt" fingering—a combination of a high fretted note (C, on the G string at the third fret) with open strings.

C) Another "stunt" fingering: a C major shape, moved up two frets, along with a single open string (G, the added 4th).

G) and H) These chords have no 3rd, so they could be played as substitutes for either a major sharp four or a minor sharp four chord.

And here are some minor chords in open position with the add4 color note.

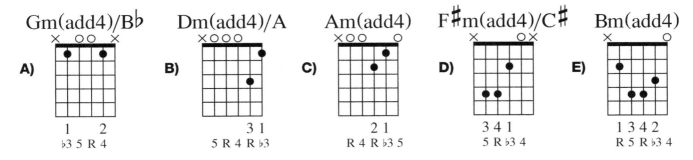

In previous chapters, I've added charts at this point to explore all the possible combinations of a new note with all of the appropriate tertiary triads. While this is possible with the add4 and add♯4 color note, it reveals little. (You might want to try it yourself and see what you discover.) Let's move on.

Common and Uncommon Add Four Chords—Practical Fingerings

The color notes we've identified as "add4" and "add♯4" are almost always added to major triads. Add4 can also be added to a minor triad, but add♯4 does not work well, nor do they work well with augmented and diminished triads, as we've seen in the previous section. It's also safe to say that you'll never see an add4 added to the unusual tertiary triads we've mentioned earlier—the 1–3–♭5 and 1–♭3–♯5 constructions. (It may be worth your own time to explore why this is so.) It's also a matter of chord-naming logic to see that there will never be a "sus" chord with an "add" suffix.

As with any four-note chord, there are twenty-four possible different voicings for each add4 and add♯4 chord, including voicings we'd name as "slash" chords but not including doubling of notes. Exploring these voicings (and confirming the impractical voicings mentioned in the previous section) is another worthwhile project for intermediate level guitarists, but not a practical one for utilitarian fingerings on the guitar. As you play the following suggested shapes (and perhaps create some of your own), keep these guidelines in mind:

- Any note (including the add4 or add♯4) can work well as the lowest note in the chord. If any note other than the root is the lowest note, the chord will be given a "slash" name. Slash chords have already been addressed, so they will not be found here.

- Chords with add4 or add♯4 will always be so named unless the new note is the lowest note in the chord, in which case the chord will given a "slash" name without the add4 appearing anywhere. For example, a C major triad with an F added above the lowest note will be named Cadd4, while a C major triad with F added as the lowest note will be named C/F.

- As you play each chord, identify each note within the chord using the analysis below the fingering. Isolate the color note from the basic chord and listen carefully to how that note colors the chord.

- Begin with just one or two fingerings for a given chord and try to play them from memory every day. Play a song or an etude that uses the chords.

- If you are unsure of naming notes on the guitar, this kind of structured work may not be for you.

Practical Fingerings of Movable Add4 Chords
Major Add4

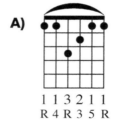 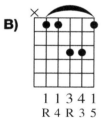 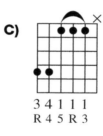 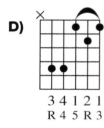 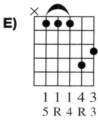

A)	B)	C)	D)	E)
1 1 3 2 1 1	1 1 3 4 1	3 4 1 1 1	3 4 1 2 1	1 1 1 4 3
R 4 R 3 5 R	R 4 R 3 5	R 4 5 R 3	R 4 5 R 3	5 R 4 R 3

Minor Add4

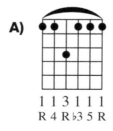 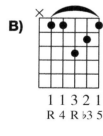 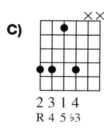 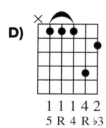

A)	B)	C)	D)
1 1 3 1 1 1	1 1 3 2 1	2 3 1 4	1 1 1 4 2
R 4 R♭3 5 R	R 4 R♭3 5	R 4 5 ♭3	5 R 4 R♭3

Major Add♯4

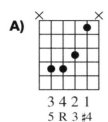

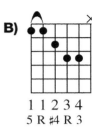

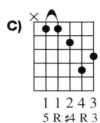

A) 3 4 2 1
    5 R 3 ♯4

B) 1 1 2 3 4
    5 R ♯4 R 3

C) 1 1 2 4 3
    5 R ♯4 R 3

Inversions, Voicings, Harmonized Scales and Etude for Add4 and Add♯4 Chords

Any of the just-introduced practical fingerings of the add4 and add♯4 chords could be further explored using our Tool Kit of chord exploration. However, if you try this tack, you might find yourself with some insurmountably hard fingerings for chords that have little practical application in traditional harmony. Commentary follows within the toolbox.

Chord Study Tool Kit:

Any time we run into a new chord, whether a new voicing of an old favorite or some rare and exotic new species, it behooves us to put it through its paces with a chord-study tool kit.

- Play the chord type in all its diatonic variations through at least the major and harmonic minor scales with root motion in ascending and descending scale steps. (This is one of the three paths of the diatonic circle, traveled in two directions.) *When taking this path with the add4 and add♯4 chords, we encounter two problems: 1) The add4 chord sounds unresolved, and 2) The diminished add4 chord is difficult to play and sounds poor in this context as well.*

- Play the chord type in all its inversions laterally across the neck. (We've ruled this out—twenty-four inversions of the add4 type aren't practical.)

- Play the chord type in all its inversions linearly up and down the neck on specific string sets. (Also largely ruled out—see above. However, one linear study follows.)

- Play the chord type in all its diatonic variations through at least the major and harmonic minor scales with root motion in ascending and descending 3rds and ascending and descending 4ths. (These are the other two paths of the diatonic circle, traveled in both directions.) *This approach suffers the same weaknesses as the first point above: a lack of resolution and the inclusion of the useless diminished add4 chord.*

- Consider what makes up the chord and create a chart to see if any other chords of that type exist beyond the major and harmonic minor tonalities. *This point has been discussed previously as well.*

Before we take leave of add4 chords, let's apply a technique similar to the one that was introduced in our study of add2 chords. The strategy behind the approach is to add a note during an arpeggio pattern at the expense of releasing an earlier note. It creates the illusion of a single chord, even though the fingering is more like two chords being played one after the other. On a guitar with no effects added to the audio signal, the first note will obviously drop out when it is released to add the later note, but with a delay-based effect, the first note can be repeated as part of the delay pattern, and the full chord will sound at one time. Andy Summers of the Police plays his signature arpeggios in "Every Breath You Take" using this technique with add9 chords, but it can work for add4 chords as well. Here's an example of this technique in action, using add4 chords. On the audio track, you'll hear the example played twice—once with a relatively dry sound, and once with a single-repeat delay added.

 AUDIO TRACK 61

Etude for Add4 Chords

CHAPTER SEVEN:

The Big Numbers— Nine, Eleven, Thirteen and "Alt" Chords

Snowmen with Five or More Body Parts

Now we come to another curious crossroad in the land of tertiary chords: *extended chords*, or chords with 3rds stacked up higher than an octave from the root. So far, we've worked almost exclusively with chords that can contain all of their pitches within an octave. To summarize our journey so far, we've worked with *dyads* (two-note intervals that often function as chords), *tertiary triads* (three-note chords built from the interval of a 3rd), *seventh chords*, and *"color" chords*. Along the way, two other chord constructions have been pointed out, with an acknowledgement that they do not get properly named in our tertiary-biased system of chord naming: *quintal/ quartal chords*, and *clusters*. We've taken all of the tertiary chords and studied their inversions and voicings and put them through their paces with sequences, progressions, and cadences. I have no doubt that many otherwise fine and aspiring guitarists will have, at this point, given up. Others may have leapt forward to this chapter in hopes of getting to "the good stuff." All is well. Knowledge of chords invariably arrives in a nonlinear way.

In tertiary chord construction, the final step in chord complexity is to consider the 3rds that stack up above the octave of the root. In constructive theory, these chords should contain five, six, or seven different note names. They begin with a tertiary seventh chord and continue with yet more 3rds stacked up from there. When dealing with these chords in snowman form, these new notes will be a 9th, an 11th, and a 13th above the root, and chords with these notes added are collectively referred to as "extended" chords. In practical application (especially on the guitar), these chords will not consist of more than six different note names (they can't) and will often be pared down to five, four, or even three notes.

Introducing the Thirteenth Chord

Rather than build an extended snowman chord with one snowball at a time, let's heap the entire blizzard of snowballs in a stack to create the towering thirteenth chord shown below.

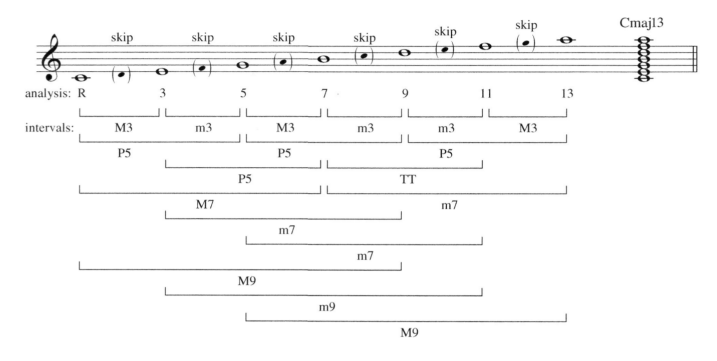

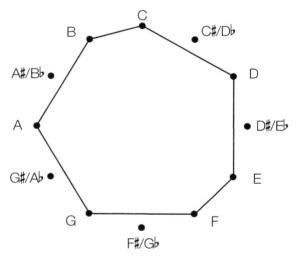

Be aware: this theoretical snowman of a thirteenth chord will hardly ever be heard in most music. Furthermore, because chord names have evolved somewhat independently of formal analysis, this specific thirteenth chord does not get the simplest name. For that, we need to flat the 7th, like this:

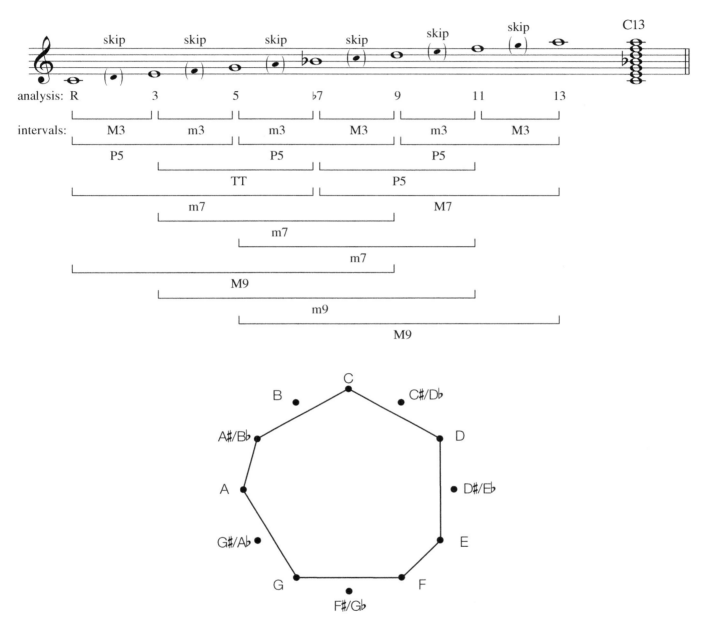

Notice that in both of these theoretical thirteen chords, a complete scale is implied. We can see this curious renumbering of the scale in this way:

	1	2	3	4	5	6	7	(8)
major scale analysis:	1	2	3	4	5	6	7	(8)
13 chord analysis:	1	9	3	11	5	13	7	(8)

This dually numbered scale shows that the note that we are now numbering as the 9th of the scale can also be numbered as the 2nd. Similarly, the 11th was previously identified as the 4th, and the 13th was identified as the 6th. In the last chapter, we added the note identified as the 2nd or 9th to triads and called them "add two" or "add nine" chords. We added the note called the 11th and called the resulting chords "add four" chords. We added the 6th and called the chords "sixth" chords. So what gives?

- What makes a chord a ninth chord instead of an add9?

- What makes a chord an eleventh chord instead of an add4?

- What makes a chord a thirteenth chord instead of a sixth?

The answer: the presence of some kind of 7th. If no 7th is present, the added notes can be identified as "color" notes, and some kind of "add" chord name will be used. If a 7th is present, the chord should be named as an extended chord.

If a chord contains a major 7th above the root, it will have "maj" somewhere in its name. If a chord has a minor 7th above the root, it won't have "maj" in its name.

Now let's backtrack to each of these chord types—ninth, eleventh and thirteenth—and explore how they can be played on the guitar.

Naming and Dissecting Ninth Chords in the Major Tonality

A ninth chord consists of some kind of tertiary triad along with some kind of 7th and some kind of 9th. Let's begin with a Cmaj9, as shown below.

Major Ninth

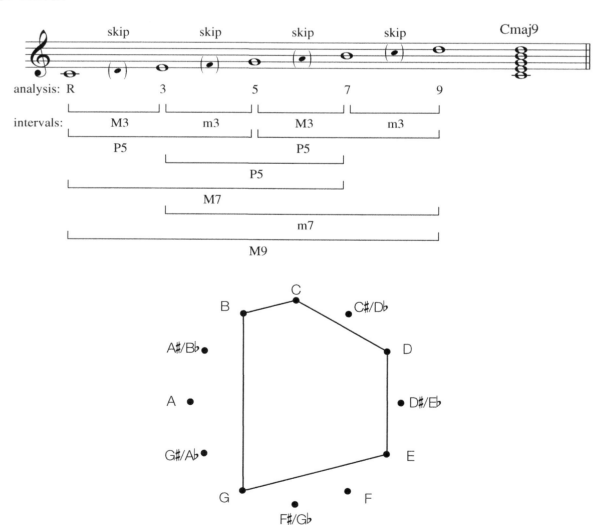

You should relate this chord back to both Cmaj7 and Cadd9 (or Cadd2), as it is essentially a melding of both of them. As such, it's a really nice, pretty chord, as we'll see when we play it on guitar. No tritones or flatted nines reside in this basic stack of snowballs. Remember, it's called Cmaj9 because it contains a *major seventh*, not because it contains a major 3rd. Now look for the root-5th dyads in this chord. You should spot three: C5, E5, and G5. Interesting—the three notes of the major triad, plus perfect 5ths above each of those three notes. If we think of perfect 5ths as powerful intervals, this is a kind of hyper-powerful major chord.

Are there triads other than C major residing within the C major ninth chord? Of course there's an E minor chord (E–G–B), as we discovered when we analyzed Cmaj7 in Chapter Five. The 9th allows a G major (G–B–D) to be found as well. C major, E minor, and G major are all simple, stable triads, and they coexist peacefully within the key of C and within Cmaj9. Another important structure to recognize: the four-note cluster of B–C–D–E. Four-note clusters are found in every complete ninth chord, and it's valuable to see how the cluster is distributed within the chord to create a traditionally useful sound. Pay attention to this when you play the Practical Fingerings of Ninth Chords beginning on p. 317.

Minor Ninth

Here's the ninth chord built on the second note of the C major scale:

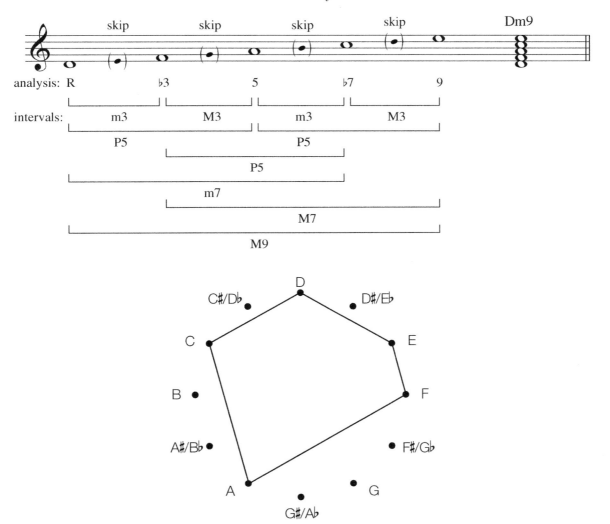

Think of Dm9 as a melding of Dm7 and Dm(add9), or Dm(add2). We found both of them to be pleasant and stable chords, and this quality extends to Dm9 as well. As we'll see with all ninth chords, there are three dyads to be found, and in the minor ninth chord, they are all strong perfect 5ths: D5, F5, and A5. Just as Cmaj9 harbored perfect 5ths above each note of the primary triad, so it is with Dm9, and it has a settled quality as a kind of hyper-powerful minor chord. As for triads besides Dm, there's F major (F–A–C) and A minor (A–C–E), all stable citizens of the C major tonality. The four-note cluster here is C–D–E–F.

Minor Flat Ninth

Here's the ninth chord built on E within the C major scale:

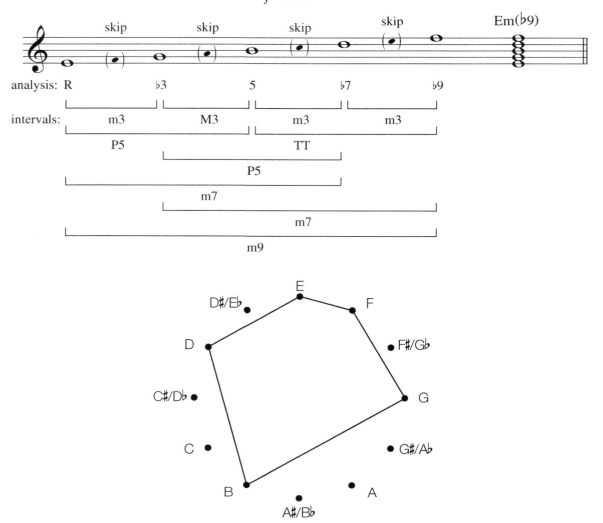

Em(♭9) joins a stable-sounding Em7 with the unstable Em(add♭9). As such, it will prove to be a difficult chord to consider stable. The ♭9 (F) is a minor 9th above the root, which is traditionally an unstable interval, and it gains no stability when placed just above the root as a minor 2nd (or ♭2). It also sits a tritone away from the 5th of the chord. Two stable dyads (E5 and G5) must now sit with the unstable tritone of B(♭5), and the stable triads of E minor and G major are joined by B°. The four-note cluster here is D–E–F–G. With E as the root, it sounds weak, but with G as the root, it sounds cool. In traditional harmony, this chord begs to be re-voiced as a G13, found later in this chapter. In short, this is not a chord for Western campfire strumming, unless you want to sit all by yourself in the dark.

Here's the ninth chord built upon F within the C major scale:

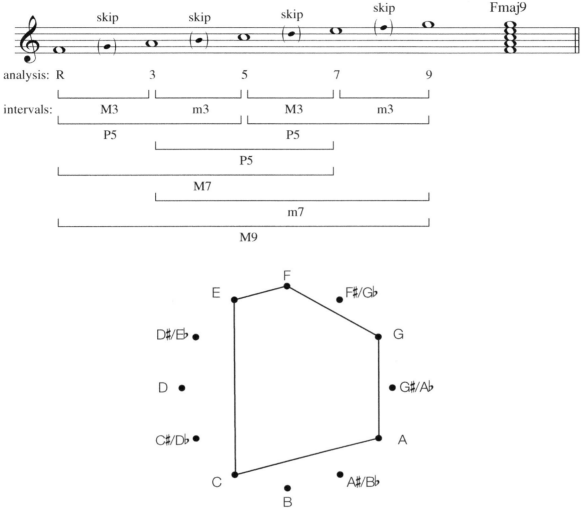

Fmaj9 is structurally identical to Cmaj9. It relates back to both Fmaj7 and F(add9), both pleasant and stable chords. Similarly, the three dyads (F5, A5, and C5) and three triads (F, Am, and C) all coexist peacefully.

Dominant Ninth

The ninth chord built upon the note G within C major is really important to know in traditional music theory. Here it is:

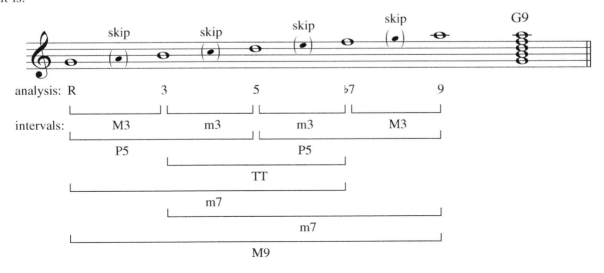

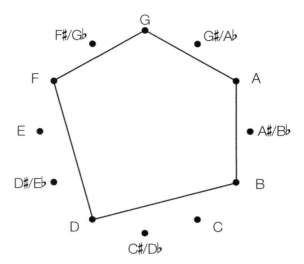

G9 mates the qualities of an exciting G7 chord with a stable Gadd9 to create a chord that has two distinct personalities. In a more traditional context, G9 is referred to as an ***extended dominant chord***—a chord that wants to move to another, more stable chord. Usually, that next chord will be a 4th above the root of the dominant chord. This is your vanilla-flavored V7–I cadence, supercharged with the added 9th in the V7 chord. In the key of C, the G9 would be preceded by a few other chords that would establish C major as the home key, then the G9 would sound, followed by a resolution to a C major chord, a Cmaj7, or a Cmaj9. Looking at the intervals of the G9 chord, we can sympathize with the traditionalists' desires to resolve it. After all, nestled between the G5 and D5 dyads is the hellion tritone of B–F, and although both a stable G major and D minor triad can be found within G9, there's that pesky B° triad just begging to move to C major. Traditionalists might also point to the cluster F–G–A–B, which suggests the largest tetrachord of the C major scale (and a reference to the peculiar whole tone scale) and insist that it all begs to resolve to something C-majorish.

But consider a more contemporary context, such as slightly sophisticated blues from about 1935 on, and all the styles spun from that thread: blues-based jazz, R'n'B, funk, rock, and contemporary dance music. In these styles, a ninth chord can easily start the party and continue to sit, happy as a clam, while all sorts of rhythmic and melodic hijinks percolate around it.

Now on to the rest of the ninth chords built upon the C major scale. Here's the ninth chord built upon the note A within the C major scale:

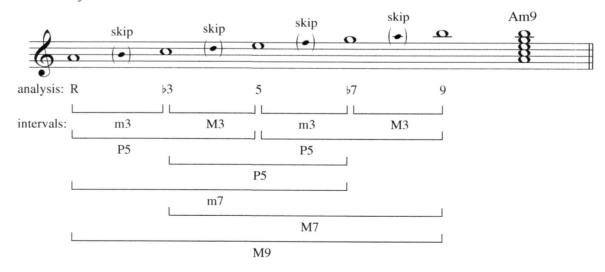

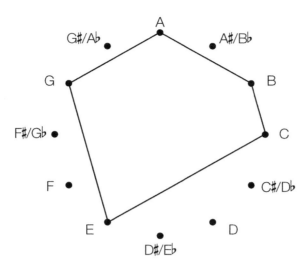

There are no surprises here; Am9 has the same structure as Dm9. It combines two traditionally pleasant and stable chords, Am7 and Am(add9), and three strong P5 dyads (A5, C5, and E5). Besides the Am triad, there are C major and E minor triads, all secure members of the C major tonality. As with Dm9, it has a settled quality as a kind of hyper-powerful minor chord.

Minor Seven Flat Five Flat Nine

Finally, let's look at the ninth chord built upon the note B within C major.

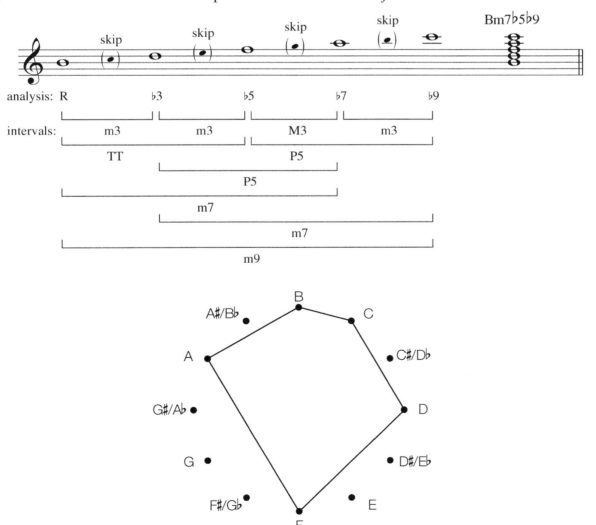

Bm7♭5♭9 is as knotty as its name suggests. It combines the unstable but functionally important Bm7♭5 with the unstable and functionally challenged B°add♭9. Looking at the dyads contained in this chord, you might think it to be relatively stable: one tritone B(♭5) along with two strong perfect 5ths (D5 and F5). Compare this with G9, which also has one tritone and two perfect 5ths. Ah, but G9's tritone is between the 3rd and the 7th of the chord, and this seems to keep it relatively stable to our ears. Bm7♭5♭9 has the pesky tritone between the root and the flatted 5th. Play with its inversions, and you might feel it tip towards a Dm13 or an Fmaj13#11. Compare it also to Em♭9—flatted 9ths are just plain unstable. The cluster A–B–C–D adds nothing in the way of insight. Also note that every note in Bm7♭5♭9 is identified in the name: B = root, m (♭3) = D, 7 (dominant or ♭7) = A, ♭5 = F, and ♭9 = C. Since chord names are supposed to be a kind of shorthand, we might wonder if this chord could be nick-named in the same way that Bm7♭5 became B half-diminished. I'm sure it could, but it would have to become part of our harmonic vocabulary first. As a chord type, the minor seventh flat five flat nine is one we don't need to explore further.

Naming and Dissecting Ninth Chords in the Harmonic Minor Tonality

Some of the stranger ninth chords will be uncovered in the harmonic minor tonality. Using C harmonic minor as our demonstration key, let's build some five-note snowman chords and see what we get.

Minor Major Nine

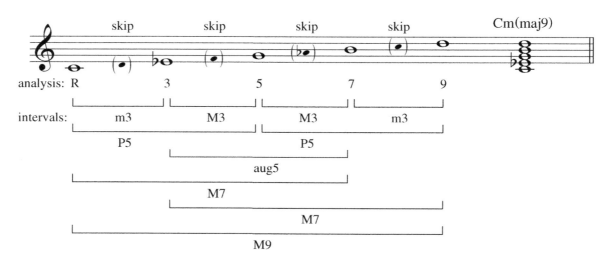

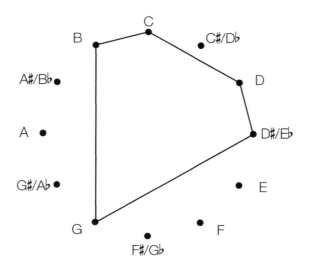

Just as Cm(maj7) presented an eerie and dark tonality, so Cm(maj9) extends that tonality. First, although there's a firm perfect 5th between the root (C) and the 5th (G) forming a C5 dyad, there's that woozy augmented 5th between the minor 3rd (E♭) and the 7th (B), which we can call E♭(♯5). Cm(maj9) also combines the qualities of the spooky Cm(maj7) with the moderately stable Cm(add9). As with all ninth chords, three triads coexist: in this case, they are Cm, E♭+, and G major. The cluster of B–C–D–E♭ suggests part of a diminished scale. This is a good campfire chord for telling ghost stories or perhaps ending a noir romantic ballad.

Now onto the ninth chord built off the second note in C harmonic minor.

Minor Seven Flat Five Flat Nine

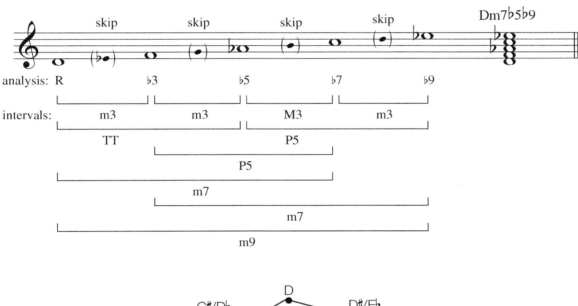

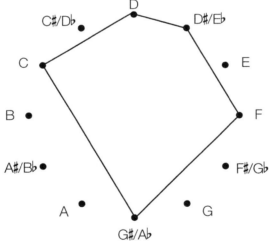

It's Dm7♭5♭9. As a collection of dyads, there's D(♭5), F5, and A♭5. It can also be looked upon as a meeting of three triads—D°, Fm, and A♭—and as two seventh chords: Dm7♭5 and Dm(add♭9). The overall effect is of a moderately unstable chord. This chord type was introduced just earlier as part of C major, so check on Bm7♭5♭9 for any further insight, then file this chord as a rare one.

Major Nine Sharp Five

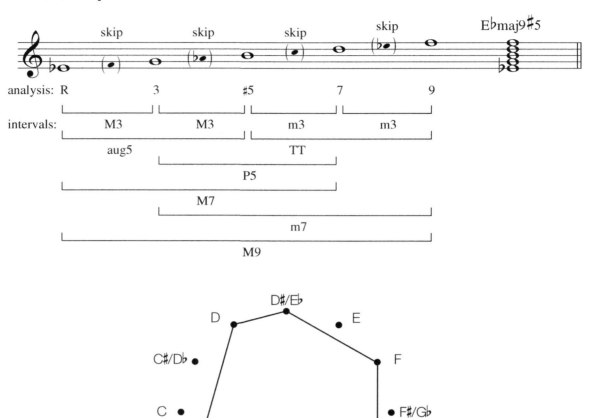

Because E♭maj9 is a relatively common and stable chord, the ninth chord built on the third note of the harmonic minor scale is given a name that reflects that commonality. Consider its alternate name: E♭+maj9. That's acceptable, but E♭maj9♯5 is probably the more common name—although "common" is not a word you'd associate with this chord. The dyads: E♭(♯5), G5, and B(♭5)—don't bode well for stability, nor do the triads (E♭+, G major, and B°) or the seventh chords (E♭maj7♯5 and G7). In fact, the G7 quality so dominates this chord (forgive the pun) that the root sounds somewhat out of place. Don't expect this ninth chord to show up on many charts.

Minor Nine

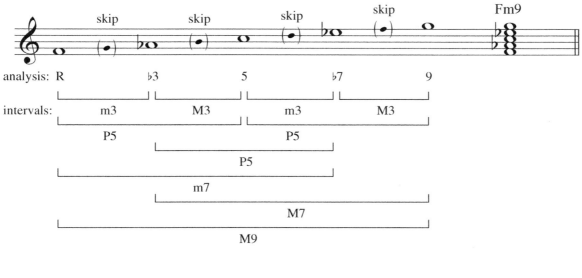

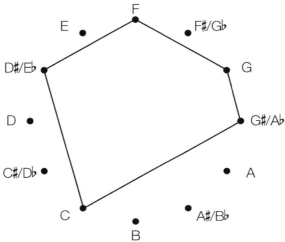

Fm9 is a chord type that was introduced in C major, so check back to Dm9 and Am9 to confirm the stable and common quality of this chord.

Seven Flat Nine

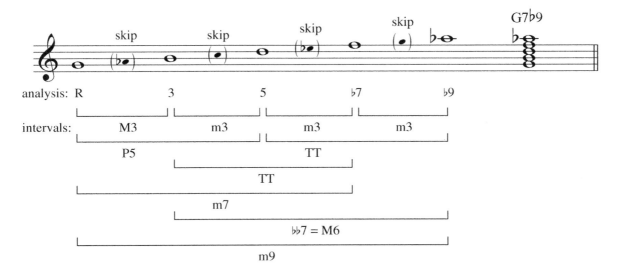

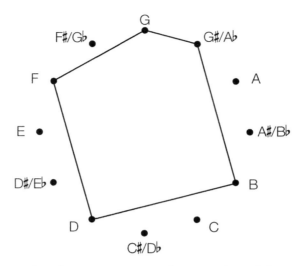

G7♭9 is full of instability and tension but functions supremely as an altered dominant chord. This is one to know well, as it works extremely well in any situation where a V–i or V–I cadence occurs (and the chord is voiced so as not to interfere with the melody). The G5 dyad is the pillar of stability, while the two tritone dyads of B(♭5) and F(♭5) point to the diminished chords found herein. G7♭9 is a teaming of G major, B diminished, and D diminished or, if you prefer, B°7 and G7. Practically speaking, think of it as a B°7 with a G added as the lowest note. Looking at the circle diagram, it's very easy to see the nearly square symmetrical structure of the four-note diminished seventh/diminished sixth chord. The root (G) is almost a color note. In fact, once you see and hear the diminished seventh/diminished sixth chord as part of this chord, you can often dispense with the root altogether.

Major Seven Sharp Nine

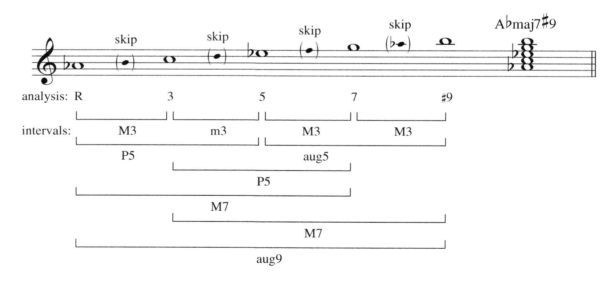

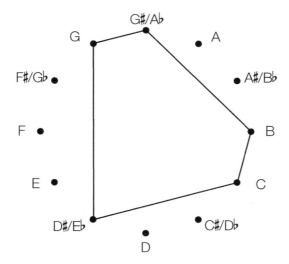

Abmaj7#9 is a possible chord, but not a probable one. The #9 sounds as a b3 (B♮ = Cb), and since the rest of the chord sounds as a pleasant and stable Abmaj7, the #9 sounds like an uninvited guest. Not recommended as a campfire chord.

Diminished Seven Flat Nine

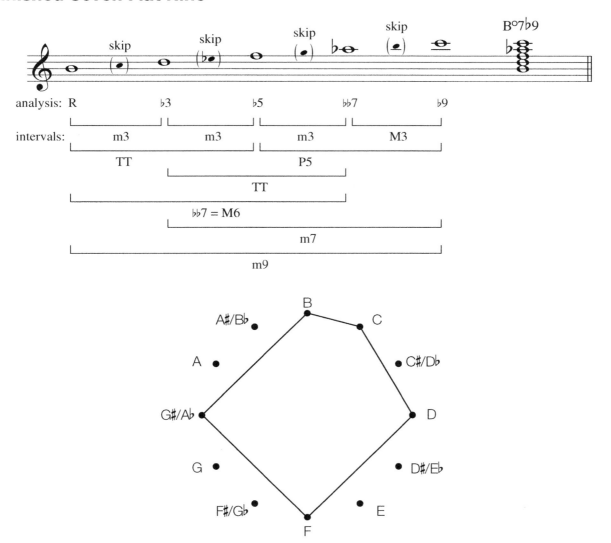

You might expect B°7♭9 to be a train wreck of useless diminution, but as long as the ♭9 (C) is voiced far enough away from the root, it functions well as an extended diminished chord. There are two tritone dyads—B(♭5) and D(♭5)—along with a stable F5. The triads here are B°, D°, and Fm. The seventh chords are B°7 and Dm7♭5.

Open Position Ninth Chords

We can begin to appreciate both the sound of the various ninth chords and the difficulty of playing complete ninth chords by creating some from open position chords. Let's begin with our old pal, C major.

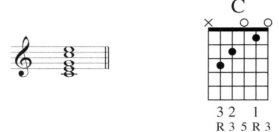

To turn this into a complete Cmaj9, we need to add a major seventh (B) and a 9th (D) without losing the root (C), 3rd (E), or 5th (G). It might seem obvious to begin by swapping out the high root and 3rd on the B and E strings for a 7th and 9th. After all, the chord already has a root, 3rd, and 5th on the A, D, and G strings. So add the major 7th by lifting your first finger from the B string, allowing the open B to ring.

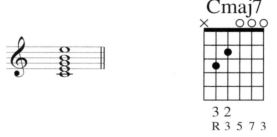

This is a Cmaj7 chord. Now all we have to do is add the 9th (D) on top… but there's no comfortable D nearby on the E string, is there? So perhaps we can leave the open E string as the 3rd of the chord and add a D on the D string by removing the second finger.

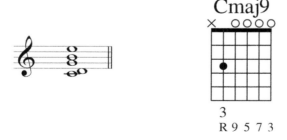

This is a complete Cmaj9 chord. It will be up to you, the player, to decide if that C–D crush works or not.

Let's build some more complete major ninth chords. Beginning with G major, can we find a way to add a major 7th and a 9th to it?

With three roots and two 3rds to swap out, it shouldn't be too hard. Let's try dropping the highest root down to add a major 7th, like this:

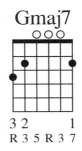

Now we need to add the 9th (A) somewhere. You might try the open A string, but I find that too muddy sounding. Instead, try adding an A on the G string and moving the fingers around, like this:

(Attempting to hold the low B on the A string would make for some miserable fingering problems.) The resulting sound is pleasing, and all the notes are accounted for.

How about a minor ninth chord? Em9 is a good candidate. (Remember that the minor ninth chord is spelled R–♭3–5–♭7–9.) Start with Em:

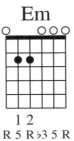

Now simply change the location of the second finger to add both the flatted 7th and the 9th.

With plenty of open strings and a full low open root note, Em9 can be voiced several other ways. For example, this fingering accentuates the dissonance of the ♭3 and the 9:

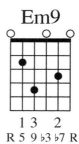

While this voicing sounds a little more open and bright:

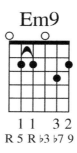

Now let's tackle the dominant ninth chord, spelled R–3–5–♭7–9. We can cheat a bit and go back to one of our earlier major ninth chords to find some demonstrative fingerings; morphing Gmaj9 into G9 works well. Here again is Gmaj9.

Just flat the 7th by moving it down one fret and you have a complete G9 chord.

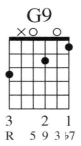

Incidentally, we can build a few complete ninth chords in close voicing by taking advantage of open strings. Here's an A9:

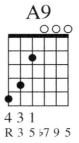

This can be easily morphed into an Am9, like this:

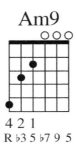

In both of the chords above, you can hear the purest form (root position, no doubled notes) by not playing the high E string.

Similar ninth chord fingerings can be constructed for D9 and Dm9.

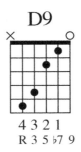

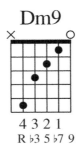

Technique Tip:

The D9 and Dm9 chords are good "yoga" fingerings. They are pleasant, stable chords that make you stretch your fingers to cover a five-fret range and require your fourth finger to reach across the fretboard—two bits of technique that differentiate an early (or a lazy) beginner from a more advanced beginning guitarist. The yoga approach to chord fingering is this:

- Be sure your posture and playing position are good. Your back should be straight, your feet should be stable, and your grip of the guitar should be stable, too.

- Finger the chord you want to work with, but don't play it. Take a deep breath through your nose, using your diaphragm to pull air in.

- As you exhale, play the chord one note at a time as a ringing arpeggio. Don't try to correct any dead or buzzing notes; simply let the chord sound.

- Repeat this two or three times at first. This should take about thirty seconds.

- Practice this regularly, and see if you can improve the sound of the chord and increase the holding of the chord to ten breaths.

All Possible Closed-Voicing Ninth Chords in Root Position

Back in Chapter Four, I introduced a chart to generate and crosscheck all the possible tertiary triads. We've used this same kind of chart to explore tertiary seventh chords and the "color note" chords. Now let's apply it to ninth chords, but with some limitations, because, from a mathematical standpoint, the number of possible ninth chord names is huge. Fortunately, as we already discovered in Chapter Five when we worked with seventh chords, there's a difference between what is possible on paper and what is practical in music.

1. We can't pair a 9th with a sus two—nine and two are different analytical names for the same note.

2. We can't pair a sharp 9th with a minor triad—sharp nine and flat three are different analytical names for the same note.

3. We won't pair a 9th with a sus four. It simply isn't done in our current chord-naming practice. That particular sound is part of the family of eleventh chords, coming up later in this chapter.

4. Certain chord names imply clusters of notes not used in our current chord-naming practice. Anything containing a root note, a major 7th, and a flat 9th would imply a three-note chromatic cluster. We just don't go there.

Let's bring back the list of seventeen different seventh chords, add as many 9ths as possible while applying the limitations just mentioned, and see what we get.

Seventh Chords from the Major Scale, Plus 9ths

Seventh Chord	Added Ninth	Resulting chord	Music notation, circle chart and commentary
Seventh chord type: major seventh	**Added ninth:** flat nine	**Resulting chord type:** Nonexistent. 7–R–♭9 implies a chromatic cluster.	
Analysis notation: R–3–5–7	**Analysis notation:** ♭9		
Example: Cmaj7	**Example:** D♭		
Seventh chord type: major seventh	**Added ninth:** nine	**Resulting chord type:** Major ninth	This is a stable and consonant chord, essential to know. It is found as the Imaj9 and IVmaj9 in the major tonality.
Analysis notation: R–3–5–7	**Analysis notation:** 9	**Resulting analysis notation:** R–3–5–7–9	
Example: Cmaj7	**Example:** D	**Example:** Cmaj9	
Seventh chord type: major seventh	**Added ninth:** sharp nine	**Resulting chord type:** Major seven sharp nine? Practically nonexistent.	
Analysis notation: R–3–5–7	**Analysis notation:** ♯9		
Example: Cmaj7	**Example:** D♯		

Seventh chord type: minor seven	Added ninth: flat nine	Resulting chord type: minor seven flat nine	
Analysis notation: R–♭3–5–♭7	**Analysis notation:** ♭9	**Resulting analysis notation:** R–♭3–5–♭7–♭9	Cm7♭9
Example: Cm7	**Example:** D♭	**Example:** Cm7♭9	E♭13 Theoretically possible as the iii♭7♭9 in the major tonality, but far more probable as an incomplete thirteenth chord, as shown. E♭13 is also pleasantly stable and plausible.
Seventh chord type: minor seven	**Added ninth:** nine	**Resulting chord type:** minor nine	Cm9
Analysis notation: R–♭3–5–♭7	**Analysis notation:** 9	**Resulting analysis notation:** R–♭3–5–♭7–9	
Example: Cm7	**Example:** D	**Example:** Cm9	This is a stable and consonant chord, essential to know. It is found as the ii9 and the vi9 in the major tonality, as the iv9 in the harmonic minor tonality, and functions well as a stable i chord in any minor tonality.

Seventh chord type: minor seven	Added ninth: sharp nine	Resulting chord type: Nonexistent. The minor 3rd (♭3) and sharp nine (♯9) are enharmonic notes.	
Analysis notation: R–♭3–5–♭7	Analysis notation: ♯9		
Example: Cm7	Example: D♯		
Seventh chord type: seven	**Added ninth:** flat nine	**Resulting chord type:** seven flat nine	C7♭9
Analysis notation: R–3–5–♭7	**Analysis notation:** ♭9	**Resulting analysis notation:** R–3–5–♭7–♭9	
Example: C7	**Example:** D♭	**Example:** C7♭9	This chord is found as the V7(♭9) in the harmonic minor scale and is a very important functioning dominant chord. Also note its nearly symmetrical square shape in the circle diagram, relating it to the diminished scale.
Seventh chord type: seven	**Added ninth:** nine	**Resulting chord type:** nine	C9
Analysis notation: R–3–5–♭7	**Analysis notation:** 9	**Resulting analysis notation:** R–3–5–♭7–9	
Example: C7	**Example:** D	**Example:** C9	This chord is found in the major scale as V9 and is a very important functioning dominant chord as well as an accepted stable chord.

Seventh chord type: seven	Added ninth: sharp nine	Resulting chord type: seven sharp nine	
Analysis notation: R–3–5–♭7	**Analysis notation:** ♯9	**Resulting analysis notation:** R–3–5–♭7–♯9	
Example: C7	**Example:** D♯	**Example:** C7♯9	Although this chord isn't properly found in either the major or harmonic minor scales, it is a very important functioning dominant chord as well as an accepted stable chord.

Seventh chord type: minor seven flat five	Added ninth: flat nine	Resulting chord type: minor seven flat five flat nine	
Analysis notation: R–♭3–♭5–♭7	**Analysis notation:** ♭9	**Resulting analysis notation:** R–♭3–♭5–♭7–♭9	
Example: Cm7♭5	**Example:** D♭	**Example:** Cm7♭5♭9	

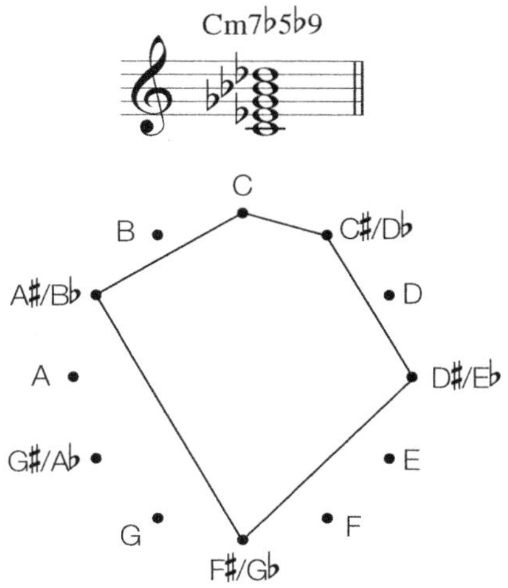

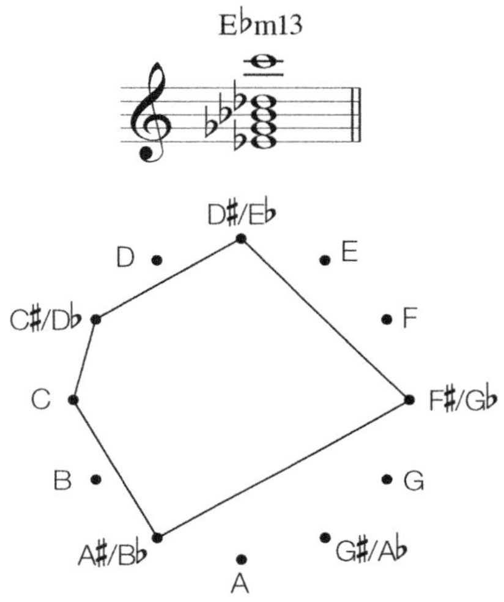

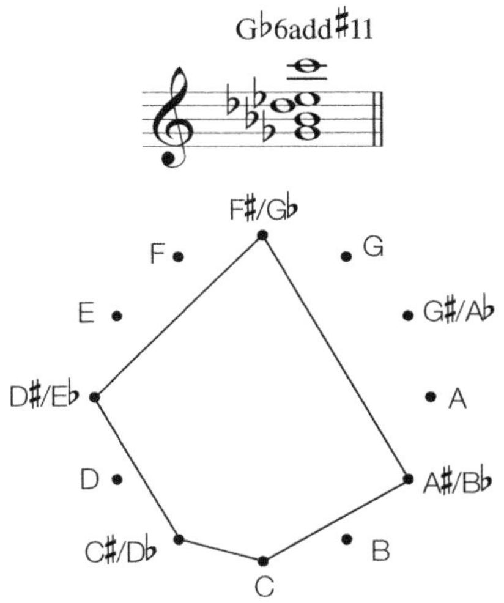

Cm7♭5♭9

E♭m13

G♭6add♯11

This chord may be used as an extended ii chord in the minor tonality. It is also theoretically possible as the vii°♭7♭9 in the major tonality, but far more probable as an incomplete minor thirteenth chord—or as a sixth add sharp eleven, as shown.

Seventh chord type: minor seven flat five	Added ninth: ninth	Resulting chord type: minor nine flat five
Analysis notation: R–♭3–♭5–♭7	Analysis notation: 9	Resulting analysis notation: R–♭3–♭5–♭7–9
Example: Cm7♭5	Example: D	Example: Cm9♭5

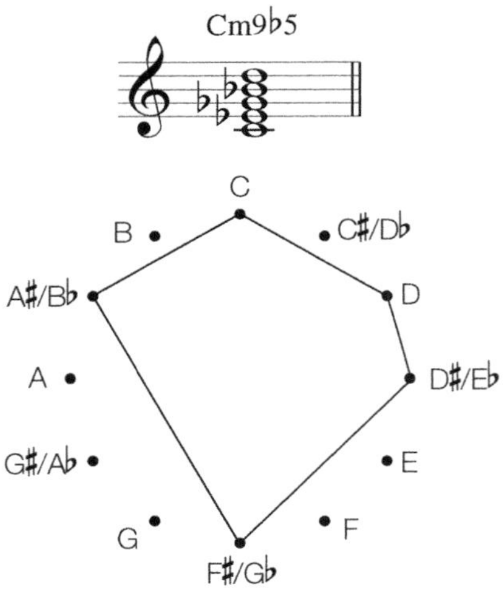

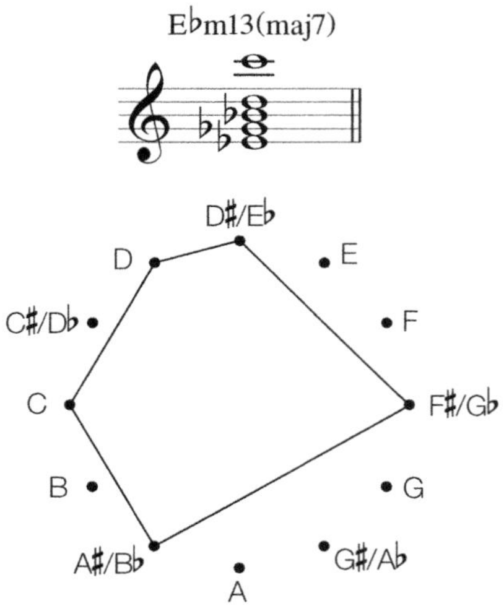

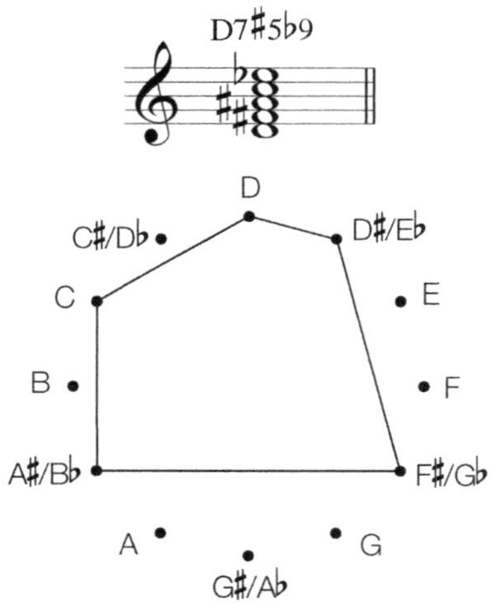

Cm9♭5

E♭m13(maj7)

D7♯5♭9

This is a moody and dark chord when played with the root as the lowest note. It could be the vi°9 of the melodic minor tonality. Re-voicing and renaming Cm9♭5 yields E♭m13(maj7) or the far more common D7♯5♭9.

Seventh chord type: minor seven flat five	**Added ninth:** sharp ninth	**Resulting chord type:** Nonexistent. The minor 3rd ($\flat$3) and sharp nine ($\sharp$9) are enharmonic notes.
Analysis notation: R–$\flat$3–$\flat$5–$\flat$7	**Analysis notation:** $\sharp$9	
Example: Cm7$\flat$5	**Example:** D$\sharp$	
Seventh chord type: seven sus two	No ninth can be added to a sus two chord, because the 2nd and the 9th are the same note. Any seven sus two chord can be considered an incomplete ninth chord.	
Analysis notation: R–2–5–$\flat$7		
Example: C7sus2		
Seventh chord type: seven sus four	If a 9th is added to a seven sus four chord, it is named as an eleventh chord.	
Analysis notation: R–4–5–$\flat$7		
Example: C7sus4		
Seventh chord type: major seven flat five	The major seven flat five chord is more commonly named major seven sharp eleven. As an eleventh chord, the 9th may or may not be added.	
Analysis notation: R–3–$\flat$5–7		
Example: Cmaj7$\flat$5		

Seventh chord type: minor seven sharp five	Added ninth: flat nine	Resulting chord type: minor seven sharp five flat nine	
Analysis notation: R–♭3–♯5–♭7	Analysis notation: ♭9	Resulting analysis notation: R–♭3–♯5–♭7–♭9	
Example: Cm7♯5	Example: D♭	Example: Cm7♯5♭9	

As named, this chord fits no common tonality. But renamed, it can be a five-note cluster from the major tonality, as shown. |

Seventh chord type: minor seven sharp five	Added ninth: ninth	Resulting chord type: minor nine sharp five	
Analysis notation: R–♭3–♯5–♭7	**Analysis notation:** 9	**Resulting analysis notation:** R–♭3–♯5–♭7–9	
Example: Cm7♯5	**Example:** D	**Example:** Cm9♯5	As named, this chord fits no common tonality. But renamed, it can be a five-note cluster from the major tonality, as shown.
Seventh chord type: minor seven sharp five	**Added ninth:** sharp ninth	**Resulting chord type**: Nonexistent. The minor 3rd (♭3) and sharp nine (♯9) are enharmonic notes.	
Analysis notation: R–♭3–♯5–♭7	**Analysis notation:** ♯9		
Example: Cm7♯5	**Example:** D♯		
Seventh chord type: major seventh sus four	If a 9th is added to a seven sus four chord, it is named as an eleventh chord.		
Analysis notation: R–4–5–7			
Example: Cmaj7sus4			

Seventh Chords from the Harmonic Minor Scale, Plus 9ths

Seventh Chord	Added Ninth	Resulting chord	Music notation, circle chart and commentary
Seventh chord type: minor major seven	**Added ninth:** flat nine		**Resulting chord type:** Cannot be named in our current system. 7–R–♭9 implies a chromatic cluster.
Analysis notation: R–♭3–5–7	**Analysis notation:** ♭9		
Example: Cm(maj7)	**Example:** D♭		
Seventh chord type: minor major seventh	**Added ninth:** nine	**Resulting chord type:** minor nine major seventh	
Analysis notation: R–♭3–5–7	**Analysis notation:** 9	**Resulting analysis notation:** R–♭3–5–7–9	
Example: Cm(maj7)	**Example:** D	**Example:** Cm9(maj7)	This is the i(maj9) chord in the harmonic minor tonality.
Seventh chord type: minor major seven	**Added ninth:** sharp nine		**Resulting chord type:** Nonexistent. The minor 3rd (♭3) and sharp nine (♯9) are enharmonic notes.
Analysis notation: R–♭3–5–7	**Analysis notation:** ♯9		
Example: Cm(maj7)	**Example:** D♯		

Seventh chord type: diminished seven	Added ninth: flat nine	Resulting chord type: diminished seventh flat nine	
Analysis notation: R–♭3–♭5–♭♭7	Analysis notation: ♭9	Resulting analysis notation: R–♭3–♭5–♭♭7–♭9	
Example: C°7	Example: D♭	Example: C°7♭9	Although this chord could be the ii°7♭9 in the harmonic minor tonality, it can also be renamed and re-voiced as D♯m13♭5.

Seventh chord type: diminished seven	Added ninth: nine	Resulting chord type: diminished nine
Analysis notation: R–♭3–♭5–♭♭7	Analysis notation: 9	Resulting analysis notation: R–♭3–♭5–♭♭7–9
Example: C°7	Example: D	Example: C°9

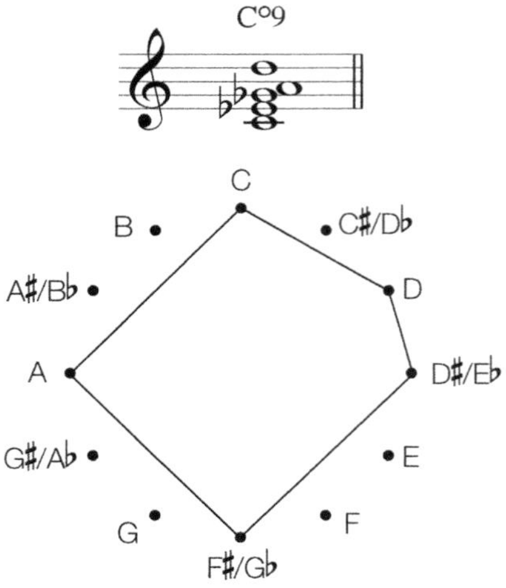

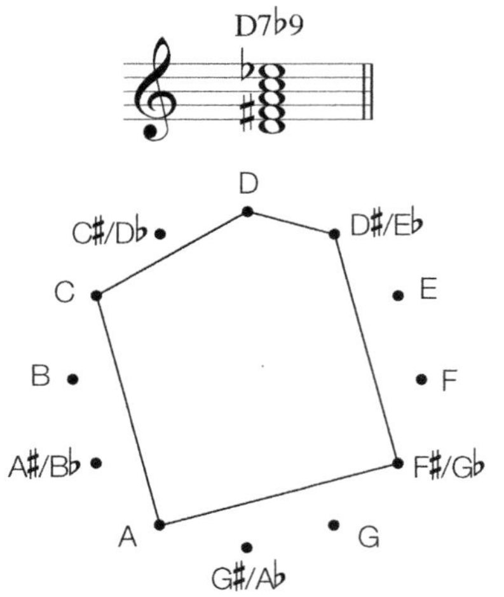

C°9

D7♭9

This chord is enharmonically equivalent to D7♭9, a far more common type. See earlier comments in this chart on the seven flat nine chord.

Seventh chord type: diminished seven	Added ninth: sharp ninth	Resulting chord type: Nonexistent. The minor 3rd (♭3) and sharp nine (♯9) are enharmonic notes.
Analysis notation: R–♭3–♭5–♭♭7	Analysis notation: ♯9	
Example: C°7	Example: D♯	

Seventh chord type: seven sharp five	Added ninth: flat nine	Resulting chord type: seven sharp five flat nine	
Analysis notation: R–3–#5–♭7	**Analysis notation:** ♭9	**Resulting analysis notation:** R–3–#5–♭7–♭9	
Example: C7#5	**Example:** D♭	**Example:** C7#5♭9	This is found as the V7#5♭9 chord in the harmonic minor scale.

Seventh chord type: seven sharp five	Added ninth: nine	Resulting chord type: nine sharp five
Analysis notation: R–3–#5–b7	**Analysis notation:** 9	**Resulting analysis notation:** R–3–#5–b7–9
Example: C7#5	**Example:** D	**Example:** C9#5

It is an essential altered dominant chord. The notes of this chord imply the ***melodic minor scale***, a scale not deeply addressed in this book but vital to know. It can be re-voiced and renamed as Bb9b5. Also note its construction as a cluster chord in the whole tone scale.

Seventh chord type: seven sharp five	Added ninth: sharp ninth	Resulting chord type: seven sharp five sharp nine	
Analysis notation: R–3–#5–♭7	**Analysis notation:** #9	**Resulting analysis notation:** R–3–#5–♭7–#9	
Example: C7#5	**Example:** D#	**Example:** C7#5#9	

The added sharp nine puts this chord outside of any traditional tonality, but it is an essential altered dominant chord.

Seventh chord type: major seven sharp five	Added ninth: flat nine	**Resulting chord type:** Cannot be named in our current system. 7–R–♭9 implies a chromatic cluster.	
Analysis notation: R–3–#5–7	**Analysis notation:** ♭9		
Example: Cmaj7#5	**Example:** D♭		

Seventh chord type: major seven sharp five	Added ninth: nine	Resulting chord type: major nine sharp five
Analysis notation: R–3–#5–7	Analysis notation: 9	Resulting analysis notation: R–3–#5–7–9
Example: Cmaj7#5	Example: D	Example: Cmaj9#5

This could be more easily named as a slash chord; Cmaj9#5 could be E7/C.

Seventh chord type: major seven sharp five	Added ninth: sharp ninth	Resulting chord type: major seven sharp five sharp nine
Analysis notation: R–3–#5–7	Analysis notation: #9	Resulting analysis notation: R–3–#5–7–#9
Example: Cmaj7#5	Example: D#	Example: Cmaj7#5#9

The added sharp nine takes this chord out of the harmonic minor tonality, and it can be more easily named as a slash chord; Cmaj7#5#9 could be Emaj7/C.

Seventh Chords from the Diminished and Whole Tone Scales, Plus 9ths

Seventh Chord	Added Ninth	Resulting chord	Music notation, circle chart and commentary
Seventh chord type: seven flat five	**Added ninth:** flat nine	**Resulting chord type:** seven flat five flat nine	
Analysis notation: R–3–♭5–♭7	**Analysis notation:** ♭9	**Resulting analysis notation:** R–3–♭5–♭7–♭9	
Example: C7♭5	**Example:** D♭	**Example:** C7♭5♭9	

This is a very common altered dominant chord. The flatted 9th pulls it out of the whole tone scale and makes it part of the diminished scale. Notice how it is equivalent to F♯7♯11, and the chord could be easily renamed F♯7/C.

Seventh chord type: seven flat five	Added ninth: nine	Resulting chord type: nine flat five	
Analysis notation: R–3–♭5–♭7	**Analysis notation:** 9	**Resulting analysis notation:** R–3–♭5–♭7–9	
Example: C7♭5	**Example:** D	**Example:** C9♭5	This is a very common altered dominant chord. The 9th pulls it out of the diminished scale and makes it part of the whole tone scale. It is a five-note cluster of whole tone scale notes. Notice how it is equivalent to D9#5; the nine sharp five chord is found earlier in this chart.
Seventh chord type: seven flat five	**Added ninth:** sharp ninth	**Resulting chord type:** seven flat five sharp nine	
Analysis notation: R–3–♭5–♭7	**Analysis notation:** #9	**Resulting analysis notation:** R–3–♭5–♭7–#9	
Example: C7♭5	**Example:** D#	**Example:** C7♭5#9	This is a very common altered dominant chord. The sharp 9th pulls it out of the whole tone scale and makes it part of the diminished scale.

As I've said before at points like this, the preceding chart is a deceptively easy way to organize chordal information—and it is information at its most undigested. Understanding ninth chords on the guitar is harder, for at least three good reasons:

1. They can almost never be played in basic R–3–5–7–9 (root position, close voicing) form.

2. They are almost never played with all five notes sounding. One or two notes are usually left out.

3. Some of these chords are far more common that others. I've already commented on this at certain points in the chart and text. We'll discuss their use later in this chapter.

First, let's work on some practical movable fingerings of ninth chords. Earlier in the chapter, I demonstrated how difficult it was to play a complete ninth chord in root position and close voicing. The few I presented required open strings, and so they don't function as movable fingerings. Complete ninth chords can be played using other voicings, but most of the time at least one note will be omitted from the chord, as you'll see in the following block diagrams. These include all of the ninth chords from the chart.

Here are the rules I'll use for ninth chord fingerings:

- All fingerings will include at least the root, 7th, and 9th.

- Some fingerings will include the 3rd and 5th, and some will omit one of these two notes.

- If the 5th is altered, it must be included; otherwise, why name it?

- Any major ninth chord that's played without the 3rd can substitute for a minor nine major seventh chord.

- All minor ninth chords shown will have the flatted or minor 3rd (♭3) in the voicing.

- Any dominant ninth chord that's played without a 3rd can substitute for a minor ninth chord.

Practical Fingerings of Ninth Chords
Major Ninth

A)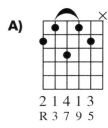

2 1 4 1 3
R 3 7 9 5

B)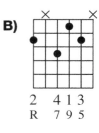

2 4 1 3
R   7 9 5

C)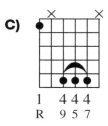

1   4 4 4
R   9 5 7

D)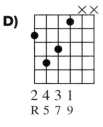

2 4 3 1
R 5 7 9

E)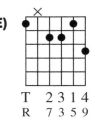

T 2 3 1 4
R 7 3 5 9

F)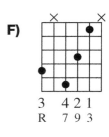

3 4 2 1
R 7 9 3

G)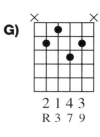

2 1 4 3
R 3 7 9

H)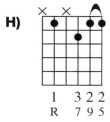

1 3 2 2
R 7 9 5

I)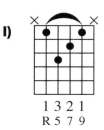

1 3 2 1
R 5 7 9

J)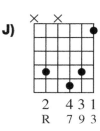

2 4 3 1
R 7 9 3

K)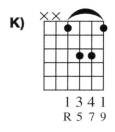

1 3 4 1
R 5 7 9

L)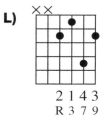

2 1 4 3
R 3 7 9

B), C), D), H), I), and K): Because these voicings do not include a 3rd, they can function as minor nine major seven chords. They can also be renamed as X/4 slash chords. For example, B), when played at the fifth fret, could be B♭maj9, B♭m9maj7, or F/B♭.

Minor Nine

A)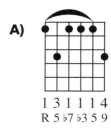

1 3 1 1 1 4
R 5 ♭7 ♭3 5 9

B)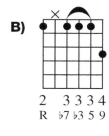

2 3 3 3 4
R ♭7 ♭3 5 9

C)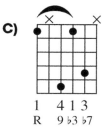

1 4 1 3
R 9 ♭3 ♭7

D)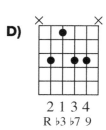

2 1 3 4
R ♭3 ♭7 9

E)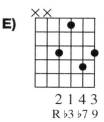

2 1 4 3
R ♭3 ♭7 9

Minor Nine Major Seven

A)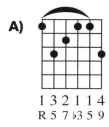

1 3 2 1 1 4
R 5 7 ♭3 5 9

B)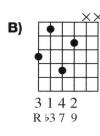

3 1 4 2
R ♭3 7 9

C)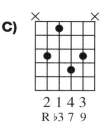

2 1 4 3
R ♭3 7 9

D)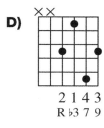

2 1 4 3
R ♭3 7 9

"Plain" or Dominant Ninth

A)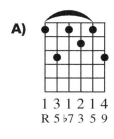

1 3 1 2 1 4
R 5 ♭7 3 5 9

B)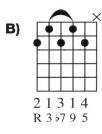

2 1 3 1 4
R 3 ♭7 9 5

C)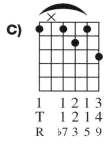

1   1 2 1 3
T   1 2 1 4
R   ♭7 3 5 9

D)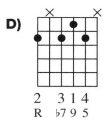

2   3 1 4
R   ♭7 9 5

E)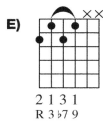

2 1 3 1
R 3 ♭7 9

F)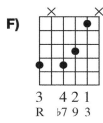

3   4 2 1
R   ♭7 9 3

G)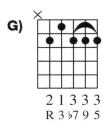

2 1 3 3 3
R 3 ♭7 9 5

H)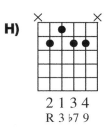

2 1 3 4
R 3 ♭7 9

I)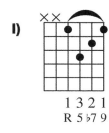

1 3 2 1
R 5 ♭7 9

J)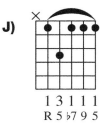

1 3 1 1 1
R 5 ♭7 9 5

K)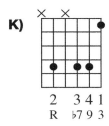

2   3 4 1
R   ♭7 9 3

D), I), and J): Because these voicings do not include a 3rd, they can function as minor nine chords. They can also be renamed as Xm/4 slash chords. For example, D), when played at the fifth fret, could be B♭9, B♭m9, or Fm/B♭.

Altered Dominant – Seven Sharp Nine

A)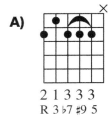

2 1 3 3 3
R 3 ♭7 #9 5

B)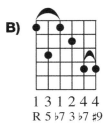

1 3 1 2 4 4
R 5 ♭7 3 ♭7 #9

C)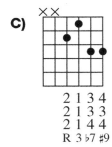

2 1 3 4
2 1 3 3
2 1 4 4
R 3 ♭7 #9

D)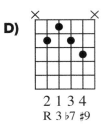

2 1 3 4
R 3 ♭7 #9

E)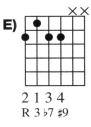

2 1 3 4
R 3 ♭7 #9

Altered Dominant – Seven Flat Five Flat Nine

A)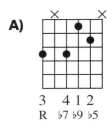

3   4 1 2
R   ♭7 ♭9 ♭5

B)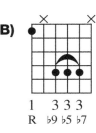

1   3 3 3
R   ♭9 ♭5 ♭7

C)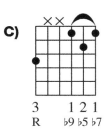

3   1 2 1
R   ♭9 ♭5 ♭7

D)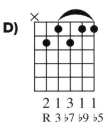

2 1 3 1 1
R 3 ♭7 ♭9 ♭5

E)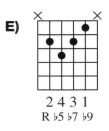

2 4 3 1
R ♭5 ♭7 ♭9

F)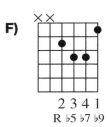

2 3 4 1
R ♭5 ♭7 ♭9

A), B), C), E), and F): Because these voicings do not include a 3rd, they can function as minor seven flat five flat nine chords. They can also be renamed as X/TT slash chords. For example, A, when played at the fifth fret, could be B7♭5♭9, Bm7♭5♭9, or F/B.

Altered Dominant – Nine Flat Five

A)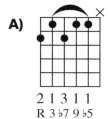

2 1 3 1 1
R 3 ♭7 9 ♭5

B)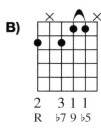

2   3 1 1
R   ♭7 9 ♭5

C)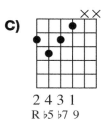

2 4 3 1
R ♭5 ♭7 9

D)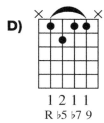

1 2 1 1
R ♭5 ♭7 9

E)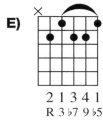

2 1 3 4 1
R 3 ♭7 9 ♭5

F)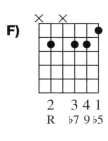

2   3 4 1
R   ♭7 9 ♭5

G)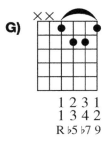

1 2 3 1
1 3 4 2
R ♭5 ♭7 9

B), C), D), F), and G): Because these voicings do not include a 3rd, they can function as minor nine flat five chords. They can also be renamed as X+/2, X+/♭7 or X+/TT. For example, B), when played at the fifth fret, could be B♭9♭5, B♭m9♭5, A♭+/♭B, C+/B♭, or E+/B♭.

Altered Dominant – Seven Flat Five Sharp Nine

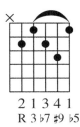

2 1 3 4 1
R 3 ♭7 ♯9 ♭5

Although this is a common altered dominant chord, it is very difficult to play all the notes in one voicing on the guitar. Focus on the minor triad created by the ♭7, ♯9 and ♭5. Then add either the third or the root of the chord as named. For example, C7♭5♯9 can be played as either D♯m/E or E♭m/C.

Altered Dominant – Seven Flat Nine

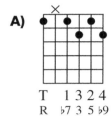

A)

T 1 3 2 4
R ♭7 3 5 ♭9

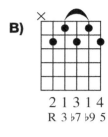

B)

2 1 3 1 4
R 3 ♭7 ♭9 5

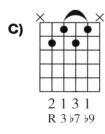

C)

2 1 3 1
R 3 ♭7 ♭9

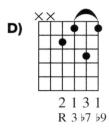

D)

2 1 3 1
R 3 ♭7 ♭9

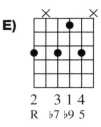

E)

2 3 1 4
R ♭7 ♭9 5

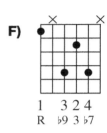

F)

1 3 2 4
R ♭9 3 ♭7

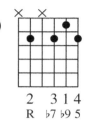

G)

2 3 1 4
R ♭7 ♭9 5

A very common stubstitution for seven flat nine chords is to not play the root and think of the chord as a dimished seven chord a minor second above the omitted root. For example, A), when played at the fifth fret, could have the low A omitted and be played as A♯dim7.

Altered Dominant – Seven Sharp Five Flat Nine

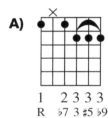

A)

1 2 3 3 3
R ♭7 3 ♯5 ♭9

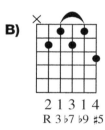

B)

2 1 3 1 4
R 3 ♭7 ♭9 ♯5

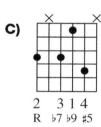

C)

2 3 1 4
R ♭7 ♭9 ♯5

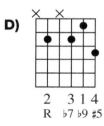

D)

2 3 1 4
R ♭7 ♭9 ♯5

Altered Dominant – Nine Sharp Five

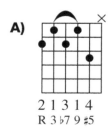

A)

2 1 3 1 4
R 3 ♭7 9 ♯5

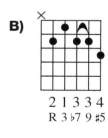

B)

2 1 3 3 4
R 3 ♭7 9 ♯5

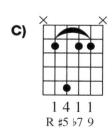

C)

1 4 1 1
R ♯5 ♭7 9

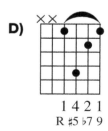

D)

1 4 2 1
R ♯5 ♭7 9

Miscellaneous

Diminished Seven Flat Nine	Diminished Nine Major Seven	Major Nine Sharp Five	Major Seven Sharp Five Sharp Nine	Major Seven Sharp Five Sharp Nine
A)	**B)**	**C)**	**D)**	**E)**
4 1 2 1 3	T 3 2 1 4	2 1 3 1 4	4 3 2 1 1	2 1 3 3 3
R ♭3 ♭♭7 ♭9 ♭5	R 7 ♭3 ♭5 9	R 3 7 9 ♯5	R 3 ♯5 7 ♯9	R 3 7 ♯9 ♯5

A Ninth Chord Cookbook: Inversions

All of the preceding chords have been shown in root position. If you need an inversion of any of these chords, there are two approaches for finding them on the guitar: *linear*, where the chord remains on the same string set but is moved up or down the neck to accommodate the new voicing, and *lateral*, where the chord remains in the same area of the neck but one or more notes are shifted to higher or lower strings.

To construct a linear inversion of a ninth chord, follow this recipe:

- Begin with a root position voicing. For a practical example, we'll begin with Cmaj9.

Cmaj9

2 1 4 3
R 3 7 9

- Draw out a Schillinger circle showing the functioning notes of the chord.

R

7   9

5   3

Notice that, although the fingering shown does not include the 3rd, it is included in the Schillinger circle.

- To move the voicing up, the string that plays the root of the chord will now play the ninth (or second), the string with the ninth (or second) will play the 3rd, and so on. The motion in the Schillinger circle will look like this:

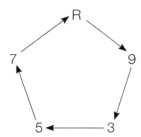

- → On the A string, the root (C) at the 3rd fret will move up to the second (D) at the fifth fret.
- → On the D string, the 3rd (E) at the second fret will move up to the 5th (G) at the fifth fret.
- → On the G string, the major 7th (B) at the fourth fret will move to the root (C) at the fifth fret.
- → On the B string, the 9th (D) at the third fret will move to the 3rd (E) at the fifth fret.
- Here's the resulting fingering and voicing:

Notice that the chord is renamed as simply as possible to show what it contains. There is no major 7th in this voicing because there was no fifth in the previous voicing.

- Perhaps this voicing is not satisfying to you; perhaps you crave the major 7th. In that case, consider either adding the major 7th on another string, as shown here…

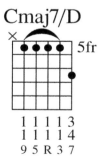

… or omitting one note and replacing it with the one you desire; the 5th could be replaced with the 7th, and this heroic fingering would be the result.

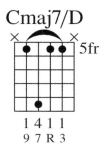

Cmaj7/D

Let's try another turn of the Schillinger circle.

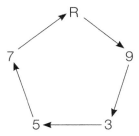

Returning to C/D, move up like this:

→ On the A string, the 9th (D) will move up to the 3rd (E).

→ On the D string, the 5th (G) will move up to the 7th (B).

→ On the G string, the root (C) will move up to the 9th (D).

→ On the B string, the 3rd (E) will move up to the 5th (G).

• Here's the resulting fingering, voicing, and—surprise!—new name.

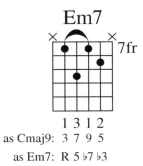

Em7

as Cmaj9: 3 7 9 5

as Em7: R 5 ♭7 ♭3

Notice that the chord no longer has the root note (C) and is named Em7.

• If you like this voicing, but want to bring the root back, try the knuckle-buster shown here.

Cmaj9

You might explore the next two turns of the Schilling circle on your own.

To construct a lateral inversion of a chord, try eliminating the lowest note and adding a note on a higher, unoccupied string.

- For example, begin with this voicing of a Cmaj9:

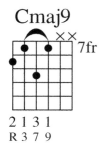

Cmaj9

2 1 3 1
R 3 7 9

- Eliminate the low root (C) from the low E string and look for another note you can add on the unoccupied B string. In this case, an appropriate note would be the 5th of the chord, the note G, which can be played at the eighth fret. Because the root is gone, the name of the chord should change to Em7, as shown. The resulting fingering and voicing looks like this.

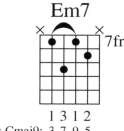

Em7

1 3 1 2
as Cmaj9: 3 7 9 5
as Em7: R 5 ♭7 ♭3

- If you miss the root note, try raising the major 7th up to the root, like this:

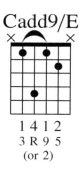

Cadd9/E

1 4 1 2
3 R 9 5
(or 2)

Since the major 7th is missing, the chord is renamed as Cadd9/E.

- If the lack of the major 7th leaves your heart empty, try adding it on the high E string with your first finger, like this:

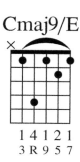

Cmaj9/E

1 4 1 2 1
3 R 9 5 7

This process of leapfrogging from lowest string to an unoccupied string can be repeated as long as you have an unoccupied string to move to. Both of these approaches to constructing inversions—the linear, up-and-down-the-neck approach and the lateral, string-to-string approach—are good exercises for getting to know any new chord.

Another Ninth Chord Cookbook: Baking Altered Dominant Ninth Chords from Friendly Ninth Chords

Even the most ambitious guitarist can be thrown for a loop when first experiencing altered ninth chords (chords with some combination of sharped and/or flatted 9ths and 5ths). A good approach to getting to know these little monsters is to apply a little modification to a plain dominant ninth chord. Most guitarists get to know the dominant ninth chord without too much difficulty—after all, this is the supreme funk chord that defines much of the music by James Brown, Prince, and countless other dance-oriented artists from the late 60's on. It is also an early "jazz" chord, usually played as part of a ii–V–I progression such as Dm7–G9–Cmaj7. By using a familiar fingering and location, altered dominant ninth chords, such as the seven flat nine and seven sharp nine, can be found. Let's begin with this C9 chord.

Rather than memorizing every note in this chord, focus on just one: the 9th (the note D, on the B string, third fret). Remember that the flatted 9th is a minor 2nd lower than the natural 9th. Since a minor 2nd is one fret on the guitar, the flatted 9th is one fret below the natural 9th. Visualize this note in the diagram, and then see if you can move your fingers around to accommodate it. The result should look like this:

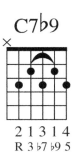

There are several more fingerings we can build from this shape, and you might find them easier to play than the previous one. If the 5th is unaltered—that is, if you don't see a ♭5 or a ♯5 in the chord name—it can often be omitted. Omitting the 5th would leave a shape with two possible fingerings:

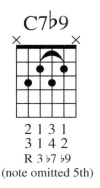

2 1 3 1
3 1 4 2
R 3 ♭7 ♭9
(note omitted 5th)

It's also quite plausible to omit the 3rd, in which case the following fingering results:

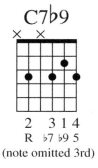

2   3 1 4
R   ♭7 ♭9 5
(note omitted 3rd)

Let's apply the same approaches to a seven sharp nine chord. Again, focus on just the 9th in a C9 chord. The sharped nine is a minor 2nd (or one fret) higher than the natural nine. If you begin with the same C9 chord as before, you should be able to visualize the sharped nine on the B string, one fret above the D—the natural nine—that's already part of the chord. If you attempt to alter the fingering of C9 to create a C7♯9, though, you'll quickly see that it's practically impossible to fret all five notes. So go ahead and omit the 5th. Your fingering will look like this:

2 1 3 4
R 3 ♭7 ♯9

An interesting lesson can be learned if we choose to omit the 3rd from the sharped ninth chord, by the way. The fingering is simple enough:

C7♯9

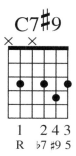

```
1   2 4 3
R  ♭7 ♯9 5
```

But the chord loses its bite. What's going on here? Well, a sharped ninth (in this case, D♯) is the same as a flatted 3rd (in this case E♭). Without the natural 3rd to rub against, this voicing of C7♯9 sounds like a Cm7 or an E♭/C. It's important to consider the context of the chord and choose the notes you use accordingly.

Now let's build some ninth chords with altered 5ths. We'll still use the C9 chord in second position, and we'll build a C9♭5 (also possibly named as C9♯11) and a C9♯5 (also possibly named as C+9). Rather than worry about the 9th this time, we'll just focus on the 5th of the C9 chord. That's the note G on the high E string, third fret. Just as the flatted and sharped 9ths were one fret below or above the natural 9th, so the flatted and sharped 5ths can be found on either side of the natural 5th. Begin by substituting the flatted 5th for the natural 5th; with a little finger-scrambling, you should find yourself with the following grip for a C9♭5 chord:

C9♭5

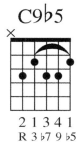

```
2 1 3 4 1
R 3 ♭7 9 ♭5
```

It's quite plausible to omit the 3rd from this chord as well:

C9♭5

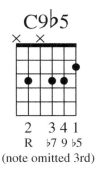

```
2   3 4 1
R  ♭7 9 ♭5
(note omitted 3rd)
```

This might lead you to consider renaming it as B♭+/C, which might lead you to ponder the symmetry of augmented triads and try D+/C and G♭+/C as substitute chords.

In the mood for a sharped 5th? Follow the same tack and simply raise the 5th by one fret. Your fingering should look like this:

C9♯5

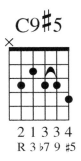

```
2 1 3 3 4
R 3 ♭7 9 ♯5
```

Once you've gotten the hang of identifying these altered notes based on the dominant ninth chord fingering, it's not terribly hard to build these terrifying altered dominant creatures:

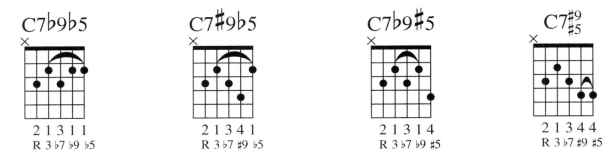

Two Etudes for Ninth Chords

Ninth chords—or any extended chord for that matter—are rarely strung together, one after the other. More often, a ninth will be used as a dominant chord to lead to a simpler home chord. Still, it's quite possible to see and hear how ninth chords can be placed sequentially in a musical context. First, consider a twelve-bar blues. The following arrangement has a somewhat sophisticated jazzy quality and is an excellent introduction to ninth chord fingerings. Once you've played it using the fingerings shown, try to recreate the same voicings on other string sets or add different voicings above or below the given ones.

Blues in C Using Ninth Chords

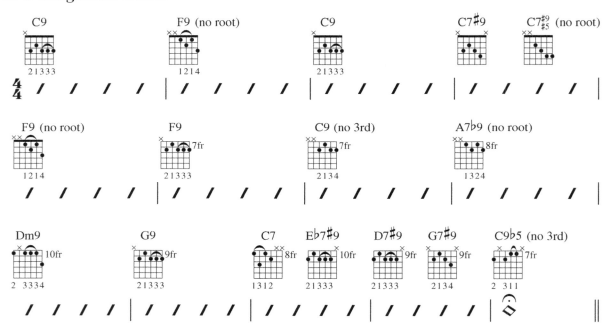

The next figure is also somewhat jazzy in quality, although perhaps more contemporary in sound, alluding to the chord voicings of Joni Mitchell or Pat Metheny. Although the chords are more sophisticated in structure, the use of open strings often makes them easier to play. Notice that the strummed guitar part covers nearly complete voicings of the chords, while the ringing arpeggiated part often plays incomplete upper voicings of the chords.

AUDIO TRACK 63

Etude for Ninth Chords

AUDIO
TRACK 63 (cont.)

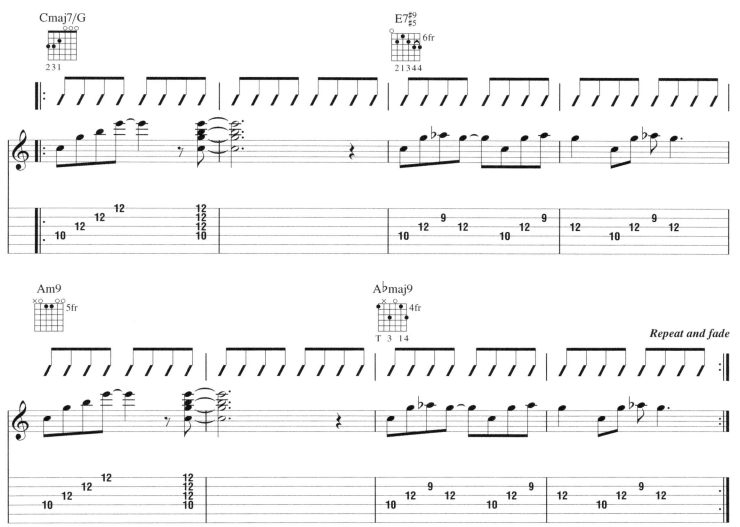

The Knotty Problems of Eleventh Chords

A new set of problems emerges as we move deeper into the world of higher numbered chords. As I pointed out in the beginning of this chapter, although an eleventh chord has six theoretical notes in it, it is almost never played that way—not on a keyboard, not with an orchestration of multiple instruments, and certainly not on a guitar with only six strings to handle the six different notes. Even the voicings that are created with five different notes are exceedingly difficult to play on the guitar. With less than five notes, the chord can be renamed in some way, as we shall see.

Here are some rules to follow as we name and explore eleventh chords:

- The root must be included.

- The appropriate 7th must be included; otherwise it will more easily named as a sus four chord.

- If the chord is based on a major triad, and the 11th is natural, it will not have the 3rd. The major 3rd and the 11th are a minor 9th apart, and this interval is avoided in traditional chords.

- If the chord is based on a major triad, and the 11th is sharp, the 3rd can and probably will be included; the 5th will likely *not* be included.

- If the chord is based on a minor triad, it will have the ♭3rd.

- If the chord has no 3rd, it must have the ninth in it; otherwise it will be named as a seven sus four chord.
- Unless the 5th is altered, it can be omitted. But if the 3rd and the 5th are omitted, it can be better named as a "slash" chord.
- To state the obvious: the chord has to have the appropriate 11th—either a natural 11 or a #11.

Why Are There No Eleventh Chords Based on Diminished Triads?

Diminished seventh chords with 11ths are almost impossible to play on the guitar. Consider C°11 as 1–♭3–♭5–♭♭7–9–11; that's six notes. Playing all six of those thorny notes at one time is a nightmare. As we remove notes to make the chord more manageable, we change the identity of the chord:

- Remove the flatted 3rd, and the resulting chord is more probably a D7#9/C.
- Remove the flatted 5th, and the resulting chord is more probably a Dm7♭9.
- Remove the double-flatted 7th or 6th (B♭♭ or A), and we're left with a cluster of notes possibly related to the diminished scale, but a headache to name as a practical chord.
- Remove the 9th (D), and we're left with an inversion of F7♭9—a far more common chord.

The same holds true of the half-diminished, or minor seven flat five chord. Consider Cm11♭5 as 1–♭3–♭5–♭7–9–11; that's still six thorny notes. As with the diminished eleventh chord, excluding a note changes the chord.

- Remove the flatted 3rd, and the resulting chord is a tangle of unconventional notes, difficult to name and rarely used.
- Remove the flatted 5th, and the chord can be more simply named Cm11.
- Remove the 7th and, again, the resulting tangle of notes is difficult to name and is rarely used.
- Remove the 9th, and the resulting chord—Cm7♭5add11—is interesting in a Duke Ellington/Billy Strayhorn kind of way but, again, hard to name and too unique to be used on a regular basis.

It's safe to say that no chord based on a diminished triad will be the basis of an eleventh chord. It's also important to consider that, while the mathematical possibilities of building eleventh chords are huge, the musical limitations become stricter, and the list of probable and useful eleventh chords becomes quite manageable. They are presented on the following pages with musical analyses, circle diagrams, and practical fingerings all given at once.

(Note that "--" indicates an omitted note. If the logic of chord-naming is not followed, the possible chord will be marked with an asterisk (°) before its name, the reason for omission will be explained, and the chord will no longer be considered.)

Eleventh Chords Based on Minor Triads

Minor Eleven Flat Nine

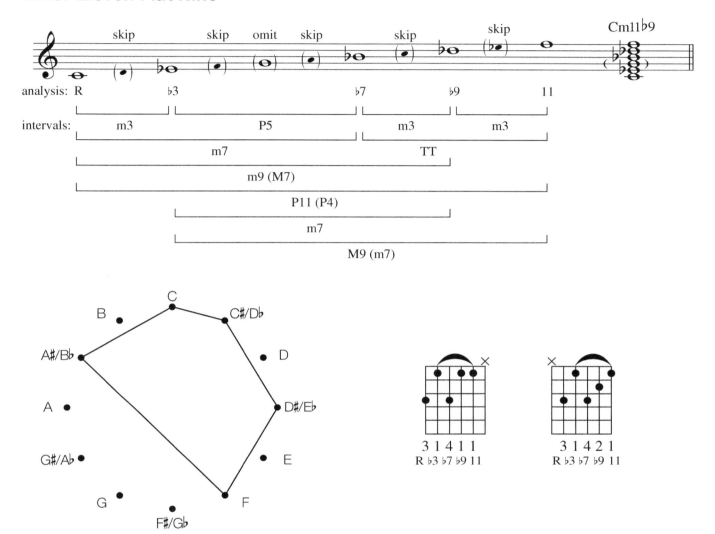

1–♭3 -- ♭7–♭9–11: This chord has a pleasant sound and is surprisingly stable. Cm11♭9 could be rethought/renamed as B♭m11/C.

Minor Seven Flat Nine Sharp Eleven

* **1–♭3 -- ♭7–♭9–#11:** This functions well as an extended m7♭5 chord, since a #11 = ♭5. However, Cm7♭9#11 is better renamed as Cm7♭5♭9, which you will find back in the section on ninth chords.

Minor Eleven

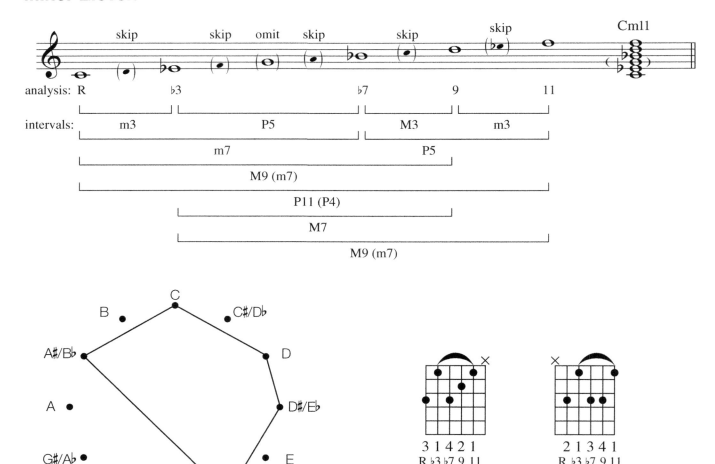

1–♭3 -- ♭7–9–11: This is the primary minor eleventh chord and is vital to know. A common substitution for the minor eleventh chord would be the minor add four. Slash chord names can also be used; for example:

Xadd4/M2, where M2 is the given root. Specifically, Cm11 can be substituted with B♭add4/C. This presents all the right notes but is a fistful for most guitarists to grab on the fly.

X/M2, where M2 is the given root. Specifically, Cm11 can be substituted with B♭/C, but notice that the ♭3 (E♭—the note that makes it minor) is missing.

Xadd2/6, where 6 is the given root. Specifically, Cm11 can be substituted with E♭add2/C.

Minor Nine Sharp Eleven

1–♭3 -- ♭7–9–♯11: This has an intriguing sound, evocative of the iv chord in the harmonic minor tonality. Note that Cm9♯11 could also be renamed as Cm9♭5, which you will find back in the section on ninth chords. Look there for an analysis and practical fingerings.

* **1–♭3 -- ♭7–♯9–11:** (no ♭3 and ♯9 in the same chord)

* **1–♭3 -- ♭7–♯9–♯11:** (no ♭3 and ♯9 in the same chord)

* **1–♭3 – 7–♭9–11:** (the 1, 7, and ♭9 create a chromatic cluster that's not used in current chord construction.)

* **1–♭3 – 7–♭9–♯11:** (the 1, 7, and ♭9 create a chromatic cluster that's not used in current chord construction.)

Minor Eleven Major Seven

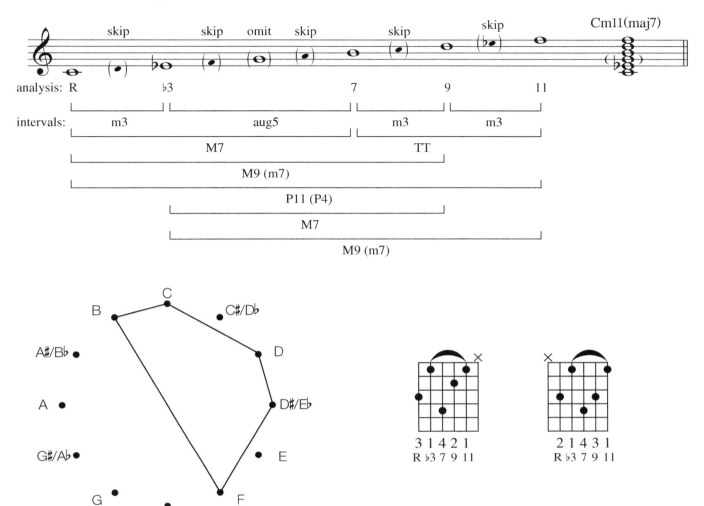

1–♭3 – 7–9–11: This has an intriguing sound based on the i chord of the harmonic minor tonality. Possible slash chord names might include the following:

Xaug/6, where 6 is the given root. Specifically, Cm11(maj7) could be substituted with E♭+/C. The 9th (D) would be missing.

Xdim/♭2, where ♭2 is the given root. Specifically, Cm11(maj7) could be substituted with B°/C. However, the minor quality—the ♭3—would be missing.

Minor Major Nine Sharp Eleven

1–♭3 -- 7–9–♯11: Another chord with an intriguing sound based on the harmonic minor tonality. Note that Cm(maj9)♯11 could also be renamed as Cm(maj9)♭5, which you will find back in the section on ninth chords.

* **1–♭3 -- 7–♯9–11:** (no ♭3 and ♯9 in the same chord)

* **1–♭3 -- 7–♯9–♯11:** (no ♭3 and ♯9 in the same chord)

Eleventh Chords Based on Major Triads

Eleven Flat Nine

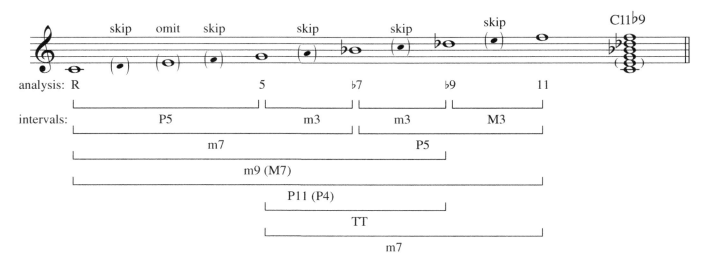

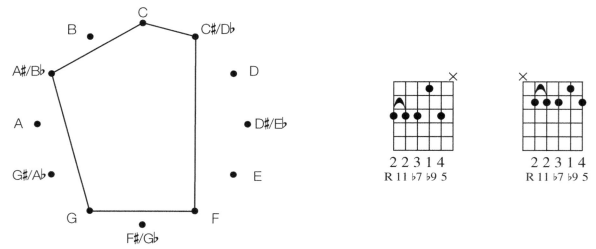

1--5--♭7--♭9--11: This could function as the V chord in the harmonic minor tonality. Consider re-voicing and renaming it as Gm7♭5/C, B♭m6/C, or even B♭m/C5.

Seven Flat Nine Sharp Eleven

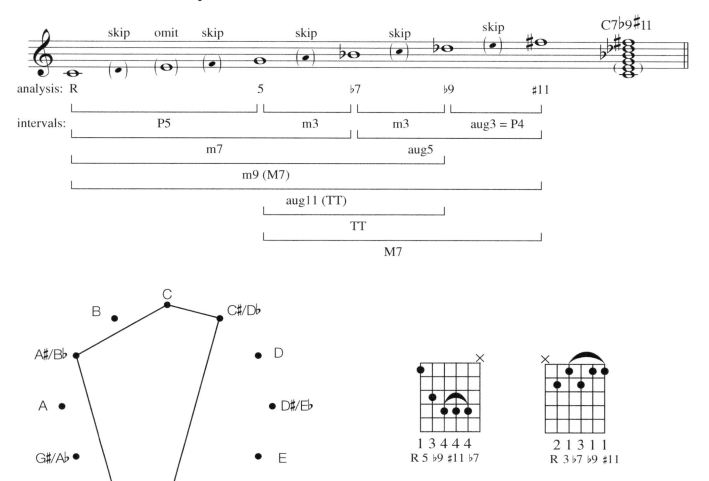

1 -- 5–♭7–♭9–♯11: A possible altered dominant chord. C7♯11♭9 can be rethought and renamed as C7♭5♭9 (see the chapter on ninth chords for more fingerings), or even F♯/C5. Perhaps the easiest name to call up this batch of notes is F♯7/C, which brings the major 3rd (E) back at the expense of the 5th (G).

Eleven

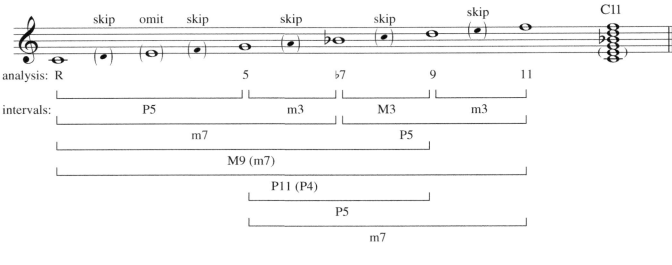

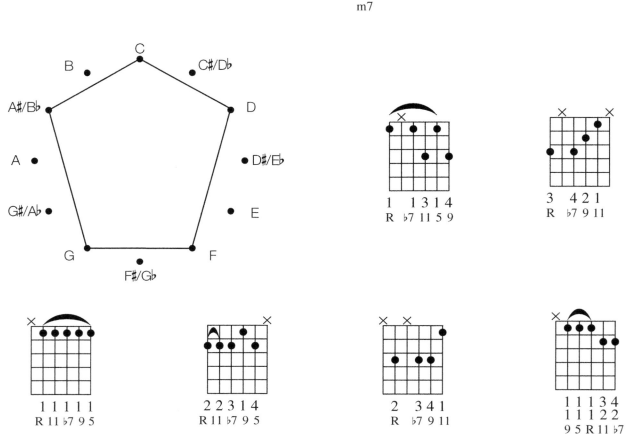

1 --5 --♭7–9–11: This is the primary dominant eleven chord and is almost always the first eleven chord to learn. It should be easy to understand, and the nature of its sound should be familiar. It's also very important to understand how this chord can be rethought and renamed as a slash chord, including the following names:

X/M2, where M2 is the given root. For example, C11 could be substituted with B♭/C. The 5th (G) would be missing.

Xm7/P4, where P4 is the given root. For example, C11 could be substituted with Gm7/C.

Another common substitution for an eleven chord might be seven sus4. C11 could be substituted with C7sus4.

Also notice the unusual inversion of C11/D. This is the quintessential quintal/quartal chord with five notes. You should notice how it is a continuous stack of perfect 4ths. If the lowest note were D, it would be spelled D–G–C–F–B♭. Re-voiced as G–C–F–B♭–D, it's the "Bill Evans" chord, made famous in "So What" by Miles Davis.

Nine Sharp Eleven

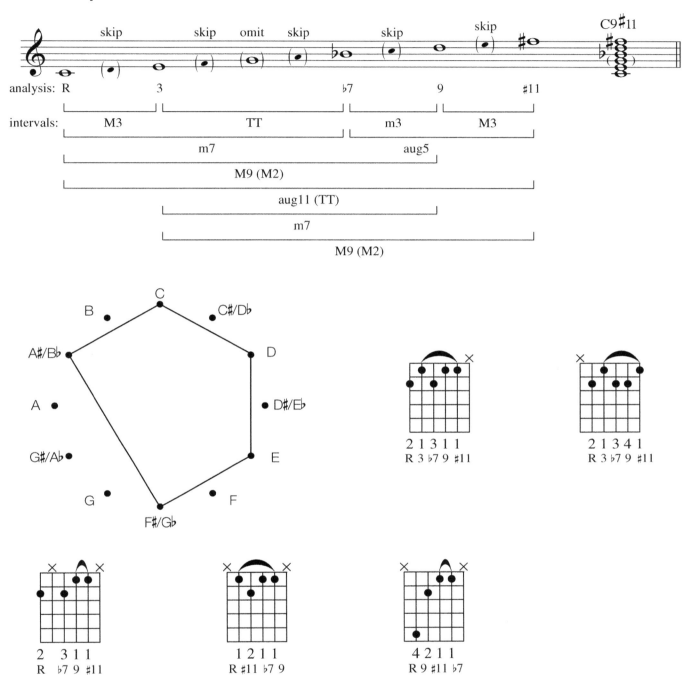

1–3 -- ♭7–9–♯11: This chord is more easily played with the 5th omitted and the major 3rd included, which follows the rules of eleven chords. If you follow that voicing, it can be rethought and renamed as a nine flat five chord, which you will find earlier in this chapter. With the 5th included, it can be rethought and renamed as a slash chord, including the following names:

Xm(maj7)/P4, where P4 is the given root. For example C9♯11 could be substituted with Gm(maj7)/C.

Xaug/M2, where M2 is the given root. For example, C9♯11 could be substituted with B♭+/C. The 3rd and the 5th would be missing. To generate some thick brain smoke, try these formulas as well: X+/m7, where m7 is the given root, and X+/TT, where TT is the given root.

* 1 -- 5–♭7–♯9–11: With no 3rd present, the ♯9 functions as a ♭3, and the chord would be renamed as minor with an added 11.

* **1 -- 5–♭7–#9–#11:** With no 3rd present, the #9 functions as a ♭3, and the chord would be renamed as minor with an added sharp 11.

* **1 -- 5–7–♭9–11:** The 1, 7, and ♭9 create a chromatic cluster that's not used in current chord construction.

* **1 -- 5–7–♭9–#11:** The 1, 7, and ♭9 create a chromatic cluster that's not used in current chord construction.

* **1 -- 5–7–9–11:** In theory, this should be a primary chord in the category of eleven chords. After all, it's the "home" chord of the major scale. However, the major 7th and the 11th create a tritone, causing the chord to sound unstable, which is not what we expect from a major 7th chord. If it were to be used at all, it would be better renamed and rethought as X7/P4, where P4 is the given root. For example, C11maj7 is better renamed as G7/C.

Major Nine Sharp Eleven

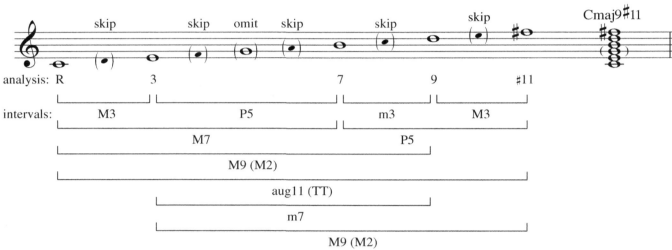

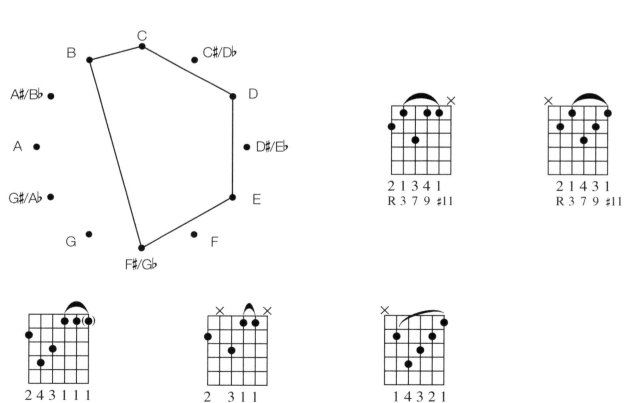

1 -- 5–7–9–♯11: This is a very important eleven chord to know and use. It is a remarkably stable chord invoking the Lydian major tonality, and it provides fascinating insight to the structure of the major scale. As I just pointed out, the previous chord (a major nine with a natural eleven) is diatonic to the major scale and is built from the root note of the scale, but as an eleven chord, it sounds unstable. This chord, with the sharp eleven in it, sounds much more stable and functions beautifully as a final resting chord in the major tonality. With the 5th omitted, it could be named as a major nine flat five. However, the scale implied by a flat five (1–2–3–4–♭5–6–7–8/1) is not the same as that implied by a sharp eleven (1–2–3–♯4–5–6–7–8/1); major nine sharp eleven is the preferred name.

With the 5th included and the 3rd omitted, the major nine sharp eleven chord can be rethought and renamed as a slash chord, including the following names:

Xmaj7/P4, where P4 is the given root. For example Cmaj9♯11 could be substituted with Gmaj7/C.

Xm/m2, where m2 is the given root. For example, Cmaj9♯11 could be substituted with Bm/C. The 3rd and the 5th would be missing.

* **1--5–7–♯9–11:** With no 3rd present, the ♯9 functions as a ♭3, and the chord would be renamed as minor with an added 11.

* **1--5–7–♯9–♯11:** With no 3rd present, the ♯9 functions as a ♭3, and the chord would be renamed as minor with an added ♯11.

Eleventh Chords Based on Augmented Triads

* **1--♯5–♭7–♭9–11:** C11♯5♭9 is better named B♭m7/C.

* **1--♯5–♭7–♭9–♯11:** Caug♭9♯11 is better named F♯add2/C.

* **1--♯5–♭7–9–11:** Caug11 is better named B♭7/C.

Nine Sharp Five Sharp Eleven

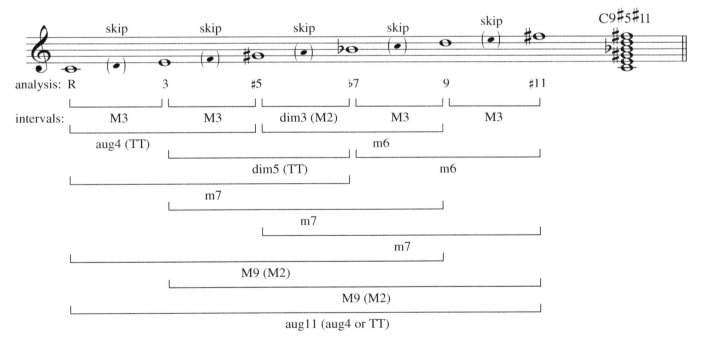

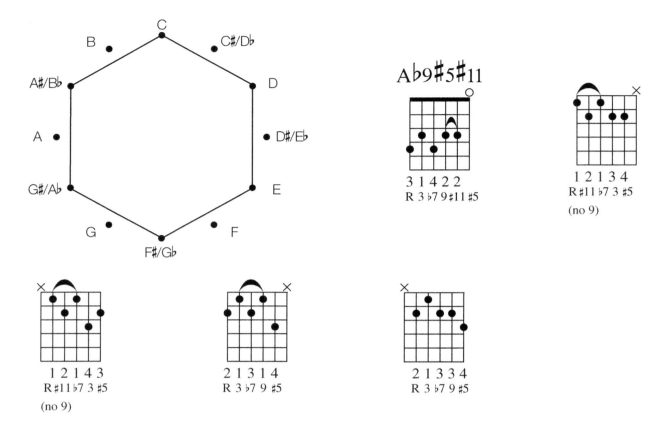

1–3–♯5–♭7–9–11: This chord is a good altered dominant chord in theory and can be seen as the mother chord of the whole tone scale. The rules of eleven chords dictate that, with a sharp eleven, this chord should have the 3rd included. And because the 5th is altered, it should be included too. But playing these six different notes simultaneously on guitar is extremely difficult. In fact, the only way I can find to play them is with singular voicings that include open strings, such as the first block diagram above. On the other hand, throw any other note overboard and you might want to rename the ship. The nine can be omitted, as in the next two fingerings above, but the chord should then probably be renamed as a seven sharp five sharp eleven. Omit the 5th, and the sharp eleven takes its place enharmonically to create a nine flat five chord, which can be found earlier in this chapter. And on, and on it goes. However, the whole tone scale is such a useful one to know that some practical approach to summoning up the sound of the scale should be addressed. Here are two suggestions:

- If the music calls for a specific voicing from within the whole tone scale, focus on the three or four notes that support that voicing, rather than clutter the page (and/or the musicians' heads) with a complicated name.

- If the music evokes the whole tone quality for any length of time—say, two or more measures—then name (or play) any smaller chord within the whole tone scale and indicate other chords that complete the scale, or simply identify the selected section as "whole tone scale."

Before we bid adieu to this curious bit of hexagonal symmetry, let's play a couple of little games. Grab any chord within the C whole tone scale, such as a simple C+, and define the three notes as if they were part of a C9♯5♯11.

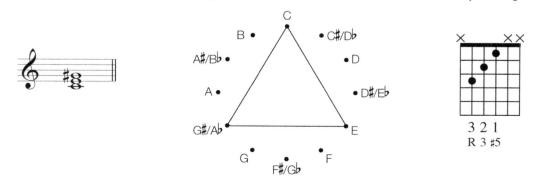

Now move the shape up two frets and define these three notes as if they were part of a C9#5#11.

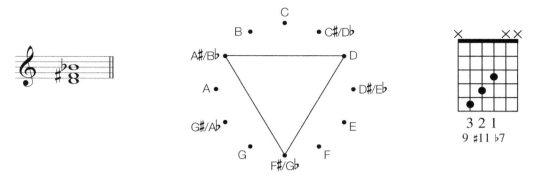

Notice that, between the two chords, you've covered all the notes within a C9#5#11 chord. The first chord provided the R, 3, and #5, and the second provided the 9, #11, and ♭7. Move up two frets again.

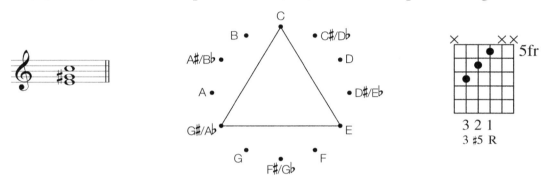

You'll notice that you've returned to an inversion of the first chord. You should see where this is heading: move up another two frets…

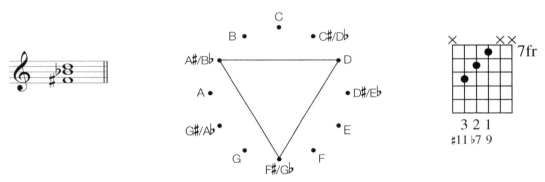

…and you'll have an inversion of the second chord. Continue in two-fret leaps, and you'll have encircled the entire cloud of whole tone symmetry evoked by the name C9#5#11.

One more game: go back to the first chord in this sequence—the C augmented triad—but define the notes as if they were a part of a D9#5#11 chord, like this:

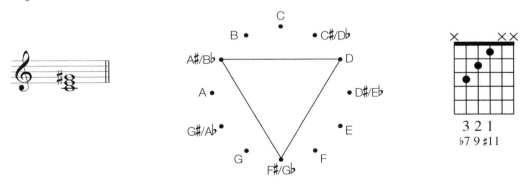

Move the shape up two frets, define these notes as if they were part of a D9#5#11 chord, and you can see that you're off on the same trip again.

Mental games like this can be painful at first, because our traditional system of music has been built around the asymmetric major scale and its transposition through the twelve different pitches of the chromatic scale. When we try to shoehorn a simple symmetry like the whole tone scale into that asymmetric system, we strain the system's limits. On the other hand, if we can experience the sound without preconception, we can bring some valuable treasures back to the conventional world. To conclude our inquiry into eleventh chords, here is a list of possible but improbable eleventh chords, and illogical spellings for nonexistent elevenths.

* **1-- #5-♭7-#9-11:** With no 3rd present, the #9 functions as a ♭3, and the chord would be renamed as minor with an added 11.

* **1 -- #5-♭7-#9-#11:** With no 3rd present, the #9 functions as a ♭3, and the chord would be renamed as minor with an added #11.

* **1 -- #5-7-♭9-11:** The 1, 7, and ♭9 create a chromatic cluster that's not used in current chord construction.

* **1 -- #5-7-♭9-#11:** The 1, 7, and ♭9 create a chromatic cluster that's not used in current chord construction.

* **1 -- #5-7-9-11:** C+(maj11) is better named as B°7/C.

* **1-3-#5-7-9-#11:** This is a chord that falls into the realm of the possible, but highly improbable. If translated to the key of C with C as the root, some mental juggling might rescramble the notes into an E9/C. It sounds as if it's struggling to sit within two keys at the same time (C major and E mixolydian). If the sound is required, pare it down to four strong notes, such as Cmaj7#5 or Bm/C.

* **1 -- #5-7-#9-11:** With no 3rd present, the #9 functions as a ♭3, and the chord would be renamed as minor with an added 11.

* **1 -- #5-7-#9-#11:** With no 3rd present, the #9 functions as a ♭3, and the chord would be renamed as minor with an added #11.

The Theoretical Limit of Tertiary Construction: The Thirteenth Chord

To restate the opening of this chapter, the final step in chord complexity is to consider all of the 3rds that stack up above the octave of the root. In constructive theory, the most complex chord possible is the thirteenth chord, which could contain seven different note names. Because our chord-naming system favors the flatted seven as the simplest chord name, chords extended above the seventh inherit this favoritism in their naming. So the theoretical construction of the simplest thirteenth chord would look like this:

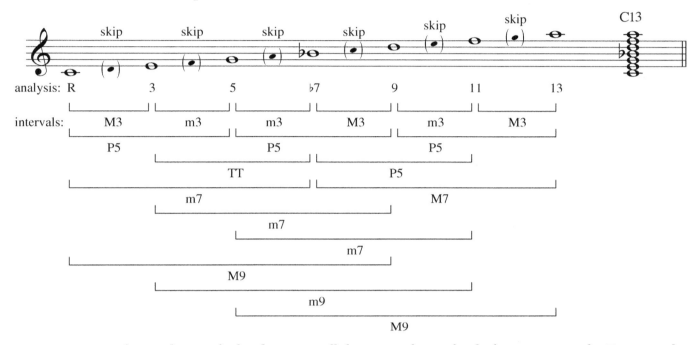

In constructive theory, thirteenth chords contain all the notes of some kind of seven-note scale. For example, if we begin with a C13 chord and drop the extended notes (the 9th, 11th, and 13th) down an octave, we get a C scale with a flatted 7th. The scale can then be analyzed in two ways: it can be numbered consecutively from 1 to 8, or it can be numbered based on the elements of a theoretical thirteenth chord, as shown below.

major scale analysis:	1	2	3	4	5	6	♭7	(8/1)
13 chord analysis:	1	9	3	11	5	13	♭7	(8/1)

In a very practical way, a thirteenth chord identifies a probable scale to play along with the given chord, and all of these notes could be heard at one time. But in most music that's come to pass as of this writing (the early twenty-first century), you'll hardly ever hear all seven notes of these theoretical thirteen chords ringing out at one time. Why is that? Opinions vary, but the consensus among people who are musically literate would probably follow these lines: If all seven notes of a thirteenth chord ring at once in a haphazard, unfocused manner, most listeners find the resulting sound to be chaotic. It takes a combination of clear intention and skilled execution to allow all seven notes of a thirteenth chord to ring out in a clearly structured and focused way, and most listeners are unresponsive to this level of intention and skill.

So, not only is the theoretical thirteenth chord a difficult sound to use and an unpopular sound to listen to when poorly played, it's quite close to impossible to get seven different notes from an instrument with only six strings on it. So in practical application (especially on a single guitar), these chords cannot consist of more than six different note names; and as we've seen with ninth and eleventh chords, they will usually be pared down to five, four, or even three notes.

Since the 13th corresponds to the sixth note of the scale we just constructed, what do we add or subtract to a thirteenth chord to make it different from a sixth chord? Just as with the ninth and eleventh chords discussed earlier in this chapter, the answer is this:

- A thirteenth chord must contain the root (although, even this is not steadfast), seventh, and thirteenth.

- Other notes can be added according to the chord name and/or the context in which the chord is played; the next most common note to add is the 3rd.

Rules of construction for thirteenth chords have developed informally over the past century. Here are some more rules to cover those "other notes:"

- If the 3rd is major, the 11th won't be added.

- If the 3rd is minor, the 11th can be added.

- If the 5th is not altered, it can be omitted.

- The 9th can be added or omitted.

Naming and Playing Thirteenth Chords in the Major Tonality

It's easy and useful to build basic thirteenth chords on each note of the major scale. These chords will consist of the appropriate root, 3rd, 7th, 13th and, in the case of the chord built on the seventh note of the major scale, the flatted 5th. Rather than show the construction of these chords with a huge line of notes in the play-a-note, skip-a-note approach I've used earlier, these thirteenth chords will be shown with octave reduction, and the 13th note of the theoretical snowman chord will appear as the 6th. However, it will be identified as a 13th in the chord block diagram analyses. As usual, we'll work in the key of C, beginning with Cmaj13.

Major Thirteenth

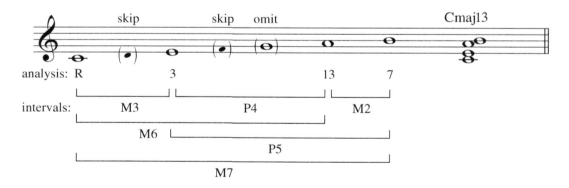

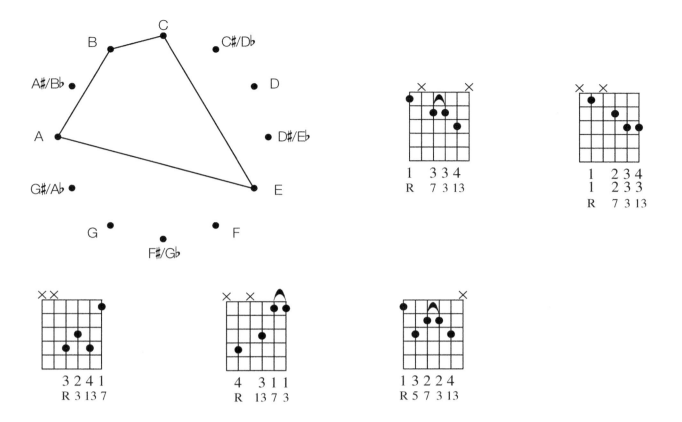

Remember, the "major" in the name (abbreviated as "maj") refers to the major 7th and not to either the basic triad (which happens to be major) or the 13th (which also happens to be major). In the extremely pared down approach of using only the root, 3rd, 7th, and 13th, two interesting structures appear in the major thirteenth chord. First, the four notes can be rearranged into a minor triad with an added 9th. Specifically, Cmaj13 can be rearranged and re-voiced as Am(add9). (You should be able to identify the notes A, C, and E as the A minor triad and B as the added ninth.) Second, the three notes above the root—the 3rd, 7th, and 13th—can be rearranged as a quartal/quintal chord (A–E–B), and the chord can be rethought as this quartal/quintal triad with an added low note. Traditionally, that quartal/quintal triad might be renamed Asus2 or Esus4, and alternate names for Cmaj13 could include Asus2/C or Esus4/C. Also notice how, in the last chord block diagram, the 5th is added.

Minor Thirteenth

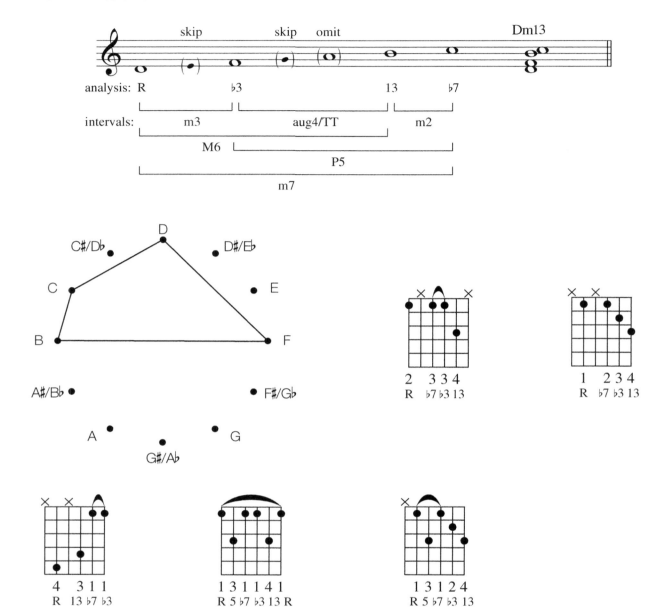

Notice that the "minor" in the name (abbreviated as "m") refers to the basic minor triad and not to the 7th (which is minor, or flatted, and therefore is not named in the chord) or to the 13th (which is major). Like Cmaj13, Dm13 can be rearranged into a triad with an added 9th. But unlike Cmaj13, the rethinking reveals a somewhat thorny B°add♭9. The quartal/quintal chord above the root (B–F–C) is similarly prickly; one possible renaming might be Fsus♯4/D.

Minor Seventh Flat Thirteen

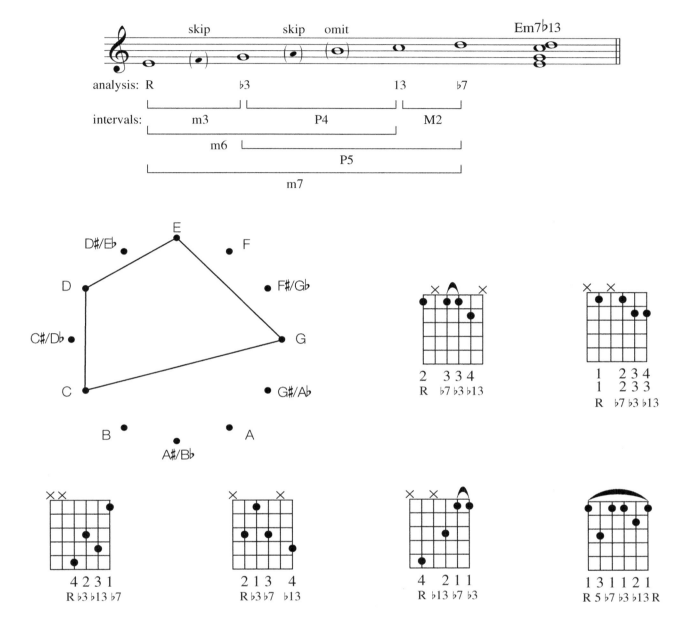

Rearranging the minor seventh flat thirteen chord into a triad with an added 9th reveals why this chord may seem rather fragile. As Em7♭13, it can be rearranged as Cadd2 or Cadd9. If you're in the key of C and you use this chord for any length of time, it will probably sound more like an inversion of the C chord with the added color note than as an E minor chord. The quartal/quintal chord above the root (C–G–D) might be traditionally named Gsus4, and an alternate name for Em7♭13 would be Gsus4/E. Adding the 5th, as in the last chord block diagram above, gives the root note more authority. Without the 5th, Em7♭13 could be renamed Em7♯5, but this would negate the idea of the thirteenth chord representing a traditional seven-note scale.

Major Thirteenth Sharp Eleven

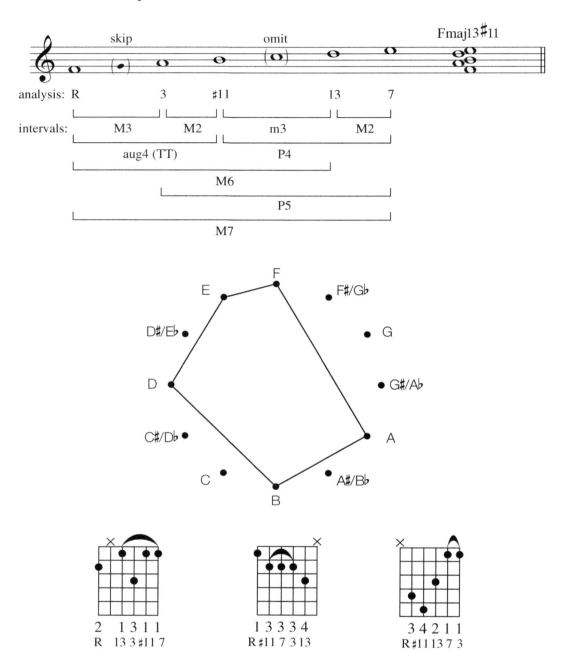

The minimalist thirteenth chord built on the fourth note of the C major scale is a major thirteenth chord (Fmaj13, spelled F–A–D–E, using the structure 1–3–13–7). Refer back to Cmaj13 for comments and analysis; Fmaj13 is cut from the same cloth. But here's an opportunity to see how other notes from the thirteenth "mother chord" can be added; in this case we'll add the ♯11th (B), which is diatonic to the key of C. It's also evocative of the Lydian tonality, which was discussed in the previous section on eleventh chords.

It's worth digressing for a moment to mention that the quintal mother chord built on F is an Fmaj13♯11. The chord is shown on the following page.

F Major Thirteen Sharp Eleven

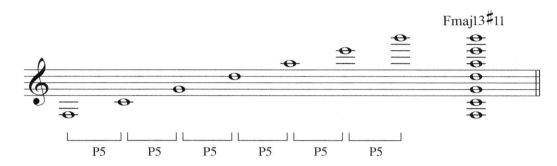

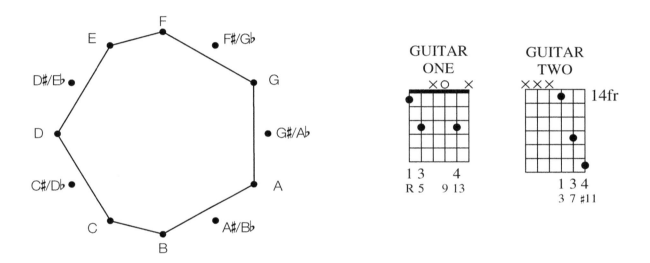

This chord is often the "proof" of the Lydian mode as the most stable and pleasing sounding scale when used in a harmonic context. While it can't be played on a single guitar in real time, it can be voiced on two guitars, as shown. This chord can be heard on Track 64.

Dominant Thirteenth

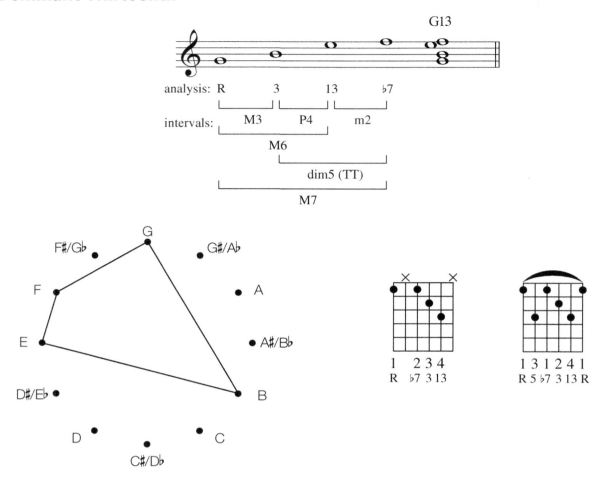

Here's the simplest named and most important thirteenth chord. Built on the fifth note of the C major scale, it is the chord that takes the traditional concept of the dominant chord as the most unstable chord and adds the idea of it also being the most complex. While all types of thirteenth chords are now in current use, this was historically the first to arrive.

The thirteenth chord built upon the sixth degree of the major scale will be a minor seven flat thirteen, identical in structure to the thirteenth chord built on the 3rd degree of the major scale. In the key of C major this will be an Am7♭13. It will have the same tendency to sound like a major chord with an added color note; specifically, Am7♭13 will sound like Fadd2.

Minor Seventh Flat Five Flat Thirteen

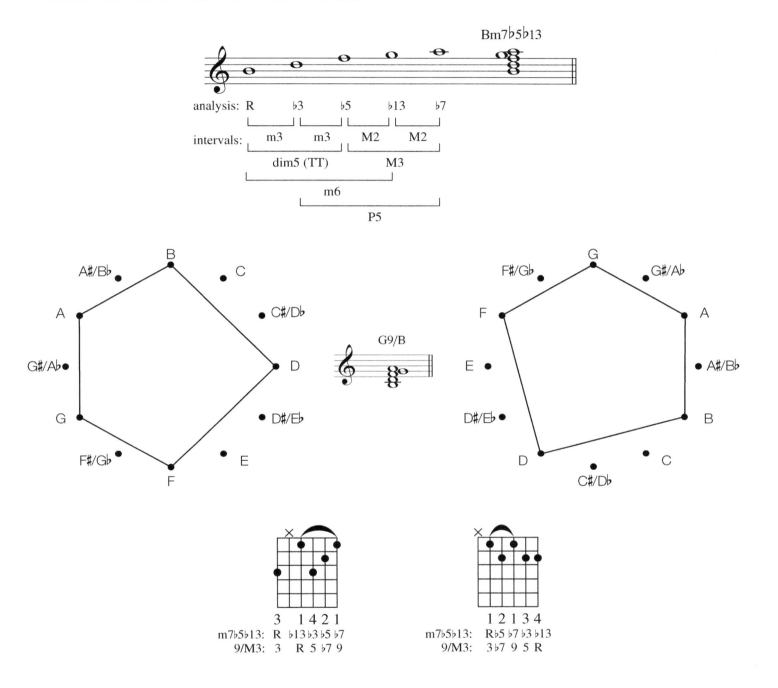

To capture all the appropriate notes of the thirteenth chord built on the seventh degree of the major scale, we have to construct a rather clumsy name. Once we experience the chord, it seems much easier to give it a friendlier name. Specifically, in the key of C, Bm7♭5♭13 can be renamed G9/B, as you can see in the figures above.

Naming and Playing Thirteenth Chords in the Harmonic Minor Tonality

The harmonic minor scale generates some very unusual thirteenth chords. Some are uncommon but useful, and some are uncommon and not so useful. Following the practice of thirteenth chord naming and construction, these chords will consist of the appropriate root, 7th, 13th and, when appropriate, a 3rd or (sometimes altered) 5th. As with the previous set of thirteenth chords, these will be shown with octave reduction, and the 13th note of the theoretical snowman chord will appear as the 6th. However, it will be identified as a 13th in the chord block diagram analyses. As usual, we'll work in the key of C harmonic minor, beginning with Cm(maj7)♭13.

Minor Major Seventh Flat Thirteen

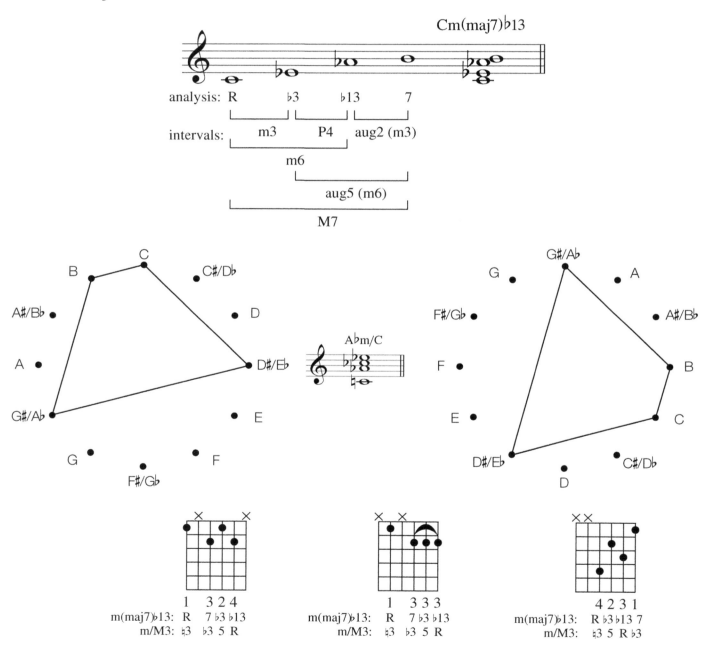

This chord is a real home wrecker. Remember, the harmonic minor scale was originally used at a time when extended chords were not, so building extended chords within the limits of such a scale can have cruel and unusual consequences. This chord is an unsettled harmony that can be more easily named as Xm/M3. Specifically, Cm(maj7)♭13 can be renamed A♭m/C, as shown in the figure above.

Minor Thirteenth Flat Five, or Diminished Thirteenth

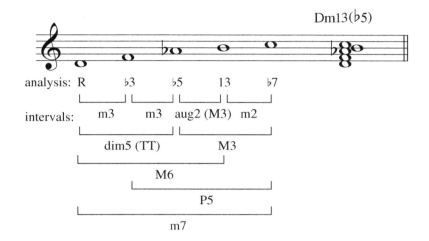

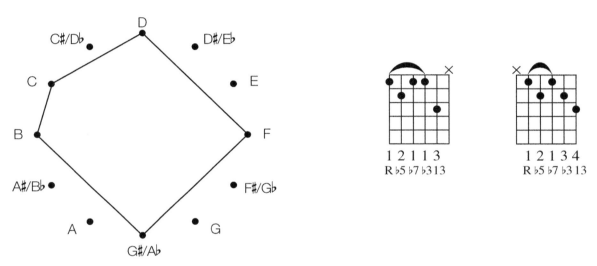

The thirteenth chord built on the second degree of the harmonic minor scale is a tense little knot of notes. The circle diagram reveals its underlying structure as a diminished seventh chord with an added note. Working around the circle, it could be rethought and renamed as:

D°13 (D°6 with an added ♭7—notice how useful the °6 name is!)
Fm6(add♯11)
Ab°add10 or Ab6add♯9
B°♭9

It functions really well as a tension chord resolving to any number of consonant, stable chords. Try these cadences:

D°13 to Cm or C major
D°13 to E♭ major
Fm6(add♯11) to G♭ major
Ab°add10 to A major
B°♭9 to A minor
B°♭9 to Cmaj7

Notice that if you take out any one of the five notes, the chord would be renamed and might lead the reader/performer to assume a different underlying scale.

Major Thirteenth Sharp Five

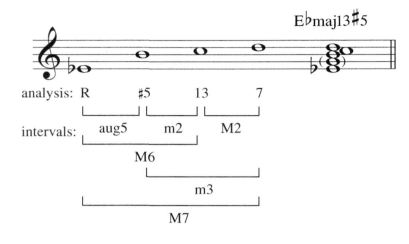

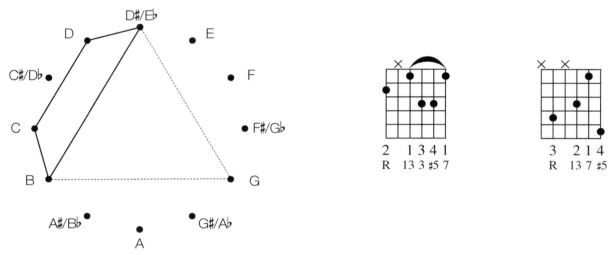

The thirteenth chord built on the third note of the harmonic minor scale presents an interesting problem in formal chord naming and a delicate and useful sound to boot. The problem in naming the chord is that the sharp five should be included in the naming and the playing of the chord to call forth the proper tonal quality of the harmonic minor scale. If the 3rd is played, as shown by the dotted line in the circle diagram and in the first block diagram, the sound of the chord leans towards a minor major nine chord in first inversion—Xm(maj9)/♭3. Which name is better? Honey, you decide. If the 3rd is omitted, as in the second block diagram, we are left with a four-note cluster: ♯5–6–7–1. Clusters are often beautiful sounds, and this one clearly calls forth the feel of the harmonic minor scale, but it's difficult to force a cluster back into a traditional harmonic function.

The thirteenth chord built on the fourth note of the harmonic minor scale is a minor thirteenth—identical in structure to the thirteenth chord built on the second note of the major scale.

Seventh Flat Thirteen

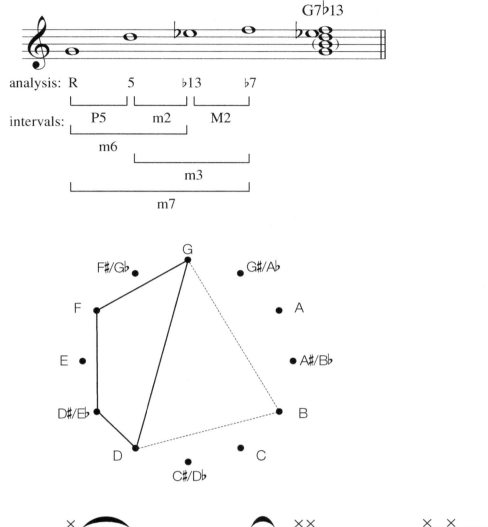

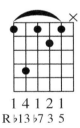

1 4 1 2 1
R ♭13 ♭7 3 5

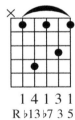

1 4 1 3 1
R ♭13 ♭7 3 5

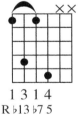

1 3 1 4
R ♭13 ♭7 5

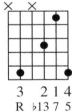

3   2 1 4
R ♭13 7 5

The thirteenth chord built on the fifth note of the harmonic minor scale is a somewhat crowded seventh flat thirteen. If the rules of naming thirteenth chords are followed, the included 3rd and omitted natural 5th would lead us to an enharmonically renamed **seventh sharp five chord**. If the 3rd and 5th were included for a more fulsome seventh flat thirteen, the first two block diagrams above would capture that sound. If the 3rd were omitted, we would arrive at yet another four-note cluster chord: 5–♭6–♭7–1, fingerings of which are shown in the last two block diagrams above.

The thirteenth chord built on the sixth note of the harmonic minor scale is a major thirteen—identical in structure to the thirteenth chord built on the first note of the major scale.

The thirteenth chord built on the seventh note of the harmonic minor scale would be a theoretical ***diminished flat thirteen chord***. A little analysis of this chord would bring you back to an inversion of a seventh flat nine chord and a much more sensible name to use. For example, B°♭13, spelled B–D–F–G–A♭ or 1–♭3–♭5–♭13–♭♭7, can be reordered as G7♭9, spelled G–B–D–F–A♭ or 1–3–5–7–♭9. Play the 3rd (B) as the lowest note, and you have G7(♭9)/B.

Adding the 9th to the Most Common Thirteenth Chords

If we consider a thirteenth chord that includes the 9th, we arrive at a cluster of 6–7–R–9, at the very least. This kind of thirteenth chord is occasionally called for, so let's look at where it might fit within the thirteenth chords we've just constructed. Annoyingly, there's no common way to name a thirteenth chord with an added 9th to differentiate it from a thirteenth chord without it. But notice how many of the following voicings fall into one of three categories:

- **Quartal/quintal chords with added low notes**. These might be thought of as quartal/quintal "slash" chords, except we don't yet have a good system for naming quartal/quintal chords.
- **Cluster chords with added low notes**. As with quartal/quintal chords, these could have "slash" names if we had a system for naming the clusters.
- **Relatively traditional chords with "slash" names**.

Major Thirteenth with an Added 9th

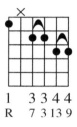

If you've gotten familiar with quartal/quintal chords, the quartal construction in the upper notes will be obvious.

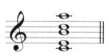
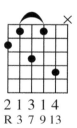

Above is another inversion of a quartal/quintal chord with an added low note.

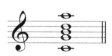
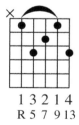

This voicing (above) brings the 5th back into the chord. This might be seen as an add nine chord with a "slash" note added. In the key of C, it could be renamed Gadd9/C.

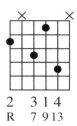

2   3 1 4
R   7 9 13

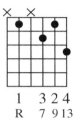

1   3 2 4
R   7 9 13

Here are the cluster voicings of 13–7–R–9.

Minor Thirteenth with an Added 9th

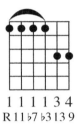

1 1 1 1 3 4
R 11 ♭7 ♭3 13 9

2 1 3 3 4
R ♭3 ♭7 9 13

The first voicing above satisfies the requirements of a nearly complete minor thirteen chord. In snowman-style construction, it would be 1–♭3–(5)–♭7–9–11–13; only the 5th is omitted.

Dominant Thirteenth with an Added 9th

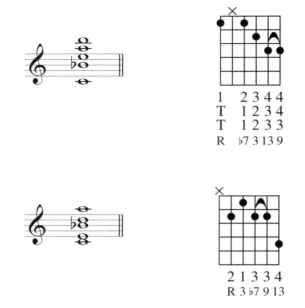

Here are two useful voicings of the dominant thirteenth chord. As a bonus, they include the 3rd, providing the juicy 3-♭7 tritone that can either be resolved or savored as your context dictates.

What Is an "Alt" Chord?

An "alt" chord—short for "altered"—is a seventh or extended chord with any number of possible alterations to the 5th, 9th, and/or 13th of the chord. We've been introducing them all along; chords like the seven sharp five, seven flat five, seven flat five flat nine, etc. are all part of the alt chord family. When the music calls for an alt chord, its calling for a chord in which any of the appropriate notes may be played. Specifically, there's an "altered scale" from which the notes may be chosen. It looks like this in the key of C:

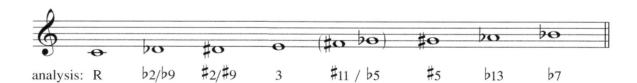

analysis: R   ♭2/♭9   ♯2/♯9   3   ♯11 / ♭5   ♯5   ♭13   ♭7

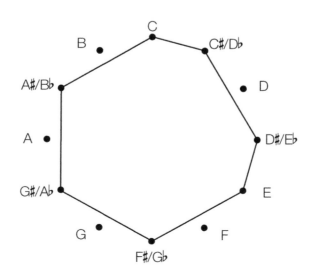

An Etude for Extended Chords

For a final look at many of the more complex chords introduced in this book, here's an etude I call "The Two–Five–One–Six Obstacle Course for Aspiring Jazzers." It's built on a ii–V–I–vi chord progression—part of the progression of roots by 4ths—and it's an extremely common progression in jazz and harmonically sophisticated pop music. The exercise begins with the chords in their simplest forms in the key of D major, and every repetition of the sequence introduces new and more complex variations on the progression. After seven sets of chords, the exercise modulates to a new, somewhat distant key (G♭ major) and reintroduces the same chords in the new key. After this new key runs its course, the music moves to a third tonal center (B♭ major), and the sequence is repeated again. The use of these three equidistant tonal centers will cause the chords to be played in multiple ways, keeping the fingers and the brain in a flexible state. Block diagrams with fingerings are given for the key of D, but after that, you're on your own!

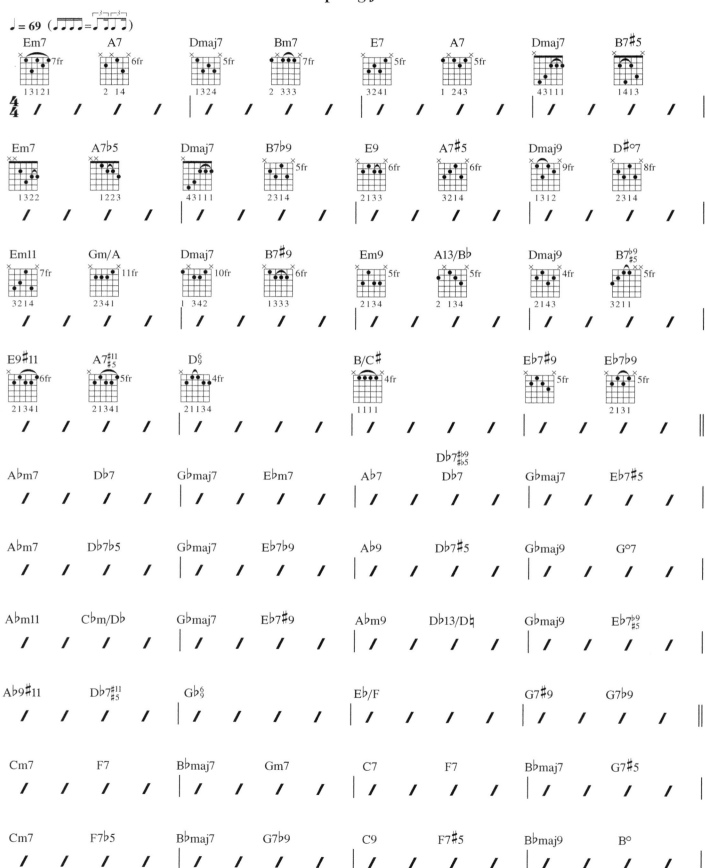

AUDIO TRACK 65

The Two-Five-One-Six Obstacle Chourse for Aspiring Jazzers

AUDIO TRACK 65 (concluded)

Cm11		Ebm/F		Bbmaj7		G7#9		Cm9		F13/Gb	
/	/	/	/	/	/	/	/	/	/	/	/

Bbmaj9		G7b9#5		C9#11		F7#11#5		Bb6/9			
/	/	/	/	/	/	/	/	/	/	/	/

Postlude

The past century has seen the sound of music (not to mention the storage and transmission of sound itself!) change radically. One hundred years ago, composers of "serious" styles were fretting over the end of tonality and how to move "forward," as if music needed to be seen as a linear progression. Meanwhile, vital and essential elements of popular music from around the world were just beginning to meld into each other in ways that many serious musicians could not imagine. Today, we pick and choose among a vast collection of ingredients to create our own personal musical identities.

The purpose of chords—collections of notes that sound good together—remains constant as the literal harmony of music, a metaphor for human harmony, and a language of musical propulsion. The skill of understanding relatively traditional chords—from two-note dyads to some highly altered thirteenth chord—is really just a part of the greater skill of playing music in harmony with others. Even within our equally tempered twelve-note system of music, and on an instrument that traditionally has six strings and a three-and-a-half- to four-octave range, there are orderly collections of notes that contain great musical power, yet have no conventional names for general use: quintal/quartal chords, diatonic clusters, chromatic clusters, and polychords, to name a few. One challenge of any serious guitarist is to explore and make use of these sounds—perhaps to even contribute to a language that names these sounds more easily.

A greater challenge, one that requires the skills of the heart as well as the head and hands, is to be a part of the sounds made possible in a performance by more than one person and to generate chords no one person could alone. Beginning with a single guitarist, current technology allows anyone with sufficient imagination to create an orchestra of themselves—a performance by one person as a multiplicity of themselves—with pitch shifting and tone shaping available to color every degree of the audio spectrum. Small groups are another beginning of this possibility. Traditionally, the chords that occur in most small groups can be coded down to a single chordal instrument. Isn't this a restriction worth transcending? The European model of the symphony orchestra, where a single person is responsible for a musical idea that's conveyed on paper to a group of subservient performers, is but one way of working as a larger group to generate sounds that no single person might recreate. A serious musician of the twenty-first century might look to Balinese gamelan and African drumming, to name but two traditions, as further models of collective music-making. The possible chords approach the infinite, and the future begins to look very bright indeed.

Get Better at Guitar

...with these Great Guitar Instruction Books from Hal Leonard!

101 GUITAR TIPS
STUFF ALL THE PROS KNOW AND USE
by Adam St. James
This book contains invaluable guidance on everything from scales and music theory to truss rod adjustments, proper recording studio set-ups, and much more.

00695737 Book/Online Audio $16.99

AMAZING PHRASING
by Tom Kolb
This book/audio pack explores all the main components necessary for crafting well-balanced rhythmic and melodic phrases. It also explains how these phrases are put together to form cohesive solos. The companion audio contains 89 demo tracks, most with full-band backing.

00695583 Book/Online Audio $19.99

ARPEGGIOS FOR THE MODERN GUITARIST
by Tom Kolb
Using this no-nonsense book with online audio, guitarists will learn to apply and execute all types of arpeggio forms using a variety of techniques, including alternate picking, sweep picking, tapping, string skipping, and legato.

00695862 Book/Online Audio $19.99

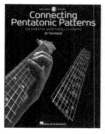

BLUES YOU CAN USE
by John Ganapes
This comprehensive source for learning blues guitar is designed to develop both your lead and rhythm playing. Includes: 21 complete solos • blues chords, progressions and riffs • turnarounds • movable scales and soloing techniques • string bending • utilizing the entire fingerboard • and more.

00142420 Book/Online Media....................................$19.99

CONNECTING PENTATONIC PATTERNS
by Tom Kolb
If you've been finding yourself trapped in the pentatonic box, this book is for you! This hands-on book with online audio offers examples for guitar players of all levels, from beginner to advanced. Study this book faithfully, and soon you'll be soloing all over the neck with the greatest of ease.

00696445 Book/Online Audio $19.99

FRETBOARD MASTERY
by Troy Stetina
Untangle the mysterious regions of the guitar fretboard and unlock your potential. This book familiarizes you with all the shapes you need to know by applying them in real musical examples, thereby reinforcing and reaffirming your newfound knowledge.

00695331 Book/Online Audio $19.99

GUITAR AEROBICS
by Troy Nelson
Here is a daily dose of guitar "vitamins" to keep your chops fine tuned! Musical styles include rock, blues, jazz, metal, country, and funk. Techniques taught include alternate picking, arpeggios, sweep picking, string skipping, legato, string bending, and rhythm guitar.

00695946 Book/Online Audio $19.99

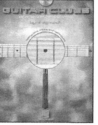

GUITAR CLUES
OPERATION PENTATONIC
by Greg Koch
Whether you're new to improvising or have been doing it for a while, this book/audio pack will provide loads of delicious licks and tricks that you can use right away, from volume swells and chicken pickin' to intervallic and chordal ideas.

00695827 Book/Online Audio $19.99

PAT METHENY – GUITAR ETUDES
Over the years, in many master classes and workshops around the world, Pat has demonstrated the kind of daily workout he puts himself through. This book includes a collection of 14 guitar etudes he created to help you limber up, improve picking technique and build finger independence.

00696587...$15.99

PICTURE CHORD ENCYCLOPEDIA
This comprehensive guitar chord resource for all playing styles and levels features five voicings of 44 chord qualities for all twelve keys – 2,640 chords in all! For each, there is a clearly illustrated chord frame, as well as *an actual photo* of the chord being played!.

00695224...$19.99

RHYTHM GUITAR 365
by Troy Nelson
This book provides 365 exerci – one for every day of the year. to keep your rhythm chops fin tuned. Topics covered includ chord theory; the fundamenta of rhythm; fingerpicking; stru patterns; diatonic and non-diaton progressions; triads; major and minor keys; and more.

00103627 Book/Online Audio $24.9

SCALE CHORD RELATIONSHIPS
by Michael Mueller & Jeff Schroedl
This book/audio pack explains ho to: recognize keys • analyze chor progressions • use the mode • play over nondiatonic harmon • use harmonic and melodi minor scales • use symmetric scales • incorporate exotic scales • and much more!

00695563 Book/Online Audio $14.9

SPEED MECHANICS FOR LEAD GUITAR
by Troy Stetina
Take your playing to the stratospher with this advanced lead book whic will help you develop speed an precision in today's explosiv playing styles. Learn the fastes ways to achieve speed and contro secrets to make your practice tim really count, and how to open your ears and make you musical ideas more solid and tangible.

00699323 Book/Online Audio $19.9

TOTAL ROCK GUITAR
by Troy Stetina
This comprehensive source fo learning rock guitar is designe to develop both lead and rhythm playing. It covers: getting a ton that rocks • open chords power chords and barre chord • riffs, scales and licks • strin bending, strumming, and harmonics • and more.

00695246 Book/Online Audio $19.9

Guitar World Presents STEVE VAI'S GUITAR WORKOUT
In this book, Steve Vai reveals hi path to virtuoso enlightenmen with two challenging guita workouts – one 10-hour and one 30-hour – which include scal and chord exercises, ear training sight-reading, music theory, an much more.

00119643...$14.9

fabulously fast quilts

amy smart

Martingale®
Create with Confidence

Fabulously Fast Quilts
© 2014 by Amy Smart

Martingale®
19021 120th Ave. NE, Ste. 102
Bothell, WA 98011-9511 USA
ShopMartingale.com

MISSION STATEMENT

Dedicated to providing quality products and service to inspire creativity.

CREDITS

PRESIDENT AND CEO: Tom Wierzbicki
EDITOR IN CHIEF: Mary V. Green
DESIGN DIRECTOR: Paula Schlosser
MANAGING EDITOR: Karen Costello Soltys
ACQUISITIONS EDITOR: Karen M. Burns
TECHNICAL EDITOR: Rebecca Kemp Brent
COPY EDITOR: Sheila Chapman Ryan
PRODUCTION MANAGER: Regina Girard
COVER AND INTERIOR DESIGNER: Connor Chin
PHOTOGRAPHER: Brent Kane
ILLUSTRATOR: Anne Moscicki

What's your creative passion?
Find it at ShopMartingale.com

books • eBooks • ePatterns • daily blog • free projects
videos • tutorials • inspiration • giveaways

Printed in China

19 18 17 16 15 14   8 7 6 5 4 3 2 1

Library of Congress Cataloging-in-Publication Data is available upon request.

ISBN: 978-1-60468-363-9

contents

Introduction

I'm addicted to making quilts. I love the entire process of choosing fabrics, playing with color, and piecing a new design. As a part-time blogger and busy mother of four, my spare time is fleeting. I also have a short attention span. I like to finish a project quickly so that I can move on to the next one as soon as possible. And let's face it: if I drag out a project too long, it may be destined for the UFO (unfinished objects) pile.

As a result, I love shortcuts: time-saving methods to help me cut, piece, and assemble my quilts quickly. I'll admit I like it when people think these deceptively easy projects look complex and time-consuming. It pains me when I find out that potential quilters are scared off by the perceived time investment that this fulfilling hobby might demand. That's why I wrote this book—to help other busy, short-attention-span quilters who want an efficient way to create something pretty.

Fabulously Fast Quilts is divided into four sections: Strip Piecing; Quick Corners; Slick Slicing; and Stack, Slice, and Shuffle. Each section takes a shortcut method and shows a few variations that can result from the technique. In some cases I've created a traditional block or pattern faster, with fewer little bits and pieces.

Get ready to amaze your friends and family with the complexity of quilts that look like they took much longer to make than they really did!

Basic Quiltmaking Techniques

I'm the first to say that making a quilt does not need to be meticulous tedium. I'm not a perfectionist by any stretch, but adhering to the four basic practices below will save headaches later, make the process more enjoyable, and help your quilts look good.

- Consistent *scant* ¼" seam allowances (this means that seam allowances should be a thread or two less than ¼")
- Careful and accurate measuring and cutting
- Pressing seams and blocks
- Squaring up blocks

I can't stress that list enough. While at first some of the tasks may seem time-consuming, practicing good habits from the beginning makes the quiltmaking process so much more enjoyable in the long run. The more you practice the techniques, the more they will feel like second nature.

If you need more information than is given here, you can visit the Martingale website and my own website as references for basic techniques. For a free downloadable resource on everything from rotary cutting to piecing, quilting, and binding, with beautiful diagrams and pictures, visit ShopMartingale.com/HowtoQuilt. For my thoughts on favorite must-have quilting tools, or how to choose colors and fabrics, visit my blog, www.DiaryofaQuilter.com, and click on the *Tutorials* tab at the top of the home page.

Since this is a book about patchwork shortcuts, there are a few techniques that I'll refer to repeatedly, so let's take a closer look at each of those.

STRIP PIECING

Many of the quilts in this book will be made using strip piecing. This is a great technique for saving time when making quilts because rather than cutting lots of small squares and rectangles and piecing them back together, you sew width-of-fabric strips together, and then cut the resulting strip

sets into smaller, presewn units. There are some important tips to help with strip piecing:

- Cut the strips accurately.
- Use consistent scant ¼" seam allowances.
- Where possible when piecing strips together, sew successive seams in alternating directions. For example, sew the first two strips together top to bottom, but join the third strip from bottom to top. This decreases bowing (curving into an arc) and stretching out of shape within the strip set.

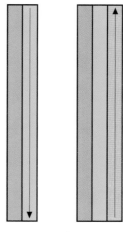

Sewing direction

- Carefully press the seam allowances to one side. I prefer pressing to one side because opposing seams will nest nicely at intersections to aid in sewing seams and matching patch corners. Press (don't iron) the seams again from the right side to make sure the pieced strips are fully open and flat.

PRESSING MATTERS

Ironing is the familiar motion of sliding an iron back and forth over a garment or fabric to remove wrinkles. In quiltmaking, pressing is a better technique. The proper motion for pressing is to lift and replace the iron on the fabric, keeping gliding motions to a minimum to avoid distorting the fabric.

When rotary cutting pieced units, use a *middle* seam as a guide rather than the top or bottom edge of the strip set. Align a marking on the ruler with a middle seam to make sure that the strip set stays square and the seams don't become crooked.

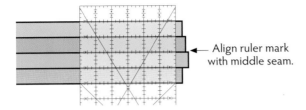

Align ruler mark with middle seam.

Adjust the ruler placement and straighten the end of the strip set after every few cuts to make sure angles and measurements are still accurate. Variation is normal; it's important to check and adjust so that your pieced units aren't misshapen.

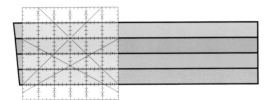

Check and square the ends occasionally.

QUICK CORNERS

Quick corners is a technique for adding triangles to the corners of a block. Adding a corner triangle is a simple way to change the look of a block and create new design elements in a quilt. Rather than cutting a corner from a square patch and sewing a triangle to the new edge, we'll simplify by beginning with a second, smaller square instead of a triangle and sewing before cutting the bias edge. Quick corners may be added to one, two, three, or all four corners of a square or rectangular patch.

Cut the large and small squares as directed in the instructions and draw a diagonal line from corner to corner on the back of the smaller square—the one that will become the corner triangle. Align the smaller square with one corner of the larger

square, right sides together, and sew on the drawn line. Use a rotary cutter to trim the excess fabric ¼" outside the seam. Press the unit open, pressing the seam allowances toward the triangle.

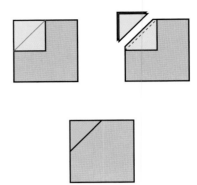

GIVE IT A SPIN

Using a rotating or revolving cutting mat will help you quickly and accurately trim quick corners.

If you need to make a lot of blocks with quick corners, save time with this simple technique to avoid drawing all those diagonal lines. You'll need a sewing machine with a bed or table that extends at least 5" in front of the needle. Carefully align a piece of tape (painter's tape or another low-tack tape) with its edge directly in front of the needle and its length extending toward the front edge of the bed or table. Use a ruler to make sure the tape is placed perfectly straight and not slightly angled. As you sew, put the leading corner of the smaller quick-corner square directly under the needle and align the opposite corner with the edge of the tape. Move the trailing corner along the tape edge as you sew the seam.

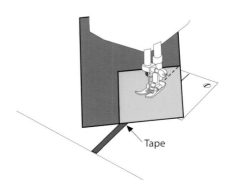

Tape

SLICK SLICING

Slick slicing begins with ordinary strip-pieced units. Rather than crosscutting them in the usual manner, you slice the strip sets at a 45° angle to create diagonal dimensions in the quilt design, without handling many pieces with sharp angles.

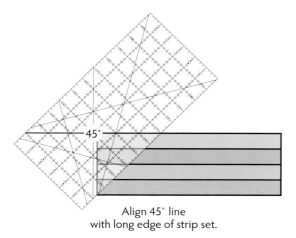

Align 45° line
with long edge of strip set.

Two of the projects—"Butterfly Effect" and "Diverging Diamonds"—are created with a tube-piecing method in which a single strip of fabric or a second strip-pieced set is sewn to the first set along both edges. After the tube is sliced, the segments are opened to reveal the pieced blocks. See the individual project instructions for details.

Some things to note. First, make sure all of the angles stay consistent as you cut. Use a ruler with a 45° line and align that with a straight seam or edge, and then use the long edge of the ruler as the cutting guide.

Second, remember that the angled edges are cut on the bias. As you piece the blocks, be careful not to pull or stretch the bias edges. Pinning will help keep the edges from stretching out of shape while you're piecing.

STACK, SLICE, AND SHUFFLE

This fun technique is like shuffling a deck of cards while performing a magic trick. Pieces are cut by stacking multiple layers of fabric and slicing through them all at once, and then "shuffling" to change the order of the prints within each stack of pieces. When they're reassembled in their shuffled order, multicolored blocks are created.

In "Quick Puss in the Corner" and "Modern Buzz Saw," pieced units are sliced and shuffled again, saving considerable time compared to cutting and piecing many small pieces of fabric one at a time. For more details, see the individual project instructions.

SQUARING UP

Squaring up pieced quilt blocks before you sew them together is vital to a crisp, well-pieced quilt. The process can seem tedious, but it's *always* worthwhile.

To accurately square up a block, find the center point of the block and trim all four sides an equal distance from the center. Remember to include a seam allowance on all four edges. For example: If the block size should be 6½" (6" finished), trim each side 3¼" from the center point. Align the ruler with an internal seam to ensure that the edges are straight and perpendicular. Using a rotating cutting mat will speed the process.

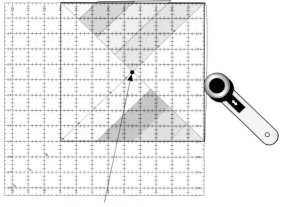

Center of block

EASY BORDERS

Adding borders correctly is an important step in preventing wavy or misshapen quilt edges. This is my favorite tried-and-true shortcut method for adding borders to quilts.

Cut border strips using the measurements given in each pattern. Sew the strips together, end to end, when required to create longer strips.

Spread the pieced quilt top on a hard surface (I usually use the floor) and lay the two side border strips, stacked together, vertically along the center of the quilt, matching one end of the strips with the top edge of the quilt. Mark the strips at the bottom edge of the quilt and rotary cut along the mark to trim the strips to size. The center of the quilt, where the blocks are all sewn to one another, is less likely to be distorted than the edges, so measuring through the center is preferable.

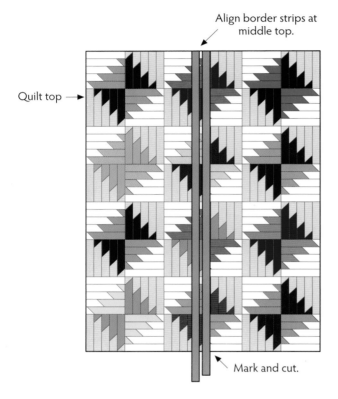

Align border strips at middle top.

Quilt top →

Mark and cut.

When you sew the border strips to the quilt, the quilt edges may be slightly longer or shorter than the border strips. Find the center of the border strip and pin it to the center of the quilt edge, and then pin at both ends. Evenly distribute any

extra fullness along the entire border and pin. The action of the sewing machine's feed dogs will ease the excess fabric into the seam without puckers if you pin carefully.

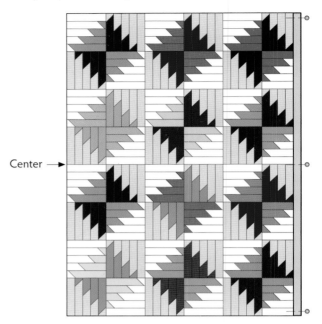

Center →

Repeat the process for the top and bottom borders: create long border strips, lay them horizontally across the center of the quilt (including the just-added borders), mark, and cut. Carefully pin and sew the borders in place. Press the seam allowances to one side, usually toward the border strip.

For additional information on finishing a quilt visit ShopMartingale.com/HowtoQuilt. These simple tips will streamline your quiltmaking process without sacrificing the quality of the end product.

fast four patch

One easy Four Patch block, alternated with colorful prints, creates a quick and cheerful quilt design.

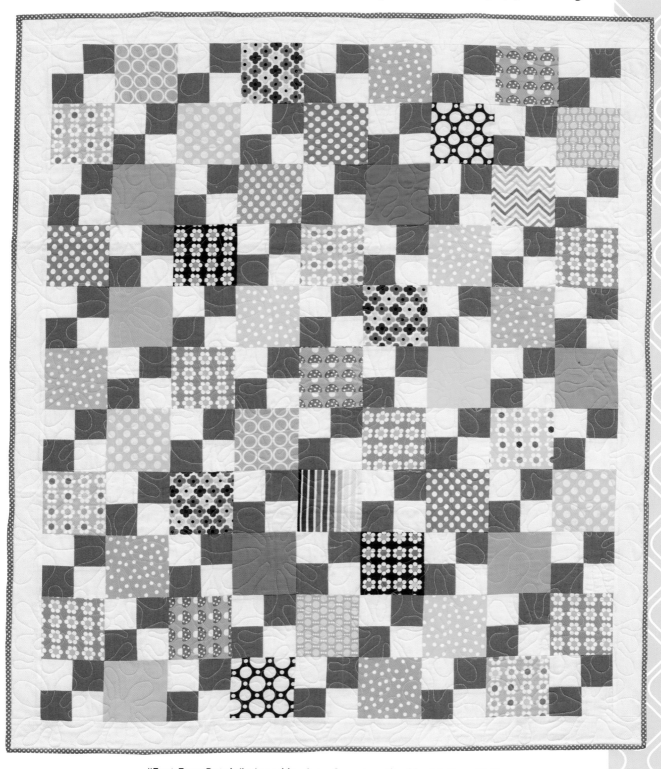

"Fast Four Patch," pieced by Amy Smart; quilted by Melissa Kelley

> Finished quilt: 40" x 48"
> Finished block: 4" x 4"

MATERIALS

Yardage is based on 42"-wide fabric.

49 squares, 4½" x 4½", of assorted prints for blocks (⅞ yard total)

1 yard of white solid for blocks and border

⅝ yard of red solid for blocks

½ yard of red polka dot for binding

2½ yards of fabric for backing*

44" x 52" piece of batting

*If your fabric is wide enough, you can purchase just 1½ yards and use a single panel for the backing.

CUTTING

From the white solid, cut:
13 strips, 2½" x 42"

From the red solid, cut:
7 strips, 2½" x 42"

From the red polka dot, cut:
5 strips, 2½" x 42"

MAKING THE BLOCKS

1 Sew a white strip to a red strip, referring to "Strip Piecing" on page 5. Press the seam allowances toward the red strip. Make seven strip sets.

2 Crosscut the strip sets into 100 units, 2½" wide.

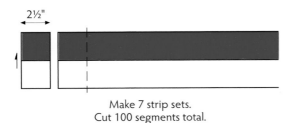

Make 7 strip sets.
Cut 100 segments total.

3 Rotate one unit from step 2 and sew it to a second unit to create a 4½" x 4½" Four Patch block. Press the seam allowances to one side. Make 50 blocks.

Make 50.

ASSEMBLING THE QUILT TOP

1 Arrange the blocks in 11 rows of nine blocks each, alternating Four Patch blocks and print 4½" squares.

2 Sew the blocks into rows, pressing the seam allowances toward the print squares.

3 Pin and sew the rows together to create the quilt top. Press all the seam allowances in one direction.

ADDING THE BORDER

1 Sew three of the remaining white strips together to make a long border strip. Make two.

2 Using the "Easy Borders" method on page 7, measure and cut the side borders from the two assembled strips. Sew, and then press the seam allowances toward the borders.

3 Measure and cut the top and bottom borders from the remnants of the long border strips and sew them to the quilt top. Press the seam allowances toward the borders.

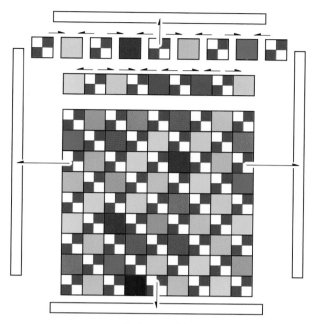

Quilt assembly

FINISHING THE QUILT

For more information on finishing techniques, go to ShopMartingale.com/HowtoQuilt for free, illustrated instructions.

1 Layer the quilt top, batting, and backing, and baste the layers together. Quilt as desired; the sample quilt uses a meandering overall design.

2 Trim the backing and batting to match the quilt top.

3 Bind the quilt using the red polka-dot strips. Add a label if desired.

zig

Turning a basic Rail Fence block on point gives this traditional block a new, modern look. Choosing one dominant accent color creates added drama in the design.

"Zig," pieced by Amy Smart; quilted by Emily Sessions

> Finished quilt: 71½" x 82"
> Finished block: 7½" x 7½"

MATERIALS

Yardage is based on 42"-wide fabric.

2⅛ yards of dark-blue print for blocks and outer border

1½ yards of orange tone on tone for blocks

1½ yards of white print for blocks and inner border

1¼ yards of blue print for blocks

1 yard of orange print for blocks

¾ yard of blue stripe for binding

5 yards of fabric for backing

76" x 86" piece of batting

CUTTING

From the orange tone on tone, cut:
20 strips, 2½" x 42"

From the orange print, cut:
20 strips, 1½" x 42"

From the white print, cut:
20 strips, 1¾" x 42"
8 strips, 1½" x 42"

From the blue print, cut:
20 strips, 2" x 42"

From the dark-blue print, cut:
20 strips, 2¼" x 42"
8 strips, 3½" x 42"

From the blue stripe, cut:
Bias strips 2½" wide, totaling at least 340"*

For details on cutting and making bias binding, see ShopMartingale.com/HowtoQuilt.

MAKING THE BLOCKS

1 Referring to "Strip Piecing" on page 5, create a strip set by sewing together, in order: one orange tone-on-tone 2½" strip, one orange-print 1½" strip, one white 1¾" strip, one blue 2" strip, and one dark-blue 2¼" strip. Press the seam allowances in one direction. Make 20 identical strip sets.

2 Cut five squares, 8" x 8", from each strip set for a total of 100 squares. Two blocks will be left over.

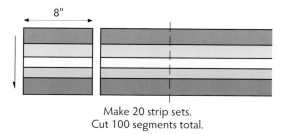

8"

Make 20 strip sets.
Cut 100 segments total.

A SQUARE DEAL

Measure the width of each strip set; it should be 8". If not, make a note of the measured width and cut the segments to match. As long as all of the strip-set segments are squares with the same dimensions, the quilt can be assembled correctly. If your strip-set widths are inconsistent, remove and restitch the seams to create 20 identical strip sets before cutting the segments.

ASSEMBLING THE QUILT TOP

1 Arrange the Rail Fence blocks on point in eight rows of seven blocks as shown in the quilt assembly diagram on page 14. Fill in between the rows with seven additional rows, each containing six blocks turned in the opposite direction.

2 Sew the blocks together into diagonal rows, pressing the seam allowances toward an unbroken strip (away from the intersecting seam allowances).

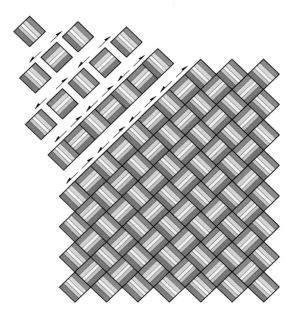

3 Sew the rows together to create the quilt top. Press the seam allowances in one direction.

4 Carefully trim the edges of the quilt top ¼" outside the seam-line intersections, creating straight edges on the quilt top.

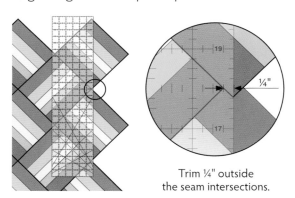

Trim ¼" outside
the seam intersections.

ADDING THE BORDERS

1 Sew two white 1½" x 42" strips together along the short edges; make four.

2 Using the "Easy Borders" method on page 7, measure and trim two of the pieced border strips and sew them to the side edges of the quilt. Repeat with the remaining pieced white strips for the top and bottom borders. Press the seam allowances toward the borders.

3 Repeat steps 1 and 2 with the dark-blue 3½" x 42" strips to make the outer borders. Press the seam allowances toward the borders.

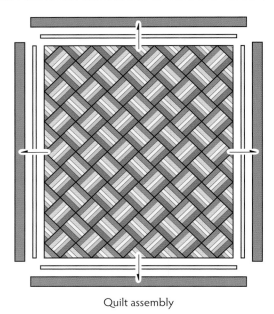

Quilt assembly

FINISHING THE QUILT

For more information on finishing techniques, go to ShopMartingale.com/HowtoQuilt for free, illustrated instructions.

1 Layer the quilt top, batting, and backing, and baste the layers together. Quilt as desired; the sample quilt uses a pattern of overlapping concentric circles, a modern version of the traditional Baptist Fan pattern.

2 Trim the batting and backing to match the quilt top.

3 Join the striped bias strips and use them to bind the quilt. Add a label if desired.

moroccan tile

By using lots of negative space and turning the blocks on point, this variation on a Four Patch block takes on a new look. The negative space lets you showcase quilted embellishment. This project is perfect for precut 2½" strips.

"Moroccan Tile," pieced by Amy Smart; quilted by April Rosenthal

Finished quilt: 62" x 83"
Finished block: 5" x 5"

MATERIALS

Yardage is based on 42"-wide fabric.

2⅝ yards of cream tone on tone for blocks

18 strips, 2½" x 42", of assorted prints for blocks (1¼ yards total)

1¼ yards of red floral for outer border

½ yard of yellow print for inner border

⅝ yard of blue print for binding

4¾ yards of fabric for backing

66" x 87" piece of batting

CUTTING

From the cream tone on tone, cut:

9 strips, 1½" x 42"

11 strips, 5½" x 42"; crosscut into:

70 rectangles, 1½" x 5½"

54 squares, 5½" x 5½"

2 strips, 8½" x 42"; crosscut into:

8 squares, 8½" x 8½"; cut into quarters diagonally to make 32 triangles (2 will be left over)

2 squares, 4½" x 4½"; cut in half diagonally to make 4 triangles

From the yellow print, cut:

7 strips, 2" x 42"

From the red floral, cut:

8 strips, 5" x 42"

From the blue print, cut:

8 strips, 2½" x 42"

MAKING THE BLOCKS

1 Referring to "Strip Piecing" on page 5, sew a print 2½" strip to each side of a cream 1½" strip. Press the seam allowances toward the print strips. Make nine strip sets.

2 Cut each strip set into 16 units, 2½" wide. You will use 140 units and have four left over.

2½"

Make 9 strip sets.
Cut 144 segments total; 4 will be left over.

3 Sew a unit from step 2 to each long side of a cream 1½" x 5½" rectangle. Press the seam allowances toward the cream rectangle. Make 70 blocks, 5½" x 5½".

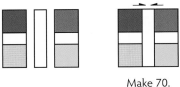

Make 70.

ASSEMBLING THE QUILT TOP

1 Arrange the pieced blocks on point in 10 rows of seven blocks as shown on page 17. Fill in between the pieced blocks with cream 5½" squares. Add the 30 cream side triangles and four corner triangles along the edges.

2 Sew the blocks together in diagonal rows, pressing the seam allowances away from the pieced blocks.

3 Sew the rows together, pressing all the seam allowances in one direction.

4 Sew the red strips together in pairs; make four. Measure and trim the pieced border strips, and then sew them as before. Press the seam allowances toward the outer border.

Quilt assembly

ADDING THE BORDERS

1 Sew two yellow strips together along their short edges; make two.

2 Using the "Easy Borders" method on page 7, measure and trim the pieced border strips and sew them to the side edges of the quilt. Press the seam allowances toward the borders.

3 Cut one of the remaining yellow strips in half. Sew a half strip to one end of each remaining yellow strip. Measure and trim the pieced yellow strips, and then sew them to the quilt top and bottom. Press the seam allowances toward the borders.

FINISHING THE QUILT

For more information on finishing techniques, go to ShopMartingale.com/HowtoQuilt for free, illustrated instructions.

1 Layer the quilt top, batting, and backing, and baste the layers together. Quilt as desired; the sample quilt uses mini medallions for the plain squares and straight-line quilting that echoes the block seams.

2 Trim the backing and batting to match the quilt top.

3 Bind the quilt using the blue strips. Add a label if desired.

simple simon

Adding a quick corner to each patch creates movement on another simple four-patch design, with twin illusions of curves and floating squares. The quilt reminds me of Simon, an electronic game that was popular when I was young.

"Simple Simon," pieced by Amy Smart; quilted by Melissa Kelly

Finished quilt: 75½" x 75½"
Finished block: 9" x 9"

MATERIALS

Yardage is based on 42"-wide fabric.

218 squares, 5" x 5", of assorted bright prints for blocks (4 yards total)

1½ yards of white solid for blocks and inner border

1¼ yards of green stripe for outer border

⅝ yard of green print for binding

4½ yards of fabric for backing

80" x 80" piece of batting

CUTTING

From the white solid, cut:

14 strips, 2½" x 42"; crosscut into 218 squares, 2½" x 2½"

8 strips, 2" x 42"

From the green stripe, cut:

8 strips, 5" x 42"

From the green print, cut:

8 strips, 2½" x 42"

MAKING THE BLOCKS

1 Using the "Quick Corners" technique on page 6, sew a white square to one corner of a 5" print square. Trim the excess fabric, leaving a ¼" seam allowance. Make 218 units with one white corner. Press the seam allowances toward the white corner in half of the units and toward the print square in the remaining units.

Make 218.

2 Sew two units from step 1 together, matching the white corners, with the seam allowances lying in opposite directions. Make 100 units; 18 units from step 1 will be used later.

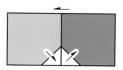

3 Sew two units from step 2 together, matching the white triangles. Make 41 blocks; 18 units from step 2 will be used in the next step.

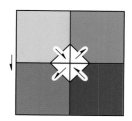

Make 41.

4 Sew a unit from step 1 to a unit from step 2 as shown to make a partial block. Make 18. Align a ruler ¼" from the point where three squares intersect and trim the excess fabric. Set aside 16 of these units to use as side triangles.

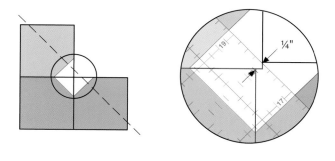

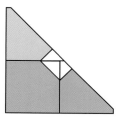

Make 18.

5 Cut the two remaining units from step 5 in half diagonally to create four corner triangles.

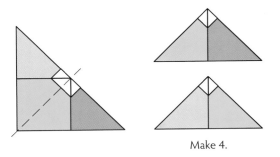

Make 4.

ASSEMBLING THE QUILT TOP

1 Arrange the 41 pieced blocks on point in a grid five blocks across and five blocks high, with additional blocks filling the spaces. Rearrange the blocks until you're pleased with the placement of the fabrics and colors.

2 Add the 16 side and four corner triangles along the edges of the layout.

3 Sew the blocks together in diagonal rows, pressing the seam allowances in alternating directions from row to row.

4 Sew the rows together in order, pressing the seam allowances in one direction.

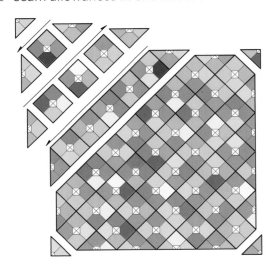

ADDING THE BORDERS

1 Sew two white strips together along their short edges; make four.

2 Using the "Easy Borders" method on page 7, measure and trim two of the pieced border strips and then sew them to the side edges of the quilt. Press the seam allowances toward the borders.

3 Measure and trim the remaining pieced white strips, and then sew them to the top and bottom edges. Press the seam allowances toward the borders.

4 Sew the green-striped strips together in pairs; make four. Measure and trim two pieced border strips and sew them to the quilt sides; repeat for the top and bottom, as above. Press the seam allowances toward the outer border.

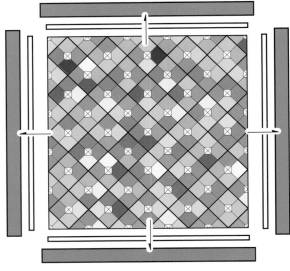

Quilt assembly

FINISHING THE QUILT

For more information on finishing techniques, go to ShopMartingale.com/HowtoQuilt for free, illustrated instructions.

1 Layer the quilt top, batting, and backing, and baste the layers together. Quilt as desired; the sample quilt uses spiral circles to emphasize the illusion of curves in the piecing.

2 Trim the backing and batting to match the quilt top.

3 Bind the quilt using the green-print strips. Add a label if desired.

roundabout

This design is easier to create than it looks, and uses traditional Snowball and Nine Patch blocks.

"Roundabout," pieced by Amy Smart; quilted by Melissa Kelley

Finished quilt: 63" x 81"
Finished block: 9" x 9"

MATERIALS

Yardage is based on 42"-wide fabric.

2⅞ yards of light floral for blocks

1 yard of black floral for blocks

1 yard of multicolored print for blocks

1 yard of red print for blocks

1 yard of large geometric print for blocks

⅝ yard of red stripe for binding

4¾ yards of fabric for backing

67" x 85" piece of batting

CUTTING

From *each* of the black floral, multicolored print, and red print, cut:

3 strips, 3½" x 42" (9 total)

2 strips, 9½" x 42"; crosscut into 8 squares, 9½" x 9½" (24 total)

From the large geometric print, cut:

3 strips, 3½" x 42"

3 strips, 9½" x 42"; crosscut into 7 squares, 9½" x 9½"

From the light floral, cut:

27 strips, 3½" x 42"; crosscut *12 of the strips* into 124 squares, 3½" x 3½"

From the red stripe, cut:

8 strips, 2½" x 42"

MAKING THE BLOCKS

1 Using the "Quick Corners" method on page 6, make 31 Snowball blocks by sewing a light-floral 3½" square to each corner of the print 9½" squares. Press the seam allowances toward the triangles.

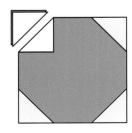
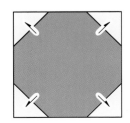

2 Referring to "Strip Piecing" on page 5, use the 3½" x 42" print strips to make three strip sets in *each* of the following combinations:

▸ Set A: black floral, light floral, multicolored

▸ Set B: light floral, red print, light floral

▸ Set C: light floral, geometric print, light floral

Press the seam allowances away from the light-floral strips in each strip set. Crosscut each group (A, B, and C) into 32 units, 3½" wide, for a total of 96 units.

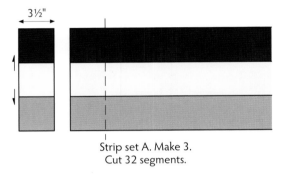

3½"

Strip set A. Make 3.
Cut 32 segments.

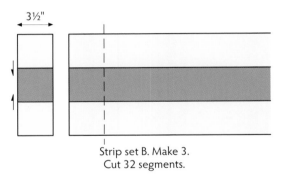

3½"

Strip set B. Make 3.
Cut 32 segments.

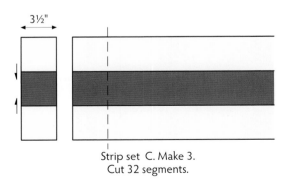

3½"

Strip set C. Make 3.
Cut 32 segments.

3 Using the units from step 2, make 20 Nine Patch blocks by joining strip-set segments in the order shown: C/A/B (block X). Make 12 Nine Patch blocks as shown for block Y: B/A/C. Press the seam allowances toward the center (A) units.

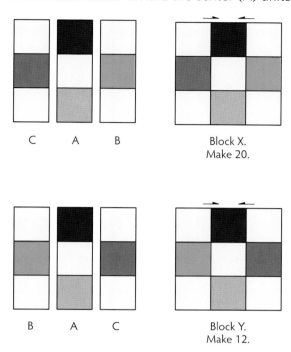

C   A   B

Block X.
Make 20.

B   A   C

Block Y.
Make 12.

ASSEMBLING THE QUILT TOP

1 Arrange the first row, alternating block X and Snowball blocks in the fabrics shown, beginning with block X. Rotate the Nine Patch blocks as necessary so that the fabric prints match between blocks.

2 Arrange the second row, beginning with a multicolored Snowball block and using block Y for alternating blocks. Continue to lay out the quilt as shown.

3 Sew the blocks together into rows, pressing the seam allowances toward the Snowball blocks.

4 Join the rows to complete the quilt top. Press the seam allowances in one direction.

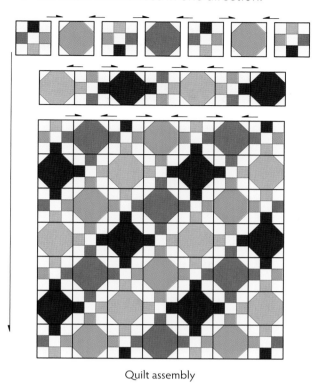

Quilt assembly

FINISHING THE QUILT

For more information on finishing techniques, go to ShopMartingale.com/HowtoQuilt for free, illustrated instructions.

1 Layer the quilt top, batting, and backing, and baste the layers together. Quilt as desired; the sample quilt uses a meandering pattern of leaves.

2 Trim the batting and backing to match the quilt top.

3 Bind the quilt using the red-striped strips. Add a label if desired.

floating shoofly

Assembling Snowball blocks from strip-pieced squares creates a scrappy look. Add sashing and cornerstones to produce these floating Shoofly blocks.

"Floating Shoofly," pieced by Amy Smart; quilted by Emily Sessions

Finished quilt: 68" x 78"
Finished block: 8" x 8"

MATERIALS

Yardage is based on 42"-wide fabric. Fat quarters are 18" x 21".

10 fat quarters of assorted orange prints for blocks and cornerstones

⅝ yard *each* of 10 different cream or neutral prints for blocks, sashing, and pieced outer border

1¼ yards of dark-orange print for inner border and binding

4⅝ yards of fabric for backing

72" x 82" piece of batting

CUTTING

From *each* of the orange fat quarters, cut:

4 strips, 3½" x 21"; crosscut into 18 squares, 3½" x 3½" (180 total; 12 will be left over)

1 strip, 2½" x 21"; crosscut into 5 squares, 2½" x 2½" (50 total; 8 will be left over)

From *each* of the cream or neutral prints, cut:

2 strips, 2½" x 42"

2 strips, 2" x 42"

1 strip, 1½" x 42"

1 strip, 8½" x 42"; crosscut into:

8 rectangles, 2½" x 8½"

3 rectangles, 3½" x 8½"

3 rectangles, 2½" x 3½"

From the leftover cream and neutral fabrics, cut a *total* of:

2 strips, 2½" x 42"

2 strips, 2" x 42"

1 strip, 1½" x 42"

4 squares, 3½" x 3½"

You will have a total of:
22 strips, 2½" x 42"
22 strips, 2" x 42"
11 strips, 1½" x 42"
80 rectangles, 2½" x 8½" (9 will be left over)
30 rectangles, 3½" x 8½" (8 will be left over)
30 rectangles, 2½" x 3½" (4 will be left over)
4 squares, 3½"x 3½"

From the dark-orange print, cut:

8 strips, 1½" x 42"

9 strips, 2½" x 42"

MAKING THE BLOCKS

1 Referring to "Strip Piecing" on page 5, use the cream and neutral strips to make eleven strip sets. In each strip set, use two 2½" x 42" strips, two 2" x 42" strips, and one 1½" x 42" strip. Vary the order of widths and fabrics in each set. Press all of the seam allowances in one direction.

2 From *each* of 10 strip sets, cut three 8½" squares and three 4½" x 8½" rectangles.

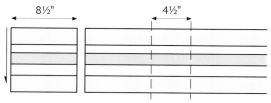

8½"   4½"

Make 11 strip sets.
Cut 3 squares and 3 rectangles
from *each* of 10 of the strip sets.

3 Cut six 4½" x 8½" rectangles from the remaining strip set. You'll need a total of 30 pieced 8½" squares and 36 pieced 4½" x 8½" rectangles. Set the rectangles aside for the outer border.

4 Use the "Quick Corners" technique on page 6 to add an orange 3½" square to each corner of the 30 pieced 8½" squares. Trim the excess fabric from each corner, leaving a ¼" seam allowance. Press the seam allowances toward the orange corners.

Make 30.

5 Using the same technique, stitch orange 3½" squares to two adjacent corners of 22 cream or neutral 3½" x 8½" rectangles to make 22 side blocks.

Make 22.

6 Lay a cream or neutral 3½" square on an orange 3½" square, right sides together. Draw a diagonal line from corner to corner on the wrong side of the lighter square and sew directly on the drawn line. Trim the excess fabric ¼" outside the seam. Press the seam allowances toward the orange fabric. Make four corner blocks.

Make 4.

ASSEMBLING THE QUILT TOP

1 Arrange the blocks, side blocks, corner blocks, sashing rectangles, and cornerstones as shown below. Alternate the direction of the strips in the centers of the Snowball blocks. Sew the pieces together in rows and press the seam allowances toward the sashing rectangles.

2 Join the rows to complete the quilt top. Press the seam allowances in one direction.

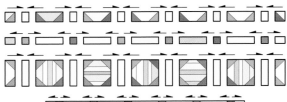

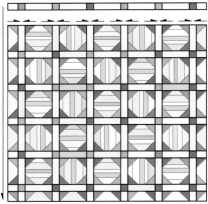

ADDING THE BORDERS

1 Sew two dark-orange 1½" x 42" strips together along their short edges; make four.

2 Using the "Easy Borders" method on page 7, measure two of the pieced border strips and sew them to the side edges of the quilt. Press the seam allowances toward the borders.

3 Measure and trim the remaining pieced strips and sew them to the top and bottom edges. Press the seam allowances toward the borders.

4 Sew nine 4½" x 8½" pieced rectangles together to create a border strip; make four. Using two pieced borders, measure and trim the outer border units and sew them to the quilt sides as before. Press the seam allowances toward the inner border.

5 Using the remaining two pieced border units, add the outer border to the top and bottom of the quilt. Press the seam allowances toward the inner border.

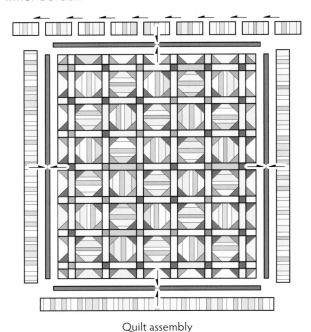

Quilt assembly

FINISHING THE QUILT

For more information on finishing techniques, go to ShopMartingale.com/HowtoQuilt for free, illustrated instructions.

1 Layer the quilt top, batting, and backing, and baste the layers together. Quilt as desired. The sample quilt uses rows of a looping figure-eight pattern.

2 Trim the batting and backing to match the quilt top.

3 Bind the quilt using the dark-orange 2½" x 42" strips. Add a label if desired.

crossing guard

This quilt is constructed from only two repeating blocks, but the fabric placement creates various design illusions. I love the way the orange-peel quilting pattern accentuates the composition.

"Crossing Guard," pieced by Amy Smart; quilted by April Rosenthal

Finished quilt: 66" x 75"
Finished block: 9" x 9"

MATERIALS

Yardage is based on 42"-wide fabric.

2⅞ yards of white solid for blocks and inner and outer borders

2⅛ yards of medium-green solid for blocks, middle border, and binding

1⅛ yards of light-green solid for blocks

1⅛ yards of chartreuse solid for blocks

4 yards of fabric for backing

70" x 79" piece of batting

Clear template plastic

CUTTING

From the light-green solid, cut:

21 strips, 1¾" x 42"

From the chartreuse solid, cut:

21 strips, 1¾" x 42"

From the medium-green solid, cut:

21 strips, 1¾" x 42"
10 strips, 1½" x 42"
8 strips, 2½" x 42"

From the white solid, cut:

7 strips, 7½" x 42"; crosscut 3 of the strips into
84 rectangles, 1½" x 7½"
7 strips, 2½" x 42"
8 strips, 3½" x 42"

MAKING THE BLOCKS

1 Using the techniques in "Strip Piecing" on page 5, make 21 strip sets from the 1¾" x 42" strips. Arrange the colors as shown above right: light green, medium green, and chartreuse.

2 Trace the pattern on page 30 onto template plastic and cut it out. Using the template, cut eight triangles from each strip set (168 total),

alternating point-up and point-down placement. Sort into piles of triangles with either a chartreuse or light-green tip.

Make 21 strip sets.
Cut 8 triangles from each.

Make 84.   Make 84.

3 Sew a white 7½" x 42" strip to each side of a 1½" x 42" medium-green strip to make a strip set; make two. Press the seam allowances toward the white strips. Crosscut into 42 units, 1½" wide.

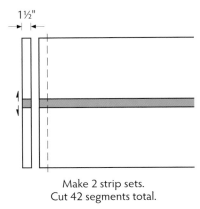

Make 2 strip sets.
Cut 42 segments total.

4 Sew a white 1½" x 7½" rectangle between two triangles from the same pile (having the same color tip). Match the raw edges at the 90° corners of the triangles, allowing the other end of the rectangle to extend beyond the triangles. Press the seam allowances toward the white rectangle. Make two.

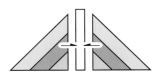

5 Sew a unit from step 3 between the two pieced triangle units. Press the seam allowances toward the rectangular unit. Keeping the 1"

green square centered, trim the corners to square up the block to 9½" x 9½".

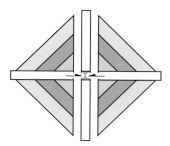

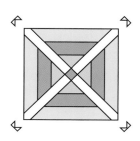

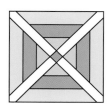 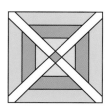

6 Repeat steps 4 and 5 to make 42 blocks total (21 of each), matching the color order of the triangles within each block.

SIZE MATTERS

If some of your blocks are smaller than 9½", square them all up to the size of the smallest block. Consistency is more important than the exact measurement.

ASSEMBLING THE QUILT TOP

1 Arrange the blocks, alternating blocks with light-green and chartreuse edges, in seven rows of six blocks.

2 Sew the blocks into rows, pressing the seam allowances to the left in odd rows and to the right in even rows.

3 Sew the rows together, pressing the seam allowances in one direction.

ADDING THE BORDERS

1 Sew two white 2½" x 42" strips together along their short edges; make two.

2 Using the "Easy Borders" method on page 7, measure and trim the pieced border strips and sew them to the side edges of the quilt. Press the seam allowances toward the borders.

3 Cut one of the remaining white 2½" x 42" strips in half. Sew a half strip to one end of each remaining white 2½" x 42" strip. Measure and trim the pieced white strips and sew them to the top and bottom edges. Press the seam allowances toward the borders.

4 Sew the remaining medium-green 1½" x 42" strips together in pairs; make four. Measure and trim the pieced border strips and sew them to the quilt sides, and then to the top and bottom, as above. Press the seam allowances toward the green borders.

5 Sew the white 3½" x 42" strips together in pairs; make four. Measure and trim the pieced border strips and sew them to the quilt sides, and then to the top and bottom, as above. Press the seam allowances toward the green border.

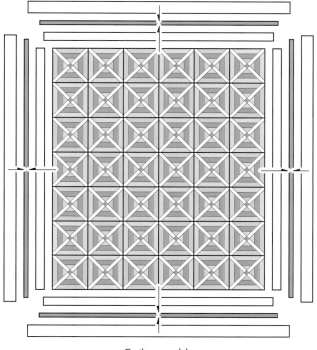

Quilt assembly

FINISHING THE QUILT

For more information on finishing techniques, go to ShopMartingale.com/HowtoQuilt for free, illustrated instructions.

1 Layer the quilt top, batting, and backing, and baste the layers together. Quilt as desired. The sample quilt uses an orange-peel motif extending from each corner of the blocks to the block centers.

2 Trim the backing and batting to match the quilt top.

3 Bind the quilt using the medium-green 2½" x 42" strips. Add a label if desired.

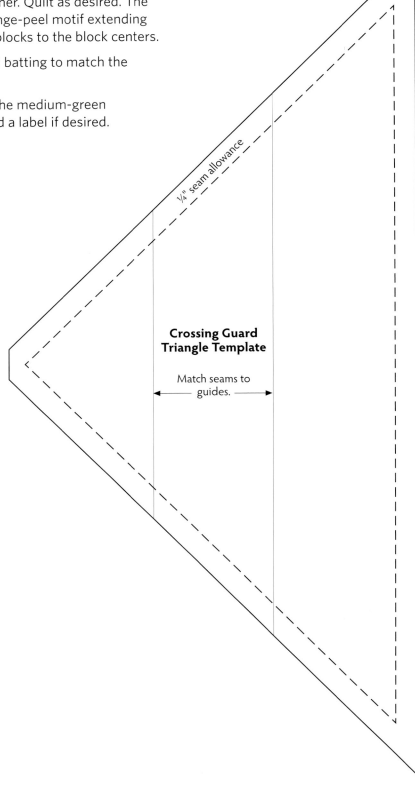

¼" seam allowance

Crossing Guard Triangle Template

Match seams to guides.

butterfly effect

Creating a fabric tube from a strip set makes fast work of these Hourglass blocks. You'll find many secondary patterns as you look at the completed quilt.

"Butterfly Effect," pieced by Amy Smart; quilted by Emily Sessions

Finished quilt: 40½" x 55½"
Finished block: 7½" x 7½"

MATERIALS

Yardage is based on 42"-wide fabric.

24 strips, 2" x 42", of assorted orange, gray, turquoise, yellow, and green prints for blocks (1⅓ yards total)

1½ yards of white solid for blocks and border

⅜ yard of gray print for binding

2½ yards of fabric for backing

45" x 60" piece of batting

CUTTING

From the white solid, cut:
   6 strips, 6½" x 42"
   5 strips, 2" x 42"

From the gray print, cut:
   5 strips, 2½" x 42"

MAKING THE BLOCKS

1 Referring to "Strip Piecing" on page 5, sew four assorted 2" x 42" print strips together to make a strip set. Press the seam allowances in one direction. Make six strip sets.

Make 6.

2 Place a strip set on a white 6½" x 42" strip, right sides together, and sew both long edges to create a tube of fabric. Make six.

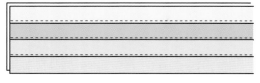

Make 6.

3 Cut six squares, 6½" x 6½", from each tube (36 total). With the seams positioned horizontally, cut each square along one diagonal as shown. *It's important to be sure the seams are always at the top and bottom—not along the sides—of the squares, and that the diagonal cut is always made in the same direction.*

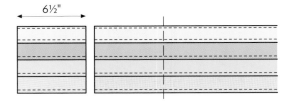

4 Open each triangle, removing the few stitches across the tip, and press the seam allowances toward the white fabric. You will need 70 triangles; two will be left over.

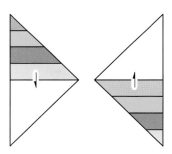

5 Sew the pieced triangles together in pairs, alternating the striped halves, to make 35 Hourglass blocks. Press the seam allowances to one side. Square up and trim the pieced blocks to measure 8" x 8".

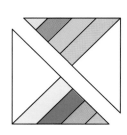 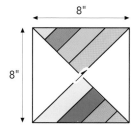

Make 35.

ASSEMBLING THE QUILT TOP

1 Arrange the blocks into seven rows of five blocks, alternating the orientation of the striped triangles as shown.

2 Sew the blocks together in rows, pressing the seam allowances away from the pieced stripes.

3 Sew the rows together and press the seam allowances in one direction.

ADDING THE BORDER

1 Cut one 2" x 42" white strip in half. Sew two full strips and a half strip together along their short edges; make two. Cut a 58" length from each pieced strip.

2 Using the "Easy Borders" method on page 7, measure and trim the 58"-long pieced border strips and sew them to the side edges of the quilt. Press the seam allowances toward the borders.

3 Measure and trim the remaining lengths of the two pieced white strips and sew them to the top and bottom edges. Press the seam allowances toward the borders.

Quilt assembly

FINISHING THE QUILT

For more information on finishing techniques, go to ShopMartingale.com/HowtoQuilt for free, illustrated instructions.

1 Layer the quilt top, batting, and backing, and baste the layers together. Quilt as desired; the sample quilt uses an allover pebble motif of circles in different sizes.

2 Trim the backing and batting to match the quilt top.

3 Bind the quilt using the gray strips. Add a label if desired.

TWIN-SIZE OPTION
Finished quilt: 66" x 81"

MATERIALS

Yardage is based on 42"-wide fabric.

56 strips, 2" x 42", of assorted prints for blocks (3¼ yards total)

3½ yards of white solid for blocks and border

⅝ yard of gray print for binding

4¾ yards of fabric for backing

70" x 84" piece of batting

CUTTING

From the white solid, cut:
  14 strips, 6½" x 42"
  8 strips, 3½" x 42"

From the gray print, cut:
  8 strips, 2½" x 42"

Follow the instructions for the main project, but make 14 strip-set tubes and 80 Hourglass blocks. Arrange the blocks in 10 rows of eight blocks; use the 3½" x 42" white strips for the border.

diverging diamonds

This diamond pattern is deceptively easy to assemble using strip-piecing techniques and a ruler with a 90° angle. This project is perfect for precut 2½" strips.

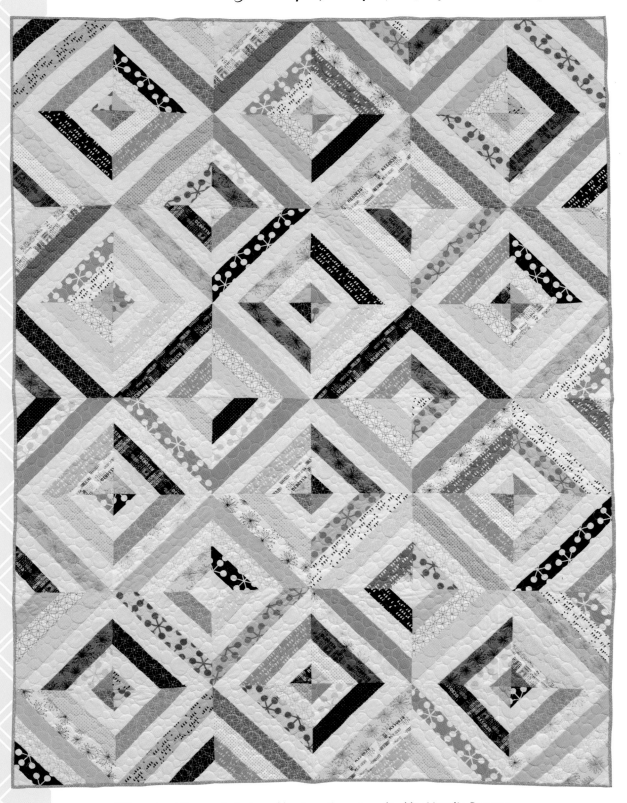

"Diverging Diamonds," pieced by Amy Smart; quilted by Natalia Bonner

Finished quilt: 63" x 84"
Finished block: 10½" x 10½"

MATERIALS

Yardage is based on 42"-wide fabric.

48 strips, 2½" x 42", of assorted light prints for blocks (3⅜ yards total)

48 strips, 2½" x 42", of assorted dark prints for blocks (3⅜ yards total)

⅝ yard of orange print for binding

5 yards of fabric for backing

66" x 88" piece of batting

CUTTING

From the orange print, cut:

8 strips, 2½" x 42"

MAKING THE BLOCKS

1 Alternating light and dark prints, sew four 2½" x 42" strips together to make a strip set. Press the seam allowances toward the dark strips. Make 24 strip sets.

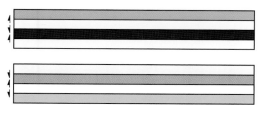

Make 24.

2 Lay two strip sets right sides together, matching a light edge to a dark edge on each long side. Stitch both long edges to create a fabric tube; make 12.

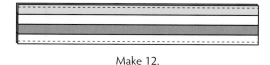

Make 12.

3 Use a rotary cutter and a large ruler to cut four 90° triangles from each pieced strip set as shown.

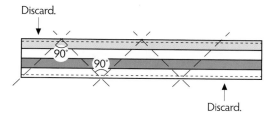

4 Remove the stitches across the point of each triangle. Open the triangular pieces to reveal pieced square blocks. Trim each block to 11" x 11", positioning the longest seam from corner to corner diagonally through the center of the block. Make 48.

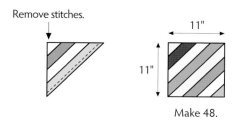

Make 48.

ASSEMBLING THE QUILT TOP

1 Arrange the blocks in eight rows of six blocks, referring to the quilt photo on page 34 or the quilt assembly diagram on page 36.

2 Before sewing the blocks together, re-press the seam allowances in alternate blocks toward the light strips (blocks 2, 4, and 6 in row 1; blocks 1, 3, and 5 in row 2; etc.). This allows the seams to nest together for better matching when assembling the blocks, and will create a smoother quilt top.

3 Sew the blocks together into rows, pressing the seam allowances to the left in odd rows and to the right in even rows.

4 Sew the rows together to make the quilt top. Press the seam allowances in one direction.

Quilt assembly

FINISHING THE QUILT

For more information on finishing techniques, go to ShopMartingale.com/HowtoQuilt for free, illustrated instructions.

1 Layer the quilt top, batting, and backing, and baste the layers together. Quilt as desired. The sample quilt uses an allover pebble design of variously sized circles.

2 Trim the backing and batting to match the quilt top.

3 Bind the quilt using the orange strips. Add a label if desired.

quick puss in the corner

This pattern is perfect for 10" precut squares. By stacking sets of complementary prints before sewing, you can quickly create multiple Puss in the Corner blocks.

"Quick Puss in the Corner," pieced by Amy Smart; quilted by Melissa Kelley

Finished quilt: 70" x 82"
Finished block: 8½" x 8½"

MATERIALS

Yardage is based on 42"-wide fabric.

30 squares, 10" x 10", of assorted prints for blocks (2½ yards total)

2⅜ yards of light print for alternate blocks and setting triangles

½ yard of pink stripe for inner border

1⅛ yards of yellow print for outer border

⅝ yard of yellow stripe for binding

5 yards of fabric for backing

74" x 86" piece of batting

CUTTING

From the light print, cut:

5 strips, 9" x 42"; crosscut into 20 squares, 9" x 9"

2 strips, 13½" x 42"; crosscut into 5 squares, 13½" x 13½". Cut into quarters diagonally to yield 20 side triangles (2 will be left over).

2 squares, 7" x 7"; cut in half diagonally to yield 4 corner triangles

From the pink stripe, cut:

8 strips, 1½" x 42"

From the yellow print, cut:

8 strips, 4½" x 42"

From the yellow stripe, cut:

Bias strips 2½" wide, totaling at least 315"*

For details on cutting and making bias binding, see ShopMartingale.com/HowtoQuilt.

MAKING THE BLOCKS

1 Divide the 10" squares into 15 pairs, selecting fabrics to provide good contrast within each pair. Working with one pair at a time, stack the fabrics carefully, right sides up and with raw edges matched; slice each 10" square into two 2" x 10" rectangles and one 6" x 10" rectangle. You'll have four 2" x 10" rectangles and two 6" x 10" rectangles in each pair; keep the pairs together. Stack and slice all 15 pairs of squares.

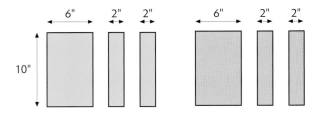

2 Again working with one pair of fabrics, sew matching 2" x 10" strips to the long edges of the contrasting 6" x 10" rectangle. Press the seam allowances toward the darker fabric. Cut two 2"-wide strips from the block, cutting perpendicular to the seams.

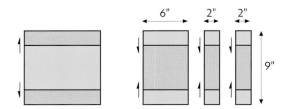

3 Sew matching 2" x 9" strips to opposite sides of the contrasting block center, creating two blocks. Press the seam allowances toward the center. Make a total of 30 blocks, 9" square.

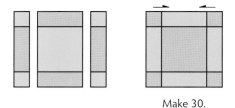

Make 30.

ASSEMBLING THE QUILT TOP

1 Arrange the blocks on point, five blocks across and six blocks down. Fill in the layout with light 9" squares. Use the 18 side triangles along the

outside edges and place the four corner triangles at the corners.

2 Sew the blocks together in diagonal rows, pressing the seam allowances away from the pieced blocks.

3 Assemble the diagonal rows to create the center section of the quilt. Press the seam allowances in one direction.

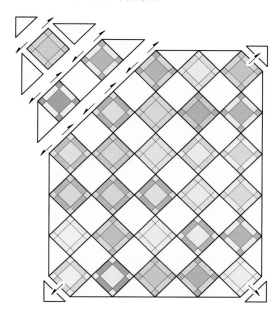

4 Trim the edges of the setting triangles to square the quilt top, leaving a ¼" seam allowance beyond the seam intersections.

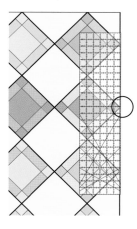

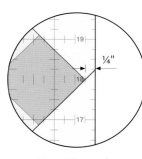

Trim ¼" outside the seam intersections.

ADDING THE BORDERS

1 Sew two pink-striped strips together along their short edges; make four.

2 Using the "Easy Borders" method on page 7, measure and trim two of the pieced border units and sew them to the side edges of the quilt. Press the seam allowances toward the borders.

3 Measure and trim the remaining pieced strips and sew them to the top and bottom edges. Press the seam allowances toward the borders.

4 Sew the yellow-print strips together in pairs; make four. Measure and trim the pieced border strips and sew them to the quilt sides, and then to the top and bottom, as above. Press the seam allowances toward the outer border.

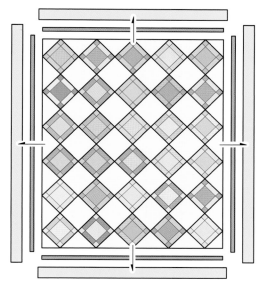

Quilt assembly

FINISHING THE QUILT

For more information on finishing techniques, go to ShopMartingale.com/HowtoQuilt for free, illustrated instructions.

1 Layer the quilt top, batting, and backing, and baste the layers together. Quilt as desired; the sample quilt uses an allover floral motif.

2 Trim the backing and batting to match the quilt top.

3 Bind the quilt using the yellow-striped bias strips. Add a label if desired.

modern buzz saw

This version of a traditional Buzz Saw block works great with precut 10" squares and produces no waste!

"Modern Buzz Saw," pieced by Amy Smart; quilted by Melissa Kelley

Finished quilt: 62" x 79"
Finished block: 8½" x 8½"

MATERIALS

Yardage is based on 42"-wide fabric.

24 squares, 9½" x 9½", of assorted prints for blocks (1¾ yards total)

2¼ yards of white polka dot for blocks and outer border

1¼ yards of gray print for blocks

½ yard of turquoise print for inner border

⅝ yard of yellow diagonal stripe for binding

4⅝ yards of fabric for backing

65" x 82" piece of batting

SIMPLE SOURCE

Precut 10" squares are a great source for the prints in this quilt. Simply trim them to 9½" x 9½" before beginning.

CUTTING

From the white polka dot, cut:

3 strips, 9½" x 42"; crosscut into 12 squares, 9½" x 9½"

6 strips, 2" x 42"; crosscut into 24 rectangles, 2" x 9"

8 strips, 4½" x 42"

From the gray print, cut:

3 strips, 9½" x 42"; crosscut into 12 squares, 9½" x 9½"

6 strips, 2" x 42"; crosscut into 24 rectangles, 2" x 9"

From the turquoise print, cut:

7 strips, 2" x 42"

From the yellow diagonal stripe, cut:

8 strips, 2½" x 42"

MAKING THE BLOCKS

1 Draw a diagonal line from corner to corner on the wrong side of each white and gray square. Lay a white or gray square on a colored square, right sides together, matching the raw edges. Stitch ¼" from both sides of the drawn line. Cut on the drawn line to make a pair of half-square-triangle units. Open both units and press the seam allowances toward the colored print. Square up the units to measure 9" x 9". Make 48.

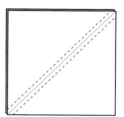

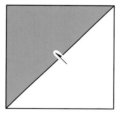 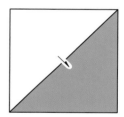

Make 48.

2 Lay a half-square-triangle unit on your cutting mat with the colored triangle at the lower right, as shown. Cut the pieced unit into four strips, 2¼" x 9".

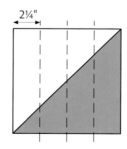 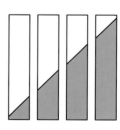

2¼"

Cut 4 segments.

3 Reverse the order of the strips as shown and piece them back together, adding a matching 2" x 9" strip at one end. Press the seam allowances in one direction.

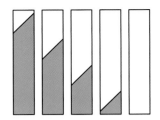 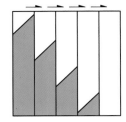

4 Repeat steps 2 and 3 with each half-square-triangle unit to make a total of 48 blocks.

ASSEMBLING THE QUILT TOP

1 Arrange alternating white and gray blocks into eight rows of six blocks. Keep blocks with matching prints together within a four-block section of the quilt and rotate the blocks as shown.

2 Sew the blocks into rows and press the seam allowances away from the intersecting seams.

3 Sew the rows together in order. Press the seam allowances in one direction.

ADDING THE BORDERS

1 Sew two turquoise strips together along their short edges; make two.

2 Using the "Easy Borders" method on page 7, measure and trim the pieced border strips and sew them to the side edges of the quilt. Press the seam allowances toward the borders.

3 Cut one of the remaining turquoise strips in half. Sew a half strip to one end of each remaining turquoise strip. Measure and trim the pieced turquoise strips and sew them to the top and bottom edges. Press the seam allowances toward the borders.

4 Sew two white strips together end to end; make two. Measure and trim the pieced border units and sew them to the quilt sides as above. Press the seam allowances toward the outer border.

5 Sew the remaining white strips together in pairs. Measure and trim the pieced white strips and sew them to the top and bottom of the quilt. Press the seam allowances toward the outer border.

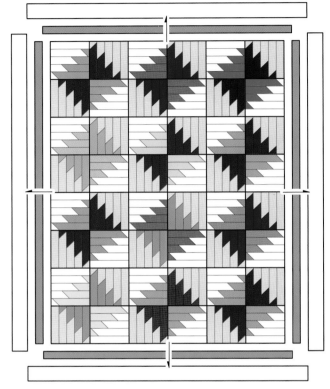

Quilt assembly

FINISHING THE QUILT

For more information on finishing techniques, go to ShopMartingale.com/HowtoQuilt for free, illustrated instructions.

1 Layer the quilt top, batting, and backing, and baste the layers together. Quilt as desired; the sample quilt uses a meandering angular pattern formed by straight lines.

2 Trim the backing and batting to match the quilt top.

3 Bind the quilt using the yellow strips. Add a label if desired.

square deal

The stack-and-shuffle method makes cutting and piecing these blocks really fast. There's a lot of freedom with this block—precision piecing isn't important here.

"Square Deal," designed and pieced by Amy Smart; quilted by Melissa Kelley

> Finished quilt: 67" x 81" (approximately)
> Finished block: 14" x 14"

MATERIALS

Yardage is based on 42"-wide fabric. Fat quarters are 18" x 21".

20 fat quarters of assorted prints for blocks and pieced outer border

⅝ yard of yellow solid for inner border

⅝ yard of red solid for binding

5 yards of fabric for backing

73" x 87" piece of batting

CUTTING

From *each* of the fat quarters, cut:
   1 square, 17" x 17" (20 total)
   1 rectangle, 4" x 18"* (20 total). Crosscut *1 rect-angle* into 4 squares, 3" x 3". Set the remaining rectangles aside for the outer border (1 will be left over).

*If the fat quarter is too small to cut a full 4" x 18" rectangle, cut the largest rectangle possible. Standardize the rectangles so that all are the same width; variations in length are acceptable.

From the yellow solid, cut:
   7 strips, 3" x 42"

From the red solid, cut:
   8 strips, 2½" x 42"

CUTTING THE BLOCK PIECES

These blocks are cut by stacking the 17" squares in groups of four and cutting through all the layers as shown. As you cut the fabric, arrange the pieces as shown in the cutting layout on page 45 so that it's easy to shuffle the fabrics without losing track of placement. A flat cookie sheet makes a wonderful stacking surface.

1 Stack four 17" print squares, right side up and matching the raw edges. From the left side of the stack, cut a 2" x 17" rectangle. Cut a 2¼" x 17" rectangle from the right side.

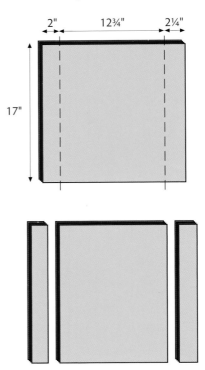

2 From the top edge of the remaining stack, cut a 2¼" x 12¾" rectangle. Cut a 2¾" x 12¾" rectangle from the bottom edge of the stack.

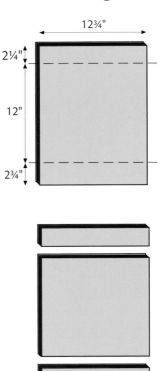

3 From the left side of the remaining stack, cut a 1¾" x 12" rectangle. Cut a 4" x 12" rectangle from the right side.

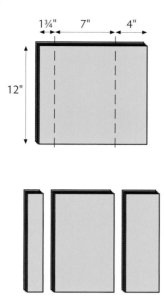

4 Cut a 2" x 7" rectangle from the top edge of the remaining stack and a 3" x 7" rectangle from the bottom edge. This leaves a 7" square for the center.

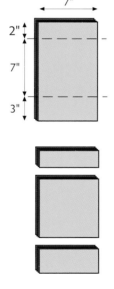

MAKING THE BLOCKS

1 Arrange the sliced group of four fabrics as shown. Leave the stack of 7" center squares as is. Move the top fabric from each of the four stacks surrounding the center square to the bottom of the stack. Move the top two fabrics from the four outer stacks to the bottom. As each block is assembled, a pattern of three concentric squares will emerge.

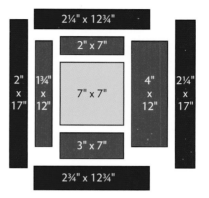

2 Working with the top fabric in each shuffled stack, sew the 2" x 7" and 3" x 7" rectangles to the top and bottom of the center square. Press the seam allowances away from the center.

3 Sew the 1¾" x 12" and 4" x 12" rectangles to the sides of the center section, matching one end of each new rectangle to a raw edge of the assembled section. Press the seam allowances away from the center. Trim the excess fabric from the new rectangles.

Align strips to top of block.
Trim excess.

4 Sew the 2¼" x 12¾" rectangle to the top and the 2¾" x 12¾" rectangle to the bottom of the assembled unit. Press the seam allowances away from the center. Trim the excess fabric.

Align strips to left side of block.
Trim excess.

5 Sew the 2" x 17" and 2¼" x 17" rectangles to the sides of the assembled unit. Press the seam allowances away from the center. Trim the rectangle ends and square up the block to measure 14½" x 14½".

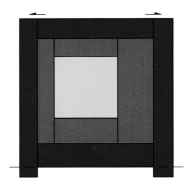

Align strips to top of block.
Trim excess.

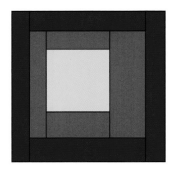

6 Repeat steps 1–5 with the remaining fabrics in the four-fabric group; use the fabrics at the top of each stack to create a block. Repeat the entire cutting and sewing process to make a total of 20 blocks, each including three different fabrics.

MEASURE UP

The "center" square is actually slightly off-center in these blocks. A little variation in the placement of the square relative to the block edges is OK, so you have some freedom when squaring up the blocks. If there's not enough fabric in some blocks to reach 14½" x 14½", square up all the blocks to match the smallest one and adjust the pieced quilt border lengths accordingly.

ASSEMBLING THE QUILT TOP

1 Arrange the blocks in five rows of four blocks as shown in the quilt assembly diagram on page 47. Rotate individual blocks so that the center square floats in different directions in adjacent blocks.

2 Sew the blocks together into rows, pressing the seams to the right in rows 1, 3, and 5 and the left in rows 2 and 4.

3 Sew the rows together and press the seam allowances in one direction.

ADDING THE BORDERS

1 Sew two yellow strips together along their short edges; make two.

2 Using the "Easy Borders" method on page 7, measure and trim the pieced border strips and sew them to the side edges of the quilt. Press the seam allowances toward the borders.

3 Cut one of the remaining yellow strips in half. Sew a half strip to one end of each remaining yellow strip. Measure the width of the quilt top between the border seams and add ½" for seam allowances. Trim each pieced yellow strip to this length. Sew a 3" square to each end of each strip and press the seam allowances toward the yellow strips.

4 Sew the assembled border units to the top and bottom edges. Press the seam allowances toward the borders.

5 Trim 18 of the fat-quarter 4" x 18" rectangles to a consistent width, as close to 4" as possible. Sew four rectangles together end to end; make two. Sew the remaining rectangles together in two groups of five each to make the longer border units.

6 Measure and trim one of the shorter border units to match the quilt width and sew it to the bottom edge of the quilt. Press the seam allowances toward the border.

7 Measure and trim one of the longer border units to match the quilt length, including the border just added, and sew it to the right side of the quilt. Press the seam allowances toward the border.

8 Add the remaining short border unit to the top and the final long border unit to the left side of the quilt in the same way. Press the seam allowances toward the borders.

FINISHING THE QUILT

For more information on finishing techniques, go to ShopMartingale.com/HowtoQuilt for free, illustrated instructions.

1 Layer the quilt top, batting, and backing, and baste the layers together. Quilt as desired; the sample quilt uses a meandering angular pattern formed by straight lines.

2 Trim the backing and batting to match the quilt top.

3 Bind the quilt using the red strips. Add a label if desired.

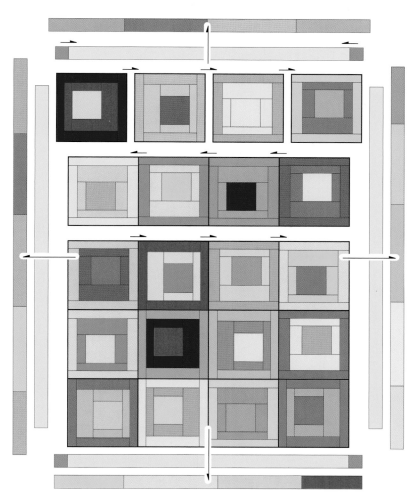

Quilt assembly

About the Author

Amy Smart loved to play with her mom's sewing machine when she was small and first learned to quilt as a girl, but she didn't begin quilting in earnest until after her first baby arrived in 1999, when she needed an artistic outlet and yearned to accomplish something that stayed done.

She worked Saturdays in a local quilt shop for seven years. She taught beginning quilting classes and found that she loved watching other people fall in love with collecting fabric, cutting it up, and sewing it back together. In 2008 she started her now-popular blog, www.DiaryofaQuilter.com, documenting her creations and sewing adventures. Amy thoroughly enjoys participating in the online quilting community and continues to be inspired by the people she has met, both virtually and in real life.

Amy lives in Utah with her patient and encouraging husband and four busy children who fortunately think nothing of random piles of fabric or seam rippers placed strategically throughout the house. As a family they like to explore the outdoors together and laugh at silly Internet videos.

ACKNOWLEDGMENTS

Special thanks to:

My mom, for teaching me to sew, quilt, and love fabric.

My husband, who encouraged me every time I thought that I was in over my head or that I was crazy for writing a blog, let alone a book.

My kids, for their ongoing patience with a kitchen table that is far too often covered with fabric, pins, and a sewing machine.

The nice people at Riley Blake Designs, Moda Fabrics, Michael Miller Fabrics, Robert Kaufman Fabrics, Dear Stella Design, and Pellon, for contributing beautiful fabrics to work with.

The makers of peanut M&M's, for providing fuel for long sewing and writing binges.

Kind blog readers, for their ongoing encouragement and support.